Scripting Justice in Late Medieval Europe

Scripting Justice in Late Medieval Europe

Legal practice and communication in the law courts of Utrecht, York and Paris

Frans Camphuijsen

Routledge
Taylor & Francis Group
LONDON AND NEW YORK

First published in 2022 by Amsterdam University Press Ltd.

Published 2025 by Routledge
4 Park Square, Milton Park, Abingdon, Oxon OX14 4RN
605 Third Avenue, New York, NY 10158

Routledge is an imprint of the Taylor & Francis Group, an informa business

ISBN: 9789463723473 (hbk)
ISBN: 9781041185857 (pbk)
ISBN: 9781003703419 (ebk)
NUR 684

Cover illustration: Detail of Court session of the trial of the duke of Alençon at Vendôme (1458). Bayerische Staatsbibliothek, Munchen: Cod.Gall.6, fol. 2v.

Cover design: Coördesign, Leiden

DOI: 10.5117/9789463723473

In memoriam

Frans Tausch	Francis Heere
1936–2004	1938–2001

De man en de vrouw aan het water

Table of Contents

List of figures, maps, plans and timelines

Figures

Maps

Plans

Timelines

Acknowledgements

No book is written alone. Both directly and indirectly my work over the past years has profited immensely from the commentary, support and general inspiration provided by others. I want to spend the next few pages thanking those without whom this book would not have been what it is today. As medieval courts realized, use of a particular language can make or break the legitimacy of one's message. To underscore the sincerity of my gratitude I have therefore tried to address people in the language generally used to speak with them.

Wie de wordingsgeschiedenis van dit boek zou willen schrijven kan deze in ieder geval terugvoeren tot de zomer van 2009, toen ik voor het eerst kennismaakte met de toen net nieuwe hoogleraar Middeleeuwse Geschiedenis aan de Universiteit van Amsterdam, een zekere Guy Geltner. Als begeleider, promotor en collega-wetenschapper heeft Guy mij sindsdien steeds weten te inspireren en heeft hij een grote invloed gehad op mijn begrip van wat het betekent om historicus te zijn. Daar ben ik hem heel dankbaar voor.

De eerste inhoudelijke basis voor dit onderzoek werd gelegd tijdens mijn onderzoek naar de Raad van Utrecht, dat later zou uitgroeien tot een van de drie poten van dit boek. Daarbij heb ik bijzonder veel gehad aan de steun en het advies van Justine Smithuis en Bram van den Hoven van Genderen. Het Utrechts Archief en zijn medewerkers hebben me bovendien de kans gegeven in alle rust het rijke bronnenmateriaal van de Utrechtse Raad in te zien.

While all large research projects can be seen as intellectual 'journeys', in my case the journey was more than just metaphorical. Residing both in York and Paris for several months in a row, I was not only able to broaden my intellectual horizons, but also to get to know a score of new people and places. Instrumental in facilitating these research stays was Michele Campopiano. His help in finding my way into alien academic contexts has been indispensable.

I have felt very welcome as visitor at the Centre for Medieval Studies of the University of York in 2013. Both its former director, Linne Mooney, and my guest supervisor, Jeremy Goldberg, have done everything in their power to make my stay as enjoyable as possible. This was also largely helped by the possibility to work in the centre's workroom. I heartily thank the then workroomers, and in particular Erika Graham, for their good company. My work in York was further facilitated by the staff of the Borthwick Institute for Archives, notably Paul Dryburgh, who was always ready to help me with any cause paper-related questions. Final thanks go out to Sarah Brown, for explaining the architectural intricacies of York Minster.

À Paris, j'ai trouvé une hospitalité equivalente en 2014 à l'École Normale Supérieur. Je voudrais remercier mon hôte-là, François Menant, pour la possibilité de profiter de toutes les ressources de l'École, tout comme son séminaire au même institut. Plusieurs autres m'ont permis de prendre un bon départ pour mes recherches Parisiens, notamment Olivier Mattéoni, Marie Bouhaïk-Gironès, Cléo Rager et Elisabeth Schmit. Aux Archives Nationales (site de Paris) j'ai trouvé le personnel toujours très serviable, rencontrant peu d'obstacles à obtenir ce que je voulais consulter. En particulier, mes recherches ont bien profiter de la possibilité m'offrant par Brigitte Lozza de consulter plusieurs documents normalement inaccessibles. Je voudrais aussi remercier les membres du Laboratoire de Médiévistique occidentale de Paris (LaMOP) pour la possibilité de partager les résultats de mes recherches avec eux dans le cadre de la Bourse Robert de Sorbon en 2018.

A great source of inspiration during all these years have been the many sessions and other activities organized as part of the Court Records Collective, an informal research collective born at the IMC Leeds 2012. I wish to thank my co-organizers Jamie Page and Sarah Crawford for past and future cooperation, as well as the many contributors to our sessions for their inspiring papers. Special thanks go out to Ian Forrest, who has chaired many of our sessions from the start, and, in the process, valiantly struggled with my last name for years in a row.

Toch is er weinig zo fijn als weer thuiskomen. En dat thuis is voor mij de afgelopen jaren de afdeling Geschiedenis van de Universiteit van Amsterdam geweest. Mijn dank gaat uit naar de vele collega's met wie ik zowel in het onderzoek als onderwijs intensief heb samengewerkt. Ik wil in het bijzonder de leden van de leerstoelgroep Middeleeuwse Geschiedenis bedanken, met wie ik gedurende al die jaren in steeds wisselende samenstelling onder meer een middeleeuws onderwijsprogramma heb verzorgd, artikelen en hoofdstukken in wording heb besproken, en pizza's heb gebakken. In niet-chronologische volgorde betreft het: Josephine van den Bent, Maaike van Berkel, Jan Burgers, Alex Collin, Janna Coomans, Valentina Covaci, Mario Damen, Lola Digard, Serena Ferente, Willem Flinterman, Erik Goosmann, Sander Govaerts, Nathan van Kleij, Christian Manger, Arend Elias Oostindiër, Marianne Ritsema-van Eck, Petros Samara, Jinna Smit, Arie van Steensel, André Vittoria, Claire Weeda, Justyna Wubs-Mrozewicz, Taylor Zaneri en Ester Zoomer.

Het is geen overdrijving om te stellen dat het meeste werk voor dit boek uiteindelijk verzet is op kamer 5.57 van het PC Hoofthuis en kamer D0.11

van het Bushuis. Ik wil de vele medebewoners van 5.57 en Do.11 gedurende die jaren bedanken voor hun directe of indirecte bijdrage aan mijn denken, schrijven en bovenal dagelijkse werkplezier. Naast een aantal reeds genoemden betreft het Mathijs Boom, Sebastiaan Broere, Alex Collin, Mano Delea, Alberto Feenstra, Daniel Knegt, Sven Meeder, Bob Pierik, Tim Verlaan en Antonia Weiss.

Delen van mijn onderzoek zijn gelezen en becommentarieerd door veel verschillende collega's, waaronder Bert Demyttenaere, Anne van Egmond, Sanne Frequin, Leonard van 't Hul, Rudi Künzel, Alice Taatgen, Yvonne Vermijn en Wouter Wagemakers. Naast anderen die ik eerder al genoemd heb, wil ik ook hen hierbij hartelijk danken voor hun volledig belangeloze bijdrage aan het verbeteren van mijn werk. Dit vormt wat mij betreft de essentie van een wetenschappelijke gemeenschap.

I have profited greatly from the suggestions of the anonymous peer-reviewers who have commented on the manuscript of this book at several stages of its coming into being. Furthermore, in the final phase of the book's gestation the valuable assistance of my managing editor, Erika Gaffney, was indispensable to bringing this project to a fruitful conclusion. I want to thank her for her helpful suggestions, lightning quick responses and infinite understanding of the time restraints of an early career academic without dedicated research time.

Ook buiten de academische wereld ben ik veel mensen dankbaar, te veel om hier allemaal te noemen. Ik wil in ieder geval Helma en Martin bedanken. Zij hebben op een heel andere wijze aan de basis van dit boek gestaan, al was het maar door het van een auteur te voorzien. Ook Jaro, Martha, Djaya en Ravi verdienen het om hier genoemd te worden; zij weten als geen ander te definiëren wat écht belangrijk is. Tot slot wil ik Léa bedanken. De intellectuele en bovenal emotionele rijkdom die ze mij de afgelopen jaren heeft geboden is en blijft een niet-aflatende bron van inspiratie. Merci infiniment.

Introduction

Abstract

Late medieval Europe saw the spread and popularization of a particular form of institutionalized socio-legal practice and logic: the law court. While generally understood in legal or institutional terms, this book presents this 'rise of the court' as a socio-cultural history of communicative interactions between producers and consumers of justice. In a world with many alternatives for resolving conflicts and countering perceived threats to social order, courts presented people with specific – and in hindsight highly successful – scripts to perform and define justice, entailing spaces, acts, texts, oral pronouncements and more. By comparing three different types of courts from different regions, this book traces their shared and individual development as scriptwriters of justice, impacting both their contemporaries and modern historians.

Keywords: medieval law courts, medieval legal practice, medieval court records, comparative history, legal communication, performativity

Justice can be an ambiguous concept. That much was clear to the Parisian poet François Villon (b. 1431) from his encounter with law courts. In 1462 the provost of Paris had sentenced him to death, following his involvement in a street brawl. Fighting the latter's decision in an appeal to the supreme royal court, the *Parlement*, Villon managed to obtain a reprieve from this harsh punishment. Yet, while granting the poet his life, the *Parlement* also decided to exile him from his home town, effectively sentencing him to a social death instead.[1] In the poem 'Ode to the Court', Villon underscored the irony of his situation. While his poem begins as a laudatory exposition on

1 On this episode in Villon's life, see Marcel Schwob, "Date de la condamnation à mort de Villon", in *Œuvres complètes*, vol. 6, *Mélanges d'histoire littéraires et de linguistique: L'Argot, Villon, Rabelais* (Paris: François Bernouard, 1928). Every trace of Villon is lost after his exile from Paris, thus leaving us in the dark as to his fate.

Camphuijsen, F., *Scripting Justice in Late Medieval Europe: Legal Practice and Communication in the Law Courts of Paris, York and Utrecht*. Taylor & Francis Group, 2022
DOI 10.5117/9789463723473_INTRO

the goodness of the *Parlement*, by the third stanza the underlying critique becomes discernable:

> And you, my teeth, each one thus loosening,
> Leap forward, offer thanks of every sort,
> Louder than organ, trumpet or bell;
> And don't worry about chewing anymore.
> Consider that I could have been dead,
> Liver, lungs and spleen that breathe again.
> And you, my body, which is vile and worse
> Than bear, or pig who beds down in the mud,
> Praise the Court before it goes worse for you,
> Mother of the good, sister of blessed angels.[2]

In calling on his loose teeth, innards and filthy body to praise the court for letting him keep the ensemble of these parts, Villon juxtaposes, in an absurdist play on the poem's use of bodily metaphors, his own sorry state with a nearly divine *Parlement* that has decided to both pardon and punish him at the same time. Such justice provided by an all-powerful court, so the poem implicitly asks, are we supposed to be grateful for it, no matter the state in which it leaves us?[3]

Villon's subtle lambasting of the *Parlement*'s justice illustrates the ambiguous feelings late medieval people could have towards law courts and legal practitioners. With the growing role of courts in daily life came numerous reactions to what were perceived as the problematic aspects of this form of institutionalized legal practice. Lawyers in particular became a common target of moral criticism by learned elites. Their perceived avarice, deceitfulness and hypocrisy led authors as diverse as Jacques de Vitry (ca. 1160–1240), Dante Alighieri (1265–1321) and John Wycliffe (1330–1384)

2 For the Middle French original, see François Villon, *Lais, testament, poésies diverses/Ballades en jargon*, eds. Jean-Claude Mühlethaler and Eric Hicks (Paris: Champion, 2004), 310–313. My English translation is based on François Villon, *Poems*, trans. Peter Dale (London: Carcanet Press, 2001), 245, but I have chosen to favour a more literal translation.

3 The poem seems to have received little attention beyond that of philologists. For the latter, see Sarah Spilsbury, "Villon's *Louenge a la court* Reconsidered", *Neophilologus* 59, no. 4 (1975): 482–493. Spilsbury's assertion that in this poem Villon is certainly not 'irreverent towards the Court' nor 'insincere in his thanks' seems to me to overlook some of the more subtle strategies of venting social critique that this poem contains. Cf. Villon's characterization of court officials in one of the stanzas of his most famous poem, the *Testament*, as people that 'drain their bones and bodies for the public good' and are in need of absolution: Villon, *Lais*, 186.

to lament the position such professional pleaders had come to play.[4] But other legal practitioners could also form the subject of these accusations, such as the scribes and notaries who were responsible for recording cases and thus susceptible to critiques of the power of the quill.[5] Law courts and their individual representatives would even occasionally become the explicit targets of violent protests.[6] Significantly, attacks need not be directed solely against individual officials, but could also involve the destruction of court documents and associated buildings, like prisons and courthouses.[7] Such reactions, however extreme or out-of-the-ordinary they may have been, reflect some of the polyvalent character of medieval understandings of justice. Fixed judicial bodies meting out sentences were not the only, nor necessarily the most accepted form of conflict resolution available.[8] Countering traditional distinctions between fundamentally rule-led and anarchic societies, historians have unearthed widespread evidence of elaborate feuding practices, forms of judicial self-reliance and extra-curial adjudication existing in tandem with legal institutions in the late medieval period.[9] These alternatives show us even more profoundly than explicit critiques of courts how people's legal literacy, that is, the way

4 James A. Brundage, *The Medieval Origins of the Legal Profession: Canonists, Civilians, and Courts* (Chicago and London: University of Chicago Press, 2008), 477–487.

5 Romain Telliez, *'Per potentiam officii': Les officiers devant la justice dans le Royaume de France au XIVe siècle* (Paris: Champion, 2005), 55–62.

6 Alan Harding, "The Revolt against the Justices", in *The English Rising of 1381*, ed. R.H. Hilton and T.H. Aston (Cambridge: Cambridge University Press, 1981).

7 W.M. Ormrod, "The Peasants' Revolt and the Government of England", *Journal of British Studies* 29, no. 1 (1990): 1–30; for similar evidence of attacks on court buildings and documents in Siena (1355) and Paris (1381), see the edited sections of the *Cronaca Senese* and the *Chronographia regnum Francorum* in Samuel K. Cohn, Jr., ed., *Popular Protest in Late Medieval Europe: Italy, France and Flanders* (Manchester and New York: Manchester University Press, 2004), 112–116, 294–299.

8 See the examples in John Bossy, ed., *Disputes and Settlements: Law and Human Relations in the West* (Cambridge: Cambridge University Press, 1983), and for the late Middle Ages, see, in particular, Michael Clanchy, "Law and Love in the Middle Ages", in ibid.

9 Clanchy, "Law and Love"; Gerd Althoff, *Spielregeln der Politik im Mittelalter: Kommunikation in Friede un Fehde* (Darmstadt: Darmstadt Wissenschaftliche Buchgesellschaft, 1997); Société des historiens médiévistes de l'enseignement supérieur public, *Le règlement des conflits au Moyen Âge: Actes du XXXIe congrès de la SHMES, Angers, juin 2000* (Paris: Publications de la Sorbonne, 2001); Paul R. Hyams, *Rancor and Reconciliation in Medieval England* (Ithaca, NY: Cornell University Press, 2003); Warren C. Brown and Piotr Górecki, eds., *Conflict in Medieval Europe: Changing Perspectives on Society and Culture* (Aldershot and Burlington, VT: Ashgate, 2003); Corien Glaudemans, *Om die wrake wille: Eigenrichting, veten en verzoening in laat-middeleeuws Holland en Zeeland* (Hilversum: Verloren, 2004); Jeppe Büchert Netterstrøm and Bjørn Poulsen, eds., *Feud in Medieval and Early Modern Europe* (Aarhus: Aarhus University Press, 2007).

they conceptualized justice and the proper ways to achieve it, extended beyond and could even at times be contrary to the institutional practices and ideology of the law court.[10]

Despite such diverging interpretations of the nature of justice, courts did manage to find a stable place in late medieval societies as prominent dispute settlers and political legitimators, forming crucial fora for individuals to make social, political and legal claims. This did not happen from one day to the next, nor do we see a uniform process between European regions. Yet the integration of courts in the socio-judicial practices of people in many if not most European regions fundamentally increased between 1200 and 1500.[11] Explanations of this change in judicial practice vary widely, relating it to processes of state-building,[12] the growth of bureaucracies, the professionalization of a social class of lawyers,[13] or changes in intellectual

10 Cf. the term 'legal consciousness' as proposed by Anthony Musson, *Medieval Law in Context: The Growth of Legal Consciousness from Magna Carta to the Peasant's Revolt* (Manchester and New York: Manchester University Press, 2001), 7–9. However, Musson's legal consciousness is strongly related to the forms of legal reasoning as practiced in law courts, and is therefore also seen to 'grow' during the late medieval period. I interpret legal literacy as referring to people's ideas and emotions about proper judicial practice more in general, regardless of the form that this idealized system takes, and thus as a constant human factor whose substance may change over time and varies between individuals and societies. In this sense my definition of legal literacy comes closer to what Paul Hyams calls a mentality of 'resentment at wrong' (Hyams, *Rancor*, 265–266), where both what is considered as a 'wrong' and how one's 'resentment' may be eased, is subject to change over time and varies between societies.

11 Anthony Musson and W.M. Ormrod, *The Evolution of English Justice: Law, Politics and Society in the Fourteenth Century* (Basingstoke: Macmillan Press and St. Martin's Press, 1999); Musson, *Medieval Law*; Brundage, *Medieval Origins*, esp. 126–163; for an exceptionally rich image of this integration of courts in practice in fifteenth-century England, see Tom Johnson, *Law in Common: Legal Cultures in Late-Medieval England* (Oxford: Oxford University Press, 2020).

12 Richard W. Kaeuper, *War, Justice, and Public Order: England and France in the Later Middle Ages* (Oxford: Clarendon Press, 1988); Jean-Philippe Genet, ed., *L'état moderne: Genese: Bilans et perspectives: Actes du colloque tenu au CNRS à Paris les 19–20 septembre 1989* (Paris: CNRS Éditions, 1990); Michelle Bubenicek and Richard Partington, "Justice, Law and Lawyers", in *Government and Political Life in England and France, c. 1300–c. 1500*, eds. Christopher Fletcher, Jean-Philippe Genet and John Watts (Cambridge: Cambridge University Press, 2015); this link with state-building is also prominent in many case studies of local legal practice, such as recently Aude Musin, *Sociabilité urbaine et criminalisation étatique: La justice namuroise face à la violence de 1360 à 1555* (Turnhout: Brepols, 2017).

13 Paul Brand, *The Origins of the English Legal Profession* (Oxford and Cambridge, MA: Blackwell, 1992); Susan Reynolds, "The Emergence of Professional Law in the Long Twelfth Century", *Law and History Review* 21, no. 2 (2003): 347–366; Brundage, *Medieval Origins*; R.H. Helmholz, *The Profession of Ecclesiastical Lawyers: An Historical Introduction* (Cambridge and New York: Cambridge University Press, 2019).

traditions or legal theories.[14] Without denying the importance of these factors in understanding socio-judicial change, I contend that these approaches risk a number of pitfalls. Developments are often explained with a specific destination in mind, like the nation state or the modern legal profession. The present-day state of affairs thus provides the primary logic for the long-term historical processes taking place.[15] Moreover, the forces that shape developments work mainly 'from above', by political and economic elites implementing specific ideas and practices among other social actors lower down the hierarchy, or are limited to the internal forum of the court, springing from the interactions within a body of legal officials or between these officials and their superiors. Even in cases where historical actors beyond the court are considered, their role is at best one facilitating specific forms of institutional organization that are effectively beyond them.[16]

Microhistory has famously reacted to such overarching and top-down historical narratives by approaching courts and their records from the opposite direction. Classic works like Emmanuel Le Roy Ladurie's *Montaillou*, Carlo Ginzburg's *The Cheese and the Worms* and Natalie Zemon Davis' *The Return of Martin Guerre* and *Fiction in the Archives* have extensively drawn on the records of various courts in order to reconstruct the daily lives and experiences of people living centuries ago.[17] Rather than attempting to trace broad institutional developments, these authors presented an image

14 Harold J. Berman, *Law and Revolution: The Formation of the Western Legal Tradition* (Cambridge, MA: Harvard University Press, 1983).

15 This tendency echoes the Weberian model of the development of rational-bureaucratic European states: Max Weber, *Economy and Society: An Outline of Interpretive Sociology*, trans. and ed. Guenther Roth and Claus Wittich (New York: Bedminster Press, 1968), esp. 641–900, 956–1005.

16 Such as the oft-repeated assumption of medieval litigants 'willingly' and 'enthusiastically' bringing their cases to court, thereby uncritically supporting the growth of these institutions: Frederik Pedersen, *Marriage Disputes in Medieval England* (London and New York: Hambledon and London, 2000), 11; and more carefully phrased: Brundage, *Medieval Origins*, 126–127. While I agree as to the critical role of litigants in shaping these institutions, said assumption risks instrumentalizing non-court actors, thus leaving them with very little actual agency to shape their interactions with law courts.

17 Emmanuel Le Roy Ladurie, *Montaillou: Village occitan de 1294 à 1324* (Paris: Gallimard, 1982); Carlo Ginzburg, *Il formaggio e i vermi. Il cosmo di un mugnaio del '500* (Turin: Einaudi, 1976); Natalie Zemon Davis, *The Return of Martin Guerre* (Cambridge, MA, and London: Harvard University Press, 1983); idem, *Fiction in the Archives: Pardon Tales and Their Tellers in Sixteenth-Century France* (Stanford: Stanford University Press, 1987). Also see more recently: Thomas N. Bisson, *Tormented Voices: Power, Crisis, and Humanity in Rural Catalonia 1140–1200* (Cambridge, MA, and London: Harvard University Press, 1998); Robert Bartlett, *The Hanged Man: A Story of Miracle, Memory, and Colonialism* (Princeton, NJ: Princeton University Press, 2004); Michael Goodich, ed., *Voices from the Bench: Narratives of Lesser Folk in Medieval Trials* (New York: Palgrave

of people's social interactions and mentalities in a court setting. However, while explicitly empowering the many people glossed over in larger historical narratives, this microhistorical prominence of individual historical actors also created new methodological problems. For in focusing strongly on a geographically and temporally narrow aspect of history, such as one town, individual or event, the relative weight of the studied phenomenon in relation to others is often assumed or otherwise unclear. Furthermore, by shifting attention explicitly away from the large machinations of power, some of these works overlook the strong institutional bias of the documentary sources used by historians to conceive of past people's lives.[18]

Building on and reacting to both historiographical trends, this book will trace the advent of law courts in the late medieval period by focusing on the mutual interaction between courts and the societies in which they operated. Instead of limiting an analysis to the development of formal institutional characteristics, it considers law courts as parts of broader communication processes, involving texts, speech, activities and spaces, through which a large variety of social actors negotiated, debated and struggled over concepts of justice, as well as the proper ways of achieving it.[19] I will argue how court officials themselves took an active part in these processes, attempting to influence people's legal literacy by propagating particular scripts of logic and practice, but will likewise stress courts' dependency on these same 'externals' for legitimizing their own position as adjudicators and guaranteers of social order.[20] As such, I will present the development and increasing popularity of

Macmillan, 2006); Steven Bednarski, *A Poisoned Past: The Life and Times of Margarida de Portu, a Fourteenth-Century Accused Poisoner* (Toronto: University of Toronto Press, 2014).

18 See in particular the methodological discussion on Le Roy Ladurie's *Montaillou* in Chapter 4 and the historiographical reflections on the field of microhistory in Bednarski, *Poisoned Past*, 1–22.

19 Cf. Marco Mostert and P.S. Barnwell, eds., *Medieval Legal Process: Physical, Spoken and Written Performance in the Middle Ages* (Turnhout: Brepols, 2011). Also see Marco Mostert, *A Bibliography of Works on Medieval Communication* (Turnhout: Brepols, 2012) for a sense of the range of media and forms of communication that have received the attention of medievalists in recent years.

20 For the value of taking into account both exogenous and endogenous influences on the development of legal systems, see Musson and Ormrod, *Evolution*, 6–7; however Musson and Ormrod's definition of 'external influences' (war, famine, disease, revolt, tyranny) and 'internal influences' (consumer demand, legal professionals, legislation) seems to echo a legalistic distinction between disorder (i.e. anything that can disrupt the smooth functioning of institutionalized justice) and order (i.e. anything that contributes to a smooth functioning of institutionalized justice), rather than a necessary distinction between what is external or internal to these institutions as such. Thus, consumer demand, which Musson and Ormrod define as an internal influence on the judicial system, would be more appropriately considered as an external influence, as it originates beyond the legal officials that constitute a judicial body. Considering consumers of justice as fundamentally

a court-centred model of justice in the late medieval period as the result of concrete interactions between many agents, be they court officials, litigants or others.[21] This book therefore traces a socio-cultural, rather than a purely legal or institutional, process in late medieval Europe, which shaped ways of conceptualizing and pursuing justice that have remained highly influential in subsequent centuries.

With its focus on the socio-cultural history of law courts, the book positions itself within a growing body of literature. Influenced by the sociology and anthropology of law, an increasing number of historians have turned to stressing the social and cultural embeddedness of medieval courts.[22] While acknowledging the institutional contexts that shaped both legal practice and the written record of this practice, these authors show the influence of broader social and cultural phenomena on the institutionalized court, such as vendetta systems, emotion discourses, ritual forms and conceptualizations of gender. So far these studies have tended to limit their scope to one locality[23] or one region.[24] However, throughout this literature very similar social and cultural processes can be seen to operate in and involve institutionalized courts. For example, engagement with 'bottom up' or communal knowledge in the form of witness testimony, or *fama*, is shown to have occupied courts from Marseilles to York.[25] What is more, examples from legal history have shown the added value of a transregional comparison between courts, even when sticking to the strict confines of one legal system only.[26] While a focus on the court as socio-cultural phenomenon

internal to a judicial system, risks limiting them to the role of 'cogs in the machine' and thus losing sight of their agency. See my critique of the idea of litigants merely facilitating institutional growth above.

21 The focus on tracing a multiplicity of agencies in interaction is influenced by the 'sociology of associations' or Actor-Network-Theory of Bruno Latour and others. See Bruno Latour, *Reassembling the Social: An Introduction to Actor-Network-Theory* (Oxford: Oxford University Press, 2005). For the implications of this sociological perspective on the study of modern courts, see Bruno Latour, *La fabrique du droit* (Paris: La Découverte, 2002).

22 Daniel Lord Smail, *The Consumption of Justice: Emotions, Publicity and Legal Culture in Marseille, 1264–1423* (Ithaca, NY, and London: Cornell University Press, 2003); Trevor Dean, *Crime and Justice in Late Medieval Italy* (Cambridge: Cambridge University Press, 2007); Patricia Turning, *Municipal Officials, Their Public and the Negotiation of Justice in Medieval Languedoc: 'Fear Not the Madness of the Raging Mob'* (Leiden and Boston: Brill, 2012); Steven Bednarski, *Curia: A Social History of a Provençal Criminal Court in the Fourteenth Century* (Montpellier: Presses universitaires de la Méditerranée, 2013); Johnson, *Law in Common*.

23 Smail, *Consumption of Justice*; Turning, *Municipal Officials*; Bednarski, *Curia*.

24 Dean, *Crime and Justice*; Johnson, *Law in Common*.

25 Smail, *Consumption of Justice*, 207–241; Johnson, *Law in Common*, 184–212.

26 Most notably Charles Donahue, *Law, Marriage and Society in the Later Middle Ages: Arguments about Marriage in Five Courts* (Cambridge: Cambridge University Press, 2007).

seems perfectly suited to combine the microhistorical interest in lived experience with a transregional sense of institutional developments, this has to my knowledge not been pursued consistently.[27]

By comparing multiple courts across geographical and legal boundaries, this book is meant to add an absent transregional perspective to the socio-cultural study of medieval law courts. To do so, I have developed three case studies with different geographic, social, political and institutional backgrounds. Next to the royal *Parlement* of Paris, encountered in Villon's poem, I will consider the archiepiscopal Consistory Court of York and the urban Council of Utrecht in the northern Low Countries. My selection of case studies is explicitly meant to cross various geographical, institutional, linguistic and historiographical boundaries that have implicitly shaped much of the scholarship on the phenomenon of the late medieval law court. In taking the communication processes surrounding these courts as a point of departure, I argue that another logic – one looking beyond many of these traditional boundaries and involving both producers and consumers of justice – is fundamental to understanding the proliferation of this particular form of judicial activity in many European societies.[28]

Studying the intersection between institutionalized courts and the many potential consumers of their justice, naturally raises the issue of sources. In late medieval Europe the development of a variety of institutions went hand in hand with increasing amounts of written documentation.[29] Historians studying law courts have therefore based their analyses strongly on written texts, and more in particular on records of court practice or 'court records'.[30] However, the means by which late medieval people negotiated definitions and practices of justice comprised a much broader range of modes of communication, including the spoken word, embodied acts, images, objects and spaces.[31] Tracing the socio-cultural history of law courts thus means on the one hand to pay serious attention to the many forms of communication that constituted these institutions beyond their written legacy, and on the other

27 A notable exception being Susan Reynolds, *Kingdoms and Communities in Western Europe, 900–1300* (Oxford: Clarendon Press, 1984), who, however, treats law courts as part of a broader socio-political history of 'collective activity'.

28 Cf. the consumerist model proposed by Daniel Lord Smail in Smail, *Consumption of Justice*, and discussed extensively in Chapter 5 of this book.

29 Michael Clanchy, *From Memory to Written Record: England 1066–1307*, 3rd ed. (Chichester and Malden, MA: Wiley-Blackwell, 2013).

30 Frans Camphuijsen and Jamie Page, "Introduction: New Approaches to Late Medieval Court Records", *Open Library of Humanities*, 5(1), no. 69 (2019): 1–26, DOI: http://doi.org/10.16995/olh.505.

31 Mostert and Barnwell, *Medieval Legal Process*.

to consider the role of the documents themselves more firmly within this contemporary multimedial context. Both approaches are pursued in this book, with the explicit purpose not only to understand the functioning of court records within a late medieval communicative context, but also to reflect methodologically on the uses made of these written fragments of medieval communication by historians.

Scripting Justice will thus develop a number of interrelated arguments, concerning sources, methodology and historical developments. First of all it argues for a socio-cultural interpretation of the 'rise of the law court' in the late medieval period. It contends that the increasing acceptance of and reliance on a specific court-centred model, notwithstanding the presence of multiple other ways to define and pursue justice, needs to be understood in terms of the history of communicative interactions between the courts as producers and the many contemporary consumers of justice. Secondly, because the influence of the development of institutionalized courts on people's lived experience can be seen to have played a role in many different regions of late medieval Europe, it is deemed relevant to trace these communicative interactions comparatively across geographical, legal and other boundaries. Doing so will help us to distinguish broader social and cultural aspects of late medieval lives from the particular institutions that developed locally or regionally. Lastly, court records, being the primary yet highly limited documentary basis for historians' view on these communicative interactions, need to be considered more firmly within their contemporary contexts of multimedial communication. To better understand people's experiences of late medieval law courts it is fundamental to consider these courts as more than text-producing entities, while also, however, recognizing the impact of the increasing number of court documents on people's lives. Each of these three arguments engages partly unique and partly overlapping historiographies and theoretical frameworks. In what follows I will further introduce them one by one, before giving an overview of the structure of the book as a whole.

Court records

In the thirteenth century, courts in north-western Europe began generating large numbers of written reports of the cases appearing before them. This was neither exclusively nor even primarily a regional phenomenon. Northern and central Italy, for instance, had seen a very similar development during the twelfth century, when communal courts began producing an increasing amount of records.[32] Nor was this development necessarily linear and evenly spread within north-western Europe. Where some courts already produced records around 1200, others have left nothing earlier than the late fourteenth century.[33] But overall a parallel practice became commonplace in courts from different legal traditions, which saw them committing more and more to writing. This broader change is in itself relevant to explore, if only because its chronology overlaps so strongly with the institutional developments that saw the establishment of law courts in these regions. Far from forming a uniform programme implemented from the top – wherever that may be – downwards, keeping court records came to be a varied and multidirectional practice, shared among many different courts from various jurisdictional hierarchies and localities.[34] The mutual development of record-keeping and other marked aspects of these judicial institutions – permanent courtrooms, specialized functionaries, and more – stand at the centre of this story.

The proliferation of court recordings did not necessarily lead to any uniformity of documentation. Differences between how courts produced and used written materials could be great, from the written acts composed by the *Parlement*, to the Utrecht Council's registers of verdicts, to records of witness testimony in York.[35] Why then consider them as one category of documents, distinct from other categories? Part of the answer has to do with understanding the role of the document as an object, rather than just a text.[36] As Chapter 4 will show, building on an interpretation of texts that has become commonplace in integrationist linguistics, court documents were essentially verbal utterances and material artefacts combined. These language-objects, through their association of two distinct practices, form

32 Chris Wickham, *Courts and Conflict in Twelfth-Century Tuscany* (Oxford: Oxford University Press, 2003), 8–9. Note furthermore that Italy had seen earlier phases of intense court record production: ibid., 8.

33 For the English royal court, for example, rolls of pleas are extant as early as 1194: Clanchy, *Memory*, 98–99.

34 For important reflections on the production, use and logic of late medieval court records, see Daniel Lord Smail, "Aspects of Procedural Documentation in Marseille (14th–15th Centuries)", in *Als die Welt in die Akten kam. Prozeßschriftgut im europäischen Mittelalter*, eds. Susanne Lepsius and Thomas Wetzstein (Frankfurt am Main: Vittorio Klostermann, 2008).

35 For a sense of the diversity of documents falling under the header of 'court records', see the various contributions to the online *Open Library of Humanities* special collection 'New Approaches to Late Medieval Court Records' and in particular the introduction to the collection: Camphuijsen and Page, "Introduction".

36 The value of treating the materiality of court records is also shown in Tom Johnson, "Legal Ephemera in the Ecclesiastical Courts of Late-Medieval England", *Open Library of Humanities* 5(1), no. 17 (2019): 1–27, DOI: https://doi.org/10.16995/olh.334.

particularly tactile forms of communication with their own communicative dynamic.[37] The objects dealt with in this context had one main locus of use, namely, the courtroom. Contrary to other legal texts, like law codes and other regulations, court records had a very physical relation to the courtroom, because they were frequently produced and often also physically used there. They thus stood closer to the daily comings and goings at court than most other documents broadly called legal, even those that only survive in the form of fair copies. In addition, from a linguistic point of view, their relation to the legal process as such was diverse, in that they prescribed, described, but also often performed this process.

The physical records themselves are thus very much part of this history. Moreover, involving them in such a way makes it possible to connect them more fundamentally to the many non-textual forms of communication that comprised the legal process. Since one of the intentions of this book is to reconstruct late medieval courts as multimedial fora, it is paramount to place these text-objects within a broader context of the speech, spaces and activities involved in the daily practice of the courts: a multimedial context both mediated by and underlying the surviving textual record. This book will therefore consider court records next to and in relation to the court as space, the often ritualized activity taking place there, and the people participating in such legal performances. This approach thus broadens our understanding of these documents and the cultures in which they were used, confronting us with the defining, albeit heavily biased, view that such records promote. Historians depend on them for much of their understanding of people's legal practices and experiences, but have to be careful not to lose sight of the logic and ideology of their production and maintenance.[38] The relation that is important to consider is thus not just between these records and the world in which they were made and used, but also between us historians, these documents of social practice and the world for which they form some of our richest sources.

Comparing courts

If offering a broader understanding of medieval court records and their uses is a major goal of this book, no less important is to explore the potential of a comparative approach towards late medieval law courts. In 1928, Marc

37 Roy Harris, "The Semiology of Textualization", *Language Sciences* 6, no. 2 (1984): 271–286.
38 For a similar approach to modern court records, see Latour, *Fabrique du droit.*

Bloch announced that the time had come to break down 'the outmoded topographical compartments within which we seek to confine social realities'.[39] Given the legal pluralism of late medieval Europe, this call for comparative history seems all the more important. The socio-legal reality of late medieval Europe was after all one where different types of courts operated next to, together with or in competition with each other.[40] Among scholars of late medieval law courts topographical compartmentalization in itself is occasionally challenged.[41] But it is not done so extensively or regularly. Nor do most studies try to bridge other forms of classification, like that between different legal traditions or types of courts. It is possible to construct an increasingly full image of city authorities' legal activities in highly urbanized areas like the Low Countries or northern Italy.[42] Likewise, the royal courts of, for example, France and England, have a rich historiography, covering centuries of scholarship.[43] And the courts from the canon law tradition are similarly well researched.[44] But these formal boundaries need not have influenced contemporaries as much as one might assume, based on modern experiences or medieval ideal types.[45] They constituted claims to a certain power and conceptualizations of an ideal legal order, but do not directly tell us everything about how contemporaries actually operated in navigating the legal pluralism surrounding them. By sticking

39 Marc Bloch, "Pour une histoire comparée des sociétiés Européennes", in *Mélanges historiques* (Paris: Fleuris, 1963), 36.

40 Musson, *Medieval Law*, 9–18.

41 See, for example, Dean, *Crime and Justice*, who compares the judicial activities of a large number of urban authorities in Italy, and Donahue, *Law, Marriage and Society*, who makes a comparison between five ecclesiastical courts from England, France and the Low Countries.

42 Wim Blockmans, "Les pouvoirs publics dans des régions de haute urbanisation: 'Flandre' et 'Italie' aux XIVe–XVIe siècles", in *Villes de Flandre et d'Italie (XIIIe–XVIe siècle): Les enseignements d'une comparaison*, eds. Élisabeth Crouzet-Pavan and Élodie Lecuppre-Desjardin (Turnhout: Brepols, 2008); Élodie Lecuppre-Desjardin, "The Space of Punishments: Reflections on the Expression and Perception of Judgment and Punishment in the Cities of the Low Countries in the Late Middle Ages", in *The Power of Space in Late Medieval and Early Modern Europe: The Cities of Italy, Northern France and the Low Countries*, eds. Marc Boone and Martha Howell (Turnhout: Brepols, 2013).

43 A rich bibliography is provided in Malcolm Vale, "Courts", in *Government and Political Life in England and France, c. 1300–c. 1500*, eds. Christopher Fletcher, Jean-Philippe Genet and John Watts (Cambridge: Cambridge University Press, 2015); Bubenicek and Partington, "Justice", in ibid.

44 Donahue, *Law, Marriage and Society*; Brundage, *Medieval Origins*; Mia Korpiola, ed., *Regional Variations in Matrimonial Law and Custom in Europe, 1150–1600* (Leiden and Boston: Brill, 2011).

45 Cf. Susan Reynolds' important argument about the transregional similarity of collective activity in medieval Europe vis-à-vis ideas of (proto-national) differences, in Reynolds, *Kingdoms*, 7–9.

too strongly to these formal jurisdictional separations, we risk losing sight of developments in broader socio-legal practice.

The comparison that this book thus intends to make goes beyond the purely geographical – York, Paris, Utrecht – but also involves more extensive differences between the three cases under scrutiny. As the first chapter shows, institutionally, all three courts found themselves in very different positions within a (theoretical) jurisdictional hierarchy, from the highest court in the Capetian realm, to the governing board of one, albeit prestigious, urban centre in the Low Countries. All three worked within different legal traditions – be it canon law, Roman law or something else altogether – that overlapped only partially. To complicate matters even more, their individual competences differed strongly, some being clearly limited to what from a modern Western viewpoint would be considered judicial activities, others claiming executive powers that had a much broader, and more strongly political character. And even between their 'purely' legal activities there were major differences. Some courts focused on accusational dispute resolution, letting litigants take the initiative to begin a legal process, while others primarily operated *ex officio*, by initiating these processes themselves. Considering such broad differences between the three courts, and thus between what is generally identified as late medieval law courts, we might rightly ask whether a comparison between entities so different is possible at all. Is it even feasible to define anything like a late medieval law court? Or are they simply a category too diverse to allow any kind of overarching characteristic to be identified?

In answering these questions we turn to one of the basic activities underlying the social role of law courts, namely, the resolution of disputes. The attempt to resolve a conflict of some sort is fundamental to most types of legal procedure that were and are practiced in the courtroom, be they accusatory or inquisitorial.[46] Yet systems of dispute resolution themselves are far from dependent on the institutionalized form of the law court. As anthropologists and social historians have come to recognize, neither the presence of central government agencies, nor even of a judging third party is a necessary condition for such a system to be in place.[47] Considering societies that are chronologically and geographically close to the ones considered

46 See furthermore Massimo Vallerani, *Medieval Public Justice*, trans. Sarah Rubin Blanshei (Washington, DC: The Catholic University of America Press, 2012), who argues that both types of legal procedure often overlapped, and cannot be strictly separated.

47 Simon Roberts, "The Study of Dispute: Anthropological Perspectives", in: *Disputes and Settlements: Law and Human Relations in the West*, ed. John Bossy (Cambridge: Cambridge University Press, 1983), 10–11.

here reveals a variety of mechanisms for dispute resolution, many of which did not involve formal courts, or attributed them with a minor role in the peacemaking process.[48] Nor is this form of social interaction exclusively limited to human groups and societies, as primatologist Frans de Waal has extensively shown.[49] The form mechanisms of dispute resolution take thus varies greatly between different times, places, societies and even species.

What connects the forms that emerged in the three societies treated here, and identifies them as law courts, was the specific role they claimed in the resolution of disputes. Considering the roles third parties can play in such processes of mitigation, anthropologist Philip Gulliver has proposed to distinguish between those of negotiators and adjudicators.[50] The fundamental difference between the two lies in the place where the power of decision is located. In case of a negotiation the parties themselves hold the competence to decide, while the third party mainly acts as a facilitating agency. In case of adjudication, however, this power is claimed by the third party.[51] In medieval practice, the distinction between these two categories was far from absolute. All courts treated here, and York's Consistory Court in particular, accepted various forms of extra-curial negotiation, regularly taking a facilitating role in processes of peacemaking. However, as Chapter 5 will show, the social claim that these courts posed did present them in a strong adjudicatory role. And in this they differed markedly from some earlier judicial bodies.[52] Where early medieval royal and seigneurial courts provided provisional fora for arbitration, the later courts studied here presented themselves consciously as third parties that held the power to judge.[53] Thus, although in practice the facilitating and adjudicatory roles often worked in tandem, ideologically the emphasis shifted to the latter.

48 Hanna Vollrath, "Rebels and Rituals: From Demonstrations of Enmity to Criminal Justice", in *Medieval Concepts of the Past: Ritual, Memory, Historiography*, eds. Gerd Althoff, Johannes Fried and Patrick Geary (Cambridge: Cambridge University Press and Washington, DC: German Historical Institute, 2002). See the contributions in: Netterstrøm and Poulsen, *Feud*, for various examples of late medieval feuding systems in northern and southern Europe. Also note Susan Reynolds' preference for the term 'assemblies' over 'courts' for many judicial gatherings before the twelfth century: Reynolds, *Kingdoms*, 24–25.

49 Frans de Waal, *Peacemaking among Primates* (Cambridge, MA: Harvard University Press, 1990).

50 Philip Gulliver, *Disputes and Negotiations: A Cross-cultural Perspective* (New York and London: Academic Press, 1979), 3–7.

51 Roberts, 'Dispute', 13–15.

52 Vollrath, 'Rebels', 92–94.

53 Cf. the relative flexibility in numbers and composition of Iberian judicial bodies in the ninth and tenth century, as treated in Wendy Davies, "Judges and Judging: Truth and Justice

At the same time, the documentary evidence plays an important role in distinguishing these courts from other forms of judicial activity. As mentioned, one of the main features of these institutionalized judicial bodies was the increasing use made of court records. The appearance of such documents between the thirteenth and fifteenth centuries is an important factor linking the different courts considered here. Such an increase in the use of written texts in the activities of the court is not an isolated development, but is, as I will show, closely related to other organizational changes in these adjudicative bodies. As suggested by Michael Clanchy in his linking of developments in literacy to those in the royal bureaucracy, the increasing use of texts formed part of the advent of particular bureaucratic ways of working and thus of a particular style of dealing with disputes or potential disputes arising from interactions in society.[54] However, as Simon Roberts has stressed, the use of texts is not a necessary characteristic of any adjudicative body, and the distinction between negotiation and adjudication cannot be paired automatically with one between formal state-directed judicial processes and informal practices of negotiation.[55] The fact that certain bureaucratic modalities, including a relatively strong reliance on texts, did form part of the bodies under scrutiny, is something to be explained rather than an inevitable consequence of their role in dispute resolution processes.

Related to these first two features, various other characteristics can be unearthed that were held in common by all three courts. One important similarity was their fixed location. Although many law courts developed out of the itinerant courts of secular and ecclesiastical magnates, by the time they took the shape of a text-producing adjudicative body, they had fixed their place of operations in one locality. And in this state they managed to survive major political upheavals and intellectual transformations, showing a strong socially embedded logic of connecting particular places with judicial activities.[56] This has important implications for the exact

in Northern Iberia on the Eve of the Millennium", *Journal of Medieval History* 36, no. 3 (2010): 193–203.

54 Clanchy, *Memory*, 18–19, 64–70.

55 Roberts, 'Dispute', 14; also see Susan Reynolds' arguments about the role of non-textual custom on legal developments in medieval Europe before the twelfth century: Reynolds, *Kingdoms*, 12–38.

56 The most striking example is probably the seat of the Parisian *Parlement*, the *Palais de la Cité*. Despite major socio-political upheavals since the end of the Middle Ages, most notable of which was the French Revolution, the modern *Palais de justice*, which houses some of the highest courts in France, is still situated at the same site, thus continuing its explicit association with legal practice for over seven centuries. Also see Katherine Fischer Taylor, "Le code et l'équité: La transformation du palais de justice de Paris au XIXe siècle", in *La justice en ses temples: Regards*

understanding of law courts. For, apart from their institutional sense, law courts can also readily be understood as spatial phenomena. The fact that we begin to see such a unity of place for these bodies in this period suggests that institutional and documentary developments were somehow related to the use of place and space in legal practice. The same goes for the legal practice proper. The attitudes and practices of these courts as regards the course of the legal process – including the use of space, the management of time and the relation towards potential audiences – often show a remarkably similar logic.

It is thus possible from the outset to point out both strong similarities and marked contrasts between the three case studies. The question that follows, however, is: What interpretive value do such similarities and contrasts hold? Do they show that these courts are mere variations on a common theme, or are they, on the contrary, locally embedded forms that happen to share one or two characteristics? Are they, in other words, defined by certain overarching structural developments, or primarily by their individual contexts? Similar considerations have been famously put forward by David Nirenberg in the context of the study of medieval minorities. In his *Communities of Violence*, Nirenberg argued for a context-driven approach to the interpretation of violence against religious and social minorities. According to Nirenberg, historians tended to overemphasize the continuity of collective discourses on minorities, while downplaying local particularities. In such approaches, individual instances of violence are strung together in a long narrative from medieval to modern times, often obfuscating the particular meanings such occasions had for contemporaries.[57]

The same critique holds for much of the historiography on law courts. In line with broader narratives on the rise of the state, law courts are often presented as paragons of a process of bureaucratic centralization and rationalization eventually resulting in the modern nation state. The tendency is particularly strong among historians of royal courts.[58] But the state-building narrative is present in other historiographies as well. Cities and their politico-legal institutions, such as law courts, are often regarded within the context of the appearance of large political constellations, either as a fundamental basis of or, to the contrary, as independent bodies resisting

sur l'architecture judiciaire en France, ed. Association Française pour l'histoire de la justice (Paris: Éditions Errance and Poitiers: Éditions Brissaud, 1992).

57 David Nirenberg, *Communities of Violence: Persecution of Minorities in the Middle Ages* (Princeton, NJ: Princeton University Press, 1996), 3–7.

58 Kaeuper, *War*; Bubenicek and Partington, "Justice".

state-based centralization.[59] The narrative can even be found underlying work on ecclesiastical law courts. Although distinct from the process of nation building, there exists a tendency to read many of the developments in late medieval church courts, such as the codification of law or the professionalization of its personnel, as constituting the institutional origins of the later secular state apparatus.[60] Like the historiography with which Nirenberg is concerned, such perspectives on the role of premodern law courts follow a teleological interpretation of history, stressing the institutional continuities that would underlie the birth of the modern nation state. Or, as Norbert Elias, a well-known spokesman of this approach, has formulated it, 'the compelling forces of social interweaving have led the transformation of Western society in one and the same direction from the time of utmost feudal disintegration to the present'.[61] I agree with Nirenberg that such approaches, in replacing a contextual analysis with a strongly directional historical narrative, can tell us very little about the activities and concerns of historical actors.

On the other hand, more than is the case for Nirenberg, whose work is largely concerned with individual instances of violence and people's interpretations of these events, the study of law courts fundamentally involves structural patterns of thought and behaviour. Such broader patterns – or at least their suggestion – were part of how judicial bodies legitimized their own existence. It was thus partly a discursive strategy utilized by successive generations of court operatives to position themselves against potential resistance to their desired role in society. Even beyond purely discursive strategies, however, courts as institutions displayed very tangible structural developments. As has been argued, their places of operation were often fixed

59 Neithard Bulst and Jean-Philippe Genet, eds., *La ville, la bourgeoisie et la genèse de l'état moderne (XIIe–XVIIIe siècles): Actes du colloque de Bielefeld (29 novembre–1er décembre 1985)* (Paris: Centre National de la Recherche Scientifique, 1988); Wim Blockmans, "Voracious States and Obstructing Cities: An Aspect of State Formation in Preindustrial Europe", *Theory and Society* 18, no. 5 (1989): 733–755; Charles Tilly and Wim Blockmans, eds., *Cities and the Rise of States in Europe, A.D. 1000 to 1800* (Boulder, CO: Westview Press, 1994); Wim Blockmans, André Holenstein and Jon Mathieu, eds., *Empowering Interactions: Political Cultures and the Emergence of the State in Europe, 1300–1900* (Farnham and Burlington, VT: Ashgate, 2009).
60 Berman, *Law and Revolution*; Brundage, *Medieval Origins*.
61 Norbert Elias, *Über den Prozess der Zivilisation* (Basel: Haus zum Falken, 1939), 438: 'Hier führt das Hebelwerk der Verflechtungsmechanismen in der Tat von der Zeit der aüßersten feudalen Desintegration bis zur Gegenwart hin die Veränderung des abendländischen Menschengeflechts in ein und derselben Richtung weiter.' For the English translation, see Norbert Elias, *The Civilizing Process: The History of Manners and State Formation and Civilization*, trans. Edmund Jephcott (Oxford and Cambridge, MA: Blackwell, 1994), 515.

for several centuries, in some cases surviving momentous political events that rocked the institution itself or at least its political underpinnings. Thus, the actual locations where justice 'was to be had' could be constant for decades, if not centuries on end. Moreover, strong continuities can also be found in the documentary material. To be sure, one needs to be careful not to project later archivists' attempts at serialization back on the institutions producing the texts. But such later attempts at standardization notwithstanding, these courts produced, used and archived specific types of texts over successive generations, which influenced these bodies' interactions with and interpretations of the world beyond the court over the long term. These and other institutional structuralities thus formed an inalienable aspect of the lived experience of contemporaries in encountering late medieval law courts, as the various chapters in this book will show.

Rather than distinguishing strongly between the structural and the particular, this book seeks to lay bare the creative tension between both. It contends that individual interactions between court officials and others, be they litigants, witnesses or audiences, were shaped by more structural features, such as the spaces of procedure, the use of written texts, or discourses on social order and disorder. However, these structural features in their turn only developed because they were put into practice through many individual occasions of interaction involving varying actors and contexts. A comparison between communicative interactions involving law courts of different types and from different regions is thus meant to negotiate between these structural and particular aspects of developing court practice. Working from individual social experiences of interacting in and with courts, this book will seek to trace broader structural patterns in these experiences both geographically, but also diachronically. Comparing multiple late medieval law courts from the perspective of communicative interaction is thus explicitly meant to unpack the creative tension between the structural and the particular, between a certain institutional obdurateness and the many instances of interaction between these institutions and broader society.

Communication, performance and scripting

The approach I will follow in tracing the development of law courts looks for explanations where judicial institutions and their respective societies interact. It looks at the legal process before all else as a communication process, a constellation of words, signs, spaces and actions through which various groups and individuals were making sense of the world around them and laying claims to its interpretation. Such a perspective has found a growing group of adherents among cultural and social historians. Some focus on the role of publicity and theatricality in the cases conducted in court.[62] Others emphasize the way in which participants in the legal process formed legal narratives or discourses.[63] Giving communication a central role in the understanding of legal practice has in fact a long history in academia. In his *De la division du travail social*, Émile Durkheim argued for a discursive interpretation of penal activity. Punishment, according to Durkheim, was essentially a show of concerted aversion by a society whose collective conscience had been infringed by a particular act. It was a means by which society told itself what it thought and valued.[64] Drawing on this interpretation of judicial activity as communal discourse, sociologists have come to emphasize the cultural and discursive elements in law. Philip Smith, for example, sees the creation of meaning as one of the central aspects of penalizing behaviour. Punishment constitutes a communicative act by which people speak about contrasting pairs of concepts, like order versus disorder and purity versus pollution, in discussing their society's moral identity.[65]

In this communicative approach to law, legal acts are essentially interpreted as speech acts, a term strongly associated with the English philosopher of language John Austin. Austin distinguished a particular type of speech, so-called performative utterances. This category constituted all those statements that do not simply describe a given action, but in effect perform the act itself, thereby bringing about an actual change in the world. Thus, when a court pronounces a verdict it is not just giving an account of the decision taken in a specific case, but brings the decision into existence.

62 Esther Cohen, "To Die a Criminal for the Public Good: The Execution Ritual in Late Medieval Paris", in *Law, Custom and the Social Fabric in Medieval Europe: Essays in Honour of Bryce Lyon*, eds. Bernard S. Bachrach and David Nicholas (Kalamazoo: Medieval Institute Publications, Western Michigan University, 1990); Smail, *Consumption of Justice*.

63 Claude Gauvard, *'De grace especial': Crime, état et société en France à la fin du Moyen Âge* (Paris: Publications de la Sorbonne, 1991); John Arnold, *Inquisition and Power: Catharism and the Confessing Subject in Medieval Languedoc* (Philadelphia: University of Pennsylvania Press, 2001); Mark G. Pegg, *The Corruption of Angels: The Great Inquisition of 1245–1246* (Princeton, NJ, and Oxford: Princeton University Press, 2001); Dean, *Crime and Justice*; Jeremy Goldberg, *Communal Discord, Child Abduction and Rape in the Later Middle Ages* (New York and Basingstoke: Palgrave Macmillan, 2008).

64 Émile Durkheim, *De la division du travail social*, 5th ed. (Paris: Félix Alcan, 1926), 76–77, translated as Émile Durkheim, *The Division of Labor in Society*, trans. George Simpson (Glencoe, IL: Free Press, 1960), 108–109.

65 Philip Smith, *Punishment and Culture* (Chicago and London: University of Chicago Press, 2008), 13–15.

Whereas the accused has until then resided in limbo between guilt and innocence, through this linguistic utterance he becomes either an offender or an innocent man. For Austin, however, the utterance of a certain type of statement by itself was not sufficient for it to count as performative. He drew up several prerequisites for what he called a 'felicitous' – we may also say 'effective' – performance. One of these was the condition of 'appropriate circumstances'. If a verdict is not pronounced by a judge in a court setting, it fails as a performative utterance, since people are unlikely to acknowledge the speaker as an authoritative performer or the context as one in which verdicts can be pronounced. For Austin there thus had to exist a certain convention between speech participants in order to make a performative utterance work.[66]

It was in further elaborating on the Austinian condition of conventionality, that the French sociologist Pierre Bourdieu developed his own theory of linguistic practice. For Bourdieu, linguistic conventions were above all socially constructed phenomena, which involved the relations between different actors in a particular linguistic arena. Following from his more general theory of practice, Bourdieu saw language use as springing from a combination of people's linguistic habitus and the specific field in which they operated. In this model, the habitus encapsulated all those pregiven socially determined factors that shape the way someone perceives, thinks of and acts in the world at a given moment, that is to say, people's historically developed frame of reference. With these preconceived notions and habits in mind, actors then engage in a field, a socio-spatial arena with its own rules, where they encounter and interact with other social agents. In these linguistic fields – often also indicated as markets – agents possess varying amounts of symbolic capital, which entails the recognition by other participants in the field of the legitimacy of the speaker's use of language. Performative utterances, Bourdieu emphasized, are only effective in so far as their speaker possesses a form of legitimacy that is external to the utterance itself.[67] Thus, in Bourdieu's understanding, the reason that a court's verdict can actually be considered a performative statement is because its speaker is recognized by others – who have learned to rely on the court in certain cases – as a legitimate pronouncer of verdicts.

66 John Austin, *How to Do Things with Words*, ed. J.O. Urmson (Cambridge, MA: Harvard University Press, 1962), 1–38. For a recent introduction into Austinian theories of performativity, see James Loxley, *Performativity* (London and New York: Routledge, 2007).

67 Pierre Bourdieu, *Language and Symbolic Power*, ed. John Thompson, trans. Gino Raymond and Matthew Adamson (Cambridge, MA: Harvard University Press, 1991), 37–89; also see Thompson's clarifying editor's introduction in the same volume.

In emphasizing the social embeddedness of language, Bourdieu crucially broadens our understanding of performative speech. Whereas Austin limited his understanding of performativity primarily to spoken language, Bourdieu's integration of linguistic activity in a broader theory of practice seeks to sensitize us to the performative qualities of the many non-vocal types of interaction. Acts like looking, dressing, moving about and positioning oneself in space all have the potential to change the perceived reality of the people involved in them, and are in that sense acts of performative communication.[68] In the same way that the pronunciation of a verdict can turn a defendant into a culprit, the public enactment of a penal measure can make the law effective for those witnessing the event. Consequently, in this book we will encounter the term 'performance' in two understandings, both concerned with the link between speech and practice. The first, working in the Austinian line of reasoning as set out above, considers as a performance those instances where an individual performs an act by speaking. In the second sense, which is closer to the understanding of the term among students of theatre, to perform is to say something by means of an act, not necessarily an oral one. Essentially then, performance is concerned with a two-sided relation between speaking and acting. Furthermore, as this book, and in particular its third and fourth chapters, will show, this relationship between the two modalities of performance is not mutually exclusive. Rather, both aspects of the relationship – acting through speech and speaking in acts – formed an essential means for the participants in the medieval legal process to claim legitimacy.

Bourdieu, like many social theorists, is mainly concerned with performative speech in a modern context. The ideas about people's habitus, linguistic fields and socio-linguistic capital on which his model is based, tend to assume the existence of modern forms and institutions, like a centralized state and legal system.[69] Consequently, the historical coming into being of specific fields or forms of linguistic capital as distinguished by Bourdieu, tends to be absent from the analysis or reduced to a strongly teleological reading. An analysis of socio-judicial communicative interaction in the medieval period, concerned as it is with a world where extensive legal pluralism and limited institutional fixation meant a fundamentally different constellation of linguistic fields, capital and habitus, allows a look beyond these modern assumptions to shed light exactly on this coming into being

68 On the role of non-linguistic forms of performance, also see Judith Butler, *Notes Toward a Performative Theory of Assembly* (Cambridge, MA, and London: Harvard University Press, 2015).
69 Thompson, in Bourdieu, *Language*, 25.

of more familiar linguistic fields and socio-linguistic capital. In other words, to understand the institutions and modes of communication that influence so much of Bourdieu's linguistic practice, their late medieval modalities form a crucial piece of the puzzle. As Chapter 5 of this book will show in more detail, my analysis of socio-judicial communicative interaction will not be limited to a social contextualization of linguistic practice, but will also involve the ways in which such a social context of linguistic fields and capital takes shape.

To attune our understanding of linguistic practice to such historic variety, it is important to stress not only the socially constructed character of this practice, but also to consider the ways in which speech acts in their turn contribute to shaping – and thereby also changing – the fields where they are performed and the socio-linguistic capital they express. In this understanding, linguistic fields and capital are not necessarily pregiven external factors, but may themselves form part of the negotiation of legitimate speech. This enriches our view of linguistic practice in several ways. On the one hand, it explains speakers' motivations for trying their hand at performative utterances in situations where the relative symbolic capital is not clearly recognizable for or accepted by everyone. This would be the case, for example, if a court pronounces a verdict in a situation where its legitimacy is disputed by other authorities or in light of a certain socio-judicial tradition; a not uncommon situation in late medieval Europe. The verdict itself may well fail as a performative utterance in a direct sense if those involved in the case do not recognize the court as a legitimate speaker. Yet by pronouncing it as such, the court also poses a claim for its legitimacy to utter this particular type of performative statement; a claim that upon regular reiteration may well succeed in structurally changing ideas about the legitimacy of its verdicts. Furthermore, this understanding of speech acts allows for an interpretation of historical changes as being not merely socially, economically or politically driven, but also the result of the performance strategies of speakers in a field. When a court at some point successfully manages to claim jurisdiction over a particular type of case, this need not only signal developments in the social, economic or political constellations surrounding it. We can also explain this change in judicial legitimacy by considering the court's and others' previous activities in the linguistic field, that is, as an effect of the posing and counter-posing of claims to legitimate speech.

This posing of claims to legitimate and authoritative speech will form the central process on the basis of which this book traces the history of late medieval law courts. In order to cover both linguistic and non-linguistic means of posing such claims, I will consider these attempts as forms of scripting. That is to say, by making performative utterances, be they bodily, vocally, textually or otherwise, one or more actors in a communicative field may suggest a specific script according to which all participants in the said field are supposed to operate in order to become legitimate speakers. Thus, to draw once more on our previous example, the judge's verdict is more than a single vocalized utterance to claim legitimacy for its speaker. Rather, it presents those witnessing the event with a constellation of spaces, acts, words and symbols, constituting what is claimed to be the proper way to do justice. Such processes of scripting explicitly extend the socio-legal communicative activity beyond the officials operating the court. Although the latter's voice is often heard most prominently, the communicative activity surrounding these courts was largely given form and meaning by the many non-officials who were in some way or another involved, be it as active participants, ostensibly passive audiences, or a combination of both. Like language in general, socio-legal performance was not only shaped by its most obvious producers, but just as much by those traditionally considered as its passive consumers.[70] By taking the communicative activity between court and broader society as the main *explanans* for these bodies' historical development, this study thus critically involves the roles of all these historical agents in an understanding of the court.

Structure of the book

The main threads of this book – the role of court records, the possibilities of comparison and the legal process as communication process – are integrated into four thematic chapters. However, since the book also encapsulates three different case studies, the Council of Utrecht, the Consistory Court of York and the *Parlement* of Paris, these cases will first be considered within their respective historical contexts. Chapter 1, 'Profiles: Three late medieval law courts', thus treats the social, political and legal environment of the three courts, presenting a case-by-case overview of developments before, during and after the period on which the focus of this book lies. This chapter provides a first consideration of the practical aspects of the

70 Bourdieu, *Language*, 38–39. Important to note in this context is furthermore Michel de Certeau, *The Practice of Everyday Life*, trans. Steven Rendall (Berkeley: University of California Press, 1984), whose ideas also concern the way in which cultural products – like language – are essentially produced by their consumers. Cf. Smail, *Consumption of Justice*.

courts, like personnel and location, and sets out their formal organization, judicial competences and the records they produced. Mapping the historical context in this way is crucial for understanding the particularities of each of the courts, and forms a necessary basis for the broader developments that I trace in the subsequent chapters.

Chapter 2, 'Legal space', provides a first thematic exploration. It proceeds from the idea that a law court, besides its character as an institution, is primarily a location where specific activities take place. Drawing on the work of Henri Lefebvre and others, it offers a spatial analysis of the law courts under scrutiny, asking how judicial activities related to the sites where they were performed. The chapter is first of all concerned with the choice, construction or reconstruction of places to be used in the legal process. As the three cases studied here illustrate, such spaces could vary widely, from churches to royal palaces to market squares and guild halls. At the same time, however, they exhibit remarkable similarities as regards the way in which people used and adapted them to accommodate both public and non-public aspects of the court's daily business. Furthermore, the court's relation to its spatial context also had a more discursive side. In speaking about aspects of space, from the stones used to repair the city wall to the boundaries of areas of jurisdiction, people used their built and demarcated environment to generate meaning in the context of the legal process. As such, space – and particularly urban space – both influenced and was influenced by the legal activities taking place within it.

From a consideration of the role of space vis-à-vis legal activity, Chapter 3, 'The rituality of court practice', shifts focus to the character of court practices themselves. Building on anthropological theories of ritual, it considers legal acts as ritualized acts, forms of activity that are given meaning in relation to perceived broader structures of meaningful activity. By analyzing particular instances of legal practice for each of the three courts under consideration, this chapter illustrates how actors in these courts linked the things they did to such broader structures of meaning. Ritualizing court activity in this way thus became a means to claim legitimacy for these practices, their actors, and the institution catering to them. Although the forms these activities could take varied greatly between the different courts, their role in performing and thus validating the court can be seen in each instance. In this we see again how considerations of the audiences to be reached with such communicative activity shaped much of what took place in court.

Chapter 4, 'Legal text and social context', zooms in on the court records that underlie much of this book. It considers the role of texts in the legal process and their complex relation to other forms of communication that took place in law courts. The creation and use of a text, here interpreted in the integrationist sense as language-objects, had a particular influence on the nature and content of the communicative activity thereby performed. The translation of socio-legal messages to the text reshaped their contents in various ways, for example, by mediating between languages and by standardizing the spoken word within written legal and narrative frames. Their subsequent presentation to various – partly non-literate – audiences in turn involved retranslation through a number of non-textual media, again influencing form and content of these socio-legal messages. That such language-objects became increasingly common in the courts' legal process is thus a particularly relevant development from a communicative perspective, fundamentally shaping the way these judicial bodies worked. In this, the chapter also engages with the social historian's challenge of searching for authentic voices 'from below' in a period when texts as a medium, despite the marked increase in their production, were used, and certainly written, by a very small section of society.

Chapter 5, 'Court and society: The production and consumption of justice', moves beyond the media used in communicating to discuss the historical actors using them and their strategies of communication. Building on Bourdieu's theory of social interaction, it attempts to contextualize the different court communities within their broader society. This is done on the one hand by tracing the habitus of the various court officials, considering social background, training and other relevant elements influencing these people's frames of reference. In addition, the chapter regards these actors' position in their communicative fields, the speech arenas in which various groups and individuals negotiated socio-legal meaning. Here it draws upon the conclusions of the previous chapters to argue where, when and through which media the courts interacted with various elements in their surrounding societies. Finally, and related to this last point, the chapter considers how the respective courts then claimed a specific position for themselves within these communicative fields. Through the use of various media, and by constructing specific socio-legal narratives, these courts put forward claims about the ordering of society and their own role therein.

The conclusion will bring these different elements together in presenting a final analysis of the development of the considered courts as communicators and communicative environments. By relating court-specific changes to more overarching processes in socio-legal practice, I will argue that the courts scripted particular forms of judicial practice and logic, thereby attempting to influence people's conception of legitimate speech and activity. In linking the various media of the court to each other in this way, I show

how a consideration of communication processes can not only elucidate the historical development of law courts, but is also crucial to understanding their surviving documents, which purport to tell us so much about medieval society.

1. Profiles: Three late medieval law courts

Abstract
The late Middle Ages were defined by an immense legal pluralism, encompassing multiple legal traditions and institutional forms. Studying late medieval law courts comparatively therefore implies balancing overarching developments with the many case-specific features of individual legal bodies. While the Council of Utrecht, the episcopal Consistory Court of York and the royal *Parlement* of Paris all developed from a ruler's judicial council into a (semi-)autonomous legal body, and all did so in an urban context, other characteristics differed markedly. In their composition, their size, the scale and nature of their jurisdiction, their spaces of operation, the textual record they produced, and the legal traditions from which they drew, these bodies constituted markedly distinctive producers of justice faced with similar challenges.

Keywords: medieval law courts, comparative history, Utrecht, York, Paris

One of the defining features of the late medieval legal landscape was its immense pluralism. This great diversity in legal forms found its clearest expression in the many different ways in which law courts came to be organized during this period. Drawing both on broader learned legal traditions, that is, those of Roman and Romano-canonical law, and – often more locally based – customary law, these courts took many shapes. In addition, extra-legal conditions, such as political configurations, communities' social composition, existing economic relations and spatial contexts, influenced the way in which the courts were organized and functioned on a day-to-day basis.

All these factors make it necessary to elaborate in some detail on the three case studies at the heart of this book. In this chapter I will therefore set out to contextualize the Council of Utrecht, the Consistory Court of York and

Camphuijsen, F., *Scripting Justice in Late Medieval Europe: Legal Practice and Communication in the Law Courts of Paris, York and Utrecht.* Taylor & Francis Group, 2022
DOI 10.5117/9789463723473_CH01

the *Parlement* of Paris from several perspectives. This first of all means a historical contextualization, asking how and why these law courts developed before and during the period treated here. Secondly, I will place them in a broader legal context, setting out the traditions of written and unwritten law on which they based themselves, the specific competences they claimed to hold, and the way in which these were subsequently translated into daily legal practice. None of the law courts considered here were purely legal institutions in the modern sense of the word. Looking beyond a modern bias, I will thus pay ample attention to the political, social and economic activities undertaken by the courts and their relation to the societies in which they operated. This also involves a consideration of these courts' spatial context, as I believe this to have been an important – and often overlooked – aspect of their institutional identity and practice. Last but certainly not least, the internal make-up of the law courts will receive an in-depth examination, both regarding their formal organization and – as far as possible – their more informal socio-political make-up. This chapter will thus form the groundwork for the subsequent parts of the book, both by gathering together the basic information from which to develop my overarching thematic arguments, and as a first exploration of the relation between the particular and the more general developments of these law courts.

The Council of Utrecht

The history of the Council of Utrecht is strongly related to the history of the city itself as a legal and political actor.[1] Since the eighth century, the settlement that would develop into the city of Utrecht had been defined mainly by its role as an episcopal see.[2] In the eleventh century, the Ottonian kings made extensive donations of goods and rights to the Utrecht bishops. Consequently, the latter would for centuries form not only the most important religious leaders in the area, but also its central secular authorities.[3]

1 For a recent general history of the city of Utrecht, see R.E. de Bruin, P.D. 't Hart, A.J. van den Hoven van Genderen, A. Pietersma and J.E.A.L. Struick, eds., *'Een paradijs vol weelde': Geschiedenis van de stad Utrecht* (Utrecht: Matrijs, 2000).

2 H.L. de Groot, "Van strijdhamer tot bisschopsstaf: De vroegste geschiedenis tot circa 925", in *'Een paradijs vol weelde': Geschiedenis van de stad Utrecht*, eds. R.E. de Bruin et al. (Utrecht: Matrijs, 2000), 29–34, 39–43.

3 K. van Vliet, "De stad van de bisschop, circa 925–1122", in *'Een paradijs vol weelde': Geschiedenis van de stad Utrecht*, eds. R.E. de Bruin et al. (Utrecht: Matrijs, 2000), 48–50.

From the twelfth century onwards, however, the city's rapidly expanding population managed to increase its influence both in political and judicial affairs. The growing role of the Utrecht urban community in regional and super-regional power struggles gave it the leeway necessary to increase its own autonomy vis-à-vis the bishops. Tied up with this increase in urban autonomy was the coming into existence of several urban institutions. A 'bench' of aldermen existed as early as 1122. To this was added an advisory organ, called the Council (*de Raad*), at the end of the twelfth century. For more than a century these two institutions were dominated by a small number of prominent families, originating in the old mercantile elite of the city. Only during the thirteenth century did other groups within the city challenge their position, as guilds of craftsmen came to play a serious – though not uncontested – political role within the city.[4] In 1304 the aldermen and guild elders (*oudermannen*) agreed on a so-called 'Guild letter'. This document gave the guilds an important formal role in the political organization of the city at the expense of both the bishop and the old mercantile elite. Together with a confirmatory and complementary letter from 1341, this document established a system of indirect elections for the members of the Council and the aldermen.[5] Rather than being selected by the bishop these officials would now be chosen by the members of the different guilds, to one of which every full Utrecht citizen was expected to attach itself.[6]

Within this new constellation the Council, which as an institution was less closely linked to the episcopal landlord than the aldermen were, began to play a much more prominent role than before. Gradually it increased its control over political, economic and judicial matters at the expense of both the bishop and many other local authorities, like the aldermen, local ecclesiastical courts and many smaller secular courts in the vicinity of the city. During the fourteenth century the Council managed to expand its competences into many different fields, including lawmaking and the most important governmental functions as well as a large range of judicial tasks. Although the focus here lies on the latter, it is important to keep this

4 K. van Vliet, "De stad van de burgers, 1122–1304", in *'Een paradijs vol weelde': Geschiedenis van de stad Utrecht*, eds. R.E. de Bruin et al. (Utrecht: Matrijs, 2000), 73–79, 82–88, 95, 107–111; Samuel Muller, ed., *De middeleeuwsche rechtsbronnen der stad Utrecht*, Introduction (The Hague: Nijhoff, 1885), 17–21.

5 Both letters have been edited in J.C. Overvoorde and J.G.C. Joosting, eds., *De gilden van Utrecht tot 1528*, vol. 1 (The Hague: Nijhoff, 1896), 52–53 and 57.

6 A.J. Van den Hoven van Genderen, "Op het toppunt van de macht, 1304–1528", in *'Een paradijs vol weelde': Geschiedenis van de stad Utrecht*, eds. R.E. de Bruin et al. (Utrecht: Matrijs, 2000), 113–117, 132–133.

multifaceted character of the Council's institutional identity in mind. Far from being only a law court, it was a governmental body in the process of establishing its authority in a variety of areas, legal as well as political.[7] This diversity also found its reflection in the Council's textual output, the volume of which increased markedly from the fourteenth century onwards. Four subsequent books of bylaws, the *Liber albus*, the *Liber hirsutus minor*, the *Roede boeck* and *Die Roese*, collected various regulations from the early fourteenth century onwards.[8] At about the same time that the earliest book of bylaws was put together, the Council also began to keep a register of verdicts, spanning the rest of the century.[9] From the early fifteenth century onwards this register was then replaced by two new series of registers, the *Raads dagelijks boek* and the *Buurspraakboek*.[10] As Chapter 4 will show, hardly any of these records was limited to one type of activity only. Rather, they contained a whole range of rules, notifications, verdicts and other entries, showing the broad involvement of the Council in legal, political, economic and even occasionally religious matters.

In the legal field the Council's authority covered both areas of instance (*accusatio*) and *ex officio* jurisdiction, that is, procedures initiated by litigants and by the court itself, respectively. Concerning the latter, its authority was more or less absolute: all acts that could be considered contrary to the common good of the community – murder, violent assault, theft, prostitution, sedition, etc. – would come before the Council. Exceptions to this were the criminal jurisdiction over clergy and nobles as well as certain minor transgressions committed in one of the nearby townships.[11] Concerning instance jurisdiction the Council's competence was less far-reaching. Especially in the fields of immovable property, debts and damages, the aldermen still had a large jurisdictional role to play. Nonetheless, over time the Council began to encroach on many of these competences as well.[12] Some historians have distinguished a third judicial category, although it has a certain overlap with the Council's other two fields of jurisdiction. Samuel Muller defined this category as 'voluntary jurisdiction', which is concerned

7 Ibid., 115–121.

8 These books are edited in Samuel Muller, ed., *De middeleeuwsche rechtsbronnen der stad Utrecht*, vol. 1 (The Hague: Nijhoff, 1883), 3–68 (*Liber albus*), 69–149 (*Liber hirsutus minor*), 151–180 (*Roede boeck*) and 181–394 (*Die Roese*), where they are divided into numbered sets of articles.

9 This register survives in two copies, titled *Th.1* and *Th.2*, at the Utrechts Archief (HUA): 701-1.226 and 1.227, respectively.

10 The *Raads dagelijks boek* is found at HUA 701-1.13, the *Buurspraakboek* at HUA 701-1.16.

11 Hoven van Genderen, "Toppunt", 120; Muller, *Rechtsbronnen*, Introduction, 126–134.

12 Muller, *Rechtsbronnen*, Introduction, 135–141.

with the making of what the sources call *willekeuren* and *loften*, that is, formal promises by individuals to do or abstain from doing something, like making a payment.[13] This type of legal action, with its 'voluntary' character, seems closely linked to the more general instance type activities employed by the Council. However, seeing that *willekeuren* are often closely linked to actions which seem to echo *ex officio* activity, it is probably too simple to consider them as another type of instance activity.[14] As this type of judicial activity is already present in the earliest textual sources left by the Council, it is not unlikely, as Muller suggests, to regard it as one of the fundamental functions in the Council's development from a simple advisory board to a full-fledged legal and political authority.[15]

The core of the Council consisted of 24 elected members. These were elected annually by the collective guild elders out of the twelve so-called *waken*, urban administrative units each containing the members of one or more guilds that had the responsibility to guard a particular section of the city wall by night.[16] The Council's basic composition could, however, expand significantly when more important decisions were to be taken. Sometimes the aldermen and elders of the guilds were involved.[17] Likewise, an appeal was sometimes made to officials – be they Council members, aldermen or guild elders – of the previous year. All this could result in a governmental body of up to 156.[18] The Council thus formed a body of elected representatives of the community – or, more precisely, of the largest stakeholders in the community – rather than a body of legal specialists, as encountered more prominently in Paris and especially York. In order to investigate some of the more juridically complex matters, the Council created special commissions from amongst its members, charged with

13 Ibid., 141–159.

14 The *Th.2* register, for example, begins by stating that it will contain cases and *willekeuren* concerning the body or parts of it as well as banishments, emphasizing the close link between the 'voluntary' character of the promise made and the penal consequences of not keeping this promise. See HUA 701-1.227, fol. 1r.

15 Muller, *Rechtsbronnen*, Introduction, 156–157. The *Th.2* register, containing entries dated between 1315 and 1403, already contains a large amount of *willekeuren*. See HUA 701-1.227.

16 Hoven van Genderen, "Toppunt", 116, 130–134; Justine Smithuis, "Gildevertegenwoordiging of oligarchie? De samenstelling van het Utrechtse stadsbestuur in de late Middeleeuwen (1304–ca. 1450)", *Jaarboek Oud-Utrecht* (2014): 209–236, at 213–216, reprinted with an English abstract in Justine Smithuis, "Urban Politics and the Role of Guilds in the City of Utrecht (1250–1450)" (PhD diss., University of Leiden, 2019), 23–60.

17 This is often the case in the *Raads dagelijks boek*, which generally contained more cases of civil law.

18 Hoven van Genderen, "Toppunt", 115.

investigating a specific case. Several of these commissions developed a more or less permanent character. Notably among them was the so-called *vive* ('the five'), a committee charged with investigating serious crimes and several related activities, such as advising the other Council members on verdicts and playing a role in their execution, but also the supervision of the city police.[19] A second category of commissions was formed by the *keurmeesters* (literally: 'masters of bylaws'). These commissioners were charged with investigating transgressions of a range of different bylaws (*keuren*) concerning – among other things – violence, the sale of wine, pigs and gambling.[20] Such diversity in responsibilities can also be seen among the functionaries called *stadsknapen* ('city servants'), charged with the practical side of the matters that concerned the Council. They would summon litigants, arrest culprits, carry messages and facilitate the Council's activities in many other ways. The *stadsknapen* thus played a crucial role in putting the Council's broad power claims into concrete practice, as considered in Chapter 5.[21]

The Council's broad range of functions – legal as well as political and economic – gave it a particular character that had important consequences for our understanding of its development and *modus operandi* in the late Middle Ages. Contrary to a modern logic of distinguishing between a legislative, an executive and a judiciary power, the Council's functions spanned all these three areas of authority. Rather than regarding the Council's authority from a modern-day perspective, we need to understand it within its contemporary context of socio-political relations. The professed focus of the Council's activity was promoting peace and quiet in the city. This goal not only straddled several forms of power nowadays divided between different spheres of authority, but also cuts across different academic subject areas: political, legal, economic and environmental history. It is thus insufficient to regard the Council's activity simply from a legal viewpoint, without involving acts of legislation, economic policy and relations to legal and political players external to the city of Utrecht.

Secondly, and on a more practical level, the Council's involvement in different theatres of power created a range of potential conflict areas, where it was forced to negotiate its interests with others. The Council increased its range of competences at the expense of other authorities in the city and its

19 Muller, *Rechtsbronnen*, Introduction, 212–220; D.A. Berents, *Misdaad in de Middeleeuwen: Een onderzoek naar de criminaliteit in het laat-middeleeuwse Utrecht* (Utrecht: Stichting Stichtse Historische Reeks, 1976), 20–21.

20 Muller, *Rechtsbronnen*, Introduction, 174–195; Berents, *Misdaad*, 21.

21 Muller, *Rechtsbronnen*, Introduction, 80–81, 210, n. 2; Berents, *Misdaad*, 24.

vicinity. These included the bishop and some of the officers and institutions that formerly played an important role in the relations between the bishop and the city, like the sheriff and the bench of aldermen. But smaller players like local courts in the direct vicinity of the city (*buitengerechten*) and the many ecclesiastical immunities which dotted the legal landscape at the time were similarly relevant factors.[22] Far from being on an unchallenged and unidirectional road to increasing authority, in the period under study the Council constantly negotiated its power with other larger and smaller authorities. And next to these semi-official relations, a more informal sphere needs to be taken into account as well. The individuals staffing the Council formed an unrepresentative cross section of Utrecht society. Several families, supported by large patronage networks, formed the socio-political elite from which the members of the Council were usually recruited.[23] Within this narrow socio-political elite, however, the new constellation of civic government as it developed during the fourteenth and fifteenth centuries led to instances of fierce party strife. Rival factions, grouped around coalitions of important families, competed over positions of authority in the city. Sometimes these struggles even came to a head when one of the factions managed to gain the upper hand, resulting in a change of power and the exile of the most important members of the losing faction.[24] As Chapter 5 will elaborate further, the Council thus formed at the same time a party in local and supra-local power struggles, and a forum on which such struggles took place.

It will be clear by now that the history of the Council was closely intertwined with that of the city of Utrecht, an interrelatedness that had a spatial dimension as well. Several locations within the city figure very prominently in the textual sources (Map 1). A particularly central role is taken by the *Buurkerk*. This church, which since the eleventh century served as the main parochial church of the city, seems to have formed the focus of much of the judicial activity of the Council. The square in front of this church was most probably the location for the regular *buurspraak* assemblies during the fourteenth and fifteenth centuries. On these

22 Hoven van Genderen, "Toppunt", 120.

23 For the fourteenth and first half of the fifteenth century, see Smithuis, "Gildevertegenwoordiging", 222–226; for the end of the fifteenth century, see D.A. Berents, "Gegoede burgerij in Utrecht in de 15^{e} eeuw", *Jaarboek Oud-Utrecht* (1972): 90–91.

24 Justine Smithuis, "Politiek en geweld in een laatmiddeleeuwse stad. Utrecht 1400–1430", *Tijdschrift voor geschiedenis* 123, no. 2 (2010), reprinted with an English abstract in Smithuis, "Urban politics", 137–157. Years in which major power changes took place were 1380, 1413–1415 and 1425–1426.

occasions the Council would publicly pronounce its verdicts and it was here that people condemned to public shaming would come to openly beg the Council for forgiveness.[25] It was probably not a coincidence then that up until the sixteenth century the residence of the Council was located opposite the *Buurkerk*, in the so-called *Schoonhuis*. Although the seat of the aldermen could also originally be found in the vicinity of the *Buurkerk*, in 1343 the expansion of this church drove them to a new residence, the *Hasenberg* house at the square called the *Plaets*, which in later centuries came to form the central governmental seat of the city.[26] Only in the early sixteenth century, when the autonomy of Utrecht and the power of its guild-led Council was definitively broken by Emperor Charles V, did the Council exchange the *Schoonhuis* as place of residence for one of the houses in this new governmental hub at the *Plaets*.[27] A final spatial feature of interest here were the city prisons. There was apparently no specific location in the city where prisoners were kept. Rather, several existing locations doubled as prisons in this period. These included some of the city gates, most notably the *Catharijne* gate to the west and one of the *Tolsteeg* gates – nicknamed the 'Red Tower' – to the south.[28] During the fifteenth century another multifunctional building was used to house inmates. The so-called *vleyshuis* ('meat house'), named after its contemporaneous use by the butchers' guild, served as a primary location for imprisonment purposes – both pre- and post-trial – after 1410.[29]

The Council would, for most of its history, be susceptible to broader power struggles at a regional and super-regional level. Especially during the fifteenth and early sixteenth century, involvement in larger political conflicts led to periods of major political – and juridical – changes within the city. During the fifteenth century, the growing influence of the Burgundian dynasty strengthened the internal divisions within the city and between the city and the bishop, as the latter's position was heavily contested between Burgundian and non-Burgundian candidates. The takeover of the episcopal see by David of Burgundy in 1449, for instance, resulted in fundamental

25 N. van der Monde, *Geschied- en oudheidkundige beschrijving van de pleinen, straten, stegen, waterleidingen, wedden, putten en pompen der stad Utrecht*, vol. 3 (Utrecht: N. van der Monde, 1846), 176, suggests that this practice was already in existence before its use by the Council, but he unfortunately provides no source for this claim.

26 Hoven van Genderen, "Toppunt", 147.

27 A.H.M. van Schaik, "Een nieuwe heer en een andere leer (1528–1618)", in *'Een paradijs vol weelde': Geschiedenis van de stad Utrecht*, eds. R.E. de Bruin et al. (Utrecht: Matrijs, 2000), 193–194.

28 Ibid., 130.

29 Berents, *Misdaad*, 44.

Map 1: Sixteenth century map of the city of Utrecht (detail). With a few exceptions, the layout still follows that of the late medieval city.

changes within the city, as the position of the guilds was seriously contested by the bishop. Despite a relative weakening of the role of the landlord after the death of the Burgundian duke Charles the Good, the succeeding Habsburg dynasty continued to infringe on the guild-dominated system of urban government. In 1528 the guild-led government came to an end, basically meaning a reversal to the power relations as they had been before the fourteenth century. The Council lost all its judicial authority to the landlord-dominated bench of aldermen and the sheriff, and reverted back to the role of advisory board that it served up until the fourteenth century.

The first court profile thus sketched is that of a multifaceted urban authority, holding extensive legal as well as a variety of other powers. Its fate was closely tied up with the guild-led governance of late medieval Utrecht, and during its bicentennial dominance in the city it formed the nucleus of both internal and external struggles for socio-political authority. Considering the legal activities of the Council thus means looking at one aspect of a broader pallet of power claims. Furthermore, compared to the other two courts studied here these claims were concerned with a geographically limited area, namely, the city and its surrounding lands. The impact of such differences in scale and political involvement will become clearer as we take a closer look at the other courts.

The Consistory Court of York

The thirteenth century was the main formative period for the archiepiscopal Consistory Court of York. In line with broader European developments, which saw a growing demand for the ecclesiastical legal process, the case load of the York archbishops began to increase markedly from the late twelfth century onwards.[30] To address this pressure, the York archbishops

30 K.F. Burns, "The Administrative System of the Ecclesiastical Courts in the Diocese and Province of York: Part I: The Medieval Courts" (unpublished manuscript, 1962), 3–8. For the broader European developments, see Brundage, *Medieval Origins*, 126–163. Brundage follows Martin Brett, "Canon Law and Litigation: The Century before Gratian", in *Medieval Ecclesiastical Studies in Honour of Dorothy M. Owen*, eds. Michael Franklin and Christopher Harper-Brill (Woodbridge and Rochester, NY: Boydell & Brewer, 1995), in stressing litigants' demands for the legal process as primary cause for these growing caseloads. Although I agree that it is crucial to consider the fundamental role of the law's consumers in its production, Brundage's subsequent contention that these increasing demands 'reflected the litigants' desire to settle their differences through legal processes, rather than a scheme by church authorities to attract more business into their courts and thus to increase their power' (pp. 126–127) underplays the role of the courts, by reducing them to a merely reactive role, while assuming that the development of a complex

gradually delegated their competences, forming three distinct law courts covering different aspects of their jurisdiction: the Court of Audience, mainly concerned with the bishop's direct audience and corrective jurisdiction,[31] the financially oriented Exchequer court[32] and the Consistory Court, which covered the growing numbers of 'ordinary' civil suits received by the episcopal administration.[33] This latter did not spring into existence from one day to the next. Whereas up until the twelfth century the different archdeacons in the northern province would form the most important judicial aides to the archbishop, from the end of the century their role was gradually taken over by a specialized episcopal functionary, called the 'bishop's official'. While at first applied in the sense of an episcopal agent in general, the term 'official' came during the thirteenth century to indicate the specific functionary charged with the execution of the bishop's instance jurisdiction.[34] As the bishop's vicar, he would be the presiding judge of the episcopal court when gathered *in consistorio*, that is, in judicial session. From the later thirteenth century onwards the further delegation and subdivision of judicial tasks from the official downwards created an increasingly independent law court in which the official, as the bishop's vicar, operated as presiding judge. What had originally been the judicial activity of the archbishop and his direct advisers, thus gradually developed into a semi-independent body staffed by legal professionals, holding multiple fixed sessions a week.[35]

The functionaries operating in this Consistory Court are first explicitly defined in the statutes drawn up under Archbishop William Greenfield (1306–1315). In his *Concilium provinciale Eboracensis* (1311), Greenfield distinguishes between several categories of functionaries. Next to the bishop's official the court would consist of two examiners, the judges charged specifically with the examination of witnesses. One of them was supposed to double as registrar, who oversaw the production and custody of all the relevant documents as performed by an unspecified number of notaries. In addition, twelve advocates and eight proctors were to be connected to the court, the first group fulfilling basically a legal advisory function, and

and far-reaching system of canon law was received unproblematically by everyone making use of it. See my earlier critique of the instrumentalization of non-court actors in the Introduction to this book.

31 Burns, "Medieval Courts", 201–228.

32 Ibid., 229–236.

33 Ibid., 117–200.

34 Ibid., 60–67.

35 Ibid., 6–7, 70–83, 122–124.

the second group constituted to speak on behalf of the litigating parties.[36] Despite their convenient clarity, in the end Greenfield's statutes are little more than a temporary glimpse of idealized court practice. What the statute gives us is basically the codification of a practice that had been developing for several decades at the least. And although it did serve as a clear guideline for later court practice, the actual character of the different functions described in the statute underwent several major changes over the fourteenth and fifteenth centuries.[37] Moreover, a group of functionaries that does not appear in Greenfield's statutes – except maybe implicitly – is that of the apparitors or summoners. These functionaries, charged with bringing the court's summons to all those required in a session, formed from an organizational perspective a crucial factor in day-to-day court practice.[38]

The Consistory Court operated within a complex variety of political, social and judicial contexts. As an archiepiscopal court it formed part of a broader ecclesiastical juridical hierarchy. Within the northern English church province, which stretched from Nottinghamshire in the south to the Scottish border, the Consistory Court was – apart from the episcopal Court of Audience – the theoretical pinnacle of the ecclesiastical court system. Yet actual jurisdiction was limited in many ways. The archbishop had first instance jurisdiction within his own diocese, which constituted only part of the entire ecclesiastical province. Within the diocese, a large number of exceptions, formed by the peculiar jurisdictions of several religious houses, (groups of) parishes and even the whole archdeaconry of Richmond limited the actual judicial authority. Also, lower courts were sometimes able to bypass the archiepiscopal claim to hear appeals from all over the province. In addition, following the longstanding conflict between the archbishops of York and Canterbury for primacy within the English church, the actual reach of York's judicial authority in the north could be seriously compromised.[39] However, given all these limitations, under normal circumstances supreme jurisdiction lay with the archbishop and his Consistory Court, leading to a steady flow of cases from all over the northern church province.[40] At

36 Greenfield's statutes are published in David Wilkins, ed., *Consilia magnae britanniae et hiberniae ab anno MDXLVI ad annum MDCCXVII*, vol. 2 (London, 1737), 409–415. See also Burns, "Medieval Courts", 98–116.

37 Burns, "Medieval Courts", 127–161.

38 Ibid., 152–155.

39 Roy Martin Haines, *Ecclesia anglicana: Studies in the English Church of the Later Middle Ages* (Toronto: University of Toronto Press, 1989), 69–105.

40 Ibid., 8–27, 37–43; Robert N. Swanson, *Church and Society in Late Medieval England* (Oxford and New York: Blackwell, 1989), 160–161.

the same time, the Consistory Court did not form the necessary end point for cases pursued through church law. There was always the possibility that a case concluded in the archiepiscopal court would be appealed to the papal curia. In practice this was a rather elaborate undertaking for litigants wanting to pursue their case further.[41] Nonetheless, the possibility to appeal a case at the papal curia, be it in theory or in practice, was an option available to litigants of the Consistory Court. Furthermore, despite its increasing independence as court of law, the Consistory Court remained part of a broader archiepiscopal administration. Though the archbishops themselves were often and increasingly absent from York, they did keep the right to withdraw certain cases from the Consistory Court. Both in the treatment of these cases and in that of the archiepiscopal criminal jurisdiction, which as a rule was not treated in the Consistory Court, the archbishops were supported by a permanent court of legal professionals, the Court of Audience or Chancery. Although not functioning as a court of appeal in the strict sense, the Court of Audience was superior to the Consistory Court. It formed a means for the archbishops – or, in their absence, their vicars-general – to involve themselves more directly in cases that they considered as having an extraordinary character.[42]

Next to, but hardly ever entirely disconnected from, the jurisdictional hierarchy of ecclesiastical courts, the Consistory Court also had to relate itself to a number of other judicial entities in local, regional and supra regional contexts. To begin with the latter, the king and his system of royal justice formed an important jurisdictional peer to take into account. With the development of both extensive common law and canon law systems from the twelfth century onwards, the English legal landscape was effectively split between two major legal constellations operating next to each other, which could result both in situations of conflict and cooperation. Where many subjects were regarded as clearly belonging to one or the other of these two systems, certain types of cases were regularly the cause of jurisdictional

41 In the twelfth century a system of papal judges-delegate developed, as local churchmen were appointed to represent the pope, increasing the availability of papal jurisdiction and unburdening the papal *curia* itself. By the fourteenth century, however, this system was already in decline. See W. Pantin, "The Fourteenth Century", in *The English Church and the Papacy in the Middle Ages*, ed. C.H. Lawrence (London: Burns & Oates, 1965), 175–178; Charles Donahue, "Roman Canon Law in the Medieval English Church: Stubbs vs. Maitland Re-examined after 75 Years in the Light of Some Records from the Church Courts", *Michigan Law Review* 72, no. 4 (1974): 670–671; James A. Brundage, *Medieval Canon Law* (London and New York: Longman, 1995), 123–129.

42 Burns, "Medieval Courts", 201–228.

controversy or conflict between ecclesiastical and royal courts.[43] On a more local level as well, the Consistory Court had to deal with numerous non-ecclesiastical courts and legal officials. Given the extensive territory over which the archbishops claimed supreme spiritual jurisdiction, it is not feasible to give anything near a complete overview of the many secular courts operating in England at the time.[44] What may be directly relevant, however, is to give a sense of the most pertinent judicial context of the Consistory Court, namely, that of the city of York itself. Similar to that other city doubling as an episcopal see, Utrecht, the jurisdictional landscape of York's municipal area was severely fragmented. Initially the fragmentation would be between those areas falling under royal and those falling under diverse religious jurisdictions and liberties. During the thirteenth and fourteenth centuries, however, the strengthened position of local civic officials and institutions, like the mayor and aldermen, put a heavy strain on the existing power relations. Whereas the thirteenth century saw several major conflicts between the city and the many ecclesiastical landholders in and in the vicinity of the city, in the fourteenth century the urban officials' success in marginalizing royal influence in the city also stimulated a narrower confinement of the ecclesiastical liberties. The direct involvement of the archbishop in these conflicts, as well as the fact that they took place in the court's direct physical vicinity, makes it a socio-judicial context not to be ignored.[45]

It was also in this context that the physical spaces used by the Consistory Court were most directly involved. As Chapter 2 will show, as early as the first quarter of the fourteenth century the Consistory Court held many of its sessions in the cathedral church of York, the Minster, which at the time was undergoing an elaborate extension and structural renewal.[46] Choosing such a place to perform the legal process had important practical and symbolic implications, which will become clearer when analysing the court's communication strategies in the following chapters. Next to

43 Swanson, *Church and Society*, 140–158; W.R. Jones, "Relations of the Two Jurisdictions: Conflict and Cooperation in England during the Thirteenth and Fourteenth Centuries", *Studies in Medieval and Renaissance History* 7 (1970).

44 For a sense of this judicial diversity in fifteenth-century England, see Johnson, *Law in Common*.

45 David M. Palliser, "The Birth of York's Civic Liberties, c. 1200–1354", in *The Government of Medieval York: Essays in Commemoration of the 1396 Royal Charter*, ed. Sarah Rees Jones (York: Borthwick Institute of Historical Research, University of York, 1997); Sarah Rees Jones, "York's Civic Administration, 1354–1464", in ibid.

46 Burns, "Medieval Courts", 124–125; Sarah Brown, *'Our Magnificent Fabrick': York Minster: An Architectural History c. 1220–1500* (Swindon: English Heritage, 2003), 11–16, 35.

this space in the York Minster, several other locations played a role in the administration and judicial practice of the Consistory Court. From the late thirteenth century onwards, the area surrounding the Minster, the so-called Minster close, was made into a walled precinct separated both physically and jurisdictionally from the surrounding city (Maps 4, 5 and 6).[47] Much of the administration of the court took place in the different scriptoria forming part of this walled precinct. It is also likely that parts of the legal process itself, like the examination of witnesses, which according to canon law was supposed to take place in a private setting, were not performed in public sessions in the consistorial place in the Minster but in one of these scriptoria. And at least from the late fourteenth century onwards evidence can also be found of the court conducting parts of the legal process in people's houses or local parish churches.[48]

The formal status of the Consistory Court as the highest court of appeal of the ecclesiastical province had a major influence on the character of its jurisdiction. Among the cases recorded by the court, matrimonial cases form the largest minority of about one-third. Other cases frequently treated by the Consistory Court concerned benefices, tithes, church rights, testamentary matters, defamation and breach of faith.[49] Such litigation predominantly concerned instance jurisdiction, either coming before the court as first instance or as appeal from a lower court.[50] Yet the court's jurisdiction was not limited to instance cases. It treated a number of disciplinary offences, ranging from attacks on clergy and violation of church property to clandestine marriages. Whereas such litigation had an *ex officio* character from the beginning, many of the cases initially entering the court through the initiative of a plaintiff also led to interventions by the judge, for example, when parties did not follow correct court procedure – which was treated as contempt of court or contumacy – or when the court considered the matter to be concerned with public morals more generally. Especially in matrimonial

47 R.M. Butler, "Notes on the Minster Close at York", *York Historian* 14 (1997): 10–18.

48 Burns, "Medieval Courts", 125–126; see, for example, BIA CP.E.138 (1387), where the sentence in a case is read in the consistorial place of the collegiate church of Beverley: *in ecclesia collegiis beati Johannis Beverlac' Eboracencis diocesis loco consistorii eiusdem.*

49 See Burns, "Medieval Courts", 162–189, who mainly concentrates on the fifteenth century. Of the fourteenth-century cases recorded in the cause papers, some 35% (88 out of 254) concern matrimonial disputes. The share of other types of cases for this century is as follows: 14% benefices (35), 13% tithes (34), 12% church rights (30), 9% testamentary matters (23), 8% defamation (20) and 6% breach of faith (14). See Appendix 2.1 for a detailed overview of the fourteenth-century cause papers.

50 45% of the cases recorded in fourteenth-century cause papers, that is, 115 of 254, concerned appeals.

cases, interventions of this kind often blurred any clear distinction between instance and *ex officio* jurisdiction.[51]

Our main source for the legal activity of the Consistory Court are its cause papers. This series of documents has survived in the form of countless dossiers, each related to one particular case, which contain a broad variety of texts used in litigation, including plaints, plaintiff and defendant statements, witness testimony and verdicts.[52] The oldest surviving cause papers date to 1301, increasing in number as the century progresses. Of the 254 fourteenth-century cause papers still found in the archive, one-third (77 dossiers) was produced between 1390 and 1400.[53] The Consistory Court also kept a series of registers called act books, briefly recording the cases appearing in court on a day-to-day basis. Unfortunately the fourteenth-century act books have largely been lost. Only two remain, containing records for the years 1371–1375.[54] Further evidence on the legal activities of the Consistory Court can be found in the general registers of the archbishops of York.[55] However, as these records were primarily concerned with the activities of the archbishops themselves, the Consistory Court only makes

51 Burns, "Medieval Courts", 176–177, 189–193. Unfortunately, for the fourteenth century, the nature of the source material – only cause papers, almost no act books – hides much of the *ex officio* activity of the court from view. However, the two act books that do survive show a picture of the court's day-to-day business similar to that which Burns presents based on the fifteenth-century act books.

52 The cause papers can be found at the Borthwick Institute for Archives (BIA): CP series, where CP.E represents the fourteenth century, CP.F the fifteenth century, etc. An extensive catalogue of the cause papers is available at https://www.dhi.ac.uk/causepapers/. The cause papers have also recently been digitized at http://dlibcausepapers.york.ac.uk/yodl/app/home/index. Unfortunately, the catalogue does not yet contain links to the image database (although the image database does contain links to the catalogue). Note also that, at the time of writing, the catalogue contains some peculiar hiatus and errors. For example, seven fourteenth-century cause papers are missing from the database, namely, CP.E.49, 72, 79, 135, 182, 188 and 235. For the fourteenth-century cause papers, also see D.M. Smith, *Ecclesiastical Cause Papers at York: The Court of York 1301–1399* (York: Borthwick Institute of Historical Research, University of York, 1988).

53 Smith, *Ecclesiastical Cause Papers*, vi.

54 York Minster Library (YML): M 2(1)b and M 2(1)c.

55 Many of these registers have been edited: William Brown, ed., *The Register of William Wickwane, Lord Archbishop of York, 1279–1285* (Durham: Surtees Society, 1907); idem, ed., *The Register of John le Romeyn, Lord Archbishop of York, 1286–1296*, 2 vols. (Durham: Surtees Society, 1913–1917); idem, ed., *The Register of Thomas of Corbridge, Lord Archbishop of York, 1300–1304*, 2 vols. (Durham: Surtees Society, 1925–1928); William Brown and A. Hamilton Thompson, eds., *The Register of William Greenfield, Lord Archbishop of York, 1306–1315*, 5 vols. (Durham: Surtees Society, 1931–1934); Rosalind Hill et al., eds., *The Register of William Melton, Archbishop of York, 1317–1340*, 6 vols. (Torquay and Woodbridge: Boydell Press, 1977–2011).

an appearance in them when they were involved in a case that directly concerned the archbishop.

The second profile thus brings us a different kind of court in several respects. There is first of all the matter of scale. Whereas the Utrecht Council was directly concerned only with a small area of jurisdiction, the Consistory Court could be involved in lawsuits from all over the northern English church province. Its character as a judicial body was also fundamentally different, standing much closer to a modern Western understanding of a law court. The Consistory Court was primarily concerned with providing verdicts in the disputes that were brought before it, and was not as directly involved in political struggles as was the Council of Utrecht. Its members, furthermore, were by and large trained and specialized in legal matters, rather than elected officials. At the same time, however, the situations of both courts also show remarkable similarities. Each had to relate itself to a variety of other legal authorities in its direct vicinity and further away. And the same can be said of their physical surroundings, as each established itself not only jurisdictionally, but also physically in an urban context.

The *Parlement* of Paris

The *Parlement* of Paris is often used as typical model for the development of royal institutions during the later medieval period.[56] Originally an itinerant royal court, the *curia regis* of the French kings began gradually both to diversify its functions and to establish itself more permanently in Paris.[57] As early as the eleventh century the *curia regis* held its sessions in the royal palace on the *Île de la Cité*.[58] The judicial sessions of the court in particular took place in this *Palais de la Cité*, which over time became both the permanent seat and symbol of the highest jurisdiction in the French kingdom.[59] It is always tricky to give an absolute starting date for

56 See the contributions to Fletcher, Genet and Watts, *Government*.

57 For a recent overview of the five-century-long history of the *Parlement*, see Françoise Hildesheimer and Monique Morgat-Bonnet, *Le Parlement de Paris: Histoire d'un grand corps de l'État monarchique XIIIe–XVIIIe siècle* (Paris: Honoré Champion, 2018).

58 Jean Guerout, "Le palais de la cité à Paris des origines à 1417: Essai topographique et archéologique: Première partie: des origines à 1285", *Mémoires de la fédération des sociétés historiques et archéologiques de Paris et de l'Ile-de-France* 1 (1949): 132.

59 Félix Aubert, "Nouvelles recherches sur le Parlement de Paris: Période d'organisation", pt. 1, *Nouvelle revue historique de droit Français et étranger* 40 (1916): 62–67; Guerout, "Le palais: Première partie", 154–155.

the development of a legal institution like the *Parlement*. What we can say, however, is that in the hundred years between 1239, when Louis IX first spoke about holding a *parlement* of justice, and 1345, when a royal ordinance by Philip VI formally ended the annual renewal of its members and fixed their number to 82, the *Parlement* of Paris transitioned from an occasion on which the *curia regis* would hold its judicial sessions into a highly diversified and permanent law court.[60]

As was the case in the Consistory Court, this process of diversification of an originally unified court was related to a sharp increase in its case load. But whereas in York changes within the legal system itself form an important explanation for this increase, in the case of the *Parlement* of Paris the physical expansion of royal jurisdiction must also be taken into account. From the late twelfth century onwards, the Capetian kings began gradually – although certainly not linearly – to expand the royal demesne into areas that had previously been held in fief by prominent vassals. This expansion of the royal demesne resulted in an increasingly large area where the king claimed direct jurisdiction. Combined with the extensive procedural reforms that took place during the reign of Louis IX (r. 1226–1270), creating a very accessible system of appeal to the royal court from the entire kingdom, this expansion of direct royal power claims markedly grew the number of cases appearing before the *curia regis*.[61]

In thinking about the role of the *Parlement* of Paris within the French kingdom, we are again severely limited by modern Western notions of what a law court is supposed to be. Although it is feasible to speak of a diversification of functions of the original *curia regis*, this did certainly not follow a post-Enlightenment logic of the threefold division of powers.

60 Aubert, "Nouvelles recherches", pt. 1, 67, 277; Françoise Autrand, *Naissance d'un grand corps de l'Etat: Les gens du Parlement de Paris, 1345–1454* (Paris: Publications de la Sorbonne, 1981), 16. For a list of court members as envisioned by the 1345 ordinance, see Félix Aubert, "Nouvelles recherches sur le Parlement de Paris: Période d'organisation", pt. 2, *Nouvelle revue historique de droit Français et étranger* 41 (1917): 57–61. Contrary to Aubert's contention, the actual number of court members would not stay fixed for long but fluctuated from anything between 70 and 142 over the next century, as shown by Autrand, *Naissance*, 411. In this it echoed the fluctuating numbers from before 1350, which could be anything from 3 to 37 for the late thirteenth, and varied between 41 and 104 for the early fourteenth century. For lists of members for this period, see Aubert, 'Nouvelles recherches', pt. 1, 75–77, 79–80, 86–88, 94–95, 98–100, 238–242, 262–265, 268–272.

61 For an elaborate overview of the history of the Capetian dynasty, see François Menant, Hervé Martin, Bernard Merdrignac and Monique Chauvin, *Les Capétiens: Histoire et dictionnaire, 987–1328* (Paris: Robert Laffont, 1999). On the procedural changes during the reign of Louis IX, see Jean Hilaire, *La construction de létat de droit dans les archives judiciaires de la cour de France au XIIIe siècle* (Paris: Dalloz, 2011).

The majority of tasks performed by the *Parlement* was connected to the judgement of legal cases, but it also had many other competences covering areas today considered as being more administrative, legislative or outright political in nature. These mostly stemmed from the broad range of powers claimed by the French kings during the later medieval period. Similar to the Council of Utrecht, the exercise of justice by the *Parlement* of Paris was closely linked to an understanding of a more general keeping of the peace in the kingdom. It thereby extended its tasks from simply judging legal cases to all kinds of policing activity, road maintenance, economic regulations and even university business, in particular in the city of Paris.[62] It would stretch too far to consider every area of intervention by the *Parlement* independently. But it is important to acknowledge the many and diverse areas of daily life in which the *Parlement* claimed some kind of authority and the large number of other legal and non-legal authorities it had to deal with as a result.

In the judicial sphere the *Parlement* interacted with other authorities on several levels. Its origins in the *curia regis* meant that the extent of its judicial authority strongly depended on the king's success in substantiating anti-seigneurial power claims in the different parts of the kingdom. The crucial role of the *Parlement* in this royal vis-à-vis seigneurial power play can most clearly be seen in the development of a new appeal procedure and the introduction of the category of 'royal cases'.[63] While forms of appeal had existed earlier, from the middle of the thirteenth century, the French kings actively promoted a strictly hierarchical system of romano-canonical based appeal procedure, which recognized the *Parlement* as its supreme court.[64] Furthermore, by claiming that certain types of cases directly touched upon the king as guarantor of public order, the judgement of such affairs was disputed with other potential judicial stakeholders.[65] These developments strongly shaped the interaction between the *Parlement* and the various regional law courts in the kingdom, leading to situations of both judicial cooperation and conflict. The same is true for the court's relation to the many ecclesiastical jurisdictions scattered across the kingdom. At least

62 Françoise Hildesheimer and Monique Morgat-Bonnet, eds., *État méthodique des archives du Parlement de Paris* (Paris: Archives Nationales, 2011), 17; for a more extensive overview, see Félix Aubert, *Histoire du Parlement de Paris de l'origine à François Ier: 1250–1515*, vol. 1 (Paris: Picard, 1894), 290–320.

63 Aubert, "Nouvelles recherches", pt. 1, 70–71.

64 Hilaire, *Construction*, 37–65.

65 Ernest Perrot, *Les cas royaux: Origine et développement de la théorie aux XIIIe et XIVe siècles* (Paris: A. Rousseau, 1910).

from the thirteenth century onwards secular and ecclesiastical authorities were locked in a continuous jurisdictional struggle over subjects like usury, marriage and testamentary matters. With its increasing claims in the realm of secular jurisdiction, the *Parlement* began to play a major role in this struggle, encroaching not just on the jurisdiction of the many royal vassals, but also on that of spiritual authorities within the kingdom.[66] In none of these cases was the expansion of royal jurisdiction a unidirectional process. The broad geographical area in which this process took place, as well as the many different local and regional authorities involved, make an explanation along the lines of a simple unopposed centralization – which still seems to underlie much of the historiography on the *Parlement* – highly unsatisfactory.

In this light it may be revealing to zoom in on what was both the political centre of the Capetian dynasty and the most direct social and jurisdictional context of the *Parlement*, that is, the city of Paris. In its development into a semi-independent law court, the *Parlement* continued to use the royal *Palais de la Cité* as a location for most of its regular business. When the kings gradually moved their main residence to the Louvre palace during the fourteenth and early fifteenth century, the *Parlement* remained behind.[67] For a long time then, the royal court had a very direct presence in the city, which, as seen above, found its reflection in the many ways in which its representatives were judicially, administratively and economically involved in the business of the city.[68] Accordingly, it closely cooperated with numerous other authorities claiming jurisdiction in parts of the city. Central among these were the many religious institutions, of whom the bishop of Paris was the most prominent. Although the advent of royal claims reduced these authorities' secular powers, their spiritual jurisdiction still gave them a serious influence in day-to-day practice for the inhabitants of the city.[69]

Next to these ecclesiastical seigneurial authorities, the citizens of Paris themselves were also a party to be reckoned with. Originating in attempts by merchants to regulate commerce on the Seine as early as the twelfth century, an urban mercantile elite began to organize itself in the city during the

66 Aubert, *Histoire*, vol. 1, 321–346; Paul Fournier, *Les Officialités au Moyen-Age: Étude sur l'organisation, la compétence et la procédure des tribunaux ecclésiastiques ordinaires en France de 1180 à 1328* (Paris: E. Plon, 1880), 94–127.

67 Jean Guerout, "Le palais de la cité à Paris des origines à 1417: Essai topographique et archéologique: Troisième et dernier article", *Mémoires de la fédération des sociétés historiques et archéologiques de Paris et de l'Ile-de-France* 3 (1951), 29–30.

68 Aubert, *Histoire*, vol. 1, 298–315.

69 Raymond Cazelles, *Nouvelle histoire de Paris: De la fin du règne de Philippe Auguste à la mort de Charles V, 1223–1380* (Paris: Hachette, 1972), 225–247.

Map 2: Sixteenth century map of Paris (detail), showing the position of the *Châtelet* and *Palais de la Cité*.

thirteenth century and acquired competences not only in the commercial, but also more general urban administrative spheres. This municipal authority was headed by the provost of merchants (*prévôt des marchands*) and a bench of four aldermen, which also functioned as a tribunal. Based as it was in a mercantile elite, its primary jurisdiction involved commerce, but from this often followed instances of dispute resolution.[70] The royal administration, although gradually overshadowing the competences of these other urban authorities, seems to have preferred cooperation to outright competition over jurisdictional issues appearing in a city of this size.[71] The main royal functionary in Paris was the provost, who was seated in the *Châtelet*, directly facing the *Palais de la Cité* on the other side of the Seine (Map 2). It was this

70 Ibid., 197–218.
71 Ibid., 249–250.

royal provost who was most directly involved in the king's business in the city. But the *Parlement*, as the highest royal court and administrative body, was – both literally and figuratively – never far away. The relation between royal provost and *Parlement* was very close, evidenced, for example, by the latter's use of the prison of the *Châtelet*. But the *Parlement* also seems to have played a large role in supervising the functioning of the *Châtelet*.[72] So even though the judicial role of the *Parlement* in Paris itself was often an indirect one, both its physical presence and its indirect influence on royal jurisdiction in the capital make this a relevant context to consider.

In turning again from the *Parlement*'s jurisdictional contexts to the institution itself, we see how the diversification of the royal court concretely took shape during the late thirteenth and early fourteenth centuries. Perhaps the most visible sign of the gradual institutionalization of the royal court's judicial meetings was the appearance of judicial 'chambers', individual legal bodies fulfilling a specialized function within the *Parlement*, and often holding their sessions in specific halls in the *Palais de la Cité*. The largest and most general of these was the *Grande Chambre*, which formed the basis of the *Parlement*, and from which the other chambers formed mere delegations of specific functions. It was here that most cases brought before the *Parlement* were treated, in first instance as well as appeals from lower royal jurisdictions, like the bailiffs and seneschals.[73] In the thirteenth century special commissions were set up to deal with specific elements of the *Parlement*'s legal process. Many of these found their origins in particular aspects of the legal process, such as the *enquête*. The *enquête* entailed an investigation by the court in the locality where a law case originated. Although the actual investigation was often performed by local officials, the increase in case load during the thirteenth century led the royal court to appoint special commissions to hear, and also often to actively gather the local information that was required for a case, not unlike the *vive* and *keurmeesters* did in Utrecht. Around the turn of the century, these originally ad hoc commissions developed into a more permanent body, called the *Chambre des Enquêtes*. At about the same time a special room was built for this commission, making it both in a physical and organizational sense a separate body.[74] A similar development can be seen for the *Chambre des*

72 Gustave Ducoudray, *Les origines du Parlement de Paris et la justice aux XIIIe et XIVe siècles* (Paris: Hachette, 1902), 703–710; Gauvard, *'Grace especial'*, 35.

73 Aubert, *Histoire*, vol. 1, 11–18.

74 Ibid., 21–33; Jean Guerout, "Le palais de la cité à Paris des origines à 1417: Essai topographique et archéologique: Deuxième partie: De 1285 à 1350", *Mémoires de la fédération des sociétés historiques et archéologiques de Paris et de l'Ile-de-France* 2 (1950), 31–32, 158–160.

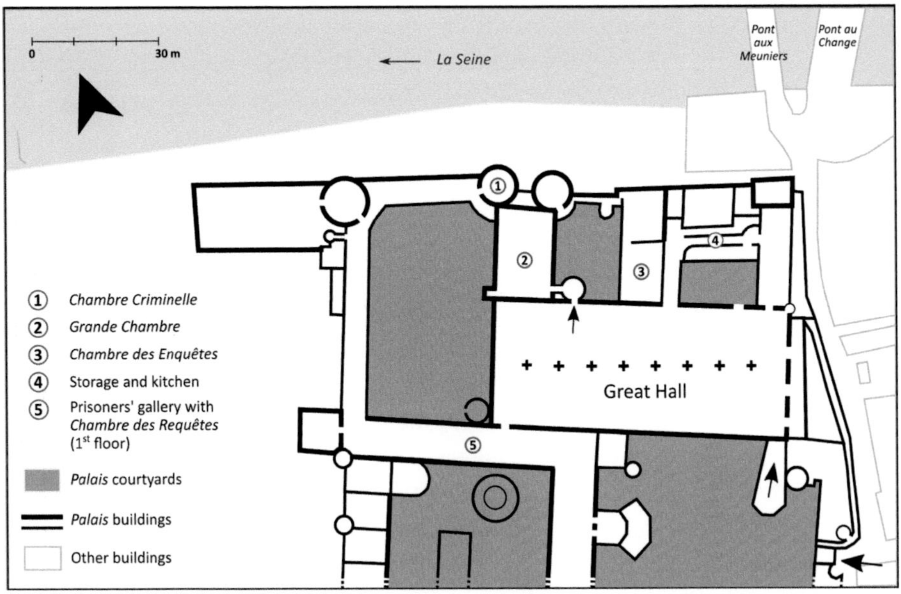

Plan 1: Northern part of the *Palais de la Cité* (ca.1360). Arrows indicate the route taken into the *Palais* by litigants whose case was heard by the *Parlement*. Dark grey spaces are palace courtyards.

Requêtes. This body received the requests for royal justice from all over the kingdom, assessing them and redirecting them to the proper judge, be it the king himself, the *Grande Chambre* or one of the bailiffs or seneschals. Again, originating in ad hoc delegations of members of the *Grande Chambre*, the *Chambre des Requêtes* developed into a permanent body, eventually also receiving its own room in the royal palace.[75] A slightly different route was taken by the body that came to be known as the *Chambre Criminelle* or *Chambre de la Tournelle*. Only in the sixteenth century does an official chamber treating criminal cases distinguish itself from the more general *Grande Chambre*. However, as early as 1312 the *Parlement*'s registers make a distinction between criminal and non-criminal cases. The first were treated by a delegation from the *Grande Chambre*, which, because of the nature of its case load, was entirely made up of lay members. These would, from 1340 at the latest, gather in one of the towers of the *Palais*, close to, but separated from the *Grande Chambre* (Plan 1).[76]

75 The *Chambre des Requêtes* was situated on the first floor of the prisoners' gallery, to the south-west of the Great Hall. Aubert, *Histoire*, vol. 1, 34–43; Guerout, 'Le Palais: Deuxième partie', 161–162; Hildesheimer and Morgat-Bonnet, *État méthodique*, 103.

76 Aubert, *Histoire*, vol. 1, 18–21; Guerout, 'Le Palais: Deuxième partie', 154–156; Hildesheimer and Morgat-Bonnet, *État méthodique*, 19.

The diversification of the legal business of the *Parlement* was not only reflected in its formal and physical organization, but also in the production of its records. An uninterrupted series of registers survives from 1254 onwards, containing records on various aspects of the legal process, including verdicts, inventories of legal documents and transcriptions of important letters.[77] In 1312 a separate register concerning criminal cases splits off from the first one, thus creating a tangible distinction between civil and criminal justice.[78] Over the fourteenth century many new series of registers began to be produced, containing among others records of the counsel and pleading sessions.[79] As Chapter 4 will show in more detail, the voluminous and immensely varied documentary material surviving for the late medieval *Parlement*, highlights the latter's size and diversified character.

As the above developments suggest, the *Parlement* was operated by a large variety of functionaries, executing the many different tasks of this legal body. A few words on the types of functionaries are therefore in order. First, the basis of the *Parlement* was formed by the *gens du Parlement* themselves, the councillors connected to the different chambers that would judge the cases coming to court. These councilmen were headed by one or more presidents, among whom the presidents of the *Grande Chambre* in particular held competences that extended far beyond simply presiding over sessions.[80] Circling around these bodies of judges were many other functionaries with crucial roles to play in the settlement, execution and subsequent administration of legal cases. As in York, the advocates and proctors of the parties pleading their case before the court again took a prominent role. The exact distinction between them is not always clear, as the two functions were often performed by the same individuals.[81] In general, however, whereas the advocate was primarily a legal adviser, proctors functioned as

77 These can be found as the X^{1A} series at the *Archives Nationales* (AN). The first four volumes of this series (AN X^{1A} 1–4) are often considered as a seperate entity, titled the *Olim* registers. A far from perfect edition of the *Olim* was published in the nineteenth century: Arthur Auguste Beugnot, ed., *Les Olim ou registres des arrêts rendus par la cour du roi sous les règnes de Saint Louis, de Philippe le Hardi, de Philippe le Bel, de Louis le Hutin et de Philippe le Long*, 4 vols. (Paris: Imprimerie Royale, 1839–1848). For a general overview of the surviving documentary material of the *Parlement*, see Monique Langlois, "Parlement de Paris", in *Guide des recherches dans les fonds judiciaires de l'ancien régime*, eds. Michel Antoine et al. (Paris: Imprimerie nationale, 1958).

78 The earliest register from the AN X^{2A} series, constituting an independent series of criminal registers, begins in 1312. Before that, criminal cases were included in the more general AN X^{1A} series. Even after 1312, however, the division is not absolute.

79 AN X^{1A}1469–8287 and X^{1A}8300A–8386.

80 Aubert, *Histoire*, vol. 1, 135–140.

81 Telliez, *Officiers*, 264–265.

actual representatives of their clients in the courtroom. Also, parties were required to make a formal request to be represented by a proctor, while advocates seem to have been considered a necessary element to any process, as they were even especially appointed by the court in cases where one was lacking for either of the parties.[82] A special category of functionaries was formed by the so-called *gens du roi*, officials who were formally linked to the king and his business, and who began to play a more important role as the person of the king became less directly involved in the business of the *Parlement*. These *gens du roi* consisted of the royal proctor and one or two royal advocates, who were not only the king's representatives in cases that involved royal interests, but had, especially in the case of the royal proctor, much broader competences in the area of the protection of public order.[83] In order to function properly, a law court the size of the *Parlement* required the support of a body of auxiliary staff. This included three registrars, that is, the heads of the registry, one for civil cases, one for criminal cases and one for the presentations brought by the parties. These registrars were aided in their business both by paid clerks, who did not form an intrinsic part of the *Parlement*, and from the fourteenth century onwards by a number of notaries from the general royal registry who were specifically assigned to the *Parlement*.[84] In day-to-day practice a crucial role was also played by the so-called *huissiers*, officials who performed various tasks related to the practicalities involved in running a court of law, like policing the courtroom, executing decisions by the court, summoning parties in a case, but also more mundane matters, such as making sure the court was heated sufficiently.[85]

Next to these formal organizational structures the character and social background of the members of the *Parlement* also underwent a notable change. Because of its origins in the *curia regis*, the thirteenth-century *Parlement* was still very much a gathering of nobles advising the king on myriad aspects of his reign. For every session its members would be selected by the king from among the many secular and ecclesiastical dignitaries in the kingdom, including archbishops, counts and dukes. Of course, actual presence in the vicinity of the *Palais* was often a criterion for selection, and there was a fairly stable basis of members who regularly acted as judges in the sessions of the *Parlement*. But in essence it was a flexible body of secular

82 Aubert, *Histoire*, vol. 1, 205–228.
83 Ibid., 141–175; Félix Aubert, "Nouvelles recherches", pt. 2, 58.
84 Aubert, *Histoire*, vol. 1, 229–248.
85 Ibid., 249–260; Aubert, "Nouvelles recherches", pt. 1, 279–282.

and ecclesiastical dignitaries.[86] In line with the changing character of the *Parlement* from an occasional judicial meeting of the royal court into a full-fledged institution, the character of its members also underwent a marked change. Next to the more eminent members of the *Parlement*, professional lawyers gradually took over much of the day-to-day business in court, leading to a shift of power both within the *Parlement* and within the royal administration more broadly. In a process that spanned the fourteenth and fifteenth centuries these professional administrators developed from a group of individually appointed regional representatives into a milieu of powerful recently ennobled families, hereditarily transferring the *Parlement*'s legal offices to its own members.[87]

Taking another step in jurisdictional size, this third profile provides us with a court that claimed to oversee the legal order of a whole kingdom. As element of the royal administration, the *Parlement* was strongly involved in the political ambitions and ideology of the French kings, providing the main jurisdictional ground for a broader royal power claim. Like York's Consistory Court, the *Parlement* was concerned with judicial business in first instance and appeal from an immense area. At the same time, the focus of its activities lay in the city of Paris, where it echoed the Utrecht case in its large variety of extra-judicial interferences. The composition of its staff also places it somewhere between the other two courts, containing both lay and religious, and legally trained next to untrained members.

A comparative study of late medieval law courts involves recognizing both major differences and similarities among the case studies. In some respects the courts under study were very much alike. All established themselves in an urban context, usually during the thirteenth century. Each of them furthermore grew out of the judicial council of a secular or ecclesiastical ruler, which increasingly came to function independently in legal matters. In other respects, differences abound. The composition of the court, for example, differed markedly from case to case, both in its members' training, in their socio-political background and in their numbers. Whereas the Consistory Court of York was made up predominantly of university-trained clergymen, the *Parlement* showed a much more varied picture, and the Council of Utrecht had no university-trained nor clerical members to speak of. The same variety can be found in the specific spaces built or selected for

86 Aubert, *Histoire*, vol. 1, 8. For edited lists of members, also see Aubert, "Nouvelles recherches", pt. 1, 75–78, 80, 86–88, 94–95, 98–100, 107–108, 238–242, 262–265.

87 Aubert, "Nouvelles recherches", pt. 2, 199; Autrand, *Naissance*, 108, 264.

the different courts to perform their legal business. A major difference exists between the purpose-built rooms in the royal palace where the *Parlement* held its sessions, the Consistory Court's use of a dedicated space in York's cathedral, and the various locations in Utrecht utilized by the Council to perform different parts of its legal process.

The coming into being and functioning of each court was shaped by a unique combination of internal and external factors. Different social, political, economic and jurisdictional contexts provided each body with specific communicative challenges. The scale of a court's jurisdiction could be a major factor. Whereas the Council of Utrecht was mostly concerned with the inhabitants of a minor settlement, York's Consistory Court and the Parisian *Parlement* dealt with an immense area containing a multitude of potential litigants and audiences. But an equally important influence was the court's relation to the broader socio-political and administrative constellation of which it was part. Forming the judicial branch of a broader episcopal administration, like the Consistory Court did, created very different circumstances from a body like the Utrecht Council, which had competences spanning the judicial, political and economic fields. Yet, despite such major differences in scale and context, each court was concerned with the production and propagation of a specifically institutionalized form of justice vis-à-vis different groups of potential consumers. In order to trace these common concerns in more detail, the following chapters will unpack the communicative interactions surrounding these three law courts. By focusing on the spaces, actions, documents, actors and discourses involved in their respective legal practices these chapters will wed the particular aspects with the structural development of these complex late medieval factories of justice.[88]

88 Cf. Latour, *Fabrique du droit.*

2. Legal space

Abstract
While often disregarded in document-focused studies, legal space formed a crucial aspect of the development of late medieval law courts. These judicial bodies took shape in interaction with an urban landscape that both facilitated and bounded their physical presence in people's lives within as well as beyond the courtroom proper. In day-to-day practice, space was involved in courts' strategies of accessibility, stimulating or impeding people to witness specific parts of a legal procedure. In addition, court procedure explicitly referenced features in the urban landscape, thus mutually investing procedures and spaces with meaning. In their own ways, the courts of Utrecht, York and Paris thus legalized their spatial environment while spatializing their legal procedures.

Keywords: medieval law courts, spatial history, urban history, medieval courtrooms, legal symbolism

Between 1400 and 1416, Nicholas of Baye filled the position of civil registrar (*greffier*) of the *Parlement* of Paris. Interspersed within the court's registers for this period he made notes on many events taking place in and outside of court.[1] They often paint a very vivid picture of daily life at the *Parlement*. On one occasion, for instance, he mentions a decision taken by the court on June 4, 1404, concerning the use of one of the courtrooms:

> On that day, because there was commotion about [the fact] that several functionaries and strangers had seated themselves in the chambers of

1 These notes are collected as the 'journal' of Nicholas of Baye in Alexandre Tuetey, ed., *Journal de Nicolas de Baye, greffier du Parlement de Paris 1400–1417*, 2 vols. (Paris: Renouard, 1885–1889). See the second volume for an extensive biographical sketch. Note that despite Tuetey's suggestion of a unified 'journal' of Nicholas of Baye, the entries constituting this 'journal' are dispersed throughout different registers, which makes it unlikely that they were originally meant to be a unified body of notes.

Camphuijsen, F., *Scripting Justice in Late Medieval Europe: Legal Practice and Communication in the Law Courts of Paris, York and Utrecht*. Taylor & Francis Group, 2022
DOI 10.5117/9789463723473_CH02

> this present council, in order to drink in the morning in the *Chambre des Enquêtes*, and thus could perceive the secrets of the court in a manner endangering and shaming the court, and that they did this while drinking too much, at overly excessive expense, and occupied [the chamber] at the time that it was to be used for counselling, [because of this] and for other reasons which have moved the court, the latter, with the two chambers combined, has ordained that henceforth while drinking in the morning in the aforementioned *Chambre des Enquêtes* none shall spend more than eight Parisian sous. And whoever does the contrary shall suffer the indignation of this court, and will be seriously punished.[2]

It appears to have been common practice then to use the room where part of the court held its sessions for certain non-judicial purposes as well. From a purely practical point of view a case could certainly be made for this double use of the *Chambre des Enquêtes*. Its vicinity to the palace kitchen and storage made it a convenient gathering place at the beginning of the day (Plan 1). The passage, however, also demonstrates how the men of the court were strongly concerned with the distinction between the room as court space and its other possible functions, linking a breach of this distinction explicitly with encroachments on the supposed secrecy of the courtroom. There appears then to have existed a tension between the practicalities of embedding a physical court space within a multifunctional royal palace, and concerns about the status of the court and the confidentiality of its legal process.

This passage calls attention to a very central, yet often overlooked, aspect of late medieval law courts, namely, the physical spaces in which its officials and litigants performed the different stages of a legal process. Such spaces could vary widely, as recent literature on late medieval courtrooms attests. For example, ecclesiastical courts all over western Europe had their seat in places as diverse as bishops' palaces and the porches and vestibules of churches,[3] while communal courts in the late medieval Low Countries

2 AN X^{1A}1478, fol. 158r; published in Tuetey, *Journal*, 90: *Cedit jour, pour ce que esclande estoit sur ce que pour boire à matin en la Chambre des Enquestes, pluseurs vallez et gens estranges se boutoient es chambres du Conseil de ceans, et povoient percevoir les secrez de la Court* in periculum et scandalum Curie, *et faisoit l'en trop grandes buveries, et y occupoit l'en le temps que l'en devoit emploier à conseiller, et si faisoit l'en trop excessive despence, et pour autres causes qui ont meu la Court, ycelle, les ij Chambres assemblées, a ordonné que d'ores en avant pour boire à matin en la Chambre des Enquestes dessusdicte ne sera despendu plus haut de viij solz parisis, et quicunques fera le contraire encourra l'indignation d'icelle Court, et sera griefment puni.*

3 Brundage, *Medieval Origins*, 421–424.

convened in a variety of demarcated spaces outside and (increasingly) inside town halls.[4] In towns in southern France, such as Marseilles and Manosque, courts often convened in marketplaces in front of a local church or seigneurial palace.[5] And Pisan communal courts were sometimes even held in Camaldolese monasteries.[6] The three law courts considered in this study show a similar diversity. Whereas the *Parlement* of Paris used the royal palace for its sessions, the Consistory Court met in York's cathedral church and the Council of Utrecht employed a variety of urban structures and outdoor spaces, including the top floor of a market hall and the square in front of a local church. Yet, despite this diversity, it is exactly in their relation to their physical context that these law courts also showed similar concerns and practices.

Modern discussions of the role of space, and in particular socially utilized space, often engage directly or indirectly with the work of the French sociologist Henri Lefebvre. In his elaborate *La production de l'espace*, Lefebvre challenges the consideration of space as stable background to or – at best – fixed end result of the activities of human agents.[7] Instead, so he argues, we should be writing a 'long history of space', focusing on the enduring bilateral influence between spaces and the people that constantly reshape them physically and mentally. Lefebvre's emphasis on the processes by which social actors produce space bodily or mentally has in its turn been criticized by Leif Jerram, for disregarding the particularly material character of a produced space.[8] For Jerram, the material obduracy of spaces, that is, the relative difficulty of changing them after they have been conceived, exerts a particularly strong influence on the lives of the social agents engaging with it, while its own malleability is crucially limited.[9] Jerram thus reintroduces some of the fixedness of space that Lefebvre denied so vehemently. However, while disagreeing on the exact nature of the influence of spaces vis-à-vis human agents, both Lefebvre and Jerram

4 Nathan van Kleij, "Beyond the Façade: Town Halls, Publicity, and Urban Society in the Fifteenth-Century Low Countries" (PhD diss., University of Amsterdam, 2021), 62–67.

5 Smail, *Consumption of Justice*, 33–34; Bednarski, *Curia*, 61–63.

6 Cécile Caby, "Hermits for Communes: The Camaldolese in the Service of the Communes of Central and Northern Italy in the Thirteenth to Fifteenth Centuries", in *Churchmen and Urban Government in Late Medieval Italy c. 1200–c. 1450: Cases and Contexts*, eds. Frances Andrews and Maria Agata Pincelli (Cambridge: Cambridge University Press, 2013), 272.

7 Henri Lefebvre, *La production de l'espace* (Paris: Éditions Anthropos, 1974), translated by Donald Nicholson-Smith as *The Production of Space* (Malden, MA: Blackwell, 1991).

8 Leif Jerram, "Space: A Useless Category of Analysis?", *History and Theory* 52 (2013), 411–412.

9 Ibid., 417–418.

consider space as a full-fledged actor in, rather than a passive background to, human activities.

It is in building on such theoretical scholarship that this chapter will foreground the role of space in the socio-judicial interactions of our three courts. In the historiography on law courts, where the study of texts and the people writing them remains dominant, such an explicit grounding of socio-judicial activity in space is often absent. However, as this chapter will show in more detail, the development of marked judicial spaces was as much a feature of the institutionalization of law courts as was their growing documentary output. For the late medieval people interacting with these courts, the 'court' was not only a body of text-producing men, but also a place where a specific kind of justice might be found. Furthermore, a consideration of the role of space in socio-judicial interaction provides us with a first methodological tool to negotiate between the long-lasting development of these institutional bodies and the many human agents interacting with and through them over time. As the Lefebvre-Jerram discussion has shown, space may encompass both the obdurate matter that frames people's interactions as well as the processes of using and conceptualizing this matter that shaped people's experience of their world. By focusing on space, this chapter will therefore seek out the link between people's socio-judicial strategies in a particular time and place, and the more obdurate forms that resulted from and in their turn shaped such strategies.

In order to achieve this, the chapter will develop two related topics. The first is concerned with the broader development of law courts as institutions in north-western Europe from the thirteenth century onwards. All three courts treated here developed from small groups of legal advisors into more extensive bodies of men judging various kinds of legal cases on a regular basis and producing abundant records. This development is usually traced on the basis of institutional and textual changes only, such as the influence of university-trained lawyers or an increase in textual literacy. Yet together with these changes in organization and practice came another that was no less fundamental. As courts came to settle more permanently in diverse localities, the obdurate physicality of the spaces they used became a factor of particular importance.[10] The first part of this chapter will therefore argue that the institutional development of the courts did not take place within a spatial vacuum. Rather, there existed a strong relationship between

10 Robert Jacob and Nadine Marchal-Jacob, "Jalons pour une histoire de l'architecture judiciaire", in *La justice en ses temples: Regards sur l'architecture judiciaire en France*, ed. Association Française pour l'histoire de la justice (Paris: Éditions Errance and Poitiers: Éditions Brissaud, 1992).

the way in which these courts came to use certain – pre-existing or newly built – spaces in diverse localities and the specific organizational form that they took over the thirteenth and fourteenth centuries. This did not only concern the buildings or outdoor spaces where sessions were held, but also the courts' relation to their broader urban context. For the fact that all three courts, at least two of which had demonstrably been itinerant up until the thirteenth century, settled in the hearts of cities, had an effect on – and was in its turn motivated by – the particular institutional form that these judicial bodies developed: a form that linked the locally particular urban landscape with broader trends of institutionalization.

Whereas the focus of the first part of this chapter is on space as a developing material arrangement, the description of Nicholas of Baye at the beginning of this chapter spotlights a second matter, namely, the way in which people engaged with this arrangement in daily legal practice. As the passage notes, the *Parlement* feared for an encroachment on the confidentiality of the courtroom. This contrasted markedly, however, with various other aspects of its legal procedure, which were made public very explicitly. As we will see in this and other cases treated in the second half of the chapter, the question of where people were at various stages in a legal process – that is, how they used the spaces involved in the process – was of prime importance for the court. Yet a courtly engagement with the material world also encompassed the meanings that were attributed to it in the legal process. Following the consideration of people's physical interaction with court spaces, we will therefore regard the ways in which these and other material arrangements, including such features as city walls, roads and churches, were conceptualized in the business treated in court, be it as socio-judicial boundaries, as material representatives of a community, or otherwise. As such I will highlight how spatial features were employed in the scripting of justice by loading both the actions performed during a legal process and the urban landscape these actions referred to with additional meanings. In tracing both the development of obdurate court spaces and their multifarious involvement in the daily legal practice of the courts under consideration, this chapter will thus sketch the spatial contours of the acts, texts and human agents that form the subject of later chapters.

The court as space

The *Parlement* of Paris provides by far the clearest example of the interdependency of the development of court space and the court as institution.

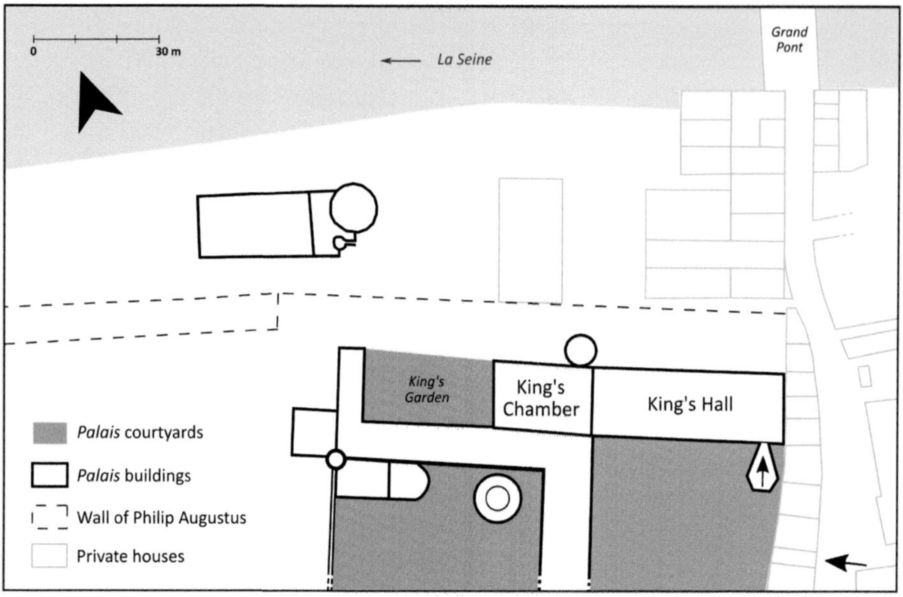

Plan 2: Northern part of the *Palais de la Cité* (ca.1292). Arrows indicate the route taken into the *Palais* by litigants whose case was heard by the *Parlement*. Dark grey spaces are palace courtyards.

In his elaborate study of the *Palais de la Cité*, Jean Guerout gives us an idea of the major architectural changes taking place in the royal palace at the end of the thirteenth and the beginning of the fourteenth century. When, from the eleventh century onwards, the *curia regis* began to use the *Palais de la Cité* for some of its public meetings, it usually met in the *aula regis*, the King's Hall, dating from the reign of Robert the Pious (r. 972–1031) (Plan 2).[11] This hall, forming one of the central buildings of the royal palace up until the thirteenth century, seems to have had a variety of uses, also functioning, for example, as a dining hall for the servants of the palace. In the second half of the thirteenth century, however, the judicial sessions of the royal court were no longer held in the King's Hall, but instead moved to what was called the Pleading Chamber or King's Chamber, a separate structure on the west side of the King's Hall consisting of two floors. Both of these floors had allegedly a double function, catering for the personal needs of the king as well as for the different types of judicial sessions of his court. The lower floor was used for the sessions of public pleading, but also functioned as the king's personal dining room. In a similar way the upper floor was not

11 Guerout, "Le Palais: Première partie", 132.

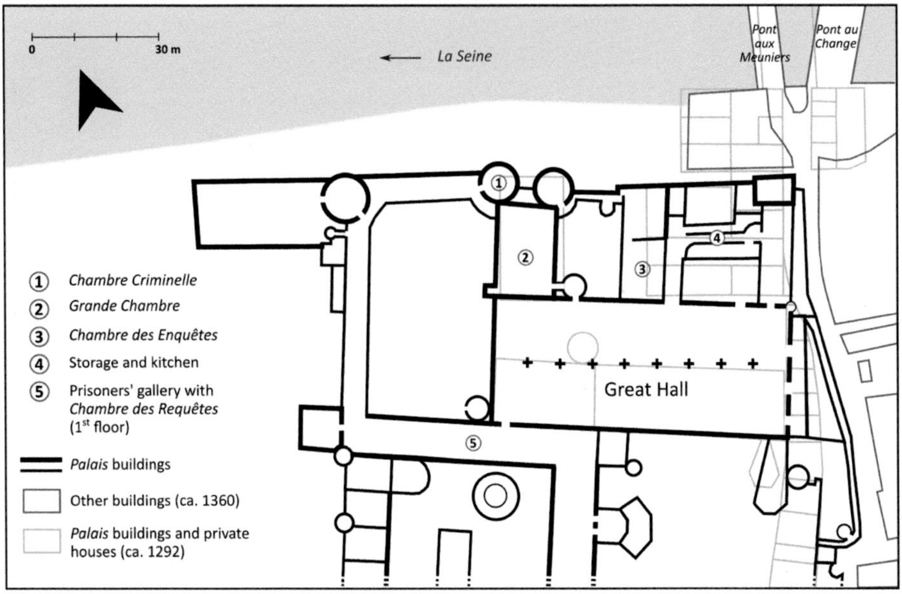

Plan 3: Northern part of the *Palais de la Cité* (ca.1360), showing *Palais* layout of ca.1292.

only the king's bedroom, but also the place where the non-public counsel sessions of the court were held. In this new setup, the King's Hall was used primarily as a waiting room for those summoned to court to plead their case.[12]

More fundamental changes took place at the beginning of the fourteenth century, when the large rebuilding campaign of the *Palais*, initiated by Philip the Fair (r. 1285–1314) and covering the first two and a half decades of the century, changed the face of the royal palace, and especially of those parts where the *Parlement* would go about its daily business (Plan 3). First, the King's Hall was expanded to three times its original size, and was henceforth appropriately called the Great Hall. This Great Hall consisted of two floors, of which the lower one was mainly used as a dining room for the palace community. The upper floor, which could be reached directly from outside by means of a landing, was used for very diverse activities, ranging from banquets to the saying of mass. But it seems also to have kept its role as a waiting chamber for the *Parlement*, judging by the presence of royal notaries in the hall.[13] The main activities of the *Parlement*, which were to listen to pleas and to deliberate over cases, were moved to a new location, just

12 Ibid., 176–177.

13 Guerout, "Le Palais: Deuxième partie", 30–31, 130–131, 138–143.

north of the old Pleading Chamber. This *Grande Chambre*, bordering on the Great Hall and constructed at about the same time, gave its name to the main body of judges who formed the basis of the *Parlement*. The double function of the old pleading and council chambers was not continued in this new layout. On the contrary, whereas in the old *Palais* royal and court spaces strongly overlapped, in the new layout the living quarters of the royal household were moved to the south of the *Palais* complex, thereby creating a separation between the activity of the *Parlement* and of the person of the king. There would remain a certain royal presence in the *Grande Chambre* through the inclusion of a throne, the *lit de justice* (Plan 5). But the close physical association between the king's private life and his public judicial functions was terminated.[14]

Another institutional division that was given physical shape in the new layout of the *Palais* was that between the main body of the court, the *Grande Chambre*, and the delegated bodies performing specific judicial functions, which eventually developed into more or less independent 'chambers' of their own. When the *Chambre des Enquêtes* was first explicitly separated from the *Grande Chambre* in 1308, this closely followed the creation of a physically separate space for the formerly delegated parliamentary commission treating the court's inquiries.[15] And the same close relationship between court and court space can be seen in the case of what would become the *Chambre Criminelle*. Long before this special commission was formally separated from the *Grande Chambre* in the sixteenth century, it already constituted a de facto separate body because of its distinct place of operations, namely, the tower that became known as the Criminal Tower.[16] The *Chambre des Requêtes* also originated in a delegated commission of the *Grande Chambre*. But when a royal ordinance of 1364 formalized its status as a separate judicial body, this was combined with a move of its members to a separate location on the second floor of the *Galerie des Prisonniers*, to the south of the Great Hall.[17] The major institutional changes of the *Parlement*, both in its relation

14 Ibid., 31–32, 36–37, 145–152. Over the fourteenth century the term *lit de justice* came to be used for a type of special court sessions at which the king did preside the *Parlement* in person. See Elizabeth A.R. Brown and Richard C. Famiglietti, *The* lit de justice*: Semantics, Ceremonial and the Parlement of Paris 1300–1600* (Sigmaringen: J. Thorbecke, 1994), 11–30. This tradition of extraordinary sessions in the king's presence is in line with my argument made in Chapter 5, that, despite the physical and practical separation of king and *Parlement*, ideologically the link between the two remained of prime importance.

15 Aubert, *Histoire*, vol. 1, 23; Guerout, "Le Palais: Deuxième partie", 31–32, 158–160.

16 Aubert, *Histoire*, vol. 1, 18–19; Guerout, "Le Palais: Deuxième partie", 31–32, 154–156.

17 Aubert, "Nouvelles recherches", pt. 2, 185–187; Guerout, "Le Palais: Deuxième partie", 161–162.

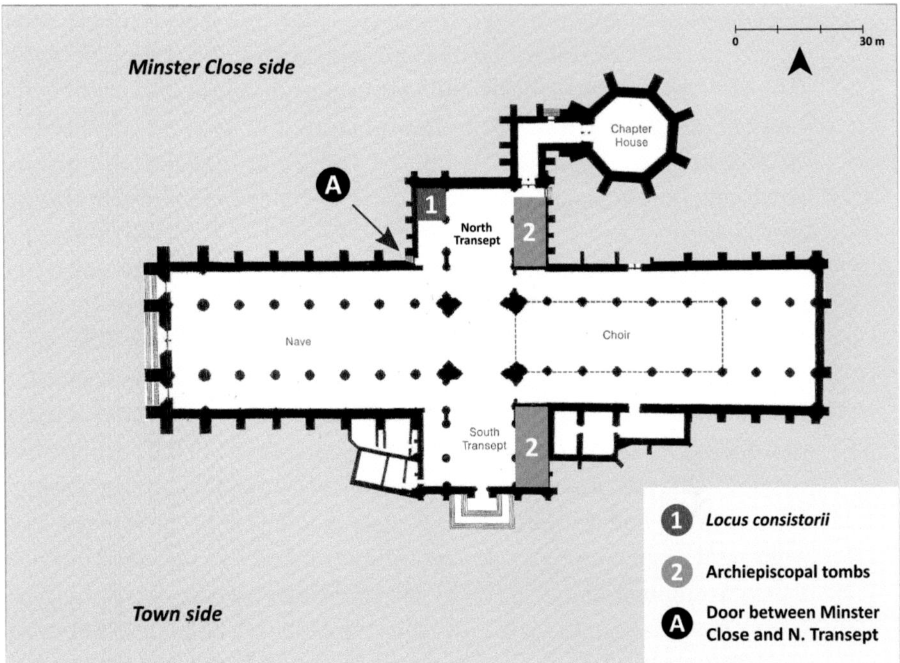

Plan 4: York Minster (late fifteenth century).

to the person of the king and in its internal organization, were thus closely intertwined with the physical development of the *Palais de la Cité* in the late thirteenth and fourteenth centuries.

Whereas the *Parlement* of Paris was closely tied up with the royal palace, one of the salient features of the Consistory Court of York was its use of the northern transept of the cathedral church as a location for its sessions (Plan 4). Like numerous cathedrals and other major building projects across Europe, this church was under constant construction between the thirteenth and fifteenth centuries.[18] From the 1220s onwards a large renovation campaign would change York's old Norman cathedral church into the building that is still visible today (Maps 4, 5 and 6). Work was initially begun on the transepts, and the northern one of these was supposedly finished around 1255.[19] There exists a chronological gap between the completion of the northern transept and the first recorded

18 For an excellent analysis of this practice of 'building-in-time', see Marvin Trachtenberg, *Building-in-Time: From Giotto to Alberti and Modern Oblivion* (New Haven, CT, and London: Yale University Press, 2010), esp. 103–283.

19 Brown, *'Our Magnificent Fabrick'*, 13–16.

mention of a 'consistory place' (*locus consistorii*) in the archiepiscopal register of 1311.[20] However, the date, circumstances and character of the expansion of the Minster provide several arguments to consider the physical development of the cathedral church to be closely related to the institutional diversification of the archiepiscopal administration, which saw the evolution of a fixed and semi-independent law court like the Consistory Court.

Explanations for the major building works on the Minster, initiated under archbishop Walter de Gray (r. 1216–1255), usually focus on its function as a religious centre. The many archiepiscopal tombs that came to occupy the eastern aisles of both transepts have been read as evidence for the liturgical, memorial and propagandistic motivation behind this early expansion of the old Norman cathedral. Following a peak in the popularity of saints' cults in the late twelfth and early thirteenth century, the archbishop decided to expand the cathedral's transepts to promote the Minster as a prominent place for pilgrimage, rivalling the position of Canterbury as primary religious centre in the kingdom.[21] However, the western aisles, lacking any tombs or other signs of pilgrimage activity, play a less evident role in this explanation. At the same time, the general rarity of double-aisled transepts in churches of this period does suggest a specific idea behind their construction.[22] Several elements, such as the integral wall benches running along their walls, make it feasible that they were meant to be places of assembly. More specifically for the northern transept, a small door, giving easy access from the archiepiscopal palace in the Minster close, confirms the idea that this part of the church was constructed with the idea of catering for assemblies that required the presence of the archbishop or

20 Noted in the records of a case regarding the election of a prior for Hexham in the register of Archbishop Greenfield, published as entry 565 in Brown and Hamilton Thompson, *William Greenfield*, 239–244, at 240. The oldest mention of a *locus consistorii* explicitly located in *maiori ecclesia Eboracensis* (that is, York Minster) dates only to 1326, and is contained in a cause paper from 1328: BIA CP.E.18. The latter is also partly published in R.H. Helmholz, *Marriage Litigation in Medieval England* (Cambridge: Cambridge University Press, 1974), 191–195. See p. 195 for the reference to York Minster. Unfortunately, no medieval plans exist to confirm the position of the Consistory Court in the Minster's northern transept. However, surviving plans from the seventeenth and eighteenth century clearly situate the Consistory Court in that place. Only in the nineteenth century did the court move to another location, namely, the former treasury built against the south side of the western choir. For reproductions of these plans, see Brown, *'Our Magnificent Fabrick'*, 271–274.

21 Brown, *'Our Magnificent Fabrick'*, 11–13; Charlotte A. Stanford, "Archbishop Melton's Donations to York Minster: Strengthening the See", *Yorkshire Archaeological Journal* 75 (2003): 84–85.

22 Brown, *'Our Magnificent Fabrick'*, 34–43.

his officials.[23] Given the expansion, diversification and establishment of the archiepiscopal administration that took place in this same period, the specific architectural development of this part of the cathedral therefore seems to point at a role in facilitating the establishment of administrative bodies like the Consistory Court, by providing them with a permanent space to congregate in. Although we lack written evidence that explicitly links the construction of the new transepts to its intended use by the Consistory Court specifically, the material evidence of this initial expansion of the Minster does suggest an intricate link between the changes that took place in the built environment and developments in the archiepiscopal administrative system more broadly, of which the institutionalization of the Consistory Court was a major aspect.

The Council of Utrecht for its part held many of its regular sessions in the building called the *Schoonhuis*. Information on this building is unfortunately very scarce.[24] Constructed in the second half of the thirteenth century, it had a variety of functions, which were facilitated by its division into two floors. The ground floor served as market hall for cloth merchants from early on, while the second floor was used by the Council for its sessions. This combination of functions was not unusual in medieval Utrecht, as the use of city gates and guild houses as city prisons attests.[25] Nor should it surprise us to find economic and legal-political functions combined, seeing that the members of the Council originally came from the old mercantile elite of the city. However, when placing the Council's use of the *Schoonhuis* in a broader regional context, the situation in Utrecht does appear exceptional. Whereas urban authorities in many other towns in the Low Countries began constructing elaborate purpose-built town halls in the fifteenth century, the Utrecht Council kept its seat on the top floor of the *Schoonhuis*.[26] Only in the early sixteenth century did the Council move north-eastwards from the *Schoonhuis* to one of the buildings bordering the *Plaets* (Map 3) that would form the basis of a new town hall.[27] This latter move, furthermore,

23 Ibid., 35.

24 The little that there is can be gathered from Tarquinus J. Hoekstra and A.F.E. Kipp, "Archeologische en bouwhistorische kroniek van de gemeente Utrecht over 1984", *Maandblad Oud-Utrecht* 58, no. 4 (1985): 174–175; Martin de Bruijn, *Husinghe ende Hofstede: Een institutioneel-geografische studie van de rechtspraak over onroerend goed in de stad Utrecht in de Middeleeuwen* (Utrecht: Het Spectrum, 1994), 279, 349; Van Vliet, "Burgers", 91; Hoven van Genderen, "Toppunt", 147.

25 Hoven van Genderen, "Toppunt", 130.

26 For the broader regional development of town halls, see Van Kleij, "Beyond the Façade", 19–25.

27 Van Schaik, "Een nieuwe heer", 193–194.

was more or less forced upon the Council as part of a campaign of political centralization under Utrecht's new lord, the Habsburg emperor Charles V, that also saw a drastic limitation of the Council's power as legal and governmental institution.[28]

It remains uncertain in how far the construction of the *Schoonhuis* in the thirteenth century already took into account its use by the Council. Given its mercantile origins, it is certainly not unthinkable that the top floor of a market hall served as gathering place for this body from early on. Yet, up until the first mention of the Council's place of residence in the *Liber albus* of 1340, we lack explicit evidence of its earliest use of the *Schoonhuis*. What does become clear, however, from the turbulent political history of fourteenth-, fifteenth- and sixteenth-century Utrecht, is the meaningful link that seems to have existed between the Council as urban institution and its place of residence. As elaborated in the next section, the *Schoonhuis* can be considered part of a hub of guild-controlled or communal buildings, also including the *Buurkerk*, that were offset in the urban landscape against other legal and political authorities and their buildings, most notably the bishop and his cathedral. The Council's attachment to the *Schoonhuis*, notwithstanding broader regional trends of town hall construction, can be read as expression of its political and juridical autonomy vis-à-vis these other spatially marked politico-judicial authorities; an autonomy that entailed the use of certain obdurate markers of guild-based communal rule, such as the *Schoonhuis* and the *Buurkerk*. Thus, when this autonomy was lost in the early sixteenth century, this had equally spatial consequences in the loss of the Council's seat in the *Schoonhuis*.

A survey of the spatial development of our three courts clearly shows that there was no ready-made trajectory for the physical manifestation of these institutions. Certain broader trends or habits can certainly be extrapolated, such as a general preference of ecclesiastical courts to hold sessions in or near church buildings, or the development of many urban courtrooms as part of new town halls. Yet specifically local circumstances could lead an individual court in a completely different direction, as the case of the Utrecht Council shows so well. Nor did courts simply impose themselves on an otherwise passive spatial context. In some cases, like the early-fourteenth-century *Grande Chambre*, the court's spaces were specifically constructed with their judicial function in mind. In others, they appeared as part of broader building activities, such as the western aisles of the new transepts of York Minster that came to house the Consistory Court. But often courts would

28 Ibid., 191–197.

simply appropriate existing spaces. This was true for many of the structures used by the Council of Utrecht, like the *Schoonhuis* or the town's towers, but can also be seen in the case of the *Parlement* before the major building campaign under Philip the Fair. Obdurate spaces could not be adapted at will, and required large amounts of resources and time to do so, as the large spatial reconstructions in Paris and York have shown. Thus, the development of these institutions as physically fixed bodies meting out justice meant necessarily an investment in the local organization of spaces, be it through fundamental physical adaptations or a reorganization of the uses made of existing ones. In that sense space was a factor that was just as defining for the shape these institutions took as broader social, political or other factors may have been.

Courts and urban space

The courts' investment in their spatial environment entailed more than the construction or appropriation of a specific building or room where people gathered in session. All three courts treated here, regardless of the scale of their jurisdiction, functioned in an urban context, which had a particular influence on their development and daily practice. This was most prominently so for the Council of Utrecht. As noted before, its legal activity was far from limited to its sessions in the *Schoonhuis*. Instead, it involved many different structures and spaces within the city, especially in the governmental hub in the north-eastern corner of the old trade settlement, the *Stathe*. Here one could find central communal buildings like the *Buurkerk* and the *Schoonhuis*, as well as central open spaces, like the *Plaets* and the churchyard in front of the *Buurkerk* (Map 3). Other spatial features of late medieval Utrecht, like its walls, roads, stairs and canal, were also linked to the Council's legal activity. Taking into account that the Council formed Utrecht's central political and legal authority between the thirteenth and fifteenth centuries a spatial history of the Council is thus very much concerned with the relationship between the growth of an independent, guild-based, urban government and the development of the city space as a whole.

The Council's investment in its physical surroundings knows a long prehistory. Some of the earliest privileges granted to the town of Utrecht by emperor Henry V in 1122 already established an explicit link between the community's political, economic and legal autonomy and its physical urban environment, in particular the city wall. Thus, Henry granted

Map 3: Detail of sixteenth century map of Utrecht, showing locations of Council activity.

freedom of toll to those who would contribute to building the city wall and submitted those who would come to trade within the limits of the wall to the jurisdiction of the aldermen. Later additions to these privileges, like the right of citizens to be judged only in their own court (*ius de non evocando*) granted in 1252, kept stressing the physical space of the city as a main reference point for the legal framework of the urban community's powers of self-governance.[29] And when these political, economical and judicial powers began to extend to an increasingly large area outside the wall, called the city's 'liberty' (*stadsvrijheid*), this in its turn had concrete physical consequences in the construction of free-standing gatehouses

29 Van Vliet, "Burgers", 75–79.

(*buitenpoorten*) to mark the boundaries of this area. Both inside the city wall and outside in the liberty, physical and legal delineation had gone hand in hand long before the Council rose to prominence.[30]

As the Council came to constitute the main urban authority in Utrecht, it drew on such longstanding associations between the town's community and urban space, articulating many of its power claims spatially. The governmental hub that saw most of its public activity contained buildings with explicitly guild- or community-tinged histories, including a guildhall like the *Schoonhuis* and the *Buurkerk*, which had formed the central church of the increasingly autonomous *Stathe* settlement since the eleventh century.[31] As suggested in the previous section, the Council's seeming attachment to this historically marked hub may well be read as a spatial elaboration of communal autonomy vis-à-vis the equally prominent episcopal presence in the area surrounding the cathedral. Furthermore, echoing some of the obligations vis-à-vis communal urban space that we saw in Henry V's privileges, the Council drew explicit links between the legal status of citizens, their guild membership and the caretaking of important urban locations. This took different forms, like the guild-based patrolling of parts of the city walls or the phenomenon where people received citizenship on the basis of their promise to take care of the maintenance of a certain bridge or public stairway in the city.[32] Building on historically developed associations between marked features of the urban landscape and the community of Utrecht's inhabitants, the Council's prominence as legal and political institution took shape not against the background of, but in active conversation with the town's morphology, stretching far beyond the Council's direct seat in the *Schoonhuis* as such.

Such mutual influence between institutional development and the physical and abstracted urban context can also be seen in the other two cases. In her recent study of land ownership and urban development in medieval York, Sarah Rees Jones stresses the important role played by what she calls the 'Minster community' in shaping and defining the face of the city in the period up to 1350. Between the twelfth and fourteenth centuries, the York Minster came to form the focal point of a community of – self-proclaimed – religious specialists, who represented the archiepiscopal authority in the city. Through the delegation of administrative, religious and judicial

30 For a recent survey of the history of the Utrecht city walls, see René de Kam, *De ommuurde stad: Geschiedenis van een stadsverdediging* (Amsterdam: Spectrum, 2020).

31 Van Vliet, "Bisschop", 64–66.

32 Ibid., 127–132.

competences, the archbishops transferred much of the growing burden of responsibilities that their position had come to entail to such functionaries and bodies as the dean and chapter of York or the official and his Consistory Court, all situated in or around the Minster.[33] During the thirteenth and fourteenth centuries, the Minster community attempted to maintain or even increase its role in the city, in which other authorities – the king, but also the civic government – contested its position.[34] Such power conflicts were concerned with urban space both in an organizational and directly physical way. For example, in order to promote the Minster's presence, many smaller churches were incorporated within a developing parochial system, subordinating them to the courts of the archbishop and other ecclesiastical authorities.[35] And in a more directly physical way, the reconstruction campaign of the cathedral and its direct surroundings also showed the attempt at defining and spatially visualizing the Minster community within the city. The cathedral formed the cornerstone of what was in a way the physicalization of its community within York's urban landscape. At the same time that the Minster was being rebuilt, the precinct around it also went through fundamental spatial changes, forming a more strictly demarcated area within the city walls. This precinct, which from the late thirteenth century onwards became known as the Minster close, was separated from the surrounding city by means of blocks of houses, with access limited to several gateways (Maps 4, 5 and 6). Within, one could find many of the central residential and administrative buildings of the Minster community, like the archiepiscopal palace, the deanery, the treasurer's house and, of course, the cathedral itself, thereby forming a distinctive and demarcated ecclesiastical hub in the midst of the city.[36] The Minster community, and in extension the resident Consistory Court, thus made a clear mark on the face of the city, both by building, rebuilding and reorganizing the spaces in which it operated.

Turning our attention to Paris, we can see that the extension of the *Palais de la Cité* also had a very direct influence on its urban surroundings. In order to be able to enlarge the *Palais*, more space was needed in an area that had over the years become clogged with houses and stores. The first step in the project of extending the *Palais* therefore consisted of the expropriation

33 Sarah Rees Jones, *York: The Making of a City 1068–1350* (New York and Oxford: Oxford University Press, 2013), 140–142.

34 Palliser, "Civic Liberties", 98–100; Rees Jones, "Civic Administration", 120–121.

35 Rees Jones, *Making of a City*, 152–153.

36 Ibid., 143–145.

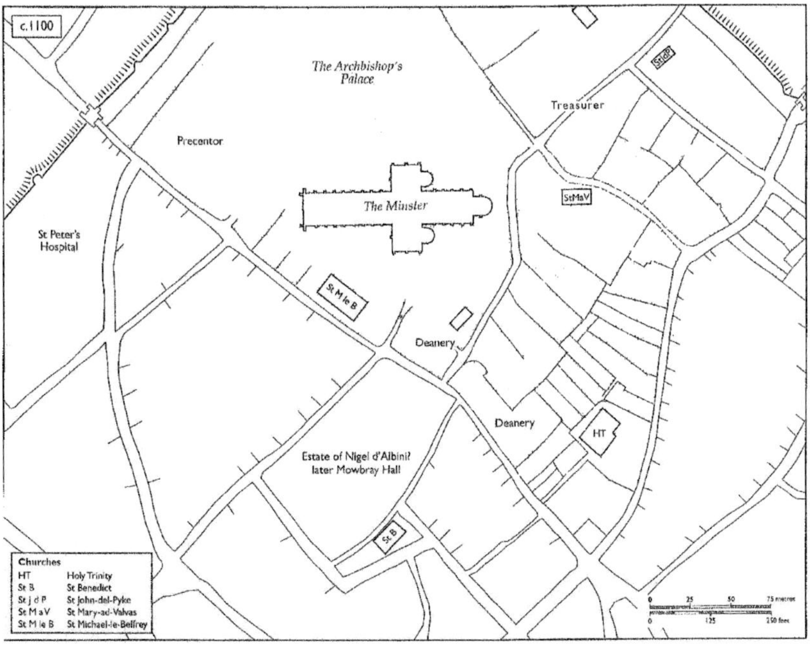

Map 4: York Minster and its direct surroundings ca. 1100.

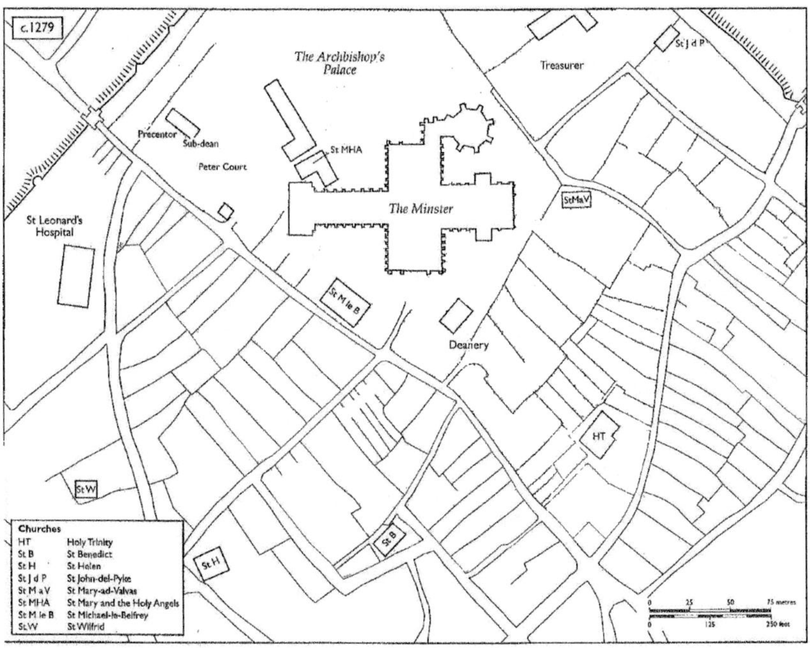

Map 5: York Minster and its direct surroundings (ca.1279), showing the beginnings of an enclosed area to the north of the cathedral church.

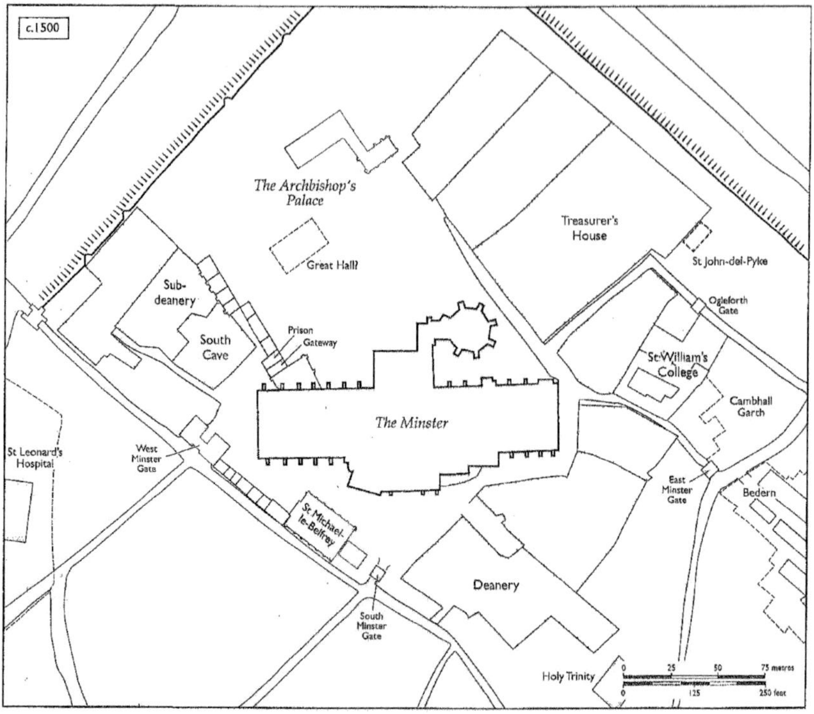

Map 6: York Minster and its direct surroundings (ca.1500), showing the Minster close as separated area, including several gateways.

and razing of many privately owned buildings in its direct surroundings (Plans 2 and 3). This required making some major financial arrangements with expropriated house owners, the records of which still survive.[37] In addition, the main road in front of the *Palais* was narrowed, to allow for larger palace buildings.[38] With the major rebuilding project begun under Philip the Fair, the king and his court thus intervened in a very direct way in the surrounding urban space. But it was not just the *Île de la Cité* where the permanent presence of the royal court could be felt. At least since Philip Augustus (r. 1180–1223), the kings' focus on Paris as their capital meant that they were particularly concerned with its built environment. The erection of the first city wall by Philip Augustus in the decades around 1200 is a case in point. The influence of this wall on the built space in the city – creating, for example, a clear physical distinction between the city and its numerous suburbs – represented a strong royal power claim vis-à-vis other urban

37 Guerout, "Le Palais: Première partie", 185–212.
38 Guerout, "Le Palais: Deuxième partie", 41–42.

authorities, like the Parisian archbishops. Later kings would continue to be actively involved in shaping and maintaining their urban environment, for example, by stimulating settlement within the walls and reorganizing the city's administrative structure.[39] When, from the late thirteenth century onwards, the *Parlement* as a semi-independent body came to exercise a portion of the king's competences, many of these directly concerned the city. For example, the *Parlement* was responsible for overseeing the guarding and maintenance of several city roads, bridges, fountains and public monuments. Other space-related matters through which the *Parlement* intervened in its direct urban context involved questions of public health – like prohibitions on the free movement of sick individuals – or the movements of social marginals, like prostitutes and vagabonds.[40] Furthermore, at least from the end of the thirteenth century, the sources show us how conflicts concerning real estate in the city of Paris would, in some instances at least, be brought before the *Parlement*.[41]

The relation between an institutionalizing *Parlement* and its surrounding built environment was not limited to the court's active involvement in the affairs of the city. As the royal court settled more permanently on the *Île de la Cité*, it made its presence felt throughout the city in much more indirect ways as well. An administrative body of this size attracted many individuals, both members of the institution itself and people who were in some way or another connected to its activities, from people whose case was appearing in court to artisans selling their wares to the royal household and its visitors. Much of the intensive building activity that can be witnessed during the thirteenth and early fourteenth century in the city was connected to the presence of a large royal administration that gradually made Paris its permanent place of residence.[42] And this effect was not limited to one specific area in the city, as evidenced, for example, by the broad distribution of houses built in this period by members of this royal administration.[43] Notwithstanding the

39 Cazelles, *Nouvelle histoire*, 13–19.

40 Aubert, *Histoire*, vol. 1, 298–301.

41 See, for example, a case from 1287, noted down in the second volume of the *Olim* register, where the conflict between a canon from Noyon and a citizen of Paris over possession of several houses in Paris is arbitrated by the *Parlement*; AN $X^{1A}2$, fol. 78v. Also see Edgar Boutaric, ed., *Actes du Parlement de Paris: Première série: De l'an 1254 à l'an 1328*, vol. 1 (Paris: Henri Plon, 1863), 255. Another example can be found in a royal letter contained in the criminal register of the *Parlement*, which is concerned with the construction of a house by the physician Pierre de Narbonne, that extended too far up the street and therefore needed to be taken down: AN $X^{2A}3$, fol. 141v.

42 Cazelles, *Nouvelle histoire*, 19–23, 33–39.

43 Ibid., 19–23.

immense size of its formal jurisdiction, the development of the *Parlement* as a fixed institution intervened most directly in the urban landscape of Paris, varying from concrete morphological changes to involvement in the way in which existing spaces were maintained and managed.

Like we have seen when considering the development of their courtrooms, the exact relation of the Utrecht Council, York's Consistory Court and the Parisian *Parlement* to their direct spatial context varied immensely. Locally specific factors, including the existing urban morphology or social and cultural valuations of specific buildings or other features, combined with broader political, economic and social considerations to shape the way these courts took form physically. In all cases, however, the groups that brought forth the courts – be it a royal household, an ecclesiastical community or an urban elite – seem to have had a longstanding relation to and particular interest in a specifically urban context. Even when not exclusively concerned with the urban community as such, as was the case both in York and Paris, the development of these courts into permanent and (semi-)autonomous judicial institutions took place in cities. While this common urban environment, with all its local variation, had a concrete impact on the particular physical form these courts took over time, its effects on daily legal practice were at least as significant. As entities that for several centuries had seen a significant population increase, cities formed the stage par excellence where courts could showcase their claim to a specific role in the socio-legal constellation. It is against this background, that is, courts' concern for people's experience of the legal process, that we now move from the spatial history of these institutions' advent, to the role of space in their daily practice.

Spatial practice and accessibility

While the role of courts' spatial context on their institutional formation has already highlighted some of the back and forth between human agents and the spaces they engage with, a consideration of legal activity shows how integral the physical environment could be to people's experiences of justice on a day-to-day basis. Drawing on Lefebvre's terminology, the law court can be seen as a 'social space', inherently linked with social relations and their development. Social space is not to be seen as an empty container of social actions, but rather as something shaped by – and in its turn shaping and defining – social relations.[44] In what follows, I will argue

44 Lefebvre, *Production*, trans. Nicholson-Smith, 85.

that the spaces related to late medieval law courts formed an integral part of the activities – and in particular the communicative activities – of the courts. As seen in the passage by Nicholas of Baye at the beginning of this chapter, a major concern of the *Parlement* centred on the tension between the publicity and confidentiality of different parts of its legal process. The fear expressed in this passage for an encroachment on the 'secrets of the court' signals a more fundamental issue of accessibility, attested for all three courts. Accessibility in this sense comprised the different ways in which the legal process could be experienced by outsiders, be it visibly, audibly, or otherwise. As will become clear, questions of accessibility were strongly connected to the courts' spaces of operation. They shaped the way in which the courts involved their spatial contexts in daily legal practice, be it by regulating access to certain spaces, by using certain spaces for public pronouncements, or in other ways.

A very explicit discussion of the uses made of the space of York Minster is found in a mandate from archbishop Zouche from February 13, 1349. In it Zouche reacts to an incident of several days earlier in which a group of people had entered the cathedral church behaving in a noisy and disrespectful manner. This leads the archbishop not only to summon the rabble-rousers before him under threat of excommunication, but also to proclaim explicitly the way in which the Minster space ought to be used. In turning vehemently against any kind of disturbance of the divine office, be it through noise or other forms of contempt for the solemnity of the place, he defines several forms of speech that should not be performed in the church, that is, *contumeliae* (disrespectful speech), *contentiones* (disputes), *publica parliamenta* (public assemblies) and *profana colloquia confabulationis* (profane speech assemblies).[45] Zouche's reaction spotlights the problem of a space where solemnity was supposed to reign, but that had a large variety of practical functions, including catering for the sessions of the Consistory Court. The Minster thus formed the locus of a variety of partly interlocking, partly incompatible practices.[46]

In considering the legal practice of the Consistory Court within the Minster, the spatial practices within the cathedral as a whole take centre

45 Published in James Raine, ed., *Historical Papers and Letters from the Northern Registers* (London: Longman, 1873), 397–399. For an extensive treatment of this episode, also see Barrie Dobson, "The Later Middle Ages 1215–1500", in *A History of York Minster*, eds. G.E. Aylmer and Reginald Cant (Oxford: Clarendon Press, 1977), 44.

46 Dobson, "Later Middle Ages", 84–86, lists a variety of uses to which the minster space could be put, including the paying of rents, the deposition of valuables for safekeeping and various kinds of political assemblies.

stage. With its gradual (re)construction over nearly three centuries, the late medieval Minster came to encompass different types of interconnected spaces, with different degrees of public accessibility (Plan 4). On the one hand there were those like the late-thirteenth-century Chapter House, the octagonal building to the north of the main cathedral building. This structure was used primarily for meetings of the cathedral chapter, although it also occasionally housed other assemblies. The Chapter House was connected to the north transept of the Minster by means of an L-shaped passage, separated from the main building by means of a double door.[47] This area of the Minster, physically separated and predominantly used for non-public gatherings, offered very limited accessibility to most people. Other parts of the Minster were, on the contrary, more accessible. Areas like the southern transept, containing the main entrance to the cathedral, and the nave, used as it was for religious services, had on many occasions a more open character. On most occasions people could – and were perhaps even expected to – freely access these spaces from outside the cathedral. Unsurprisingly, most of these areas were located on the south side of the Minster, which faced the city, while the north side was oriented towards the Minster close. These areas of the church saw major public activity, like the performance of religious ceremonies and the movement of large numbers of pilgrims, attracted as they were by the chapels of various saints and the remains of several notable archbishops.[48]

Of particular interest here is a third category of spaces, which had a semi-public character. The northern transept fell – at least partially – within this category, as did the choir. The physical separation of such spaces from the freely accessible areas of the cathedral was less absolute than in the case of the Chapter House. Essentially, they formed part of the same physical space, located under the same roof and without thick stone walls separating them from other parts of the Minster. But they could on occasion be divorced physically from the surrounding church space. The choir, for example, could be closed off by means of a portal.[49] As regards the *locus consistorii*, for the seventeenth century there is evidence of wooden screens used to separate this area from the surrounding church and create a semi-secluded space.[50]

47 Brown, *'Our Magnificent Fabrick'*, 46–85, esp. 58.

48 Dobson, "Later Middle Ages", 85–86; Brown, *'Our Magnificent Fabrick'*, 36–43.

49 Archbishop Zouche's mandate mentions *ostia chori* (the choir's doorways), which were closed after the divine office was finished *ut moris est*. See Raine, *Historical Papers*, 398. The current enclosed choir was only finished in the fifteenth century. See Brown, *'Our Magnificent Fabrick'*, 168–215.

50 As shown on the map in Brown, *'Our Magnificent Fabrick'*, 274.

Even if we assume that such screens were already in use in the medieval period, it is unlikely that such a separation of the *locus consistorii* was very absolute. Although the screens may have reduced visibility, sound could pass from the outside to the inside and vice versa, creating a partly separated, partly accessible area dedicated to the legal process.[51]

In attempting to grasp the logic behind such a semi-secluded space, it is helpful to briefly return to the role of the Minster within its broader urban context. The Minster formed the physical centrepiece of the so-called Minster close, where a religious community had its base of operations. Where the close as a whole served to distinguish between the spheres of lay and spiritual activity, the Minster seems to have functioned as intermediary space between both worlds. It was here that ordinary believers met and interacted with diverse religious specialists, be it in the context of a religious service, or other social activities. Within these spatial economies of the Minster as a whole, the north transept above all had a role as intermediary space. This is, for example, evidenced by the many small entrances leading from the Minster close into the north transept.[52] Whereas a lay public would enter the cathedral from the south, the religious residing in the Minster close had their own entrances from the north, turning the Minster's northern transept into the logical meeting point of two separate but also inherently intertwined and co-dependent worlds. That the Consistory Court held its sessions in such a communicative twilight zone therefore highlights its concerns over controlling the accessibility of the legal process. Outsiders could – and were arguably expected to – experience certain aspects of this procedure, such as the reading of sentences (see Chapter 3), but only to such a degree as the court chose to show.

In its layout York Minster echoed many of the spatial practices also seen for the *Palais de la Cité*. Before the large rebuilding campaign at the beginning of the fourteenth century, the *Palais* already encompassed spaces with different levels of accessibility. The two floors that made up the King's Chamber created a physical distinction as regards the accessibility of different parts

51 Evidence for the practice of separating large spaces by means of wooden screens can also be found in the case of York's late medieval guild halls, as well as in many late medieval courtrooms situated in town halls. See Katherine Giles, *An Archaeology of Social Identity: Guildhalls in York, c. 1350–1630* (Oxford: Archaeopress, 2000), 62–63, and Van Kleij, "Beyond the Façade", 60–67, respectively. In all these cases separation was far from absolute, blocking a full view of what happened behind the screens at most.

52 That is, the door on the west side of the transept, leading to the *locus consistorii*, a door on the east side, and the double doors between the main cathedral and the vestibule of the Chapter House. See Brown, *'Our Magnificent Fabrick'*, 274.

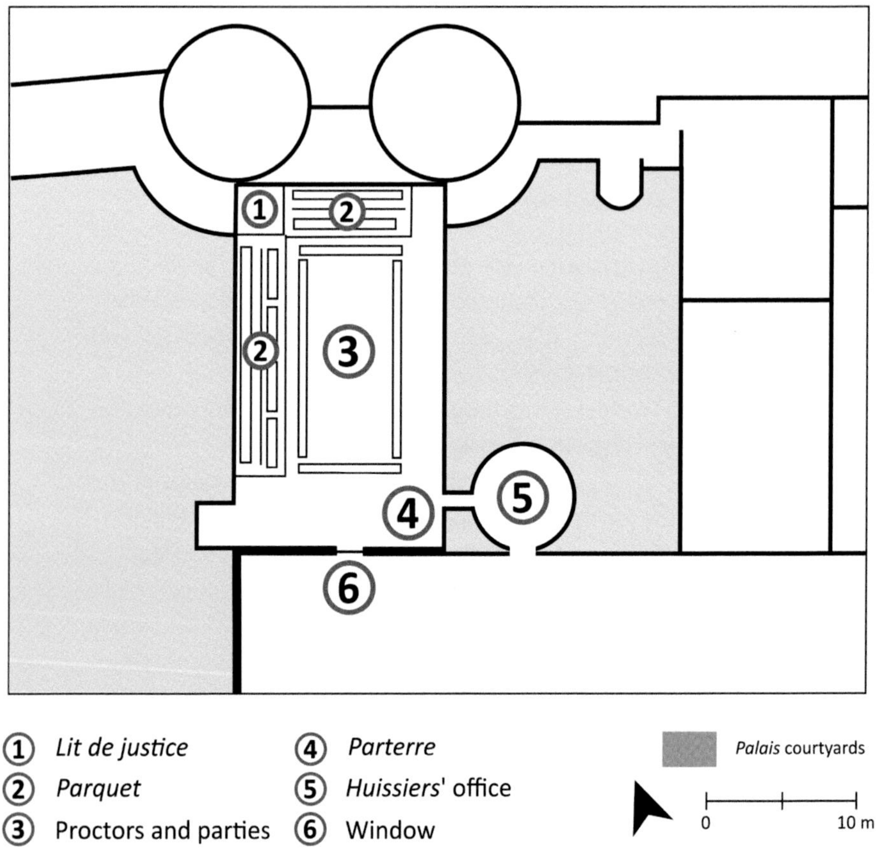

Plan 5: Detail of the northern part of the *Palais de la Cité* (ca.1360), showing the *Grande Chambre* and its direct surroundings.

of the legal process. The lower chamber, being the place where people would come to plead their case, posed obstacles to the free coming and going of individuals, as entry was restricted to people involved in a certain case. The upper or council chamber was even more limited in its accessibility, as it was intended for the non-public sessions of the royal court. The King's Hall on the contrary had a much more public character, functioning not only as a waiting room for litigants, but also catering for a variety of other uses.[53] Between the King's Hall, the Pleading Chamber and the Council Chamber, an increasingly limited accessibility reflected the court's concerns over the opacity and publicity of specific parts of the legal process.

53 Guerout, "Le Palais: Première partie", 176–177.

The large rebuilding campaign of the early fourteenth century rearranged the spatial economy of the *Palais de la Cité*, but did not fundamentally change the general concern for the division into and management of public, non-public and semi-public spaces. As described earlier, the layout of the new *Palais* created a strong physical separation between the king's personal and public personae, situating the royal household in the southern part of the *Palais* and making the *Grande Chambre* the workspace of the *Parlement*. Although the latter move meant combining two formerly separated aspects of the legal process – that is, pleading and counsel – in one space, a concern for demarcating the two types of legal practice – with their different levels of accessibility – remained the same. Rather, where formerly the separation between the public, semi-public and non-public aspects of the legal process was achieved by situating the pleading and counsel parts of the legal process on different floors, now other means were used to bring the distinction into practice. The most important method was temporal demarcation. The *Parlement* set specific days in the week for public audiences, during which litigants or their proctors could come before the court to plead their case. On other days, and sometimes immediately before or after the public pleadings, the *Grande Chambre* would be used for non-public counsel regarding the cases under scrutiny.[54] In its spatial layout as well, the *Grande Chambre* divided court practice and participants by means of visible boundaries (Plan 5). The court itself, consisting of the king, if he was present, and his ecclesiastical and lay councillors, occupied an area called the *parquet*, which bordered on the north and west walls of the *Grande Chambre*. This *parquet* was separated from the rest of the room both in height – by being partly raised above ground level – and by means of an enclosure, which could be accessed through two small doors. Outside of this enclosure were placed the benches for the advocates, proctors and parties engaged in the lawsuit. And beyond those, in the so-called *parterre*, there even appears to have been room for a broader public to witness the legal procedures.[55] Although contemporary visual evidence for the divisions within the *Grande Chambre* is lacking, visual evidence from similar sessions held elsewhere suggests that these spatial divisions will have had certain effects on the visibility, if not necessarily the audibility, of the process for the large majority of those present in the *Grande Chambre* (Figure 1). Thus, both through temporal barriers and the internal layout of the *Grande Chambre* the different parts

54 Aubert, *Histoire*, vol. 1, 180–187.

55 Guerout, "Le Palais: Deuxième partie", 145–152. For more on the role of audiences during sessions, see Chapter 3.

Figure 1: Court session of the trial of the duke of Alençon at Vendôme (1458), showing a layout similar to that of the sessions in the *Grand Chambre* in Paris. Illumination by Jean Fouquet in a manuscript of Boccacio's *On the fates of famous men* (ca. 1459-1460).

of the legal process as well as the different categories of participants were spatially separated.

A strong physical distinction did continue to exist between the Great Hall and the *Grande Chambre*, echoing that between the former King's Hall and the King's Chamber. The upper floor of the Great Hall, catering as it did for a wide range of activities, was one of the most accessible spaces in the *Palais*, probably rivalled only by the ground floor of the *Sainte Chapelle*. It could be entered directly from the *Palais* courtyard, and is likely to have been the place where people with court-related business were received by the court's notaries.[56] The distinction between this public Great Hall and the multifunctional *Grande Chambre* was physically emphasized by the lack of any direct connection between the two spaces. The only way from the Great Hall into the *Grande Chambre* led through a tower in the small courtyard to the north of the Great Hall, called the antechamber of the *Parlement* and later the office of the *huissiers*. Here, as evidenced from the late fourteenth century onwards, two officials kept guard, managing the human traffic according to the type of session that was held, either a secluded counsel or a public audience. Ordinarily the doors of this antechamber were closed, turning the *Grande Chambre* into a secluded space fit for the private deliberations of the court. During times of pleading, however, the doors were opened, turning the *Grande Chambre* into the semi-public space discussed above, still separated from the Great Hall, but more easily accessible for a larger public.[57] At least from the end of the fourteenth century, a small window also connected the *Grande Chambre* to the Great Hall, which was used for making public announcements from the former into the latter.[58]

A central role in the spatial economy of the *Palais* was played by the court officials called *huissiers*. As Chapter 5 will show, the *huissiers* of the *Parlement* were concerned with many of the more practical aspects of its daily business. However, judging by their name (*huissier* meaning 'doorkeeper') and a royal ordinance of 1345 which laid out the rules of their functioning, their main role entailed the management of the spatial practices and divisions within the *Palais*.[59] The six *huissiers* named in the ordinance were all assigned specific tasks related to the spatial practices surrounding the *Grande Chambre*: two for guarding the entrance to the Great Hall, two for guarding the doors of the *parquet* in the *Grande Chambre* and two for ensuring order within the *Grande Chambre* itself, especially in the publicly accessible *parterre*. That this latter task was more than a formality is highlighted by the confession of a man called Regnaut de Valois in 1350, who admitted having pickpocketed several people in the

56 Ibid., 137–138, 142–143.

57 Ibid., 143–144.

58 Ibid., 151–152.

59 The royal ordinance of March 11, 1344, was published in Eusèbe Jacques de Laurière et al., eds., *Ordonnances des roys de France de la troisième race, recueillies par ordre chronologique, avec des renvoys des unes aux autres, des sommaires, & des observations sur le Texte*, vol. 2 (Paris: Imprimerie royale, 1729), 219–228; the articles concerning the *huissiers* are to be found on p. 225.

Grande Chambre.[60] Significantly, the *huissiers*' role involved more than just guarding the ideal typical division between the non- or semi-public court space and the public world outside the courtroom, by refusing entry to those who had no business in the *Grande Chambre*, but also comprised the communication between both spaces. The *huissiers*, so the ordinance tells us, were responsible both for publishing proclamations coming from the *Grande Chambre*, as well as calling out the cases that were to be treated in court. In this way the *huissiers* took on a role as spatial intermediaries, managing both the accessibility of and the interaction between the spaces used in the legal process of the *Parlement*.[61]

Like York Minster, the *Palais de la Cité* was many spaces in one, catering for a large variety of activities related to the functioning of the royal court. A discussion of the spatial practices in and around the *Grande Chambre* only sheds light on a small part of the spatial divisions and overlaps contained within the overarching context of the *Palais* as a whole. The description of Nicholas of Baye at the beginning of this chapter, which highlights some tensions surrounding the *Chambre des Enquêtes*, has shown another example of the extensive spatial dynamics of the place where the *Parlement* of Paris went about its daily business. What is especially relevant to note here – both for the Consistory Court and for the *Parlement* – is the way in which these spatial divisions did not necessarily lead to any kind of strict compartmentalization of legal activities. The presence of intermediary spaces, where levels of publicity intermingled, as well as spatial intermediaries, who attended to the accessibility of and communication between separated spaces, shows how the spatial practices of these courts knew many grey areas, where any division between secrecy and publicity was far from absolute. What is more, both cases have also shown, albeit indirectly, how courts' idealized vision of accessibility could be challenged by other participants in a legal event. Both archbishop Zouche's reprimand against disturbances in York Minster and the order keeping responsibilities carried out by the Parisian *huissiers*, point at these courts' perceived need to actively guard the boundaries of accessibility as they had envisioned them.

Information on the Council of Utrecht's spatial practices as related to the *Schoonhuis* is again comparatively scarce. What is there, however, seems to point to its use as a secluded or at most semi-public meeting place, where,

60 AN X^{2A}4, fol. 231r–232v (December 17, 1350); edited in Monique Langlois and Yvonne Lanhers, eds., *Confessions et jugements de criminels au Parlement de Paris (1319–1350)* (Paris: S.E.V.P.E.N., 1971), 185–188.

61 Guerout, "Le Palais: Deuxième partie", 144, 151–152.

ideally, council members, aldermen and guild elders convened in a respectful and – above all – peaceful manner. Judging by the predominantly fourteenth-century books of bylaws the meetings in the *Schoonhuis* – called *stat huys* or simply *huys* in the sources – were subject to strict rules concerning the behaviour of the councillors and – to a lesser extent – its accessibility to outsiders. Several articles speak, for example, of punishments – both monetary and other – for fighting, shouting, insulting and carrying weapons during council meetings.[62] Regardless of the actual behaviour of the councillors, what these prescriptions suggest is a distinction made between behaviour inside and outside the courtroom, creating a boundary of tolerated social practice. Limits to the accessibility of the courtroom were also implemented to distinguish it spatially from the world outside. In an article in the *Liber albus*, which was repeated in the *Roede boeck* at the end of the century, the legislator prescribed that no more than four people could accompany anyone coming before the aldermen, the Council or the guild elders at the *Schoonhuis*. The *stadsknapen* – taking on a role similar to the *huissiers* of the *Parlement* – were responsible for making sure that this measure was enforced and could themselves be fined if they allowed more people entry than was prescribed.[63] There was thus a very real concern to distinguish the court space and the practices carried out there physically from other spaces and practices.

At the same time, public space could also play a fundamental role in the Council's legal – as well as politico-economic – practice. The urban environment was actively involved in the messaging inherent to the legal process. A case in point are the public rituals regularly performed as part of the punishment of certain offenders, which Dirk Berents called the 'procedure of forgiveness'.[64] In a typical performance of this kind, the offender would be ordered to come from one location in the city – usually one of the prisons – to the *banklok*, the clock of the *Buurkerk* which was used as a means of public communication by the urban authorities. Here he would have to publicly beg forgiveness for his deeds, wearing no more than a simple shirt and pants, the typical garb of a penitent.[65] These rituals

62 Muller, *Rechtsbronnen*, vol. 1, 5–6 (*Liber albus* I.10–12), 94–96 (*Liber hirsutus minor* XLIII.1–6), 154 (*Roede boeck* II.1–9). The entries in the *Roede boeck* are copied from the first two books, showing their continued relevance in the later part of the fourteenth century.

63 Ibid., 19 (*Liber albus* XXVIII.1).

64 Berents, *Misdaad*, 41.

65 Frans Camphuijsen, "'*In hemde ende in broeck*': The Performance of Justice in Late Medieval Utrecht", in *La Permission et la sanction: Théories légales et pratiques du théâtre (XIVe–XVIIe siècle)*, eds. Marie Bouhaïk-Gironès, Jelle Koopmans and Katell Lavéant (Paris: Classiques Garnier, 2017), 219–247. See Chapter 3 for a more extensive treatment of these forgiveness rituals.

formed part of the broader practice of holding a regular *buurspraak*, public sessions of the Council supposedly open to all citizens and held in front of the *Buurkerk*. On such occasions the Council would publicly proclaim verdicts it had reached as well as more general measures and regulations that were of interest to the urban population at large. The *buurspraak* occasions, and more in particular the penal rituals that often formed part of them, show a clear consideration of the effectiveness of public space in communicating socio-legal messages. The functioning of the legal process was visualized within an area as public as open urban space. Sight, sound and movement through space were all exploited to make a large public experience this particular aspect of the legal process.

The three cases studied here show that, although these were very different law courts inhabiting a diversity of spaces, in their spatial practices and considerations these courts often echoed similar concerns. The spaces used by these courts reflect how the question of the accessibility of – meaning the ability to view, hear, physically participate in or otherwise approach – certain parts of the legal process was of central importance in their relation to society at large. Who could and who could not experience specific parts of the legal process and how, was something that these courts actively tried to manage – sometimes successfully, sometimes unsuccessfully – through the employment of a variety of physical and non-physical spatial measures, from actual walls or wooden screens to movement regulations or restrictions. In these attempts, space and spatial practices were mutually influential. Court spaces were constructed or arranged with a certain legal practice in mind, comprising public, semi-public and non-public areas and thus giving physical shape to abstract ideas about the accessibility of different parts of the legal process. At the same time, however, existing spaces and the uses made of them fundamentally shaped the way in which people experienced the legal process. Physical limits to sight, hearing and the more general experience of parts of the legal process had a crucial influence on the ways in which people could and did interact with the court. Significantly, rather than suggesting a strict distinction between public and non-public uses of space, the analysis above has instead shown how many layers of accessibility existed between and within the physically demarcated spaces involved in these courts' legal procedure. If anything, this supports the Lefebvrian idea of the flexibility and intertwinement of social spaces, which overlap, coexist and occasionally collide with each other, and often extend beyond purely visible boundaries.[66]

66 Lefebvre, *Production*, trans. Nicholson-Smith, 86–87.

Space and socio-legal messaging

As I have argued above, the legal process was inherently a communication process in which different social actors posed their claims to a specific understanding of legal truth. This meant that, while courts' engagement with their spatial environment often took the form of physical activity, it could also involve verbal interaction. References to various spatial entities were used to suggest meaning for certain decisions reached or punishments meted out. This could involve concrete objects, such as the attribution of a specific relevance to certain buildings or parts of them. But the legal process also engaged more abstractly with geographical boundaries, by means of the inclusion or exclusion of individuals. In what follows I will trace these two types of linguistic manifestations in the legal process where we encounter space and spatiality as meaning-giver.

First we turn to York. Archbishop Greenfield's statutes of 1311 contain several regulations regarding the behaviour expected of the staff of the Consistory Court and, in particular, of its proctors. One of the regulations runs as follows:

> On the penalty for refusing to contest the suit.
> If indeed, postponements being quashed and notwithstanding them, the official or his commissary determines that the suit must be contested and any proctor under the president's orders refuses to contest the suit, let him be suspended from the proctor's office until he pays half a Mark, to be used for the fabric of our church of York.[67]

While the expectations of proctors as expressed in this regulation merit a consideration of their own, what is most striking in the context of the current chapter is the fact that the entry allocates a fine imposed on an unwilling legal functionary explicitly to the building activities of York Minster. In a sense this should not surprise us, as this same period saw major construction works on the nave of the Minster.[68] From a very practical point of view, any money that could contribute to the costly undertaking of the cathedral works was more than welcome. Similar measures appear around the same time,

67 Wilkins, *Consilia*, vol. 2, 411, article 19: *De poena recusantis litis contestationem. Si vero cassatis dilatoriis, et eis non obstantibus, officialis, vel ejus commissarius litem forte decreverit contestandum, ac procurator quicunque ad jussum praesidentis litem recusaverit contestari, a procuratoris officio suspendatur, quousque dimidiam marcam solverit, fabricae nostrae Eborum ecclesiae applicandam.*

68 Brown, *'Our Magnificent Fabrick'*, 86–136.

both in Greenfield's statutes and elsewhere, for instance, in the series of archiepiscopal registers that had been kept since the thirteenth century.[69] But the explicitness with which such regulations state the intended goal of the monetary fine suggests that this can be read as more than a measure of convenience. It is unlikely that such a fine, based as it was on the violation of a specific procedural rule by unwilling legal functionaries, guaranteed a reliable flow of money for the construction works of the church. In considering these fabric-related penalties, it is therefore also relevant to take note of the implications that the explicit spatial dimension of the fine had for the character of the measure as a whole.

To grasp the signifying context of these fines it may be fruitful to connect them to another means by which funds were frequently gathered for the (re)building of the Minster, namely, indulgences.[70] Archiepiscopal registers, for instance, contain proclamations of indulgences for monetary contributions to specific ecclesiastical – but also non-ecclesiastical – structures.[71] Several of them, especially from the early fourteenth century onwards, are explicitly meant for the fabric of York Minster.[72] However, regarding such space-related indulgences only as parts of the financial strategy of the church, we overlook the central religious significance that they incorporated. The connection that is suggested in these indulgences between the physical structure of the cathedral church and the spiritual well-being of individual believers, is part and parcel of a broader connection between the religious community as such and its physical representation through church buildings. A contribution to the building and maintenance of a church – and certainly one as central as the York Minster – was not only an act of individual piety, but also contributed to the well-being of the religious community.[73]

With this socio-cultural context in mind, the explicit connection between procedural offence and Minster space takes on an extra layer of meaning. The symbolic compensation implicit in the fine could be

69 Brown, *John le Romeyn*, vol. 1, 367–368 (August 13, 1287); Brown and Thompson, *William Greenfield*, vol. 2, 42–44 (September 20, 1307).

70 Robert N. Swanson, *Indulgences in Late Medieval England: Passports to Paradise?* (Cambridge: Cambridge University Press, 2007), 149–160.

71 See the list of indulgences contained at the beginning of the register of John le Romeyn, in Brown, *John le Romeyn*, vol. 1, 1–15.

72 Brown, *Thomas of Corbridge*, vol. 2, 30 (June 3, 1304); Brown and Thompson, *William Greenfield*, vol. 1, 4–5 (May 21, 1306). See also James Raine, ed., *The Fabric Rolls of York Minster* (London and Edinburgh: Surtees Society, 1859).

73 Cf. Swanson, *Indulgences*, 350–351, on the more general role of indulgences in late medieval Christian *caritas*.

directed at the presiding judge who the unwilling proctor does not obey. Or it could be for the archbishop himself, whose authority is damaged indirectly by the proctor's refusal. However, in light of the socio-cultural context sketched above, the party that can be considered to have been damaged the most is the religious community as a whole. This also accords with Greenfield's stated intention in drawing up the statutes in the first place, namely, to prevent 'fraud and obstruction, unnecessary delays and any other impediments', for all those coming to the court from the city, the diocese or the province.[74] Notwithstanding further possible motivations behind the statutes, a key message that the text seems to propagate is the importance of an accessible and well-functioning court to the benefit of the religious community. Within this context, the emphasis on spatially signified means of punishment underscores this broader message, linking the legal process before the Consistory Court through the maintenance of a communal cathedral church with the well-being of the religious community.

Notwithstanding the clear link between indulgences and fabric fines, forms of space-signified punishment were certainly not limited to ecclesiastical courts. In Utrecht the sources of legal practice show a similar kind of space-signification as we have seen for York, playing a very prominent and far-reaching role in the legal process. Returning once again to the penal rituals treated earlier in this chapter, we see how not only in a practical sense – that is, through the active involvement of physical space in the ritual process – but also in a much more symbolic sense, space took on a very central role in the legal messaging of the Council. Crucial here is the oft-repeated notion of a fine being levied in an amount of 'stones'. For example, after two brothers, Gherit and Eerst, had been arrested in 1398 for fighting on a Saturday, they were sentenced to appear publicly before the Council to beg it for forgiveness, and pay the city a compensation of 10,000 'stones' each.[75] This seemingly puzzling wording is clarified in several entries in the books of bylaws. A regulation from 1444 contained in *Die Roese* states how all fines that had so far been levied in stones were now

74 Wilkins, *Consilia*, vol. 2, 409: *fraudibus et cautelis, dilationibus supervacuis, et aliis quibuslibet impedimentis*. Also see Burns, "Medieval Courts", 100.

75 HUA 701-1.16: BSB 1396–1402, fol. 191v. There was a more general connection between the occasions of ritualized punishment and the naming of such stone fines. For the period under study only two occasions mentioned in the *Buurspraakboek*, one in 1411 and one in 1412, show a stone fine being levied outside of a ritualized context: HUA 701-1.16: BSB 1410–1414, 73r and 87v. Likewise, only 7 of the 135 (5%) mentions of fines in such a ritualized context concern a directly worded monetary fine rather than a stone fine.

to be levied in lengths of wall, meant as they were to repair the city wall.[76] In an earlier entry from the same book, the Council stated how offenders confronted with a fine in stones were supposed to pay the city an amount of money with which it would be able to buy the stated number of stones from the city's brick makers.[77] And even the *Buurspraakboek* itself, which is usually silent about the intended goal of the stone fines, on one occasion in 1424 mentions how part of the stone fine levied for damaging a certain sluice is to be used for its repair.[78] The money received through stone fines seems in short to have had an explicit built-in purpose for the construction and repair of the city wall and other urban structures.[79]

We can, of course, interpret these fines in a purely practical way. The city wall – and supposedly other urban structures as well – required regular maintenance, which would explain the need for considerable numbers of 'stones'. However, there is more to these fines than a purely practical interpretation would exhaust. As they are almost exclusively found in relation to the broader forgiveness ritual, it would have been a very irregular and unreliable source of income for construction works.[80] Furthermore, if the intended goal of these fines was clearly fixed, it seems redundant to state its purpose so explicitly over and over again. As in the case of the space-related fines in York, tracing a broader signifying context may help us understand the role of these stone fines within the legal process in Utrecht. The relation between the development of an autonomous urban community and the physical space of the city has been pointed out earlier in this chapter. This relationship is also very marked in the many ordinances pronounced in the *Buurspraakboek*. Numerous regulations are concerned with the maintenance of urban space, like regulations against free-roaming pigs in the streets.[81]

76 Muller, *Rechtsbronnen*, vol. 1, 352–353 (*Die Roese* CCXL.11). Also see Muller, *Rechtsbronnen*, Introduction, 76.

77 Muller, *Rechtsbronnen*, vol. 1, 200 (*Die Roese* XLVIII.1).

78 HUA 701-1.16: BSB 1418–1425, 212v.

79 These stone fines were not unique to Utrecht and can be found all over the Low Countries during the late Middle Ages. For examples from Antwerp, Brussels, Louvain, Nivelles, Amsterdam, Brielle, Delft, Haarlem, Dordrecht, Gouda, Leiden and Schiedam, see Jan van Herwaarden, *Opgelegde bedevaarten: Een studie over de praktijk van opleggen van bedevaarten (met name in de stedelijke rechtspraak) in de Nederlanden gedurende de late Middeleeuwen (ca 1300–1550)* (Assen and Amsterdam: Van Gorcum, 1978), 187, 232, 245, 256, 275, 279, 284, 287, 301, 309, 321, 342. Although Van Herwaarden treats these fines primarily in the context of imposed pilgrimages, he also shows that there exists no necessary link between these two forms of penal practice.

80 As Appendix 1.1 shows, the total amount of money received yearly through stone fines varied heavily.

81 For regulations on pigs, see, for example, HUA 701-1.16 BSB 1418–1425, 11v. Also see Frans Camphuijsen and Janna Coomans, "De middeleeuwse stad en zijn varkens", *Madoc* 28, no. 3

Others make an explicit connection between urban maintenance and an individual's social status within the city, for example, by relating the granting of citizenship to the maintenance of public stairways or bridges. In 1413 the *Buurspraakboek* notes a decision by the Council to grant Aernt Mugge citizenship on the condition that he will maintain and regularly clean a particular stairway on the Lijn Market. The close relation between Aernt's citizenship and this communal duty is confirmed by the directly preceding entry. It notes how the old shoemaker Peter son of Vrederik has just lost his status as citizen on account of his failure to perform this same stairway duty.[82] Central in all such measures is the idea of communal responsibility for the urban surroundings: free-roaming pigs and badly maintained structures are considered an impediment both to the 'flow' of daily business in the city and to the prestige of the urban community as such.[83] The stone fines seem to reflect these same ideals of shared responsibility for the maintenance of the city space. The offender, having violated certain social norms, is called upon to contribute to the communal project of maintaining the built environment. Although he is not expected personally to take care of specific maintenance activities, the explicit semiotic link between his fine and such activities gives the punishment an extra layer of meaning, contributing to the changing web of possible meanings that these public rituals entailed. The explicit inclusion of such a spatial signifier within the context of these public rituals thus significantly increases their potential reach by embedding them more strongly in a broader communal discourse on shared responsibility and the common good.

Inclusion and exclusion

Whereas the stone fines can be said to have had a socially inclusive character, emphasizing social reintegration through a spatially signified contribution to communal welfare, another common punishment in Utrecht was based rather on spatially signified exclusion. One of the most frequent punishments in the sources of legal practice in Utrecht were banishments. Both in the *Th.2* register and in the *Buurspraakboek*, banishments form the majority

(2014), for recent work on pig regulations in the medieval Low Countries.

82 HUA 701-1.16: BSB 1410–1414, 168r.

83 Camphuijsen and Coomans, "Varkens"; cf. Janna Coomans, "In Pursuit of a Healthy City: Sanitation and the Common Good in the Late Medieval Low Countries" (PhD diss., University of Amsterdam, 2018), 162–169.

of punishments meted out.[84] Many things can and have been said about the role of banishments in late medieval urban societies.[85] The social consequences of banishment could be very serious in such societies, based as they were on ties of kinship and patronage. Banishment, especially for longer spans of time, meant cutting someone loose from many crucial social resources, condemning the individual to a socially marginal position, at least for the duration of the exile. From an authority's point of view, deciding on banishment could also have very practical reasons. In order to remove a serious offender from public sight, exile was a much more effective and cheaper means than any kind of prolonged imprisonment.

However, in light of the communicative potential of punishment, another aspect of banishment is also relevant. Seen within a broader discursive context, banishments contained a multiplicity of implicit messages, relating the punishment of an offender to the boundaries of the urban community and its physical surroundings. The definition and demarcation of different spatial boundaries, that played a central role in the development of an autonomous urban community, was also reflected in the banishments. Considering the wording of the sentences as presented in the *Buurspraakboek* shows two basic variants: one which defines the area from which the offender is exiled as the city borders, and one which concerns exile from the city plus a certain extra distance from it, usually called 'the mile'. It appears that there was little difference in actual practice. A pronouncement from 1364, contained within the *Th.2* register, states that any banishment from the city automatically included the city's mile.[86] However, the entries in the *Buurspraakboek* do make the distinction, and increasingly so.[87] Furthermore, the area around the city that was included in the banishment could also

84 For the first 40 years of the *Buurspraakboek* (1385–1425), among the 786 entries concerned with punishment of some sort, we encounter 518 verdicts of banishment, often concerning multiple individuals at once. Taking account of the missing register for the years 1392–1395, this makes an average of fourteen verdicts of banishment per year. See Appendix 1.2 for details.

85 Peter Raymond Pazzaglini, *The Criminal Ban of the Sienese Commune, 1225–1310* (Milan: A. Giuffrè, 1979); Hanna Zaremska, *Les bannis au Moyen Âge*, trans. Thérèse Douchy (Paris: Aubier, 1996); Christine Shaw, *The Politics of Exile in Renaissance Italy* (Cambridge: Cambridge University Press, 2000); Alison Brown, "Insiders and Outsiders: The Changing Boundaries of Exile", in *Society and Individual in Renaissance Florence*, ed. William Connell (Berkeley: University of California Press, 2002); William Chester Jordan, *From England to France: Felony and Exile in the High Middle Ages* (Princeton, NJ: Princeton University Press, 2015); Edda Frankot, *Banishment in the Late Medieval Eastern Netherlands: Exile and Redemption in Kampen* (Cham: Palgrave Macmillan, 2022).

86 HUA 701-1.227: *Th.2* register, fol. 29v.

87 See Appendix 1.2.

be described differently. Definitions sometimes speak of the area outside the city 'as far as the city takes its excise' (*zo verre alse de stat horen sijs neempt*), or the 'land' of Utrecht.[88] Although these variations may well have indicated the same area around the city, the wording distinguishes between different criteria on which the Council based the reach of its authority. Beyond specific developments in the wording over time or their relation to actual practice, what these sentences show us is how the removal of an offender from the community was related to the explicit definition of spatial limits, based on economic, legal or political power claims. Such banishments, therefore, essentially confirm the spatial boundaries relevant to the Utrecht community, or are at least presented as such. And these spatial signifiers operated in line with, but were not exclusively limited to real physical features, such as the city walls or the free-standing gatehouses that marked the limits of the city's liberty.

Spatial restriction as an element in penal practice is not limited to the case of Utrecht. In the records of the *Parlement* of Paris we encounter numerous restrictions to the comings and goings of people condemned for a certain crime. Some of these restrictive measures concern banishments, as in Utrecht. However, another type of restriction is much more common, namely, the *élargissement*.[89] Usually forming the intermediary stage in a legal process rather than a final sentence, the *élargissement* was – in a spatial sense – the complete opposite of exile. Whereas banishment denied an individual entry into a certain spatial entity, like a city or kingdom, the *élargissement* precluded movement outside of a specific area. The sources often present such *élargissements* as a type of 'open' prison sentence, that is, the mitigation of imprisonment to an area beyond the strict confines of the prison cell. This area could vary widely, from the direct surroundings of the prison, to the whole city of Paris or even the whole kingdom.[90] The spatial limitations could also change during a case. On September 28, 1340, Guillaume of Moreauville and his wife were granted *élargissement* 'between the four gates of Paris' (*intra quatuor portas parisiensis*). Only a few days later their *élargissement* was extended to the whole viscounty of

88 As Appendix 1.2 shows, the area around the city is included in 182 verdicts (35%) which is indicated as 'mile' in 125 cases (24%), the reach of the city's excise in 32 cases (6%) and its 'land' in 25 cases (5%).

89 See Louis de Carbonnières, *La procédure devant la chambre criminelle du Parlement de Paris au XIVe siècle* (Paris: Champion, 2004), 255–299, for an extensive treatment of the *élargissement*, based mostly on late-fourteenth-century material.

90 Ibid., 263–265.

Paris.[91] Temporary exceptions could also be made to the limits set in an *élargissement*. In a case spanning the years 1345 and 1346, Pierre le Large, granted *élargissement* in Paris, was allowed to dine outside of the city one evening, given that he would be escorted there and back again by one of the *Parlement*'s *huissiers*.[92] Another noticeable arrangement is found in a case from 1341, where Barthélemy of Vaux is granted *élargissement* in the city of Paris, with the added stipulation that he may leave the city during the day, but has to return *intra portas* by night.[93] The *élargissement* was usually granted on the condition that the accused would reappear in court on the day that his case continued. If this promise was broken the offender could be punished in several ways. In 1331, a certain Henry the Monk had to return to prison for breaking his *élargissement*.[94] A decade later, the *Parlement* grants another litigant *élargissement* 'so he may better pursue the process and his case' (*ut negocia et causam suam melius prosequi valeat*). However, if he does not live up to the court's expectations, he will – in a somewhat ironic fashion – be banished from the French kingdom.[95]

Both in the granting of legal privileges, like the mitigation of imprisonment through *élargissement*, and in penalizing the violation of these privileges, the *Parlement* made prominent use of spatial limitations. In this it clearly showed the important role of space and spatial boundaries for its legal messaging, as well as the importance of the legal process – and its inherent rituality – for assigning specific meanings to different spaces. The limits of the kingdom became more than an abstract entity. For those under *élargissement* it could be a very real border, not to be passed if one ever wanted to return. And for the *Parlement*, representing after all broader claims of royal authority, it was a concrete way of demarcating an ideal legal and political unity. Considering the fairly recent political annexation of many territories under the Paris-based royal government, as well as the tense times in which many of these political constructions were again called into question, the spatial claims inherent in such legal measures as *élargissements* and banishments gain an extra layer of meaning.

On a smaller scale, the practice of granting *élargissements* also shows the strong symbolic connection the *Parlement* made to its urban context.

91 AN $X^{2A}4$, fol. 11 (September 28, 1340); ibid., fol. 12 (October 2, 1340).

92 Entries regarding this case can be found spread throughout the $X^{2A}5$ register: see AN $X^{2A}5$, fols. 3v, 4v and 47v.

93 AN $X^{2A}4$, fol. 33v (March 19, 1341).

94 AN $X^{2A}3$, fol. 119 (April 24, 1331).

95 AN $X^{2A}4$, fol. 37–37v (April 23, 1341). Carbonnières, *Procédure*, 291–294, only names exile as punishment for breaking an *élargissement*.

In the legal process, Paris became much more than a simple piece of built land surrounded by a stone wall. For those involved in a specific case the city and its gateways were a limit to their freedom of movement. And in a related fashion, the *Parlement* thereby used the city space to pose its power claims. The ability to limit one's movement, as well as the ability to subsequently restore some of this freedom, formed a spatially signified way of claiming such power. Many of these measures furthermore implied a specific conceptualization of the role of this space called Paris vis-à-vis the rest of the kingdom. In occasionally extending the area of *élargissement* from the surroundings of the prison to the city, and from the city to ever larger spatial entities, the *Parlement* suggested a certain spatial hierarchy within the kingdom – that is, from Paris outwards – as well as its proper claim to controlling all of it. As was the case for Utrecht, in the legal process of the *Parlement* the physical environment and mental conceptualizations were combined in giving the city space a certain unity filled with meanings related to social, legal and political power claims.[96]

The examples from York, Utrecht and Paris underscore the central importance of space as meaning-giver in the late medieval legal process. In similar ways, these courts explicitly engaged their spatial context in suggesting a specific meaning for certain legal actions undertaken in court. Conversely, the involvement of such spaces in the legal process contributed to shaping the urban environment semantically. For the litigant involved in a process before York's Consistory Court, the space of operations, York Minster, was more than simply a large building. It could become – or so the court suggested – a physical representation of the religious community, combining within its walls multiple aspects of the life of this community, including religious service, church administration and the legal process. Using specific spatial references in the legal process created a link between the legal case under scrutiny and the role – or rather roles – that the Minster space was supposed to fulfil in society. In a similar way, the built space in Utrecht was linguistically involved in the legal process. By making explicit references in its legal process both to physical structures and to less physical spatial limits, the Council reinscribed the social, political and legal unity of the city of Utrecht and its community, as well as its own role in preserving it.

96 A similar judicial engagement with the physical environment can be seen in the omnipresent medieval phenomenon of legal sanctuary. See William Chester Jordan, "A Fresh Look at Medieval Sanctuary", in *Law and the Illicit in Medieval Europe*, eds. Ruth Mazo Karras, Joel Kaye and E. Ann Matter (Philadelphia: University of Pennsylvania Press, 2008); Karl Shoemaker, *Sanctuary and Crime in the Middle Ages, 400–1500* (Ashland, OH: Fordham University Press, 2011).

And the same process of demarcating social and political space is found in the records of the *Parlement* of Paris, reflecting different power claims and ideal hierarchies in a period when many political boundaries were in flux. By using spatial references in the legal process, these courts did not only try to suggest certain meanings for the actions performed in this process, but also attempted to influence the communal discourses that made the denoted spaces into what they were perceived to be by contemporaries.

Conclusion: Legal space and the legalization of space

With a subject that has predominantly been regarded from a formal institutional or textual perspective, the first goal of this chapter has been to place late medieval law courts back in space. For although their ways of working and means of writing were unique and game-changing, the fact that these courts were also fundamentally places of assembly, makes a consideration of their physical environment, as well as the variety of ways in which they and others engaged with this environment, crucial for understanding both their advent and daily practice. In courts' development from royal, episcopal or seigneurial advisory bodies to semi-independent legal authorities, changes in court space both echoed and influenced changes in institutional structures and legal practices. While buildings and rooms were sometimes purpose-built according to the needs of the court, the obdurate physicality of existing spaces – meaning the large investment in time and money required to fundamentally alter them – could well limit this constructional freedom. Often courts adapted in one way or another to their physical environment instead of the other way round, contributing to the diversity of shapes courts could take as seen in the first part of this chapter. Significantly, this mutual influence between institution and space was not limited to the courtroom itself, but also involved the cities where they settled permanently from the thirteenth century onwards. For, while all three courts were legally concerned with areas of very different sizes, the day-to-day reality of each took shape within an urban context. This positioned them before some very similar issues as well as gave them opportunities to use the city space to their own socio-political advantage.

In daily practice, the courts' engagement with their spaces formed part of broader communicative concerns and strategies. The matter of the accessibility of the courts and their legal process was of paramount importance for their relation with society. In the ways in which they made use of their physical surroundings, they strongly echoed this concern for the management of accessibility. The question as to which parts of the process were to be visible, audible or otherwise available for people to experience, and which parts should on the other hand remain opaque, was at the heart of such spatial practices. By attempting to regulate the sight, hearing and physical presence of different publics, these courts tried to script people's experiences of the legal process. In addition to physical practices, space had an important role to play in providing – or at least suggesting – meaning to legal communicative actions in and by the law courts. By referencing specific structures or geographical boundaries, entities that carried a variety of implicit meanings through their integration within broader communal discourses, the court sought a means to suggest certain meanings for the penal acts it performed. In its turn – and here the Lefebvrian interpretation of space as both precondition and result of social structures becomes all the more relevant – this referencing within the legal process provided the physical environment itself with possible meanings it did not necessarily entail beforehand. In this sense late medieval law courts did not simply operate in space, but were actively involved in legally scripting the spaces they used, which in their turn influenced these courts' socio-legal practices.

A spatial analysis thus lays a significant basis for a broader consideration of the communicative logic and practice of late medieval law courts. It first of all provides a concrete stage on which to analyse these bodies' legal practices and discourses, showing the physical environment where the people involved in a legal process – be it officials, litigants or audiences – went about their business. But it also shows us some of the ways in which the courts engaged with the world around them. As the following chapters will show, questions concerning the accessibility of the legal process, or the uses made of referential systems to suggest particular meanings for words or deeds, were at the heart of the many forms of communicative action that took place in these courts. What is more, in analysing both the courts' spatial context and their linguistic and performative engagement with it, this chapter has provided a first example of the fundamental relation between the physical and non-physical aspects of the particular communication process of late medieval law courts. In what follows, this link between matter, activity and language will turn out to be crucial not only in a spatial sense, but from a whole range of perspectives.

3. The rituality of court practice

Abstract

In addition to their legal spaces and documents, late medieval law courts took shape above all in the regularized performance of specific sequences of acts, be they forgiveness procedures, sentence readings, audience sessions or other forms of legal practice. Regarding these acts through the lens of ritual theory shows their role in a complex of scripted communication between courts, litigants and audiences, where a specific grammar of acts linked individual instances of court practice to broader socio-cultural activities and phenomena, from penitence practices to political expansion. These forms of legal theatre, while reinforcing the court as forum for 'doing justice', were shaped by the acts and interpretations of a multitude of actors, including court officials, litigants and various audiences.

Keywords: medieval law courts, medieval legal practice, ritual theory, performance, legal theatre

In January 1387 a man called Jan de Rode was convicted of manslaughter in the city of Utrecht. While the sources tell us little about the details of the killing, we know all the more about its legal consequences. As part of the penal procedure, the Council of Utrecht ordered Jan to come from the city prison in the Red Tower, where he was being kept, to the bell tower of the *Buurkerk* (see Map 1). He would do so, the court explicated, dressed only in a simple shirt and pants. Furthermore, after arriving at the indicated spot, Jan was expected to publicly beg the Council for forgiveness and pay the city a fine of 50,000 'stones'.[1] The previous chapter has argued how instances like these, when read from the perspective of the development and use of urban space, show courts' intricate connection with the socio-cultural

1 HUA 701-1.16: *BSB* 1385–1391, fol. 56r: *Want Jan de Rode enen man doot ghesleghen heeft binnen der stat daer omme heeft hi gheleghen inden Roden Toorn ende is hier ghecomen in hemde ende in broeke ter klocken ende zel den rade bidden verghifnisse ende gheven der stat tebeteringe* L^{M} *steens.*

Camphuijsen, F., *Scripting Justice in Late Medieval Europe: Legal Practice and Communication in the Law Courts of Paris, York and Utrecht.* Taylor & Francis Group, 2022
DOI 10.5117/9789463723473_CH03

practices and discourses beyond a strictly legal setting. In using their physical context, courts like the Paris *Parlement*, York's Consistory Court and the Council of Utrecht engaged with broader ideas about what these spaces – and consequently the activities they hosted – meant. Yet this intertwinement between activities in and out of a legal setting stretches beyond the sites used for their performance. The sequence of actions Jan de Rode was supposed to go through, involving specific movements, clothing and spoken words, was loaded with references to practices, values and power relations beyond the legal occasion proper. Turning from the site of judicial activity to court practice itself, we will see that acts like pleading, testifying, judging and punishing did not form isolated instances of value-free truth finding, but were shaped by the social, political and economic relations and motivations of their participants.

The observation is hardly new. In his *Surveiller et punir: Naissance de la prison* (1975), Michel Foucault questions the strict division between legal actions and other forms of social activity, as presented by legal authorities themselves.[2] Treating the changes in penal practice over the last 200 years, he situates punishment within a broader 'scientifico-juridical complex', a set of extra-judicial assessments that extends far beyond the simple judgement of a specific crime and involves broader ideas of normality, causality and change.[3] Similar ideas have been voiced in legal anthropology. Lawrence Rosen, in his study of Moroccan *qadi* courts between the mid-1960s and mid-1980s, sees law as an integral part of broader cultural constellations. People's scope of legal practice – that is, what can and cannot be done – and their interpretation of these actions is part of more general systems of social activity and conceptualization.[4] In the same way that a consideration of court space has sensitized us to the spatial embeddedness of legal institutions, considering legal action as a form of social action emphasizes the close

2 Michel Foucault, *Surveiller et punir: Naissance de la prison* (Paris: Gallimard, 1975), translated by Alan Sheridan as *Discipline and Punish: The Birth of the Prison* (London: Penguin Books, 1991).

3 Foucault, *Discipline and Punish*, 16–21.

4 Lawrence Rosen, *The Anthropology of Justice: Law as Culture in Islamic Society* (Cambridge: Cambridge University Press, 1989), 4–5. Rosen elaborates on his interpretation of legal culture in Lawrence Rosen, *Law as Culture: An Invitation* (Princeton, NJ: Princeton University Press, 2006), building on Clifford Geertz' cultural approach to law: Clifford Geertz, *Local Knowledge: Further Essays in Interpretive Anthropology* (New York: Basic Books, 1983). For a general overview of the scholarly literature on the theme of legal culture, see Sally Engle Merry, "What Is Legal Culture? An Anthropological Perspective", *Journal of Comparative Law* 5 (2010); Susan S. Silbey, "Legal Culture and Legal Consciousness", in *International Encyclopedia of the Social & Behavioral Sciences*, eds. Neil J. Smelser and Paul B. Baltes (Amsterdam: Elsevier, 2001).

relationship between the law court and society. It sees the court as an integral part of society, rather than an abstract entity observing it from a distance.

Accepting that legal action is simply a specific type of social practice does not yet explain why people would then engage in this kind of activity. For the fact that people invested time and other resources in pursuing a legal suit, means that the legal process as a constellation of actions offered them something they did not readily find in other forms of dispute settlement.[5] This in turn begs the question as to what it was that made legal action an extraordinary form of social action. Providing an answer to this general question is complicated. Both the entities involved in such actions – law courts, judges, litigants, etc. – and the activities themselves have varied widely over space and time. One might even argue that the attempt to distinguish a specific type of activity as legal actions, forces too much of a predetermined (modern) analytical categorization on otherwise undifferentiated social practices.[6] At the same time, the spatial analysis of three law courts has shown how certain actions performed in and by these courts were loaded with significance. To understand the specific character of these legal actions, this chapter explores processes of ritualization. It shows how activity in and by the courts was organized in certain ways so as to suggest its importance over and above the particular instance itself. As socio-legal performances, in the sense of attempts to speak through acts, what was done in court formed a central part of the complex of scripted communication that also found its expression in the court spaces and documents considered in the previous and following chapter.

In order to analyse legal practice from the viewpoint of ritual it is imperative first to focus on the latter phenomenon itself. While legal ritual as a theme has certainly been addressed in medieval history, the use of this concept often serves to emphasize structures over practices. Decades of anthropological scholarship, on the other hand, have focused specifically on ritual practices, while drawing on fieldwork in contemporary societies rather than the documents, paintings and other textual and visual intermediaries analysed by historians. The first part of this chapter will, therefore, consider how anthropological understandings of ritual have developed over the last century, and how this may profit a historical approach to the rituality of

5 A similar question as to people's motivations to use the courts is posed by Smail, *Consumption of Justice*, 4–17.

6 Cf. the cautionary tone vis-à-vis historians' use of the modern concept of 'ritual' when analyzing medieval texts, in Philip Buc, *The Dangers of Ritual: Between Early Medieval Texts and Social Scientific Theory* (Princeton, NJ, and Oxford: Princeton University Press, 2001).

legal action. In the second part I will elaborate on several types of legal action encountered in the three courts under study, analysing a specific act or constellation of acts for each of them. In Utrecht I will consider the sequences of actions that people like Jan de Rode went through in more detail. For the Consistory Court the occasions of sentence reading, that is, when it brought the decision it had reached in a case orally before audiences of varying sizes, take centre stage. In the Parisian case the organization of audience sessions is analysed, showing the *Parlement*'s attempts at stipulating time, place, participants and procedure of these occasions, as well as their translation to a different context in the form of the *Grands Jours*. Based on these three cases, I will argue that the ritualization of activities constituted a key medium for communication between courts, litigants and audiences. At the same time, by facilitating such interaction, courts also laid claim to socio-legal legitimacy.

Ritual and legal action

Within medieval studies, various authors have approached legal practices through the lens of ritual. Applications of this concept vary widely, according to the specific types of socio-legal action that scholars have considered. Gerd Althoff, in his analysis of dispute resolution among high medieval German nobles, places ritual action within a broader field of public communication, encompassing all kinds of demonstrative gestures, rituals and ceremonial acts. Althoff distinguishes this public field, for which he uses the Habermasian term *Öffentlichkeit*, from a more confidential one, which was based mainly on verbal communication. In both dispute resolution and various other forms of socio-political communication these two fields complemented each other. First, nobles would negotiate their positions verbally in a confidential context, thus creating mutual willingness for a resolution. Subsequently, the decision reached in confidence would be performed in the public field in the form of – largely non-verbal – rituals. The communication in this field was subject to mutually accepted rules and signs, so as to render it calculable for both parties. By communicating on these two levels, both confidentially negotiating and ritually staging the conflict, disputing parties sought to avoid uncontrolled violence on a large scale.[7]

Claude Gauvard and Robert Jacob provide another interpretation. For them ritual has a broader social role to play. They connect ritual action

7 Althoff, *Spielregeln*, 9–13, 255–257.

– and judicial rituals in particular – to social myths, the stories societies tell themselves about themselves and about the world in which they exist. Whereas these myths were constantly subject to change and reinterpretation, rituals, by resisting substantial alterations in form, provided myths with a relatively constant and unified basis and limited the possibilities for individual divergences. In a judicial context, Gauvard and Jacob argue, rituals were primarily concerned with the foundational myths of social order. People performed legal rituals to (re)construct this ideal-typical order. At the same time, this role in constituting social myths also made ritual the medium par excellence to challenge them, as well as the established order that had put them in place.[8] Similar interpretations are found in the work of other historians who stress the socially constructed and/or constructive character of medieval ritual. In their work Gauvard and others consider legal rituals as events that were shaped by and required the consent of authorities, the public and often even the condemned himself.[9]

Both perspectives on medieval legal ritual – the one related to practices of dispute resolution, the other in the context of broader myths of socio-legal order – stress the role of ritual in structuring legal communicative behaviour. For both, ritual constitutes a more or less fixed – or at least preliminarily agreed upon – system of verbal and/or non-verbal communicative actions that can be tapped into by social actors to achieve certain goals. Although I agree with an interpretation of ritual in terms of communicative behaviour, in this chapter I will focus on how people engaged with these ritual systems, rather than on the systems as such. For this I base myself on recent anthropological theories, thus sharpening the interpretation of the exact communicative functioning of ritual behaviour. One of the major theoretical shifts in the anthropology of ritual is that from a concept of 'ritual action' to that of 'ritualized action'. The former use, which could be found in the work of many theorists of religion and society in the early and mid-twentieth century, began from the assumption that ritual constitutes a particular type of action, differing from other actions in kind.[10] Later scholars, however,

8 Claude Gauvard and Robert Jacob, "Introduction: Le rite, la justice et l'historien", in *Les rites de la justice: Gestes et rituels judiciaires au Moyen Âge occidental*, eds. Claude Gauvard and Robert Jacob (Paris: Léopard d'or, 2000), 5–9.

9 Cohen, "To Die a Criminal"; Claude Gauvard, "Pendre et dépendre à la fin du Moyen Âge: Les exigences d'un rituel judiciaire", in *Riti e rituali nelle società medievali*, eds. Jacques Chiffoleau, Lauro Martines and Agostino Paravicini Bagliani (Spoleto: Centro Italiano di Studi sull'alto Medioevo, 1994); Bednarski, *Curia*, 57–59.

10 Most notably Arnold van Gennep, *Les rites de passage: étude systématique des rites de la porte et du seuil, de l'hospitalité, de l'adoption, etc.* (Paris: Émile Noury, 1909); Émile Durkheim,

have questioned this binary opposition between ordinary and ritual acts. Jonathan Z. Smith, for example, has argued for understanding ritual first and foremost as a means to make ordinary things significant. Ritual, he argues, places a focusing lens on certain actions by routinizing and rationalizing them, which provides these actions with a special significance.[11] One should therefore not think of ritual as a fundamentally different type of action, but as a specific quality that ordinary actions may or may not entail. This way of looking at ritual questions the strict division between ordinary and ritual action, considering the latter primarily as a ritualized version of the former.

The shift from 'ritual' to 'ritualized action' has important consequences for our understanding of the relationship between ritual and ritual actor. The older approach considers rituality as a preliminary given to the performed act; the act is fitted within a pre-existing communication system, that provides it with a certain significance. The approaches of both Althoff and Gauvard and Jacob to medieval legal ritual tend to follow this interpretation, considering the system formative in shaping individual actions. A Smithsonian interpretation of ritual, however, puts more focus on these individual actions, by placing the ritual element within the performance of the act itself, rather than in a pre-existing system to which individual actions are attuned. Several scholars have elaborated on this relation between individual actions and ritual structures. Catherine Bell, for example, stresses the circular process of the production of ritual schemata, which are, on the one hand, formed through the sequential performance of individual acts while in their turn providing these individual acts with – the suggestion of – an overarching significance.[12] Caroline Humphrey and James Laidlaw instead focus on the qualitative exceptionality of an individual act as suggested by its ritualization. For them ritualization essentially entails an actor's denial of the authorial intentions behind her or his act, by suggesting that the act's identity takes shape external to those individual intentions.[13] Such interpretations, while acknowledging some of the formative role ritual

Les formes élémentaires de la vie religieuse: Le système totémique en Australie (Paris: Alcan, 1912); Edmund Leach, *Political Systems of Highland Burma: A Study of Kachin Social Structure* (London: G. Bell, 1954); John Beattie, "Ritual and Social Change", *Man, new series* 1 (1966); Victor Turner, *The Forest of Symbols: Aspects of Ndembu Ritual* (Ithaca, NY: Cornell University Press, 1967); for a general overview of the broad range of applications of the concept of ritual, also see D. Parkin, "Ritual", in *International Encyclopedia of the Social & Behavioral Sciences*, eds. Neil J. Smelser and Paul B. Baltes (Amsterdam: Elsevier, 2001).

11 Jonathan Z. Smith, "The Bare Facts of Ritual", *History of Religions* 20 (1980): 112–117.

12 Catherine Bell, *Ritual Theory, Ritual Practice* (Oxford: Oxford University Press, 1992).

13 Caroline Humphrey and James Laidlaw, *The Archetypal Actions of Ritual: A Theory of Ritual Illustrated by the Jain Rite Worship* (Oxford: Clarendon Press, 1994).

structures may play, strongly emphasize the agency of the ritual actor in using ritual as a medium for communication.

This brief discussion of the anthropology of ritual provides us with a number of insights with which to approach the many forms of legal action found for the three courts studied here. First, it emphasizes the processual character of ritual action. Rather than considering a ritual as a pre-determined entity that is provided with concrete shape in the form of actions, these theories take the ritual act itself as a point of departure. They focus on the way in which an otherwise ordinary act is provided with special significance by relating it to other practices in – what is suggested to be – an overarching constellation of activities. Echoing the theory of performative action as set out by Austin and others, this interpretation of ritual thus sees the performance of the act as constitutive of the ritual itself.[14] Accordingly, the setting in which an act is ritualized gains more emphasis. The specific ritual actors, but also their audiences, gain a leading role in the construction of the ritual structure of which their activity appears to be simply a manifestation. Interpreting legal acts as ritualized activity makes them more than a fixed procedural framework, limiting the options of the one performing it. Instead, such acts are part and parcel of the discursive construction of this idealized framework itself. As the following case studies will show, participants in the legal process of the Utrecht, York and Paris courts were actively shaping the procedural structures of these law courts rather than simply being subjected to them.

Utrecht: Forgiveness rituals

At the beginning of this chapter, we have seen how the conviction of Jan de Rode for murder in 1387 involved a whole series of actions to be undertaken by this Utrecht culprit: a tour from prison to the *Buurkerk* in specific clothing, followed by a public plea for forgiveness and payment of a stone fine. This description of a specific sequence of actions is common in the sources. For the period under study, some 220 mentions of this kind of procedure survive in the *Buurspraakboek*, an average of about six per year.[15] Not

14 See the introduction to this book for a discussion of performance theory.

15 Equalling about 28% of all entries concerned with punishment for this period. Some 174 mentions of this kind of procedure can be found in the *Raads dagelijks boek* (52% of punishment-related entries), but these often overlap with the entries in the *Buurspraakboek*. See Chapter 4 for an extensive discussion of the relation between these two sources.

every description contains exactly the same elements. When Snellaert the sawyer was subjected to the procedure in 1401 as a result of his public nightly misbehaviour (*ondafte bi nachte*), he had to make a formal promise (*willekeur*) not to behave in like manner, rather than pay a stone fine.[16] And in a case from 1402, in which Lambert of Zulen and his wife, Enghel, were convicted of ordering a woman to be beaten up, both were subjected to the forgiveness procedure, but only Lambert was told to do so in a simple shirt and pants.[17] In several cases the procedure was given an extra edge. When Jorden Walmer was convicted of attacking a city official in 1416, he appeared before the Council not only in a simple garb, but also carrying a bare sword, proclaiming his life forfeit.[18] Despite this variety, a certain core procedure consisting of the elements of 'appearing before the Council bareheaded or in shirt and pants' and/or 'begging the Council for forgiveness' is ordained in all these cases.[19] In the scholarly literature, this sequence of actions is often interpreted as no more than an aggravating element of other punishments.[20] Here, however, I will take the forgiveness procedure itself as point of departure, as the suggested repetition and explicit performance of certain actions gave it a particularly ritualized character. By contextualizing the various elements constituting these ritual occasions, I will reconstruct the sphere of possible meanings of which they took part.

A first element to single out is the movement undertaken from the prison space to the square in front of the *Buurkerk* tower (coming '*ter clocken*', as it is called in the sources). Several buildings in Utrecht were used as prisons during the fourteenth and fifteenth centuries: the meat house (*vleyshuis*), which was also used by the butchers guild, the *Plompetoren* to the north of the city, the tower of the southern gate called the Red Tower, and the prison in the western *Catharijne* gate.[21] With the exception of the meat house, all these buildings were located on the edges of the city (see Map 1). This meant, as noted in Chapter 2, that the prescribed movement of culprits to the place where their sentence would be proclaimed, took them through much of the city, guaranteeing a high degree of exposure. And even in

16 HUA 701-1.16: *BSB* 1396–1402, fol. 308v.

17 HUA 701-1.16: *BSB* 1402–1405, fol. 10r. This may be an indication of the role of gender differences in the execution of the procedure, as this is also one of the few cases in which a woman is subjected to the forgiveness ritual.

18 HUA 701-1.16: *BSB* 1414–1418, fol. 126v; HUA 701-1.13: *RDB* 1414–1425, fol. 50r.

19 See Appendix 1.3 for a full overview of the core procedure and its many variants. This specific sequence of events also forms the subject of Camphuijsen, "Performance of Justice".

20 Berents, *Misdaad*, 41.

21 Ibid., 44.

case of imprisonment in the meat house, the one prison not located on the town's edges, the culprit's route passed through a central place like the square in front of the aldermen's house, called the *Plaets*, making his or her movements visible to many. Such visualization of punishment within the urban landscape was a common feature in many other late medieval cities as well, strengthening the impression from Chapter 2 that space was actively and strategically used by authorities and others in Utrecht to communicate their socio-political messages.[22] This judicial performance involved not only the court and the culprit, but also the audience witnessing the latter move through the city on its way to beg the former for forgiveness. In their role as interpreters of the ritual messaging, these audiences thus had a very real influence on the form such occasions took.

This can also be seen in the specific outfit of the forgiveness-seeking culprits, as they made their way through the city. There are basically two variants in the descriptions of the culprit's appearance during these occasions: either they would go bareheaded or in 'shirt and pants' (*in hemde ende in broeck*). Prescribing this attire was in fact common penal practice, in both a regional and trans-regional context. The legal records of several other cities in the late medieval Low Countries show similar cases of bareheaded or austerely dressed culprits. For example, the *Correctieboeken* of Leiden, which have survived from the fifteenth century onwards, include on several occasions bareheaded movement from one location to another as part of the punishment for an offence.[23] But the same dress appears in quite different contexts. In northern France, for example, thirteenth- and fourteenth-century descriptions of both penal and diplomatic occasions regularly contained elements of bareheaded, barefooted or otherwise markedly dressed movement. This could concern poor women found to have carried a bastard child as well as a lord losing a suit over a parcel of land to an abbey.[24] Nor was this attire necessarily a late medieval phenomenon. In Pope Gregory VII's description of his reconciliation with – or, depending on

22 See, for example, the ritualized 'running' of offenders in Toulouse, as evidenced in Turning, *Municipal Officials*, 149–153.

23 Gemeentearchief Leiden (GAL), Oud rechterlijk archief (ORA) 4-4P: *Correctieboeken, 1392–1778*. For example, GAL ORA 4A, fol. 233 (1447): '[Gerrit Willemsz] will come before the court at the city hall before tomorrow's sunrise, bareheaded and ungirded, and beg the court to forgive him, for God's sake, anything else in which he has wronged the city.' I am grateful to Janna Coomans for drawing my attention to these instances of bareheaded movement in the Leiden archives.

24 Mary C. Mansfield, *The Humiliation of Sinners: Public Penance in Thirteenth-Century France* (Ithaca, NY, and London: Cornell University Press, 1995), 113, 264. Mansfield names many similar examples in her book, for example, at pp. 127, 268, 274 and 279.

one's perspective, humiliation of – the German king Henry IV at Canossa in 1077, he famously described the latter as having appeared barefoot and dressed in woollen clothes.[25] And these same elements can even be found in non-legal contexts. Richard Trexler, for example, describes a prayer ritual undertaken by a fifteenth-century Florentine attempting to reconcile himself with his recently deceased son. On this occasion the father was dressed in 'a nightgown with knees bare, nothing on his head, and around his neck a *corregia* or halter'.[26] The descriptions of bareheaded or austerely dressed culprits in the Utrecht records thus seem to fit within a much larger complex – both geographically and chronologically – of similarly ritualized attire.

In her work on public penance in thirteenth-century France, Mary C. Mansfield suggests an important broader context for the forgiveness procedures as described in the Utrecht records, namely, religious penance. Questioning the strong divide that is often suggested between theologically grounded ecclesiastical penances and the public shaming punishments of secular authorities, she regards public penance as a particularly adaptable form of punishment, which gave it an important role to play in the grey area that existed between spiritual and secular justice.[27] While most famously theorized in theological and liturgical works, in practice the political and social context of thirteenth-century public penances was predominantly urban. There both bishops in their function as secular lords and non-ecclesiastical authorities borrowing a certain spiritual gesture language, used these types of public penance in penal practice.[28] The specific attire encountered in the descriptions of Utrecht's forgiveness procedures thus

25 Ephraim Emerton, ed., *The Correspondence of Pope Gregory VII: Selected Letters from the Registrum* (New York: Columbia University Press, 1932), 112. Also see Vollrath, "Rebels", 97.

26 Richard C. Trexler, *Public Life in Renaissance Florence* (New York: Academic Press, 1980), 176–179.

27 Mansfield, *Humiliation*, 128. Mansfield reacts to authors like Paul de Win, *De schandstraffen in het wereldlijk strafrecht in de Zuidelijke Nederlanden van de Middeleeuwen tot de Franse Tijd bestudeerd in Europees perspectief* (Brussel: Paleis der Academiën, 1991), 35, who suggests a strong distinction between secular shaming processions (*schandtochten*) and ecclesiastical penance processions (*boetetocht*). A similar overlap between penitential and legal practices in the context of imprisonment is evidenced in Guy Geltner, "*Detrusio*: Penal Cloistering in the Middle Ages", *Revue Bénédictine* 118 (2008); Guy Geltner, *The Medieval Prison: A Social History* (Princeton, NJ, and Oxford: Princeton University Press, 2008), 77–80. That the linking of penitential and politico-legal practices had a much longer history is evidenced in Mayke de Jong, *The Penitential State: Authority and Atonement in the Age of Louis the Pious, 814–840* (Cambridge: Cambridge University Press, 2009); Rob Meens, "Penitential Varieties", in *The Oxford Handbook of Medieval Christianity*, ed. John Arnold (Oxford: Oxford University Press, 2014).

28 Mansfield, *Humiliation*, 248–287.

hint at the ritualization of these events in two related ways. By visualizing the extraordinary status of the culprit, his outfit contributed to the public performance of the legal process. Engaging the socio-cultural knowledge and expectations of an urban audience, this appearance suggested a specific penance-related meaning for the event as a whole. Furthermore, the procedure drew upon a long tradition of occasions where a similar attire was used in relation to spiritual penitence. In this way, the ritual actors – both Council and culprit – related their activity to many other situations that had gone before, thus suggesting its inclusion in a broader constellation of spiritual and legal practices.

The suggested link between Utrecht's forgiveness rituals and broader practices of public penance, is further strengthened when focusing on a third element of these penal occasions. After having visibly and recognizably moved through the city, the culprit would beg the Council for forgiveness for his deeds. More often than not this was followed by the payment of a stone fine.[29] Begging for forgiveness in combination with an explicitly signified fine strongly echoed the common penitential scheme of public submission and public satisfaction.[30] In penitential theory, when an individual had violated the established cosmic order by sinning, he or she would have to re-establish this order through submission to a spiritual authority, like the bishop, and to satisfy it in one way or another, for example, by undertaking a pilgrimage. Likewise, in begging the Council for forgiveness, the culprit in Utrecht was forced to acknowledge this body's authority as a representative of the urban community. And by paying a fine that was explicitly presented as a contribution to something as communal as urban space, he would furthermore have to satisfy his violation of the social order.

Collectively then, the elements of Utrecht forgiveness rituals contain ample references to a much larger penance-related ritual scheme. Although originally stemming from theology and liturgical theory, its strategic use by ecclesiastical authorities had brought these ritual forms within the scope of many secular authorities.[31] Elements from this ideal scheme, like exposed movement, recognizable clothing and the act of begging for forgiveness,

29 See Chapter 2 for an extensive analysis of these stone fines.

30 Mansfield, *Humiliation*, 124.

31 Ibid., 127–128. For broader ideas on the influence of theology and ecclesiastical law on European practices of penal shaming, see Jörg Wettlaufer and Yasuhiro Nishimura, "The History of Shaming Punishments and Public Exposure in Penal Law (1200–1800): A Comparative Perspective (Western Europe and East Asia)", in *Shame between Punishment and Penance: The Social Usages of Shame in the Middle Ages and Early Modern Times*, eds. Bénédicte Sère and Jörg Wettlaufer (Florence: SISMEL edizioni del Galluzzo, 2013), esp. 202–209.

could be and were applied in various urban settings.[32] At the same time, there were important local differences in the application of such penitence-related punishment. Compared to the available evidence for such instances of public penance in other urban communities in the late medieval Low Countries, the frequency and apparent standardization of a specific sequence of actions in the Utrecht source material is uncommon. Notwithstanding our still very limited view of the role of these penitential elements in the penal practice of many urban communities, the general impression that the literature and available sources offer is that of a rather fragmented and varied procedure, often forming only a minor part of other penal occasions.[33] A much more common form in which we encounter penitence-related punishment in the southern and northern Low Countries are pilgrimages.[34] Although often combined with occasions of publicly witnessed penance, pilgrimages, by taking the penitent away from home, were ostensibly concerned with a culprit's spiritual well-being, rather than his relation to society. Instead of the local audience engaged in the forgiveness procedures, pilgrimages entailed first and foremost a performance before God. In this context, it is striking how rare mentions of the imposition of pilgrimages are in the Council's sources.[35] A choice was evidently made between various penitential activities regularly applied in secular penal practice. In Utrecht certain elements were singled out and frequently combined in a set sequence of actions, while others were not. Thus, while hinting at a broader constellation of penitential practices, the forgiveness procedure essentially constituted a unique local form of legal practice.

In this context it is relevant to take into account some characteristics of Utrecht as an urban community. In contrast to most neighbouring cities, Utrecht was – and had for centuries been – the seat of a bishop, who was the community's most direct ecclesiastical and secular authority. Over the thirteenth and fourteenth centuries the latter aspect of the bishop's authority

32 No definite overview of the practice of public penances in the Low Countries is available to my knowledge, but a first general impression can be gained from Jan van Herwaarden's doctoral thesis on the related theme of obligatory pilgrimages: Van Herwaarden, *Bedevaarten*, which shows various elements to have existed in the penal practice of Antwerp (p. 196), Leuven (pp. 242, 247), Brielle (pp. 279, 283), Delft (p. 285), Haarlem (p. 290), Leiden (p. 325) and Schiedam (p. 347). For evidence of such practices in fifteenth-century Malines, see Louis T. Maes, *Vijf eeuwen stedelijk strafrecht: Bijdrage tot de rechts- en cultuurgeschiedenis der Nederlanden* (Antwerp: De Sikkel and The Hague: Martinus Nijhoff, 1947), 433–435.

33 In the examples provided by Van Herwaarden, *Bedevaarten*, forgiveness rituals generally form part of the broader punishment of obligatory pilgrimage.

34 Mansfield, *Humiliation*, 282–287; Herwaarden, *Bedevaarten*.

35 Berents, *Misdaad*, 50.

in particular came under attack, first by an increasingly influential merchant elite and from the late thirteenth century onwards by the guild-based government that made the Council such a prominent institution. As seen in Chapter 1, these two elements – the important role of an ecclesiastical landlord and the internal power struggles that spanned most of the period under consideration – formed the background for the political development of the city in the late medieval period. In this respect the situation in Utrecht strongly echoes the situation that Mansfield describes in the northern French cities where public penance became an important part of urban penal procedure in the thirteenth century. In these places, she argues, urban penances 'characteristically arose from divisions within cities and especially from divisions between bourgeois and clerics or among bourgeois families'.[36] In her view the use of public penances in northern France was therefore strongly related to struggles for legitimacy between different stakeholders in the cities. Based as it was on a common gesture language, these urban penances emphasized the spiritual legitimacy of the party applying it.[37]

There is, however, also a marked difference between the situation in Utrecht and the northern French towns. In the latter case, the party imposing the penance was generally a bishop or another ecclesiastical authority, whose influence in this region was fairly strong. Public penance was therefore a particular weapon for ecclesiastical authorities, who used it to legitimize the specifically spiritual type of power they claimed.[38] Although the Utrecht sources do occasionally mention the bishop as overlord, the penitentiary language of the forgiveness procedure almost exclusively emphasizes the city and the Council – not the bishop – as authorities to be re-acknowledged.[39] Adding to Mansfield's suggestion that such public penances were related to authorities' struggles for legitimacy, the case of Utrecht thus shows that in the late fourteenth century the legitimizing potential of such acts was actively and consistently incorporated by a secular authority as well.

The uncommon frequency of the forgiveness procedure in Utrecht begs the question as to why this specific ritual language became so popular in legal practice. Again the socio-political context of late medieval Utrecht

36 Mansfield, *Humiliation*, 251.

37 Ibid., 248–252, 262–269.

38 Ibid., 267. For a similar use of public penance by ecclesiastical authorities in late medieval England, see James Masschaele, "The Public Space of the Marketplace in Medieval England", *Speculum* 77, no. 2 (2002): 407–412.

39 See Appendix 1.3. Only on three occasions is the bishop named as recipient of a compensation in such a forgiveness procedure: HUA 701-1.16: *BSB* 1385–1391, fol. 207r (1391); HUA 701-1.13: *RDB* 1402–1408, fol. 108r (1407); HUA 701-1.13: *RDB* 1408–1414, fol. 104r (1412).

provides part of the explanation. One of the entries in the *Liber albus*, the oldest of the Council's surviving books of bylaws, records a verdict given by the bishop of Utrecht in 1346 regarding an attack on the Council and its functionaries by a group of men. The bishop, who was called upon by the citizens and guilds to judge the case, gave his decisions on the resolution of a variety of issues: punishments to be meted out, damages to be paid and peace treaties to be concluded. One of the punishments meted out to a group of offenders was to come before both the bishop and the Council in a simple garb of linen clothing, bareheaded and barefooted, with a drawn sword in hand, and begging, first the bishop and then the Council, for mercy.[40] This is as far as I know the earliest recorded example for Utrecht of the by now familiar movement in a humble garb to beg an authority for forgiveness for serious misdemeanour, which is here, as in several other cases, underlined symbolically by carrying a sword. In contrast to the many later cases encountered in the *Buurspraakboek*, here the episcopal landlord drew on this sequence of actions in his attempt at resolving an internal struggle within the Utrecht community.

Considering this instance in the light of the regularity with which the same pattern of actions reappears in the Council's sources from the later fourteenth century onwards, leads to two observations. First, that in 1346 the bishop, after the Guild letter of 1304 and the complementary ruling of 1341 had markedly decreased his actual power in the city (see Chapter 1), seems to have used this penitence-related punishment to claim an authority that he was rapidly losing. Here we discern an echo of the situation in thirteenth-century northern France as described by Mansfield, where such penance-related punishment was a much-used means of legitimization for bishops and other ecclesiastical authorities.[41] It is thus a concrete indication of the way in which Utrecht was part of a broader religious semantic network, where a specific kind of ritual language was commonplace.

Secondly, focusing on the penal occasions themselves, such instances also point at the role these broader semantic schemes could play for ritual actors – be it the Council, the culprit or others – in reaching specific socio-legal goals. For the Council, these occasions formed part of its claim for legitimacy. Tapping into a ritual grammar predominantly familiar from an

40 Muller, *Rechtsbronnen* vol. 1, 57–60: *Voert segghe wi, dat Louwe Stommekiin,* [...], *binnen dreen daghen na desen daghe comen sellen, ten ersten voer ons ende na voer den ghemenen raet vander stat ende voer die clocke, horeliic in enen bloten paer linnen cleder bloetshoefts ende barvoet, ende yeghelic van hem sel een baer swaert in siin hant hebben ende sellen bidden ons voer ende den rade na, also alse gheseghet is, dat wi hoers liifs ghenade hebben willen;*[...]'

41 Mansfield, *Humiliation*, 267.

episcopal context, suggested the continuity of the bishop's legal authority by the Council; the position of forgiveness-granter that had previously been taken by the bishop, was now explicitly and structurally claimed by the Council. By appropriating the spiritual legitimacy of these penance-related practices, the Council attempted to recreate some of the link between lay and ecclesiastical authority that had traditionally been embodied by the bishop-as-landlord. For the culprit it could also be profitable to suggest a link between his individual passage through the city and penitential practices. Given the nature of some of the offences for which this procedure was imposed, varying from the public misbehaviour of Snellaert the sawyer to Jan de Rode's act of manslaughter, one can imagine the sticky situation in which some of these culprits found themselves. An offence like manslaughter could just as well lead to permanent exile from the city, thus not only separating the offender from his social and economic means of existence, but also presenting him as a communal pariah. In this light a spiritually sanctioned reconciliation, suggesting both a personal and communal appeasement, may well have been a more inviting option, facilitating – formally at least – the offender's social reintegration.

The procedure of forgiveness exemplifies the ritualization of legal practices in late medieval Utrecht. These locally specific penal occasions referred to a broader constellation of mainly penitential acts. Frequently reappearing sequence of actions, these procedures' explicit references to broader systems of practice provided the things that were done with a certain significance. By referencing, rather than simply following a predetermined ritual scheme, actors could appropriate such broader implications, while still keeping a degree of freedom in performing the acts themselves. These occasions were thus a particularly embodied means of legal communication, partly shaped by the ritual language that was used – that is, the penitential references in dress and action – yet also dependent on the interaction between ritual actors and their direct audiences. The legal actors – both Council and culprit – strategically drew on larger communication structures – in this case penitential practices – to suggest a link between individual penal occasions and broader schemes of ritualized action, in an attempt to legitimize both action (the punishment) and the actors themselves.

York: The performance of judgement

The language of penitence also features in the legal proceedings of York's Consistory Court. In one of the court's few surviving fourteenth-century act books, a scribe noted how the official convicted a certain Thomas Candeler for contumacy, that is, for not appearing in court when summoned, and some other unspecified offences. Thomas was ordered to walk at the head of the procession in York Minster for twelve days, and around the local market square for six days. He would do this *more penitentis*, in the manner of a penitent, thereby emphasizing the spiritual character of the occasions.[42] Thus, a similar ritualization as seen in Utrecht, northern France and elsewhere, was available in York, too.[43] However, despite some evidence for these practices in the Consistory Court, they are not as extensively documented as in Utrecht. This is primarily an issue of sources. The court's act books survive only fragmentarily for the fourteenth and fifteenth centuries, while the much more numerous cause papers concern mainly instance jurisdiction, which did not – or only secondarily – involve penitence-related punishment.[44] With such limited information, it is difficult to gain a proper impression of the exact role of such practices in the Consistory Court. There was, however, another much better documented practice that illustrates how specific actions in court were ritualized to provide them with a broader relevance. These were the sentence readings, that is to say, occasions on which a court official would read out the judgement reached in a case.

The court's sentences have survived for some 34% of the fourteenth-century cause paper dossiers.[45] As this includes some cases, predominantly

42 YML M 2(1)b, fol. 2v.

43 Similar cases of penitence-related punishment are found in the courts of the dean and chapter of York Minster: Sandra Brown, *The Medieval Courts of the York Minster Peculiar* (York: University of York, 1984), 25–26. For other ecclesiastical jurisdictions, such as Canterbury, Rochester and Lincoln, there is also ample evidence of such punishments in the late medieval period: Helmholz, *Marriage Litigation*, 182; Masschaele, "Public Space", 407–412; Dave Postles, "Penance and the Market Place: A Reformation Dialogue with the Medieval Church (c. 1250–c. 1600)", *The Journal of Ecclesiastical History* 54, no. 3 (2003): 443–447; R.H. Helmholz, *The Oxford History of the Laws of England: The Canon Law and Ecclesiastical Jurisdiction from 597 to the 1640s* (Oxford: Oxford University Press, 2004), 622–624.

44 For the fourteenth century only the act books for the years 1371–1375 have survived: YML M 2(1) b and c. For the fifteenth century the years 1417–1420, 1424–1427, 1428–1430 and 1484–1489 are covered: BIA Cons. AB 1, 2, 3 and 4, respectively.

45 In absolute numbers, it concerns 87 out of 254 cases. The fourteenth-century cases with surviving verdicts are: BIA CP.E.1, 2, 3, 6, 15, 17, 18, 23, 24, 26, 28, 37, 46, 50, 71, 72, 76, 77, 79, 80, 82, 84, 85, 87, 89, 92, 95, 98, 102, 103, 105, 106, 107, 111, 112, 113, 114, 116, 117, 118, 124, 126, 130, 135, 138, 155, 157, 158, 159, 161, 169, 170, 171, 177, 178, 185, 188, 191, 193, 194, 196, 198, 201, 202, 203, 204, 208, 211, 214, 221, 224, 226, 228, 231, 233, 235, 238, 239, 242, 245, 251, 253, 255, 259, 263, 268, 270, 274 and 275. Whether the survival of sentences should be considered incidental is unclear, as cases could supposedly be settled out of court before a verdict was given. See Pedersen, *Marriage Disputes*, 105–118, for evidence on extra-curial legal procedures. There is likely to be a relation between appeal cases and the survival of sentences. While only 115 (45%) of all fourteenth-century

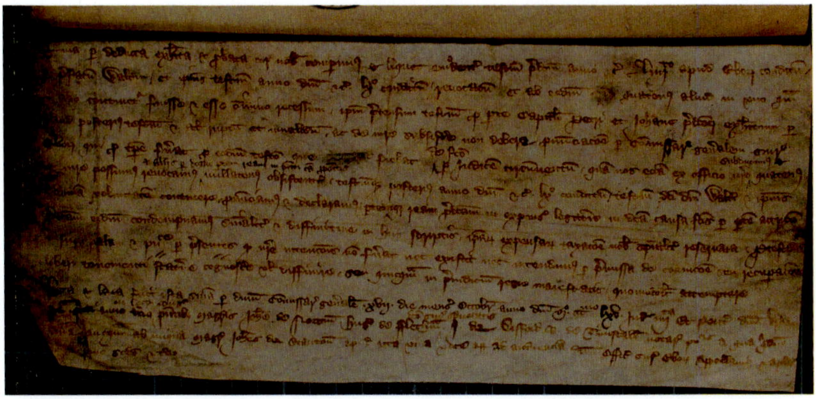

Figure 2: Fragment of sentence from cause paper CP.E.169, including *lecta et lata*-entry (four bottom lines).

appeals, with multiple verdicts from the different stages the case went through, the total number of individual sentences noted down in the cause papers for this century amounts to 118. Of these some 36% (42 sentences) date to the last decade of the century. Individual sentences generally consist of two parts: one detailing the case, the verdict and the process leading up to the verdict, the other noting the day and place on which the aforementioned was read and brought (*lecta et lata*), possible further steps taken by one of the parties and the people present at the reading of the sentence. For an example of the second, in a long-drawn-out testamentary case between the abbey of St Albans on the one hand and Peter Fleming and Joan, the sister of the testator, on the other, one of the written sentences included in the cause paper dossier explicitly mentions how the court's commissary general read and brought said sentence on October 27, 1365, in the cathedral's consistory place in the presence of the advocates John Norton and Hugo Fleetham and public notaries J. Gifford and R. Tunstall (Figure 2).[46] There is thus clear textual evidence of a fairly consistent practice of oral pronunciations as part of the legal process before the Consistory Court. As in the case of Utrecht it is crucial to realize that we are looking here at a biased textual account of these legal performances, that is, the court summarizing its own sentence reading. These descriptions can never provide us with a full account of the interpretations and experiences of all people witnessing or participating

cases concern appeals, of all cases with sentences 53 (60%) are appeals. For precise numbers of sentences per type of case (e.g. matrimonial, related to tithes, etc.), see Appendix 2.1.

46 BIA CP.E.169; Peter and Joan subsequently appealed to the official, whose sentence, pronounced on April 26, 1368, is also included in this same dossier.

in such occasions. But even if they show the court's own interpretation of these events, this in itself provides us with some sense of the way in which it tried to conceptualize actions in court as part of larger communicative schemes. The aspects of these readings that it recorded were the ones that mattered, as they formed part of the attempt at ritualization. It is therefore worthwhile to examine these descriptions in more detail.

Some indication of the physical location of the sentence readings is given in 42% (50 out of 118) of the sentences. The wording for this location varies. In some cases the entry notes only that the sentence was read in the court of York (*in curia Eboracensis*) or in the consistory of York (*in consistorio Eboracensis*).[47] This gives only a very limited indication of the actual place, as the terms *curia* and *consistorium* could hint both at a physical location and at the court as a jurisdictional body. In other cases the entries are less ambiguous, stating, as in the example above, that the reading took place 'in the place of the consistory' (*in loco consistorii*).[48] Others are even more explicit, such as the sentence in a 1360 tithe case between John Raven, rector of the parish of Normanton on Soar, and Thomas Milner, which situates the action 'in the place of the consistory in the cathedral church of York' (*in loco consistorii in ecclesia cathedrali Eboracensis*).[49] In addition, a few cases that do not name the location of the sentence reading itself, nonetheless specify that the appeal following the reading of the sentence – and which is for that reason also noted down – will be received in the *locus consistorii*. This makes the sentence readings the part of the Consistory Court's legal activity that can most clearly be situated within the cathedral church. As seen in Chapter 2, the Minster was a multifunctional and multi-signifying place, catering for a whole range of social activities and representations. To have the sentence readings take place within the cathedral – and furthermore to note this down explicitly in the records – was more than simple convenience. Visibility and more general accessibility of these occasions were heightened compared to many other parts of the legal process, like the hearing of a testimony that took place behind closed doors. And in a similar vein, the location of the cathedral placed – what Jonathan Z. Smith would call – a 'focusing lens' on the sentence readings taking place within it.[50] A judgement orally

47 Like in BIA CP.E.226 and BIA CP.E.275.

48 BIA CP.E.169. For a similar wording of the location of sentence reading see the 1382 marriage case between Ellen de Layremouth and Isabella de Holm, on the one hand, and William de Stokton, on the other, in BIA CP.E.126.

49 BIA CP.E.80.

50 Cf. Smith's development of the idea of temples and other sacred places as ritual focusing lens, in Smith, "Bare Facts", 113–115.

performed in the house of God likely shared in the religious significance of many of the other activities taking place there, most notably the singing of mass. In the emphasis on the location of the readings we thus discern, like in Utrecht, both the role of a witnessing audience and of the suggestion of broader structures of practice in this particular place.

Another element that provides us with some information on the setting of these sentence readings are the so-called *presentibus* clauses. In 83 (70%) of the individual sentences preserved for this period such a clause is included, making it the most regularly noted practical information apart from the date of the reading. *Presentibus* clauses are usually contained as a last element of the 'read and brought' entries at the end of written sentences (see above) and specify the names and often also the function of some of the people who were present at the reading. The named people encountered in these entries vary from court officials like advocates, proctors, apparitors, examiners and public notaries, to more general *magisters*, lords and clerics. But many entries end by stating that others (*aliis*) were present as well. The number or character of these *aliis* remains guesswork, but it does show the presence of more than just the named attendants. In a few cases the scribe identifies an even larger audience. Thus, the sentence in a 1381 marriage case between John Topcliffe and Emma Earl notes how the reading took place among a great crowd (*in multitudine copiosa*).[51] *Presentibus* clauses therefore suggest two related aspects of ritualized action. First, they record how in most cases audiences of various sizes were present to witness the sentence readings. Even in the most conservative estimation of the numbers of unmentioned *alii*, a sizeable audience beyond the court and litigants was present. These were events to be witnessed, even if they were not entirely open. In addition, by explicitly recording the presence of audiences and by highlighting some of their members, the entries suggest the importance of audiences in legitimizing the occasion.[52] The presence of these people – and most prominently the legal specialists and clerics – made the performance into a valid sentence reading, earning thereby an explicit notification by the scribe. Once again, the circumstances under which the judgement was brought formed an intricate part of the significance of the sentence itself.

51 BIA CP.E.124. The same expression is used to describe the attendees to the 1372 sentence reading in a major case concerning church rights between the vicar of the parish of Rampton and the archdeacon of Nottingham in BIA CP.E.107. Also see Helmholz, *Marriage Litigation*, 119, n. 16, for other examples of this wording from York and several other English church courts.

52 For a similar argument, see Clanchy, *Memory*, 298, who interprets these *et alliis* clauses as recording first and foremost 'the impressiveness of the occasion at the time'.

Moving from the second to the first part of the written sentences, i.e. from the setting of the readings to the sentences themselves, their extreme focus on the legal procedure is striking. A typical sentence begins by noting how the court has 'heard and understood' (*auditis et intellectis*) the case before it, naming the judge, both parties and the proctors involved in the case. Thus, in a case concluded in 1306 concerning an assault on the prioress of Handale, Ivetta, by two men, Nicholas Marske and Gilbert son of Letitia, the sentences of both men open in an identically formalized manner:

> In the name of God, having heard and understood the worthy cause concerning violent apprehension [*iniectione manuum violenta*] brought before us, the official of the court of York, between the prioress of Handale, appearing as plaintiff through her proctor, William Twyford, on one side, and Nicholas Marske, appearing as defendant through his proctor Walter Whitby, on the other, [...].[53]

Both sentences then continue by elaborating on the many procedural steps taken in the case, from the plaintiff's bringing of her formal complaint or libel, the production, swearing and hearing of witnesses, to the conclusion of the case and the final verdict decided upon.[54] The conclusions are limited to mentioning that Ivetta sufficiently proved her case in court and that the consequences of this verdict for Nicholas and Gilbert consist of major excommunication. As was common practice in medieval law courts, the legal reasoning underlying the final verdicts is absent.[55] The formulaic and content-wise very limited character of sentences like these has led many scholars to disregard them in favour of other parts of the legal procedure that are richer in detailed information, like witness depositions. However, the sentences also form that part of the case where the judicial role of the court – and thus its legitimacy as adjudicator – is most explicitly involved. While initially the plaintiff, defendant and witnesses would take centre stage, providing the case with legal substance in the form of a formal plaint, contestations and witness statements, in pronouncing a verdict the court itself took the active role in this final part of the procedure. To encounter

53 BIA CP.E.3. The assault on the prioress of Handale also appears in the records of the Court of Common Pleas, which shows some of the complex routes a conflict could take in the plural legal landscape of late medieval England: William Paley Baildon, *Notes on the Religious and Secular Houses of Yorkshire*, vol. 1 (London: Yorkshire Archaeological Society, 1895), 86–87.

54 See Brundage, *Canon Law*, 129–134, for an introductory overview of the different steps of formal procedure in canon law.

55 Ibid., 134.

here such a focus, not on the legal argumentation underlying the verdict, but on the procedural steps that preceded it, highlights which aspects of the whole procedure the court wanted to bring to the fore, including the judges' role therein.

In his discussion of marriage cases before the ecclesiastical courts of late medieval England, Richard Helmholz notes how legal procedure was very flexible in practice. Although canon law prescribed a strict procedural pattern, on the basis of the evidence gathered from different English church courts Helmholz argues that in reality the wishes and judgement of the parties and judge involved in a case had a much larger influence on the actual procedure that was followed. By compressing or outright renouncing certain procedural steps, the process as a whole was often shortened significantly in favour of a quick resolution of the case.[56] Formal steps were simply skipped if informal oral negotiations made them superfluous: 'What mattered to [the parties and their lawyers] was reaching an acceptable result, not following a fixed procedural pattern.'[57] In day-to-day practice the formal procedure thus formed no more than a general framework within which legal actors sought out a practical and satisfactory way to resolve their disputes. Still, the wording of the sentences suggests that in the valuation – or one should say narrativization – of this daily practice formal procedure did have an additional importance. By explicitly referencing this procedure in its sentences, the court provided its verdicts with a much stronger legitimacy than the elaboration on legal argumentation would have done. Like the forgiveness rituals in the case of Utrecht, the Consistory Court's sentences drew a link between the actions that had been performed in actual practice and the idealized scheme of actions that was formal canon law procedure. In this they were relevant both for the court pronouncing them and for the parties involved. For it was this ritualization of the different actions undertaken in the context of the case that gave them their significance as extraordinary – that is, legal – actions. Thus, for the litigant pursuing a canonically sanctioned decision in a dispute, both the suggestion that the actions performed in the legal process formed part of a broader ritual whole, and its confirmation in the explicitly staged performance of a judgement, were of the utmost importance.

The role of such a ritualization of actions in court is made even clearer when considering the broader context of dispute resolution within which much of the legal activity before the Consistory Court took place. As in

56 Helmholz, *Marriage Litigation*, 112–123.

57 Ibid., 113.

most medieval societies, so in York, asking for the formal sentence of an ecclesiastical judge was only one of several options available for the settlement of a dispute.[58] Many cases were settled out of court, and since they did not ordinarily produce any records, it is impossible to assess how common they were.[59] What may, however, give us some indication of the commonality of such practices is the large amount of cause papers that lack a sentence. Survival rates aside, the fact that only 34% of the fourteenth-century cause papers contain sentences as against, for example, 60% in the case of depositions, suggests a fair amount of initiated but not formally finished cases. Add to this the many invisible disputes that were not brought to court at all, and one gains an impression of the peculiar position of the formal sentences and their reading within the much broader economy of dispute resolution. Parties involved in a dispute had several choices of how to resolve it, only one of which led through court. In this context the legalization of actions, and in particular the court's sentence reading action, explicitly propagated the 'way of the court' as against other means of resolution that could be followed by the disputants. The actions that constituted a court case were situated within an overarching procedural framework that could in the eyes of the litigants make them a particularly valid and effective strategy for dispute resolution, backed up as it was by the social, political and cultural power claim of the institutionalized church. At the same time, procedural ritualization helped the court concretize the ideal legal order that it represented, thereby supporting its claim as authority in the resolution of people's disputes.

In 1311, Archbishop Greenfield ordered every official who would from then on preside over the court to proclaim its statutes annually at the first session after Michaelmas.[60] This yearly attempt to legitimize the court, by suggesting its integrity to potential litigants, worded in an explicit manner what the sentence readings performed on a day-to-day basis. Through the ritualization of court activity, referring back to the overarching scheme of acts that was formal canon law procedure, the court performed its position as authoritative settler of disputes. The significance of these occasions was emphasized through their setting and audience. Located as they often were within the cathedral church, the sentence readings profited from the

58 Ibid., 135–138; Brundage, *Canon Law*, 134. See the introduction to this book for more on traditions of extra-curial dispute resolution.

59 Some evidence for extra-curial procedures is given in Pedersen, *Marriage Disputes*, 105–118. However, Pedersen's conclusion on p. 118 that 'the cause paper evidence [...] suggests that the church monopoly on the settlement of matrimonial disputes was never seriously challenged' seems to overlook the inherent institutional bias of his material.

60 Wilkins, *Consilia*, vol. 2, 413; Burns, "Medieval Courts", 113–116.

multifarious functions and denotations that people attributed to this place. In the same way, their extraordinary character was emphasized by the presence of an audience of varying sizes, among whom several notable figures, such as legal specialists and clerics. As the climax of many legal cases, sentences in the Consistory Court were not just written down. They also formed the nucleus of the occasions on which the court could make its voice heard, most explicitly through the visible and oral performance of its judgements.

Paris: Performance and presence

Judicial performance was also at the heart of the activities of the Parisian *Parlement*. As in York, a fair amount of the court's daily activities involved holding audiences, during which the different parties – sometimes through their proctors – would argue their case. In the earliest surviving royal ordinance concerning the *Parlement* (1278), the king used many articles to stipulate the details of these occasions, concerning time, place, participants and procedure.[61] The parties involved, so the ordinance tells us, would come to the royal palace during the time set for the treatment of cases coming from their bailiwick.[62] For this the *Parlement* set a strict order, dividing each legal year into eleven time slots of different lengths, each reserved for one or several bailiwicks or other jurisdictional entities (Figure 3).[63] Parties presenting themselves on one of the days of their bailiwick's time slot were supposed to wait in the King's Hall, which would in the early fourteenth century be turned into the Great Hall, until they were called into the chamber where the pleading took place, at first the lower floor of the King's Chamber (Plan 2) and later the *Grande Chambre* (Plan 1). They – and only they, so the ordinance states – would enter the chamber through the door leading to the King's Hall, the accuser briefly presenting his case and the defendant his response. These would be written down and sent to the

61 The originally Latin ordinance has only survived in various Middle French translations, edited in P. Guilhiermoz, *Enquètes et procès: Étude sur la procedure et le fonctionnement du Parlement au XIVe siècle* (Paris: Alphonse Picard, 1892), 600–610, and in C. V. Langlois, ed., *Textes relatifs à l'histoire du Parlement depuis les origines jusqu'en 1314* (Paris: Alphonse Picard, 1888), 95–99.

62 Guilhiermoz, *Enquètes*, 604, art. II.

63 This division of the legal year according to the bailiwicks and other jurisdictional entities constituting the French kingdom can also clearly be seen in the registers of the *Parlement*'s registry (*registres du greffe*), which have been kept from 1319 onwards to note down the activity taking place in the *Parlement*. The register for every new year begins by prescribing the different time frames for the reception of cases from the various bailiwicks.

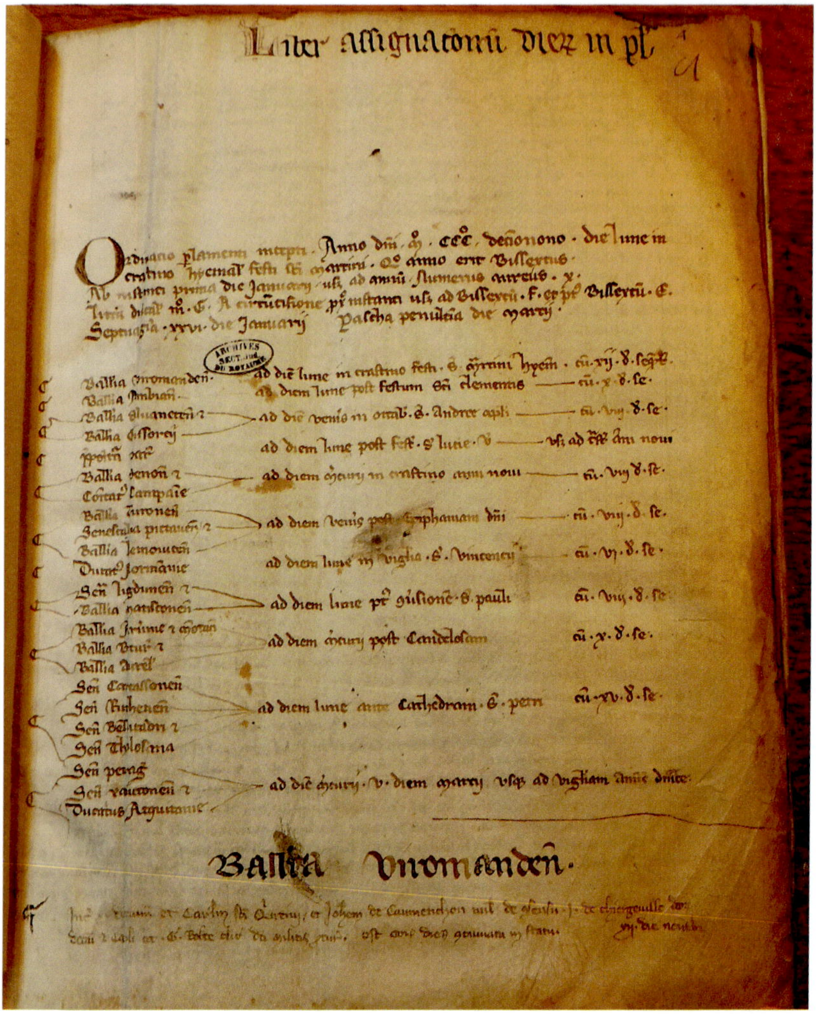

Figure 3: List of bailiwicks and other jurisdictional entities in the *Parlement's* register for 1319 (AN X1A8844, fol.4r). Each entry indicates the period during which the *Parlement* will receive cases originating in the concerned area.

auditors judging the case. The parties were then supposed to leave the chamber through the door leading to the palace garden, which was opposite the one they entered through.[64]

Several decades later, another royal ordinance – variously dated to 1296 or 1302 – further expanded these instructions.[65] It put even more

64 Guilhiermoz, *Enquêtes*, 604, art. III–VIII.

65 This ordinance has been published in Langlois, *Textes*, 161–167.

emphasis on the temporal aspects of court ritual, stressing the importance of strictly following the order of days set for the various bailiwicks, without intermingling them.[66] Whoever failed to appear on the days assigned to his bailiwick would be considered to be in default.[67] The ordinance further determined that the assemblies in the pleading chamber would take place in the morning and last until midday.[68] Much attention was also paid to the people supposed to be present in the pleading chamber, including at least one baron and one prelate and a number of explicitly named laymen and clerics.[69] At the same time, others were excluded from being present at the said occasions, like seneschals and bailiffs, that is, the intermediary legal officials of the kingdom.[70] Such ordinances, in presenting an idealized setting and procedure for the business of the court, linked individual audience sessions to the idea of a broader structure of activities. Here ritualization took place on several levels. By framing sessions as events structured according to timing, space, persons present and activity, the ordinances assign participants a fixed role and limit their agency to a set of standardized actions. At the same time, at the level of the judicial year, these individual sessions were clustered according to the judicio-political logic of the bailiwicks, again suggesting a broader framework of practices of which these activity sequences formed part. That the legal organization of the kingdom as a whole was taken as basis for the legal year, furthermore implied the geographical comprehensiveness of this system of activities. The judicio-political entity of the kingdom was presented as an interconnected whole of legal practices. The ordinances thus presented the activities taking place in court as parts of a larger entity of practice, both on the level of the individual sessions and in the relation between sessions.

However, it was more than legal interconnectedness that was at stake in these audience sessions. An aspect that recurs time and again is the physical presence and participation of court members, parties and audiences. The two ordinances cited above pay much attention to the presence and roles of the different actors – litigants and their proctors as well as court members – on these occasions. As seen above, they sometimes specify in particular detail who was supposed to be present at the sessions and who

66 Ibid., 165 (§ 16).

67 Ibid. (§ 19).

68 Ibid. (§ 18). During the fourteenth century the increase in case load led the *Parlement* to hold several afternoon sessions each week as well: Hildesheimer and Morgat-Bonnet, *État méthodique*, 43.

69 Langlois, *Textes*, 162–163 (§ 7–§ 9).

70 Ibid., 163–164 (§ 11).

was not. The registers of the *Parlement* also emphasize the importance of participation in court sessions. They regularly note how the court declared people to have been in default, even though they provided an excuse for their absence. For example, when Pierre de La Vaunage from Nîmes failed to turn up on May 4, 1330, on account of illness, the court did not consider this a sufficient excuse for his absence.[71] The same is true for the measure of *élargissement*.[72] Grants of *élargissement*, by precluding movement outside of a certain area, were meant to ensure that their recipient would be able to appear in court personally on the day that his or her case would be heard. It was also deemed important that certain actions would not be performed at any other time than during a court session. Another royal ordinance, originally published in 1310 by Philip the Fair and reproduced in 1318 under Philip the Tall, stipulated that members of the *Parlement* should not receive any information or 'private words' (*paroles priveez*) from parties except in pleading during a court session.[73] This provision is clearly meant as a way to discourage practices perceived as corrupt, like making external agreements between one party and individual members of the *Parlement*. At the same time, however, it also shows us the idealized function of the court sessions as perceived by the king and his advisers. What made an action – like receiving information in a case – a valid one, was its performance in person in the setting of the Pleading Chamber.

The importance of physical presence for the performance of legitimate legal actions also emerges from the stipulations regarding proctors. In contrast to the almost self-evident role that proctors seem to have played in the Consistory Court of York, the *Parlement* placed limits on the use of such functionaries by the parties appearing before it.[74] As Aubert has shown, from the beginning of the fourteenth century various treatises set out the rules concerning the representation of parties by proctors. Central in these stipulations was the parties' – or at least the accusers' – obligation to request a royal letter of pardon in order to be allowed to plead a case by means of a proctor. Notwithstanding the many exceptions that the authors of these tracts allow for – such as those for the proctors of certain ecclesiastical and secular dignitaries – their writings underscore the court's efforts to preclude parties' personal absence during the pleading sessions, unless explicitly

71 AN X^{2A}3, fol. 114r. For a similar case see AN X^{2A}4, fol. 47v.

72 See Chapter 2 for more on the *élargissement*.

73 This ordinance has been published in Langlois, *Textes*, 183–186. The stipulation referred to here is § 11 at p. 186.

74 For the role of proctors in the Consistory Court of York, see Chapters 1 and 5.

approved by the royal administration.[75] These theoretical considerations echo what we can grasp from daily court practice in the early fourteenth century. Both the X^{1A} and X^{2A} registers for this period regularly contain entries concerned with the question of appearing in person or by proctor. This could, for example, be in the form of a penalty for only sending one's proctor. On March 14, 1330, the day assigned to cases from the bailiwick of Sens, a certain Jean Bruiant was supposed to appear in the *Parlement*. Since only his proctor showed up, the court decided to consider him to be in default.[76] At the same time the registers also contain mentions of royal letters of grace accorded to specific litigants for reception through proctor. So for December 12, 1330, the register mentions how the king has given Jean de Culhem, a citizen of Saint-Omer, permission to be represented by his proctor in the case in which he is involved.[77] And in a case from 1341, a certain Tristan de Maignelay was allowed to be represented by a proctor up until the specific procedural step of responding to the articles in the case.[78] Although representation by proctors was certainly not forbidden on a major scale, with such procedural requirements the court encouraged litigants to appear in person before the court, thus taking an active part in performing the legal process.

The role of a witnessing public is less directly evidenced in the sources for the *Parlement*. However, the spatial layout of the *Grande Chambre* in particular provides clear indications for the presence of variously sized audiences playing an active part in at least some of the sessions. For instance, as Chapter 2 has shown, one area of the *Grande Chambre*, called the *parterre*, was available during certain sessions for a larger public to witness the proceedings.[79] Although visual evidence of these audiences is lacking for the medieval period, textual sources attest the active presence of these groups as early as the first half of the fourteenth century. An ordinance by Philip VI from 1344 provided several guidelines for the functioning of the court officials called the *huissiers*.[80] Two of them were supposed to 'remove

75 Aubert, "Nouvelles recherches", pt. 1, 282–284. Aubert's main source on this matter are several stipulations in the *Stilus curie Parlamenti* by the early-fourteenth-century advocate Guillaume du Breuil, edited as Guillaume du Breuil, *Stilus curie parlamenti*, ed. Félix Aubert (Paris: Alphonse Picard, 1909), 81–84.

76 AN $X^{2A}3$, f. 105r. For a similar case, see AN $X^{2A}4$, f.32v.

77 AN $X^{2A}4$, fol. 22r. For similar cases, see AN $X^{2A}3$, f. 117r. For similar cases from the late fourteenth century, see Carbonnières, *Procédure*, 168–176.

78 AN $X^{2A}4$, fol. 42r. On the procedure of drawing up the articles in a case, see Carbonnières, *Procédure*, 434–440.

79 Guerout, "Le Palais: Deuxième partie", 145–152.

80 De Laurière et al., *Ordonnances*, vol. 2, 225.

and prevent the noise from behind the benches and from everywhere in the Chamber of the *Parlement*'.[81] Anyone making noise or otherwise hindering an audience session was to be imprisoned.[82] These provisions hint at the essential role of the public during audience sessions, while at the same time showing the *Parlement*'s attempt to let those present play the role it had envisioned for them: that of a witnessing yet otherwise passive audience. Rather than precluding anyone from witnessing these sessions, as was done when the *Parlement* sat for counsel in the same chamber, the court explicitly recognized the audience as part of the ideal setting for these occasions, appointing two *huissiers* for this purpose. At the same time, the public was given the specific role of witnessing the session and not impeding its progress. The presence of two *huissiers* to enforce this particular role can, of course, be seen as an indication that it was not necessarily accepted by everyone attending.

Like the sentence readings in York and the occasions of public penance in Utrecht, the *Parlement*'s audience sessions allowed the court's socio-legal claim to be physically and orally performed. By drawing a link between the organization of courtroom activity and broader kingdom-wide legal and political structures, the former were presented as a confirmation of the latter. Furthermore, through its attempts to manage the physical presence of court members, litigants and audiences, the *Parlement* showed a desire to turn the audience sessions into legal performances that validated the acts that took place there. At the same time, however, the effectiveness of such site-specific ritualizing efforts will in many cases have been incompatible with the reality of a central royal court like the *Parlement*, which engaged with litigants and culprits from all over the kingdom. In part, the impediment of distance between court and litigants was dealt with through the use of proctors, who could represent litigants residing far from the capital. However, as seen concretely in the restrictions set for the use of proctors, the royal court also seriously limited this form of absenteeism in the cases appearing before it, stimulating litigants to appear in person.

It is in this context that a special type of court session deserves attention. For if the litigants did not come to court, the court could always come to the litigants in the form of what by the fifteenth century would be called *Grands Jours*.[83] The precursor of these special parliamentary sessions seems to be the

81 Ibid. (§ 1): [...] *oster et garder la noisse de derriere les bancs et de toute la Chambre du Parlement.*

82 Ibid. (§ 3).

83 The historiography on the *Grands Jours* is highly fragmented. For a more general impression of this phenomenon, see, most recently, Elisabeth Schmit, "'En bon trayn de justice': Les grands

royal practice of occasionally upgrading ducal or comital legal assemblies to the level of a supreme court of law, something which was done every now and then from the thirteenth century onwards. This was especially – though not exclusively – true for the highest judicial assemblies in the county of Champagne, regularly held in the city of Troyes and therefore known as the *dies Trecensis* or *Jours de Troyes*.[84] In 1284 Philip the Fair married the heiress of Champagne, Jeanne of Navarre, initiating a period of direct royal control over the county, Philip acting both as King of France and Count of Champagne. One of the areas where this control became most clearly visible was in the organization of the *Jours de Troyes*. These provincial judicial assemblies were turned into a sort of delegated branch of the Parisian *Parlement*: many of its judges now came from Paris and also had a seat in the *Parlement*, and its procedure and session schedule came to mirror those at the *Palais de la Cité*.[85] For one, the sessions at Troyes were strongly calibrated to the *Parlement*'s calendar of sessions at Paris, never taking place at the same time. Furthermore, the legal activity employed in Troyes also closely resembled that of the Parisian context, consisting of alternating pleading and counsel sessions. And even in the registers of these sessions themselves the material seems to be ordered according to a more general parliamentary logic.[86] The late-thirteenth- and fourteenth-century *Jours* of Troyes thus essentially transported the court activity of the *Parlement* to a different time and place.

It is crucial not to overstress the development of the *Jours* as part of a linear history of legal centralization, despite later attempts to present it as such. The development of these and similar precursors of the fifteenth-century *Grands Jours* is simply too varied and rugged to be simplified in such terms, forming more of a series of institutional experiments by a royal administration dealing with a rapid expansion of the king's demesne.[87] What

jours du parlement de Paris au lendemain de la guerre de Cent Ans (1454–1459)" (PhD diss., Paris I Panthéon-Sorbonne University, 2019). While focusing on their fifteenth-century instalment, in her introduction Schmit also takes stock of the history of and the historiography on the medieval *Grands Jours* more in general.

84 Schmit, "Grands jours", 23–42, explicitly places the *Jours de Troyes* in the context of a variety of royal 'institutional experiments' in the late thirteenth century, also including the development of the Exchequer of Normandy and the *Parlement* of Toulouse.

85 John F. Benton, "Philip the Fair and the Jours of Troyes", *Studies in Medieval and Renaissance History* 6 (1969): 281–292.

86 Schmit, "Grands jours", 23–42; see ibid., 411–414, for an extensive outline of thirteenth- and fourteenth-century sessions at Troyes in relation to Parisian sessions and those of the Exchequer of Normandy.

87 Schmit, "Grands jours", 15–61.

is more, practical considerations do not account fully for the motivation to occasionally manifest the *Parlement* in another place. While this will surely have made it easier and more affordable for people living close to Troyes to bring their appeals to the royal court directly, the fact that these *Jours* were always held in the same place, and only for some six to eight weeks every couple of years, makes it highly unlikely that this was the only, let alone the most important consideration, for organizing them. Rather, we may seek such motivations in the area of judicio-political communication. The French kings, having acquired the title of Count of Champagne, had a very real interest in tying this region – not just technically, but above all ideologically – to the royal demesne. In a late medieval context the physical presence of the monarch or his representatives in a locality were a common way of claiming such an ideological link between ruler and ruled, as the tradition of Joyous Entries – comprising the festive entrance of a ruler in a city – in this same period professes.[88] That such a show of presence was in the case of the *Jours* modelled along the lines of an extraordinary session of the *Parlement* implies not only the importance of this institution, but above all of its judicial activities in suggesting a certain idealized image of royal governance.

Considering the general development of the *Parlement* of Paris from the late thirteenth to the early fifteenth century exposes the importance attached to the ritualization of court activity, that is, attempts at suggesting a broader structure for people's movements and actions during court sessions. As in the cases of Utrecht and York, the explanation for ritualization is twofold. The setting of the court as a validating context for specific social actions could make it an attractive option for people seeking an institutionally backed resolution for disputes. The *Parlement* formed one avenue – though, again, not the only one – that people could take in pursuing their interests in a dispute, thereby seeking resolution validated in relation to this specific authority. At the same time, the royal court,

88 For more on the practice of Joyous Entries, see H. Soly, "Plechtige intochten in de steden van de Zuidelijke Nederlanden tijden de overgang van Middeleeuwen naar Nieuwe Tijd: Communicatie, propaganda, spektakel", *Tijdschrift voor Geschiedenis* 97 (1984); Élodie Lecuppre-Desjardin, *La ville des cérémonies: Essai sur la communication politique dans les anciens Pays-Bas bourguignons* (Turnhout: Brepols, 2004); Kim Overlaet, "The 'Joyous Entry' of Archduke Maximilian into Antwerp (13 January 1478): An Analysis of a 'Most Elegant and Dignified' Dialogue", *Journal of Medieval History* 44, no. 2 (2018). On the role of personal presence in royal legitimization strategies in late medieval France, see Léonard Dauphant, "'Si grant charté a Paris [...] par defaulté du roy': Governmental Practice and the Customary Geography of the Absence and Presence of the King in France (1364–1525)", in *Absentee Authority across Medieval Europe*, eds. Frédérique Lachaud and Michael Penman (Woodbridge: The Boydell Press, 2017).

as a potentially validating authority, also had interests in ritualizing the activities taking place in the *Palais* and beyond. The actions themselves functioned as a medium through which the *Parlement* posed specific claims on the socio-political order of the kingdom. By ordering the session days per bailiwick and requiring the presence or absence of specific judicial stakeholders in the kingdom (barons, prelates, seneschals, bailiffs) an ideal legal order and its connected power relations were physically performed. Physical presence was therefore particularly relevant, setting limits to the allowed absenteeism of those involved in court cases and attempts to involve and manage a witnessing public. The same role of court action as a medium in and of itself can furthermore be seen in the way in which the *Parlement* tried to transport its activities to other places in the kingdom in the form of the *Grands Jours*. By explicitly modelling the sessions of these events on the Parisian sessions, the court used references to an idealized system of practices to press its claims on the political and jurisdictional integration of different parts of the French kingdom. Again the ritualized performance of justice before a local audience took centre stage in the communicative activity of the *Parlement*.

Conclusion: The language of legal acts

Continuing the argument from Chapter 2, it has been the contention of this chapter that socio-legal messaging of and before late medieval law courts was not limited to the voluminous texts that these institutions have left behind. While historians' views of these courts are strongly based on such written remains, for contemporaries the things that took place in and around the courtroom were at least as prominent an aspect of the communicative practices that linked these bodies to the societies in which they participated, providing a language of their own. Through the ritualization of such activities, that is, their insinuation into broader networks of linked practices, this language of acts obtained a specific grammar. The alleged connection between what happened in the here and now and what had taken or would take place in other contexts gave these acts a range of possible denotations. In all three cases considered here, legal actors related their activity more or less explicitly to broader constellations of practices and ideas, from acts of penitence to politico-legal structures, thereby suggesting a particular relevance for what they were doing and legitimizing their own role in doing so. The Utrecht forgiveness rituals saw the linking of a local penal procedure to broader penitential practices, both within and beyond a legal setting. In York the reading of the Court's sentences referenced the legal and non-legal activities of the religious community, encompassing aspects as diverse as the saying of mass and the idealized practice of canon law. For Paris, finally, we have seen similar references to kingdom-wide structures of legal activity, incorporating the ideal of this judicio-political construct in the organization of daily practice in Paris and beyond. Despite major differences of character and scale between these three courts, one of the most common occasions when contemporaries will have met either of them was during such individual ritualized events. What is more, the similarity of some of the ritual languages encountered in these courts, such as the penitence-based punishments seen both in Utrecht and York, suggests that concrete grammars of acts could actually be shared among courts with a very different character.

The ritualization of legal practices was never a matter for the court alone. In each of the three cases considered here, other legal actors and audiences played a role in shaping these events. The attempt by the Council of Utrecht to stake its claim to justicial authority in occasions echoing spiritual penitence depended on the willingness of culprits to follow the script as envisioned for them. In the same way, the Consistory Court's sentence readings ultimately relied on people bringing their disputes to this particular court and following the process to its conclusion, rather than seeking other or extra-curial solutions. And the stress put by the *Parlement* on the personal presence of litigants in the courtroom also signals the latter's role in validating the court's audience sessions. People's own interests in engaging in particular instances of judicial ritualization, therefore, had an impact on the orchestration of these events. Whereas these examples mainly show that the category of ritual actors can be interpreted more broadly than just the courts' officials, extending this consideration to audiences brings a whole different kind of participation into view. Although the public witnessing the performance of legal acts did not always have an explicit role in their progression, and is therefore often not explicitly distinguished in the records, their influence on such occasions was nevertheless substantial. As aspects of communicative practice, the courts' ritualized activities relied both on their senders and receivers in order to become a felicitous speech act. Thus, for the legal actors to successfully transmit the desired semantic implications of their legal performance, they depended on their audiences' ability to interpret it 'correctly'. Because, in order to achieve this effect, they took into account the horizon – to use the Bourdieuan term – of their public, seeking a recognizable and clearly understandable act language, the latter

had a no less significant effect on the form and suggested content of these legal performances than the actors themselves did.

All this has consequences for our understanding of the role of legal ritual in manifesting the court and its model of justice in the socio-judicial landscape of the late Middle Ages. In the interpretations of legal ritual as encountered at the beginning of this chapter the emphasis generally lies on their public aspect, either as enacted confirmations of negotiated resolutions in disputes (Althoff) or as affirmations or challenges of a broadly recognized myth of social order (Gauvard and Jacob). Such rituals are thus in the first place concerned with a public performance of social norms and values. However, these views leave little room for the agency of individual ritual actors, assuming occasions of ritual activity to be uncomplicated public adoptions of a pre-existing grammar of acts. Based on the discussion in this chapter of three markedly different courts in light of the anthropological concept of ritualization, this reading seems limiting. Although these ritual occasions were certainly public performances concerned with social norms and values, they were shaped by a multiplicity of ritual actors, audiences and circumstances. These legal rituals were the occasions par excellence where individual socio-legal strategies encountered the public discussion of norms. One the one hand, legal ritualization could validate an individual's actions by suggesting a link with other meaningful activities. Thus, a culprit in Utrecht could publicly perform his repentance by echoing broader penitential practices, while a litigant in York could try to legitimate his position in a dispute by following a procedural sequence of actions in court. But at the same time the performance of said actions also contributed to scripting proper socio-legal activity itself, that is, it helped suggesting what were legitimate practices of achieving justice and – consequently – what were not. It was in the ritualization of activity itself that the court took shape, not only as physical entity in the urban landscape (see Chapter 2), but also as a specific sequence of actions to achieve justice. This ritualization, this inscription of the court in the socio-judicial landscape, depended on innumerable actors, be they court officials, litigants, culprits or audiences, collectively negotiating a specific grammar of acts.

4. Legal text and social context

Abstract
Records of court practice constitute some of the richest and most numerous written sources for the later Middle Ages, echoing the broader documentary revolution of this period. Using these documents as historical sources, however, one needs to take into account their role as text-objects produced and used within the multimedial communicative context of late medieval courts. By prescribing, describing or performing legal practice, these documents translated a, mainly oral, social world into textualized legal discourse. Such discourses, and the documents containing them, were subsequently communicated back to various audiences, in an attempt to reinforce specific scripts of justice as envisioned by the court. Rather than unproblematic reflections of social practices, court records are the physical remains of a socio-legal negotiation over their interpretation.

Keywords: medieval law courts, medieval court records, textuality, orality, legal discourse

> He who wants to get to know the peasant of ancient and very ancient regimes lacks no grand syntheses – regional, national, occidental. [...] What is wanting, however, is the direct gaze: the testimony, without an intermediary, that the peasant provides about himself. [...] Fortunately for us, yet unfortunately for them, a man, during the fourteenth-century demographic growth, has given speech to a group of villagers, and even to a whole village for that matter.[1]

With these words Emmanuel Le Roy Ladurie opened what has become one of the most widely acclaimed studies in social history in our time. He presented what was and still is a very familiar frustration for many historians: the lack

1 Translated from Le Roy Ladurie, *Montaillou*, 9.

Camphuijsen, F., *Scripting Justice in Late Medieval Europe: Legal Practice and Communication in the Law Courts of Paris, York and Utrecht.* Taylor & Francis Group, 2022
DOI 10.5117/9789463723473_CH04

of direct and reliable voices from many of the individuals from the past societies that interest us so much. For, prior to the modern era, the majority of texts were produced by, for and about a small social elite, leading to a strong evidential bias. For Le Roy Ladurie a solution to this problem came in the form of the records of the inquisitorial court of Jacques Fournier, the bishop of Pamiers, who organized a vigorous persecution of heresy in his diocese at the beginning of the fourteenth century. Basing himself on the extensive confessions and witness testimonies recorded by this court, Le Roy Ladurie wrote his famous microhistory of the small French village of Montaillou.

Montaillou is one of the most famous examples of the potential value of late medieval court records for those interested in past societies.[2] These records, so Le Roy Ladurie argues, bring us as close as one can get to the daily lives of the non-literate majorities of premodernity. Both their social practices and mentalities shine through in the answers they provided the court with. Yet, at the same time, the passage cited above also signals a fundamental problem with too strong a reliance on these types of records. As Le Roy Ladurie's critics have long asked, do such popular voices really come to us 'without an intermediary'? It was the court that drew up these documents, based on predetermined sets of leading questions posed to the witnesses that appeared before it, many of whom were under physical, emotional and financial duress. Moreover, these Latin records were copies of translations and, more importantly, textual reinterpretations of the actual words spoken by contemporaries. Thus, the texts themselves already form a fundamental intermediary between the experiences of the medieval peasant and their interpretation by the modern historian.[3] Although the three case studies considered here concern institutions that differed significantly from Fournier's inquisitorial court, being more permanently established and having less of an ad hoc character, the matter of textual intermediacy is nevertheless crucial to take into account. This chapter will accordingly examine the role of the textual record, both for historians and for the contemporaries who produced and used them.

2 For more work in the microhistorical vein, see the introduction to this book.

3 For an extensive review of *Montaillou* addressing such issues, see Leonard E. Boyle, "Montaillou Revisited: *Mentalité* and Methodology", in *Pathways to Medieval Peasants*, ed. J.A. Raftis (Toronto: Pontifical Institute of Medieval Studies, 1981). Later work on inquisitorial records, which takes account of and voices such critiques, is James Given, "The Inquisitors of Languedoc and the Medieval Technology of Power", *American Historical Review* 94, no. 2 (1989), esp. 347–351; Pegg, *Corruption*, esp. 45–62; Arnold, *Inquisition*, esp. 1–15.

Contrary to the last two chapters, where I have tried to reach beyond the records in reconstructing the non-textual aspects of the communication processes involving three courts, in what follows the texts themselves take centre stage. Such a focus on texts inevitably brings with it a series of methodological questions. As the main source used by historians to understand the comings and goings at court, these documents have had a particularly dominant influence on what we know about late medieval law courts and the people with whom they interacted. This strong dependency on a particular type of lens to look at the past means that we cannot restrict our analysis to the things we observe through it, but also involves a consideration of the lens itself. Thus, rather than regarding texts only as sources to be used in reconstructing a social 'reality' beyond them, this chapter will approach them as objects produced and used in the context of the multimedial communication processes involving the court. By asking how and why these texts came to play the role they did in courts' daily practice, I will connect the methodological questions as to their value as sources for historians with a consideration of their implication in and influence on the legal process as propagated by late medieval law courts.

The textual practices of the three courts did not stand on their own, but formed part of a major growth in the importance of texts in European societies during the medieval period. As such, the chapter will begin by relating the development of the courts' documentary practices to broader processes of document use. Subsequently, attention will shift to the place of the records within the court's legal practice. These documents related in a number of ways to the extra-textual practices for which they form our main source, be it by prescribing, describing or even performing specific acts. Treating this link between legal texts and acts shows the fundamental role of the former in the development of law courts as particular forms of socio-legal practice. As seen above, one of the main topics in recent scholarship on court records is the way in which they relate to the social activities and mentalities of the people represented in them. In the last part of this chapter I will therefore trace this relationship in two directions. In considering translation and other ways in which non-textual activities and ideas were reshaped by their transition to a text, the role of documents in legally framing the world outside the courtroom comes to the fore. By subsequently focusing on the courts' various attempts at publishing the physical texts as well as their contents, this chapter will also trace the process the other way round, showing how the strategies of validating the court and its text-based legal process went hand in hand.

Textualization

Before considering the role of texts in late medieval law courts, it is necessary on the one hand to define what we mean when speaking of texts, and on the other to indicate why the particular period under study is so relevant from the perspective of these texts. In linguistic theory the term 'text' has been interpreted variously, from a focus on the written text as opposed to oral discourse, to the text as a broader catch-all term for all cultural messages.[4] In his work on the semiology of textualization, Roy Harris, one of the proponents of the school of integrationist linguistics, argues for understanding texts primarily as combinations between linguistic utterances and material artefacts. These two aspects of the text – language and physical matter – have a different relation towards one another in every individual situation. If the exact same statement is written down in a book or spray-painted on a wall, its interpretation and valuation by various audiences will differ markedly. The one may consider the graffiti-text an illegitimate form of expression, while for the other this specific appearance makes it into a statement of resistance against the powers that be, regardless of its precise contents. The integration of language and matter is thus fundamental for the existence and implications of a text, as it is the relationship between the two that shapes the way in which it is used and interpreted in communicative practice. In such an understanding of texts, the process of textualization means the combination of two distinctive practices, that is, the uttering of verbal signifiers and the production of material objects, creating a particularly physicalized form of communication with its own communicative dynamic.[5]

In considering late medieval law courts, Harris' linguistic-materialist interpretation of texts sensitizes us to the communicative significance of one of the major changes in legal practice. For in tandem with the spatial, institutional and practical changes described in the previous chapters, the main development that characterizes the coming into being of law courts in the late medieval period is the survival of ever larger numbers of these 'language-matter entities' that we tend to call documents. Even when taking into account the eventualities of survival, it is hard to deny that all the courts treated here began to produce, use and keep a growing number of textual records originating from daily legal practice. Some numbers from these courts

4 For a general overview of linguistic theories and definitions of texts, see P. Colilli, "Texts: Semiotic Theory", in *Encyclopedia of Language & Linguistics*, 2nd ed., vol. 12, ed. Keith Brown (Oxford: Elsevier, 2006).

5 Harris, "Semiology".

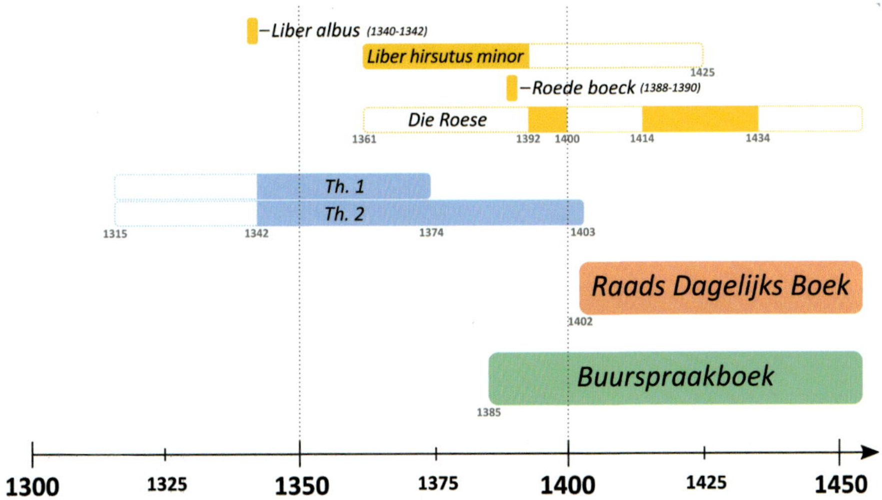

Timeline 1: Council registers and books of bylaws (yellow) in Utrecht between 1300 and 1450. Dotted lines indicate periods for which entries were included retroactively in a particular corpus (*Die Roese* and *Th.1*/*Th.2*) or which saw only very occasional additions to a corpus (*Liber hirsutus minor*).

offer an indication of the scale of these developments. When studying the penal practice of the Council of Utrecht, one register of banishments, together with occasional entries in the city's books of bylaws, forms the main source for most of the fourteenth century, averaging about two folia per annum.[6] From the late fourteenth century, when the *Buurspraakboek* comes into use, the number of written folia rises drastically to an average of 40 per year. And this increases even further when adding the material in the volumes of the *Raads dagelijks boek* which survive from the early fifteenth century onwards (Timeline 1).[7] The York cause papers show a very similar trajectory. Focusing only on the 254 dossiers surviving from the fourteenth century, we see a marked rise in their numbers. The vast majority (75%) of the dossiers comes from the second half of that century, while the last decade alone equals nearly one-third of the available material.[8] For the *Parlement* the rise in documented material is even more striking. For the late thirteenth and the first few years of the fourteenth centuries only the four well-known *Olim*

6 This concerns the *Th.1* and *Th.2* registers, consisting of two copies of the same register, that can be found at HUA 701-1.226 and 227, respectively.

7 *Buurspraakboek*: HUA 701-1.16; *Raads dagelijks boek*: HUA 701-1.13. See Chapter 1 for an overview of the Council's available sources.

8 The fourteenth-century cause papers can be found as the BIA CP.E series. See Chapter 1 for an overview of the sources surviving for the Consistory Court. See Appendix 2.1 for details on the number of surviving cause papers per decade.

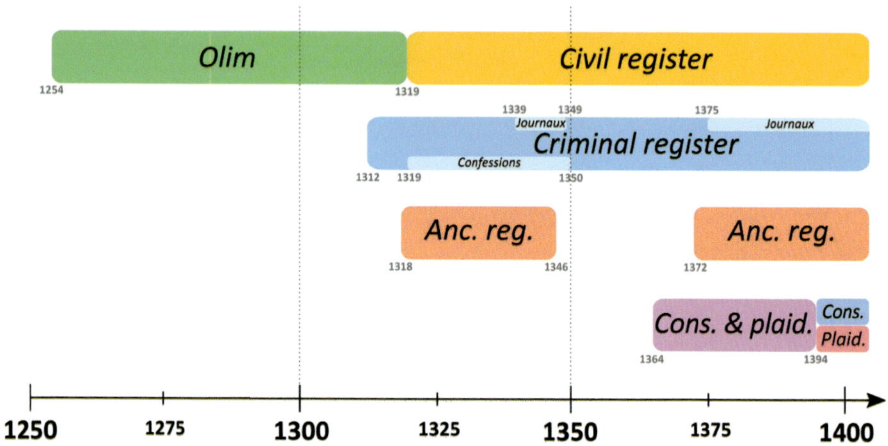

Timeline 2: Textual output of the Parisian *Parlement* between 1250 and 1400, including the *Olim*, the civil and criminal registers, the *anciens registres du greffe* (*Anc. reg.*), and the counsel and pleading register (separate from 1394 onwards).

registers have survived, amounting to about 900 folia for a period of some 65 years. Although the entries in the *Olim* begin in 1254, almost two-thirds of the material in these registers concerns the 20 years between 1298 and 1318, indicating a marked increase in documentation towards the end.[9] Beginning in 1312 a second register, the Criminal register, splits off from the *Olim*. For the first 40 years of its existence this criminal register alone covers over a thousand folia. To this is added a staggering 3400 folia from the Civil register, which formed the direct continuation of the *Olim* registers from 1318 onwards. Thus, whereas the last half of the thirteenth century gives us a yearly average of some six folia, for the first half of the fourteenth this has increased over fifteenfold to a hundred folia per annum. And after 1350 the numbers only rise further, as both the criminal and civil registers continued, while several new ones, like the counsel and pleading registers, were added to the procedural output (Timeline 2).[10] These staggering numbers form the most direct material evidence of the changes taking place in the courts under scrutiny.

Whereas the material reality of the increasing numbers of textual records from these courts seems thus hard to deny, the interpretation of this development, especially as related to broader processes in late medieval society, is

9 The *Olim* registers can be found at AN X^{1A}1–4.

10 The Civil register is kept in the AN X^{1A} series from X^{1A}5 onwards, while the Criminal register forms the AN X^{2A} series. See Chapter 1 for an overview of the surviving records of the late medieval *Parlement*.

open for discussion. Michael Clanchy connects the increasing use of texts in post-Conquest England to two interrelated processes, bureaucratization and the growth of what he calls a 'literate mentality'. He sees a shift from the predominant use of oral means of communication to a reliance on the written word in many areas of daily life. Spearheading this development was the royal bureaucracy, where written documents began to play an increasingly prominent role from the twelfth century onwards. From the royal court, Clanchy argues, this 'pragmatic literacy' trickled down along the administrative ladder of lower courts and authorities, until increasingly large numbers of people began to use and – more importantly – trust written documents in their daily lives.[11] Other explanations have been given for the increasing use of writing in different contexts. Jeroen Benders, in his comparison between several late medieval towns in the north-eastern Low Countries, suggests a link between increasing institutional textualization – or documentalization, as he calls it – and the greater administrative and judicial liberty that these towns managed to secure from the thirteenth century onwards.[12] In a different context, namely, late medieval Languedoc, James Given links the increase of written material in inquisitorial courts to their strategies of power. Together with courts' use of imprisonment and inquisitorial procedure, the production, archiving and referencing of documents formed an instrument both of knowledge and coercion, as people's words could now effectively be used against them.[13]

Such explanations risk some common pitfalls. Although not limiting their discussion exclusively to the creation of documents, this coming into being of the texts certainly receives most attention. It is above all the explanation of the growth of the production of documentary material, rather than their consumption, that forms the thread of these arguments. However, in explaining the particular importance of the proliferation of texts in the late medieval period an exclusive focus on the production side of documentary culture carries the risk of institutional bias. When agency

11 Clanchy, *Memory*. The exact causal relationship Clanchy sees between bureaucratization and the increase of texts is difficult to assess based on his work, as he sometimes suggests that the increase in documents caused bureaucratization (p. 329), while elsewhere bureaucratization is considered the main driving force behind the increase in documentation (pp. 19 and 334).

12 J.F. Benders, *Bestuursstructuur en schriftcultuur: Een analyse van de bestuurlijke verschriftelijking in Deventer tot het eind van de 15e eeuw* (Kampen: IJsselacademie, 2004); idem, "Urban Administrative Literacy in the Northeastern Low Countries: A Comparison of Groningen, Kampen, Deventer, and Zutphen, Twelfth–Fifteenth Centuries", in *Writing and the Administration of Medieval Towns*, eds. Marco Mostert and Anna Adamska (Turnhout: Brepols, 2014), 102–103.

13 Given, "Inquisitors".

is placed predominantly with the institutions producing the texts, be it a royal bureaucracy, urban authorities, inquisitorial courts or others, the use of written documents becomes something implemented gradually but steadily from the top downwards. However, following the definition of texts as suggested by Harris – that is, texts as language-objects playing a specific part in more general communicative behaviour – it becomes necessary to reassess our interpretation of them. The effective use of texts relied on their consumers' proficiency to understand and, certainly in the case of legal texts, their willingness to consider as valid these specific material-linguistic objects next to, and sometimes even in place of other forms of communication. The question is therefore not just why the courts began to produce ever larger amounts of documents, but also how and why the participants in the socio-legal communication process began to incorporate this particular physicalized form of communication as legally valid utterance. In this, texts formed part of the courts' broader claims to a prominent – if not dominant – role in society's socio-legal practice. However, as in earlier chapters, it will become clear that in order to press such claims, the courts depended on many groups and individuals from the societies with which they engaged. But before considering the role of these social actors, we will first discuss the character of the texts produced within the court, to understand what they were and what they – or at least the courts through them – tried to do.

Texts in court practice

The term 'court record' as employed so far suggests a fairly uniform type of source. However, examining the surviving documents of legal practice for the respective courts, it is above all their great variety – in form and content – that strikes one.[14] Differences abound between a register of public announcements, like the Council's *Buurspraakboek*, those with legal acts, such as the civil and criminal registers of the *Parlement*, and the Consistory Court's dossiers of procedural documents. Yet all of them were produced and used in the context of these courts' daily practice. In order to assess these documents' role in the legal process, in what follows I will consider their 'positioning' as texts, that is to say, how their authors related them vis-à-vis the many non-textual aspects of court activity.

Such text-act relations are of three kinds: descriptive, prescriptive and performative. A descriptive relation places the text after the act, recording something that – according to the text – has already taken place. Thus, when

14 Cf. Camphuijsen and Page, "Introduction", 3–6.

the clerk of York's Consistory Court noted down the deposition of Margaret Stainford in a matrimonial case in 1337, he claimed to describe the words that had been spoken by Margaret earlier during her interrogation.[15] Likewise, when, in the same year, the Council of Utrecht mentioned the banishment of Reynaer, a tailor of undergarments, in its register, it presented the act of exiling Reynaer as something which had already happened.[16] Prescriptive texts take the exact opposite position, preceding the extra-textual acts, and often instigating people to perform or abstain from those activities. Typical examples are the many regulations interspersed within the Utrecht Council's registers, for example, forbidding people to let their pigs roam the streets unsupervised.[17] But the same is true of some of the royal letters transcribed by the *Parlement* in its criminal and civil registers, such as one from 1334 charging the examiner of the *Châtelet* to make an inquiry and several arrests in the case of the death of Raoul Mauchevalier.[18] The third and final relation considered here pertains to my earlier discussion of Austinian performativity.[19] Some texts, rather than positioning themselves as preceding or following from an extra-textual act, claim to be that act. They claim to actually change something in the world, thereby effectively denying any discrepancy between text and act. This relation can most clearly be seen in the written sentences found for York in particular. Thus, a York sentence from a 1335 appeal case between John son of John, from North Dalton, and Emma, daughter of John Driffield, pronounces that, because the court has found the appeal unjust, it confirms the original verdict 'sententiously and definitively in writing this' (*sententialiter et definitive in hiis scriptis*).[20] In such cases the court presented the textual verdict through its wording and form as the defining act, making its decision a reality with real-life consequences. In what follows, I will analyse the surviving texts of the three courts from this perspective of their positioning vis-à-vis extra-textual activity. As the analysis will show, these positionings hardly ever follow the strict division as suggested above. Nevertheless, identifying such text-act relations is not only helpful to understand which role courts had in mind for these linguistic-material objects, but also reminds us of the different ways of reading that each of these texts requires from historians.

15 BIA CP.E.37.

16 HUA 701-1.227: *Th.2* register, fol. 4v.

17 Many pig-related regulations can be found in the Council's *Buurspraakboek* from the oldest surviving volume onwards. For the measures in the oldest surviving volume, see HUA 701-1.16: *Buurspraakboek* 1385–1391, fol. 12v, 13v, 27r, 28r, 39v, 72r, 87r, 115r, 138v, 190v. Cf. Camphuijsen and Coomans, "Varkens".

18 AN $X^{2A}3$, fol. 1v.

19 See the introduction to this book.

20 BIA CP.E.28.

Over its long history the *Parlement* of Paris has left us an immense corpus of texts. This mass of documents regularly underwent changes, where new series of documents were begun and old ones changed form or were discontinued (Timeline 2). Its character and internal structure were often complex, reflecting changes in institutional practice and in the logic of recording, as well as occasional adaptations to the unpredictability of daily legal practice. For the earliest documents of legal practice, the series of civil and criminal registers (X^{1A} and X^{2A}), the large majority of texts concerned legal acts, that is, textualized decisions taken by the court or the king. These texts were generally performative, purporting to change something in the world by themselves, rather than simply describing or prescribing court activity. Of the three main categories of texts in these series, *arrêts, jugés* and *lettres*, all three were to a certain extent concerned with such legal acts. Both *arrêts* and *jugés* (only encountered in the X^{1A} register) were transcriptions of the decisions taken by the *Parlement* in the cases coming before it. The *arrêts* were decisions – often only interlocutory – taken in cases that involved pleading sessions before the *Grande Chambre*. Thus, when in 1345 the *Parlement* pronounced an *arrêt* in a case concerning a violent attack in the jurisdiction of Isabelle de Blanot, lady of Uxelles, which will be treated in more detail in Chapter 5, this decision was part of a decade-long procedure involving extensive inquiries, arrests and subsequent *élargissements* of suspects, and numerous court sessions where the respective parties pleaded their case (Figure 4).[21] The *jugés*, while not radically different, originated in cases involving mainly textual procedure, like inquiries, which were therefore handled by the *Chambre des Enquêtes*. More importantly, the *jugés* generally had a final character, while *arrêts* could be either final judgements or interlocutory decisions in a continuing process. The *lettres* section of the registers, finally, saw more variety in the types of texts included, such as the prescriptive warrant of apprehension and inquiry in the case of the death of Raoul Mauchevalier seen above. However, the *lettres* also contained many interlocutory decisions in cases, formulated in the form of – often royal – letters.[22]

21 AN $X^{2A}5$, fol. 74r. No less than 29 procedural steps in this case are contained in the fourth and fifth X^{2A} register, spanning at least ten years of procedure: $X^{2A}4$, fol. 12r, 74r, 79r, 79v, 83r, 84v, 88r, 98r, 98v, 103r, 122r, 151r, 155r, and $X^{2A}5$, fol. 9v, 14v, 16v, 18r, 56r, 74r, 133v, 146v, 148r, 157r, 181r.

22 The complex character of the *arrêts, jugés* and *lettres* is evidenced by the variety of ways in which the literature has tried to make sense of them. See, for example, the various descriptions given by Alphonse Grün, "Notice sur les archives du Parlement de Paris", in *Actes du Parlement de Paris: Première série: De l'an 1254 à l'an 1328*, vol. 1, ed. Edgar Boutaric (Paris: Henri Plon, 1863), CXXXI–CXXXIX; Monique Langlois, "Parlement de Paris", 81–84; and Hildesheimer and Morgat-Bonnet, *État méthodique*, 50–52. The *arrêts, jugés* and *lettres* can be found together both

Figure 4: *Arrêts* in the Criminal register from 1345 (X^{2A}5, fol.74r), including an *arrêt* in the case of Isabelle de Blanot (see Appendix 3.2).

in the series of civil registers (AN X^{1A}5–156) and criminal registers (X^{2A}1–900, 906), although the latter does not make the distinction between *arrêts* and *jugés*. The *Olim* (X^{1A}1–4) also does not distinguish as clearly between *arrêts* and *jugés*, but its main division between registers of *enquêtes* and registers of *arrêts* is the precursor of this later distinction. See Grün, "Notice", CXXXI–CXXXII.

Given the dominance of textualized acts in these documents, a distinction that deserves further elaboration is that between minutes and registers.[23] In the procedure as followed by the *Parlement* a textual act would first be written down in the form of a free-standing original, kept by the court and possibly also copied for the parties involved. These originals would then be collectively inscribed into the *Parlement*'s registers. Whereas the minutes stood close to – and even formed a fundamental part of – the legal activity performed in court, the form in which we encounter these acts in the registers could be transcribed and possibly even edited long after the fact. Although, for the fourteenth century at least, royal ordinances seem to have tried to limit the time lapse to no more than a few days, there could be a significant delay between the moment the minute was written down and the moment of its inscription in the registers.[24] Grün has furthermore argued that, at least in the case of the *arrêts*, it is unlikely that all decisions noted down in a minute also found their way to the registers, implying that a certain selection took place.[25] The latter is difficult to substantiate, as almost no minutes have survived from before the sixteenth century.[26] But it is nevertheless important to take the possibility of selection into account, as it reminds us that the registers available for this period are basically an edited intermediary between us and the written legal acts themselves. The main source material available for the early *Parlement* can thus be characterized as texts referencing other texts, which have been used in – and often form the conclusion of – a legal process. Although these registers place us at some distance from the activity going on in the courtroom, they do offer evidence of another crucial practice of the court, namely, archiving. By selecting specific texts to be transcribed in a register, the court made a conscious choice to increase their likelihood of survival, thus reflecting its ideas on the role of different kinds of texts in the legal process.

23 Grün, "Notice", XII–XVIII, considers the distinction between minutes and registers inconvenient as it is based solely on the material aspects of the texts. However, as the focus of this chapter is exactly on these material aspects, the distinction – and what it tells us about the production of the *Parlement*'s documents – becomes particularly relevant.
24 Ibid., XII–XVIII, CXXXIV; Langlois, "Parlement de Paris", 84; Hildesheimer and Morgat-Bonnet, *État méthodique*, 23.
25 Grün, "Notice", CXXXIV, CXXXVIII. This selective character is even stronger for the four *Olim* registers, which consisted of a – predominantly later – selection and edition of parliamentary acts, assembled by a succession of royal clerks. See ibid., LXVI–LXXXV.
26 A relevant exception is the series of *accords*, that is, settlements concluded between parties before the *Parlement*, which have only survived in the form of minutes from 1320 onwards. See AN X^{1C}1A–265.

Despite the dominance of performative text-act positions in the series of *arrêts, jugés* and *lettres*, the documents produced and used in the *Parlement* were certainly not limited to these legal acts. Various other types of texts have survived as part of or separate from the X^{1A} and X^{2A} series, and their share significantly increases over time. For the late thirteenth and early fourteenth centuries, entries of different kinds were regularly intermingled in between the textualized acts in the registers. The *Olim*, for example, occasionally contains entries that purport to prescribe or describe court activities, including inventories of all kinds of – now lost – records of legal practice, lists of documents treated in court and transcripts of royal ordinances.[27] The later continuations of the *Olim*, both the X^{1A} and X^{2A} registers, could contain a similar intertwining of text positions, sometimes incidentally, sometimes more structurally. Some particularly clear examples are provided by the fourth volume of the criminal register ($X^{2A}4$), spanning the years 1339–1344. In this register, the court begins to include – for the first time in the X^{2A} series – a record of its proceedings in criminal cases, variously called *journaux* and *proces-verbaux des séances* in the literature. Although this practice disappears after a few years, later in the same century it crops up again in the X^{2A} registers, this time permanently.[28] Furthermore, at the end of this same volume we find an unusual addition spanning over 60 folia. It concerns a series of records containing the confessions and judgements of a number of Parisian prisoners between 1319 and 1350, together with occasional witness statements and the report of enquiries concerning these cases.[29] The X^{1A} and X^{2A} registers thus contain numerous texts that place themselves in a descriptive relation to the activity of the court, presenting both one-off and – eventually – more regular deviations from the general pattern of transcribed legal acts.

In the $X^{2A}4$ register such alternative entries are still the exception, but in others they become the rule. An early example are the registers often called *anciens registres du greffe* in the literature, surviving from 1319 onwards.[30]

27 Such royal ordinances would in a later period be transcribed in a specific register of their own, kept as AN X^{1A}8602–8843. See Françoise Hildesheimer, "Les deux premiers registres des 'ordonnances' ou la logique floue de l'enregistrement", *Histoire et archives* 12 (2002).

28 Langlois, "Parlement de Paris", 92–93. For an overview of the general contents of the X^{2A} registers, see the tables in ibid., 139–142; and in Brigitte Labat-Poussin, Monique Langlois and Yvonne Lanhers, eds., *Actes du Parlement de Paris: Parlement criminel, règne de Philippe VI de Valois: Inventaire analytique des registres X^{2A} 2 à 5* (Paris: Archives Nationales, 1987), 14. Both works omit the first of the X^{2A} registers for reasons of complexity, but see Claudine Bloch and Jean-Marie Carbasse, "Aux origines de la série criminelle du Parlement: Le registre $X^{2A}1$", *Histoire et archives* 12 (2002), for an extensive discussion of its history and structure.

29 Langlois and Lanhers, *Confessions*.

30 AN X^{1A}8844–8851bis.

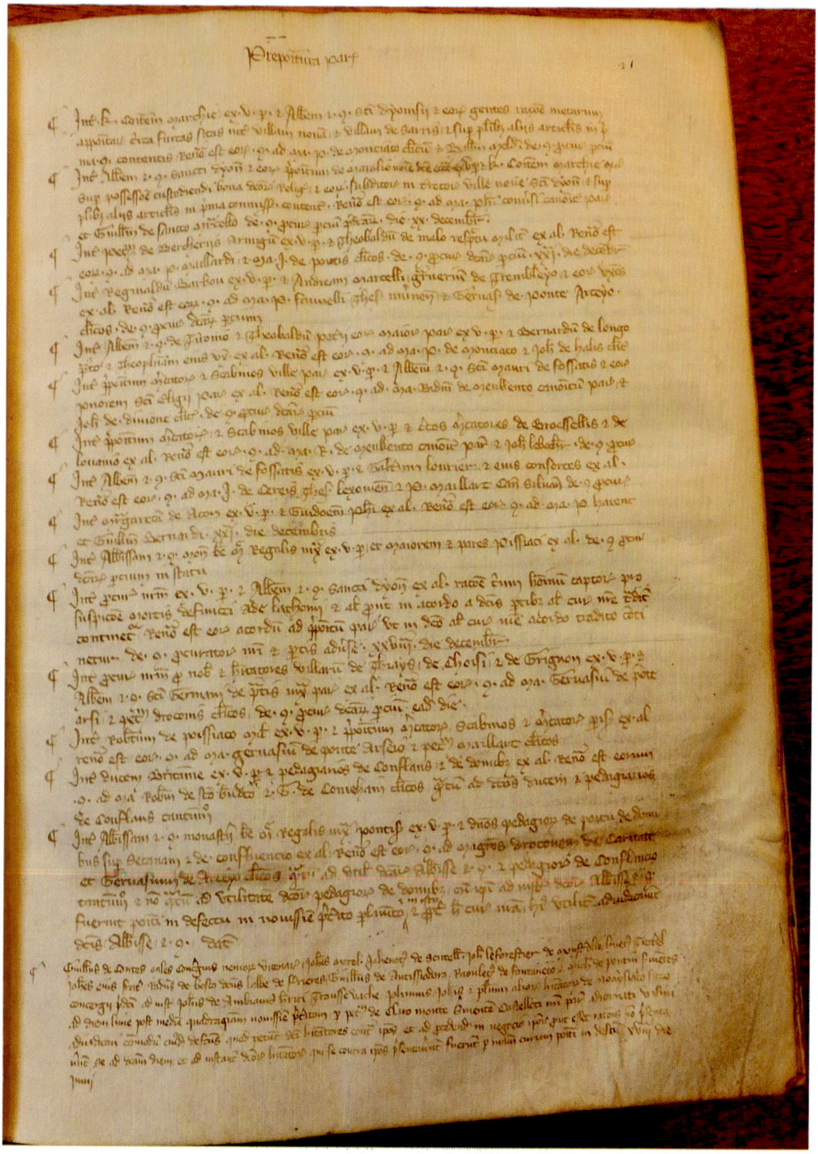

Figure 5: List of cases from the *prévôté* of Paris in the *Parlement's* registers of 1319 (AN X[1A]8844, fol.21r).

These registers contain long lists of cases coming before the *Parlement* on the days assigned to specific bailiwicks (Figure 5).[31] Such entries generally consist of short notices stating some basic information about the case, like

31 See Chapter 3 for the organization of court sessions according to bailiwicks.

the names of the parties, as well as the procedural steps undertaken. In the first five of these registers such lists are interspersed with transcriptions of legal acts in the form of letters, as seen for the *lettres* section of the X^{1A} and X^{2A} registers. When, after an intermission of several decades, this register continues in 1372, it no longer contains the transcribed letters and is limited to lists of court proceedings.[32] At around the same time, a new series of counsel and pleading registers appear. These written reports of the counsel (*conseil*) and pleading sessions (*plaidoiries*) of the *Parlement* form a substantial addition to the civil and criminal registers, spanning hundreds of volumes for the late fourteenth and fifteenth centuries alone, and indicating a major change in documented text-act relations.[33] Whereas earlier record-keeping had predominantly focused on textualizing legal acts, that is, producing texts that claimed to perform specific legal decisions, during the fourteenth century the *Parlement* also began to structurally describe the proceedings in court as they took place from day to day.

These developments in textual practice signalled a change in the way in which the *Parlement* regarded the role of texts within its broader communication process. As the occasional survival of prescriptive and descriptive texts in the earliest sources of the *Parlement* testifies, these forms of text-act relations were not beyond the imagination of the court. Yet, the predominance of legal acts in the series of *arrêts*, *jugés* and *lettres* shows a clear preference for the explicit textual performance of the legal process, echoing the non-textual performances seen in Chapter 3. After all, the court took the trouble of keeping these specific texts, by selectively copying them from minutes into registers.

These textualized judicial performances were of potential interest both to the court, supporting its own position as adjudicator and peacekeeper, and to the litigants, whose interests could profit from such an institutionally backed decision manifested in material form. During the fourteenth century the role of texts gradually expanded to include various descriptive text-act relations more structurally. The predominantly descriptive registers appearing in this century emphasized not so much the procedural end result, that is, the court's decision, but also tried to capture the legal process leading up to it. Rather than claiming to change something in the world by means of a written utterance, with these texts the *Parlement* instead fixed in writing

32 Langlois, "Parlement de Paris", 107.

33 Up until 1395, the pleading and counsel registers were combined in AN X^{1A}1469–1477. After that date two separate registers record the pleading and counsel sessions. See Hildesheimer and Morgat-Bonnet, *État méthodique*, 43–49.

Figure 6: Consistory Court sentence written on the backside of a piece of parchment containing depositions (BIA CP.E.18).

Figure 7: Consistory Court depositions on the frontside of the same piece of parchment. (BIA CP.E.18).

a specific interpretation of what had gone on there. As such, both types of texts, performative legal acts (*arrêts, jugés*) and descriptive reports (*journaux, conseils, plaidoiries*) contributed to – and arguably strengthened – the court's judicial scripting, the first by performing a direct intervention in, and the other by presenting an authoritative interpretation of the world beyond the text.

The documentary material from York contains some overlap with the types of texts surviving for the *Parlement* of Paris. Like the *Parlement*, the Consistory Court kept a variety of legal acts in written form, like sentences, (copies of) deeds and other documents that purported to perform an action, rather than describe or prescribe it. In contrast to the *Parlement*, however, the Consistory Court has left no evidence of a systematic transcription of these acts into special registers.[34] It does, however, happen regularly that we encounter such legal acts written down together with other aspects of litigation. The sentences, for example, appear in various forms in the surviving dossiers: on their own, but also written on the same piece of parchment as the depositions, the libel or other procedural pieces (Figures 6 and 7).[35] As these concern pieces stemming from different stages of a case, it is likely that in such instances the original acts were copied into a kind of case file at a later date, similar to the *Parlement*'s practice of transcribing legal acts into judicial registers. Some sentences have survived in the form of letters, sent to dignitaries elsewhere to notify them of the verdict decided on in a certain case. For example, in 1391 the sentence in a matrimonial case between William Tupman and Ellen del Grene is contained in a letter which states that the court has read and brought the final verdict in the case under scrutiny, and followed by a full transcript of said sentence.[36] A written original of the act supposedly formed the basis for such letters, although none survive for the dossiers concerned. In several other cases what has survived does seem to be the original written act or minute.[37] Contained on a single sheet of parchment or paper – often little more than a

34 The exception was formed by the occasional transcription of verdicts in the archiepiscopal registers. See, for example, Brown, *Thomas of Corbridge*, 103–104.

35 See BIA CP.E.3, CP.E.18, CP.E.87 and CP.E.105 for examples of sentences' combination with depositions. In CP.E.6 the sentence is found together with the libel. CP.E.170 has both the sentence from the first instance before the commissary general and of the appeal before the bishop's official written down on one folium. In CP.E.23 we even find all documents pertaining to the case copied onto one composite piece of parchment, including the libel, the depositions, the exceptions and the sentence.

36 BIA CP.E.178. A similar sentence contained in a letter can be found in BIA CP.E.158, treated later in this chapter.

37 For example, BIA CP.E.50, CP.E.71, CP.E.263, CP.E.268.

Figure 8: Consistory Court sentence on single piece of parchment, possibly a minute (BIA CP.E.263).

Figure 9: Draft of Consistory Court sentence (BIA CP.E.71).

small strip – such minutes very likely stood quite close to the extra-textual legal process, forming the actual documents used in this process, rather than their later transcription for purposes of preservation or long-distance communication (Figure 8).

Concerning their material characteristics the sentences also vary widely. A number of them seem to be drawn up as fair copies, as much attention has been paid to aspects of form, such as the quality of the parchment or the elaboration of its initials, as well as its legibility.[38] Other surviving pieces on the other hand give the impression of being drafts or working copies, either because the handwriting appears more sloppy, suggesting faster writing, because parts are crossed out or contain corrections, or because the quality of the parchment used appears to be inferior (Figure 9).[39] Such material characteristics cannot tell us conclusively which place each individual document occupied in the legal process, if only because characteristics suggesting either a draft or fair copy often overlap (Figure 10).[40] However, these varieties do point to the wide range of different forms in which the court's legal acts could exist, hinting at a process of coming into being from first draft to fair copy to a later transcription in letters or case files, similar to that from minutes to registers in the case of the *Parlement*. Furthermore, in the specific case of the sentences this process of coming into being is clearly evidenced in the 'read and brought' clauses they end with.[41] The main part of the sentence and the note of its reading regularly form a stylistic unity, making it likely that they have been written down together at the same moment.[42] In other cases, however, there exists a marked difference in style between the main part of the sentence and the 'read and brought'-clause, the latter being written in a quicker and more casual manner.[43] Such clauses give the impression of being later additions – as is the case with many of the corrections – and signal the way in which such written sentences came into being in multiple stages. A likely scenario in such cases would see a written sentence being drawn up, subsequently read in open court (see Chapter 3) and then complemented

38 See, for example, BIA CP.E.126, CP.E.116.

39 Examples: BIA CP.E.71 (various types of handwriting, corrections, parchment quality), CP.E.169 (corrections).

40 See, for example, BIA CP.E.116, whose sentences are written in a very clear and structured hand while at the same time containing various later additions and corrections, as well as being written on pieces of lesser-quality parchment.

41 See Chapter 3 for more on these clauses.

42 For example, BIA CP.E.126 and CP.E.159.

43 For example, BIA CP.E.71 and CP.E.84.

Figure 10: Fair copy of Consistory Court sentence (BIA CP.E.116).

with a note on the particularities of its reading and any further procedural steps undertaken by the parties. This draft sentence could then be copied in a variety of forms, be it as letters, collected case files or otherwise, as the stylistically unified versions seem to suggest. More clearly than in the case of the *Parlement*, the records from the Consistory Court show us how legal acts were textualized in subsequent stages involving multiple potential audiences. Thus, while the draft sentence may have formed the basis for the semi-public sentence readings in the cathedral's consistory place, its contents could subsequently find a different audience when they were copied into letters to provincial dignitaries or included in an appeal procedure.

Such processes, furthermore, need not be limited to texts professing a performative text-act relation, like the sentences. For, as hinted at before, the surviving documents from the Consistory Court concern more than just legal acts. The depositions in particular have formed a welcome source for many historians.[44] These represent the – often simplified – reports of witness interrogations, and are meant as descriptions of the witnesses' answers to specific predetermined questions for the sake of the court's decision-making process. They were the outcome of an extensive procedure, for which an extraordinary amount of textual material has survived. Forming one of the

44 See Appendix 2.1 for more details on the fourteenth-century depositions.

most important types of evidence in ecclesiastical court cases, the process of taking witness testimony was a detailed undertaking. First a series of articles would be submitted by the plaintiff, stating the arguments intended to be proven through the testimony.[45] Subsequently, the defence could submit interrogatories, that is, additional questions to be posed to the witnesses in an attempt to undermine the plaintiff's case. On the basis of these documents the court's examiners would formulate a set of questions to be posed to the witnesses in private. The results of these examinations were then reworked into written depositions and read aloud in open court.[46] Notwithstanding the descriptive nature of the depositions, their role in the legal process was far from purely post hoc. On the contrary, the process of gradual text construction as seen for the sentences and other legal acts, was also clearly present in the procedure of drawing up the depositions. Despite the specific ways in which the documents presented their relationship to extra-textual court activity – be it performative, descriptive or otherwise – the physical evidence from the cause papers shows us the fundamental back and forth between texts and acts in the production of these documents.

Some texts from the Consistory Court did have a more remote position from daily court practice. The Act Books, for example, being a fragmentarily surviving register of the courts' day-to-day activities, presented only a later summary of the legal actions that had taken place in court, fulfilling a role not unlike the *anciens registres du greffe* in Paris. These exceptions notwithstanding, what makes many of the surviving records of the Consistory Court particularly important, especially in comparison with those from the *Parlement*, is their material vicinity to the extra textual legal process. Contrary to the Parisian registers, which comprise by and large – supposedly edited – later copies of the documents originally used in court, the various types of texts surviving for the Consistory Court often physically took part in the legal process itself, just like the spaces used for court sessions (Chapter 2), the various human actors ritually manifesting court procedure and the audiences witnessing this ensemble (Chapter 3). Libels, positions and articles formed the basis for the examination of witnesses, while depositions and sentences were read out in court. These were concrete text-objects with recognized functions in court practice. Only later would they be turned to textual depositories by means of their collection into case-specific dossiers. Furthermore, the particularly varied character of the cause papers accentuates the difference between how a text professed to be related to

45 For examples of articles in the fourteenth-century cause papers, see BIA CP.E.26.

46 Helmholz, *Marriage Litigation*, 17–20.

extra-textual activity, and how it actually seems to have been used as part of this activity. Strengthening the impression gained from the case of the *Parlement*, these documents again show how texts became involved in courts' scripting of justice. They could do so through performing an extra-textual intervention, that is, by claiming to fundamentally change an extra-textual reality, or they could descriptively suggest a specific interpretation of acts in the world beyond them. Yet what the Consistory Court documents, through their proximity to actual court practice, show even clearer than the Parisian documents do, is the role of the material presence of texts on a daily basis in manifesting the court and its particular model of justice.

Some of the oldest surviving materials related to the administrative and judicial activities of the Council of Utrecht were its books of bylaws. Four in number and spanning a period of nearly a century and a half, these books were essentially expanding collections of regulations intended to govern a variety of sectors of Utrecht society: political, legal, economic and more.[47] Although the majority of texts contained in these books was of a prescriptive nature, their flexible and multifarious character makes it difficult to consider them as law codes in a strict sense. The first of these books, the *Liber albus*, usually considered as the most 'law code-like' of the four, already records a number of verdicts pronounced by the Council and the bishop against specific people.[48] The slightly later *Liber hirsutus minor* also contains various case-specific entries, often describing people who had formally sworn before the Council to keep the peace or to abstain from further transgressive behaviour. So it may happen that one encounters, in between general regulations concerning the recording and range of aldermen verdicts, the description of a peace made in 1367 between Baudekiin van Rutenberch and Ghisebrecht the baker.[49] Presumably, such descriptions of individual verdicts and legal acts were considered as judicial examples on the basis of which to make later decisions. Nevertheless, it added a fundamentally descriptive element to an otherwise prescriptive selection

47 The four books identified by Muller are the *Liber albus*, the *Liber hirsutus minor*, the *Roede Boeck* and the book called *Die Roese*; despite the catch-all term of 'books of bylaws' often used for these four documents, Muller clearly shows that each book had a fundamentally different character, springing from a perceived practical need to organize the expanding amount of Council decisions and bylaws at different points in time. See Muller, *Rechtsbronnen*, Introduction, 353–388.

48 Muller, *Rechtsbronnen*, vol. 1, 39–40, 57–63; also see ibid., Introduction, 358–359.

49 Muller, *Rechtsbronnen*, vol. 1, 87; also see ibid., Introduction, 365, n. 2, for other examples of verdicts copied into the *Liber hirsutus minor*.

of texts, and suggests a relatively high degree of interaction between these 'law codes' and the legal process for which they formed the basis.

Just as the books of bylaws could contain specific descriptions of individual cases, so the surviving court registers regularly comprised prescriptive measures. At about the same time as the codification of the Council's bylaws in the *Liber albus* appeared, a separate register of verdicts began to be kept, surviving in two copies, titled *Th.1* and *Th.2*. This register at first contained only verdicts in some of the more serious cases, which could lead to far-reaching punishments like corporal punishment, long-lasting banishment or the loss of citizenship, and notifications of the formal pledges (*willekeuren*) made by culprits not to repeat a specific transgression. Over time the selective character of this register decreased, as more moderate verdicts, such as shorter banishments, came to be included as well.[50] Thus, where on its first page the register states it is concerned only with banishments of a 'hundred years', as early as 1347 we see a group of women banished for only one to ten years.[51] In addition, the register also increasingly contained more general regulations decided upon by the Council, such as a 1359 interdiction to process animal corpses at certain places in the town.[52] This at first occasional, but later on more regular inclusion of regulations added a certain prescriptive element to an otherwise descriptive text (Figure 11). That there was a close relationship between this oldest register of punishments and the books of bylaws is furthermore evidenced by the fact that the *Liber hirsutus minor* is basically a collection of the most important regulations written down in the register between 1361 and 1392.[53]

The registers and books described above were predominantly written in the fourteenth century. By the beginning of the fifteenth century most of these series of documents were discontinued. That is to say, no new additions were made to them, while new series and books built upon or even completely replaced those of the fourteenth century (Timeline 1).[54] Most important in this respect were the *Raads dagelijks boek* and the *Buurspraakboek* (Figures 12 and 13). Both are first attested in the late fourteenth century, but only survive in consecutive volumes from the beginning of the

50 HUA 701-1.226 and 1.227. Also see Muller, *Rechtsbronnen*, Introduction, 363–364.

51 HUA 701-1.227: *Th.2* register, fol. 7r–v.

52 Ibid., fol. 15v.

53 Muller, *Rechtsbronnen*, Introduction, 364–365.

54 The only exception is the book of bylaws called *Die Roese*, which saw major additions in the early and late fifteenth century. See Muller, *Rechtsbronnen*, vol. 1, 181–394.

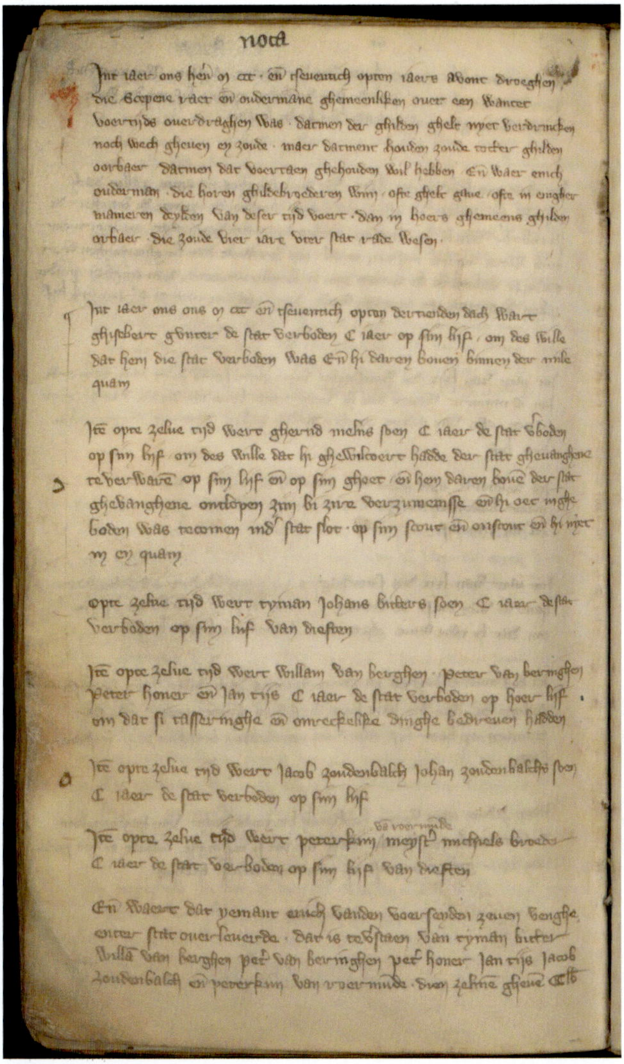

Figure 11: Page from the Council's *Th.2* register of 1370 (HUA 701-1.227, fol. 41v). This page contains mostly verdicts of banishment, but the first entry concerns a measure decided upon by the aldermen, Council and guild elders.

fifteenth century.[55] The relation between these two registers is particularly important to take into account. Not only do both sources appear in about the same period, but the overlap between the two suggests an internal

55 The earliest surviving register from the *Buurspraakboek* begins in 1385; in the case of the *Raads dagelijks boek* this is 1402, but the book of bylaws *Die Roese* contains evidence that a *Raads dagelijks boek* was in existence as early as 1369, see Muller, *Rechtsbronnen*, Introduction, 375–377.

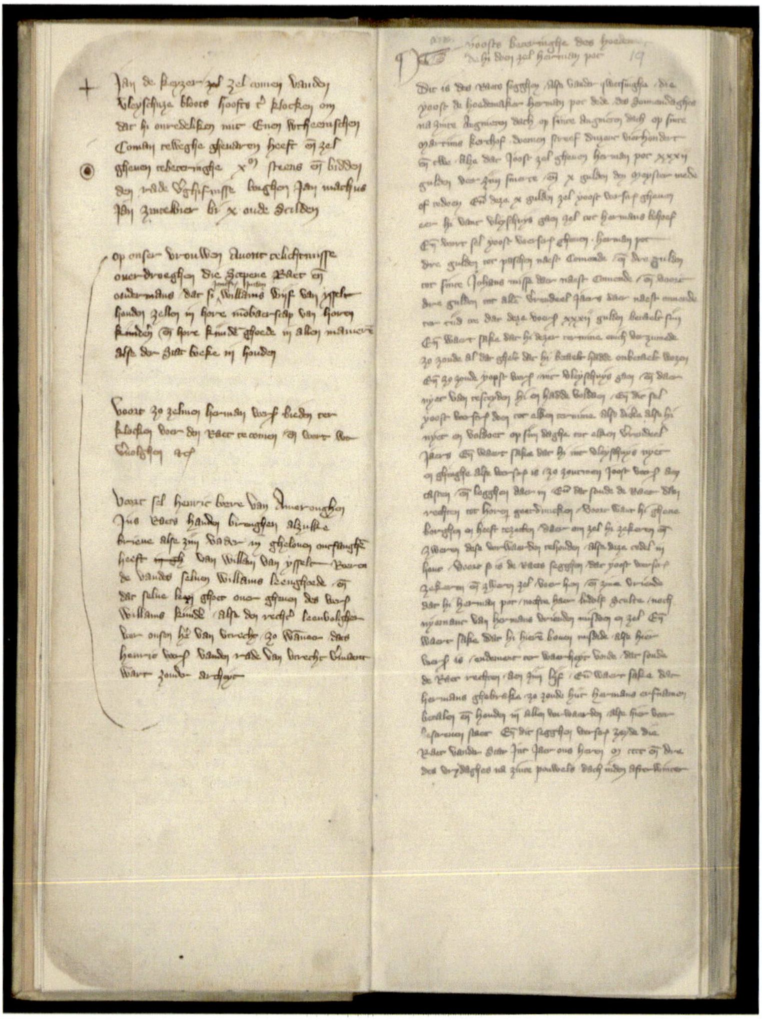

Figure 12: Pages from the *Raads dagelijks boek* of 1403 (HUA: 701-1.13: *RDB* 1402-1408, fol. 18v-19r). The case of Jan de Keyzer is the first entry on fol. 18v.

cohesion central to the smooth running of the Council. The *Raads dagelijks boek*, taking the role of daily register for the Council, describes a variety of actions performed by or before the court. This included regulations on various topics, *willekeuren* taken by people, names of guarantors, a variety of verdicts and more. Some entries in the *Raads dagelijks boek* also appear in the *Buurspraakboek*. This was the register in which the Council would write 'all *buurspraken* [...] which are pronounced at the clock'.[56] It was thus

56 HUA 701-1.16: *Buurspraakboek* 1396–1402, fol. 3r: *Dit is der stat buerspraec boec daermen al die buerspraken in scrijft diemen ter klocken uut kundicht* [...].

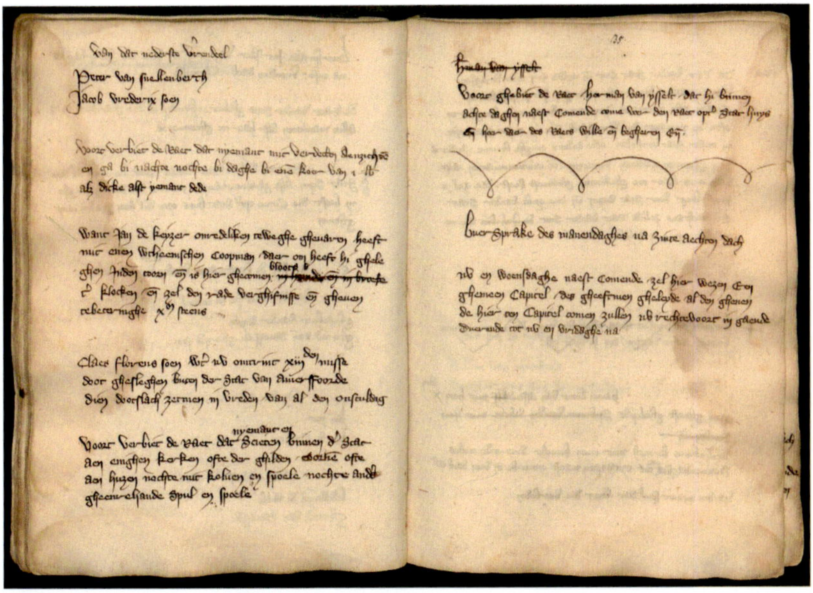

Figure 13: Pages from the *Buurspraakboek* of 1403 (HUA: 701-1.16: *BSB* 1402-1405, fol. 34v-35r). The case of Jan de Keyzer is the third entry on fol. 34v.

closely involved in the public *buurspraak* occasions at the *Buurkerk*, treated in Chapter 3.

The exact position of the *Buurspraakboek* and *Raads dagelijks boek* vis-à-vis the extra-textual events they mention is particularly relevant, as it leads us to question the strict distinction between the different text positions distinguished earlier in this chapter. Reading these registers, one's first impression is that we are dealing here with purely descriptive texts, recording events that have already happened. Although for many entries this may be the case, counter-examples are also abundant. This is especially true for the many verdicts contained in both registers. So a verdict in the *Raads dagelijks boek* from 1403 reads:

> Jan de Keyzer shall come bareheaded from the meat house to the clock, because he has illegally taken off with a foreign merchant and shall give a compensation of 10,000 stones and beg the Council for forgiveness.[57]

57 HUA 701-1.13: *Raads dagelijks boek* 1402–1408, fol. 18v: *Jan de Keyzer zel comen vanden vleyschuze bloots hoofts ter klocken om dat hi onredeliken mit enen uutheemschen coman teweghe ghevaren heeft ende zel gheven tebeteringhe* X^M *steens ende bidden den rade verghifnisse* [...]. The entry is followed by the names of his guarantors. It is unclear what the curious expression *te weghe varen* (litt.: 'taking off') means exactly. It may well have stood for an attempt to avoid

The *Buurspraakboek*, which contains an entry on the same case, states:

> Because Jan de Keyzer has taken off illegally with a foreign merchant, he has lain in the tower and has come here bareheaded at the clock and shall [beg] the Council for forgiveness and give a compensation of 10,000 stones.[58]

Apart from the curious fact that the place of safekeeping of Jan seems to have changed, there is a clear difference in the way in which both texts position themselves vis-à-vis the activity taking place. In neither case they suggest a purely descriptive relation. The *Raads dagelijks boek* places itself in a position preceding the events related to the resolution of the case, thus making it more akin to a prescriptive relation, while the *Buurspraakboek* seems to be situated in the midst of the proceedings, somewhere between the moment when Jan has arrived at the clock and the moment that he would beg the Council for forgiveness. That we are not just dealing with administrative standardization, but that such wordings were a conscious choice, is suggested by a case from 1408, in which Koenkijn van Damassche is punished for defaming two other men. Originally the *Buurspraakboek* notes how he 'shall come to the clock' and 'shall beg the Council for forgiveness'.[59] The phrasing stems from the way in which the *Raads dagelijks boek* structured its entries, namely, by placing the punishment completely in the future tense. The scribe, however, appears to have noted his mistake, as the first 'shall' is corrected to 'is', thereby placing the text itself after the act of coming to the clock and before the act of begging forgiveness, as was customary for the *Buurspraakboek*. The character of such entries therefore hovers between the purely prescriptive bylaws, stating what has to happen in a given occasion, and the descriptions of punishments meted out in the fourteenth-century registers (*Th.1* and *Th.2*). In this sense, they formed both a script, that is, how the occasion was supposed to progress, and a textual interpretation thereof in the scope of one entry. As I have argued elsewhere, this could provide the Council with important means to script these judicial occasions, by

toll in trading with a foreign merchant. As the exact meaning of the expression is uncertain, I have chosen to provide a literal translation here.

58 HUA 701-1.16: *Buurspraakboek* 1402–1405, fol. 34v: *Want Jan de Keyzer onredeliken teweghe ghevaren heeft mit enen uutheemschen coopman daer om heeft hi gheleghen inden toorn ende is hier ghecomen blootsh*[*oofts*] *ter klocken ende zel den rade verghifnisse* [*bidden*] *ende gheven tebeteringhe X*^{M} *steens.*

59 HUA 701-1.16: *Buurspraakboek* 1405–1409, fol. 100r: [...] *daer om sel hi comen in hemde ende in broec ter cloc ende sel den Rade verghiffenisse bidden.*[...]

textually fixing both the idealized schemata of such events in general and a specific interpretation of individual events that had actually taken place.[60]

Surveying the source material available for the Council illustrates how, as in Paris, the text-act relations of the series of surviving documents changed over time. Whereas the *Parlement* saw the shift from a predominance of legal acts to which were increasingly added more descriptive texts, the textual record of the Council moved from a general – though far from absolute – separation of prescriptive (the books of bylaws) and descriptive relations (*Th.1* and *Th.2* register), to registers that combined both elements. Although the separation had never been absolute, the strong intermingling of these positions in the latter registers in particular shows the potential of these texts to script the extra-textual events they were referring to. The Utrecht material is often many things in one, forming a suggested script for the course of events, while likewise providing them with a specific interpretation. What is more, and here the parallel with the York material becomes evident, many of these documents show a clear material vicinity to the legal process as it was performed by Council members, culprits and contemporary audiences. As in York, scripting justice 'in the way of the court' did not only involve prescribing or describing events in a text, but also materially manifesting the court's legal process by integrating these documents into day-to-day judicial practice.

The surviving documents of the Parisian *Parlement*, York's Consistory Court and the Council of Utrecht show us some of the many ways in which written texts became involved in late medieval legal procedure, be it as registers describing what had happened in court and beyond, regulations prescribing general behaviour or judicial procedure, written acts performing some aspect of a legal process, or, more often than not, a combination of these three. Documents might intervene in the legal process from several positions, scripting what had happened, what was to come or what actually took place when people came together to pursue some form of justice. The material fact that for all three courts considered here the numbers of surviving documents increase markedly when we move from the thirteenth to the fourteenth and subsequently the fifteenth century, should therefore be read as more than administrative convenience on the part of legal authorities from which historians can unproblematically reap the harvest. These texts were just as well instruments in shaping a specific concept of justice and idealized ways for people to achieve said justice, operating in tandem with some of the other aspects of socio-judicial activity distinguished in

60 Camphuijsen, "Performance of Justice", 242–243.

earlier chapters. Thus, the effect of the symbolic references implicit in the Utrecht stone fines depended not only on the socio-spatial world to which they referred (Chapter 2) or their ritualized proclamation during a *buurspraak* (Chapter 3), but also on the oft repeated textual descriptions of these occasions when a stone fine was pronounced. While this reading of court records as socio-judicial instruments is crucial to understanding the complex relation between what a text purports to do, be it describing, prescribing or performing activity, and its functioning in daily court practice, this may also lead to the impression that court officials had a free hand in turning these written instruments to their own purposes. In what follows, I will question this assumption, showing how multiple socio-judicial actors were involved both in producing and subsequently using these written means of communication.

From society to text: Varieties of translation

Having gained an impression of the ways in which the texts stemming from the courts could relate to the non-textual activities taking place in them, it is time to situate these documents more conclusively within the socio-legal communicative activity surrounding late medieval courts. As the use of texts in socio-judicial practice was strongly related to the specific format of legal practice as propagated by the court, their involvement in such communicative activity formed a major part of courts' claim to socio-legal authority. A study of late medieval court documents thus concerns both the influence of broader communication processes on the formation of these documents, as well as their role in shaping what people considered to be legally valid speech. To illustrate both claims, I will first consider the ways in which – mostly oral – messages and information from broader society found its way into the textual sources of these courts, as well as the processes of translation inherent to moving from the spoken to the written word. Secondly, I will trace these processes the other way round, asking if and in which form various groups and individuals encountered the messages and information noted down in these documents, by considering courts' strategies for publicizing them. In both cases the texts will be considered in light of the interaction between courts and the groups and individuals in society with which they were concerned, either as active participants in the legal process or as its audience.

For the first part of this analysis of the courts' textual material, the element of translation takes centre stage. Underlying the already huge basis of textual materials surviving for these three courts is an even broader font of oral communication, that is, people talking about other people and their social activities. When the examiners of York's Consistory Court drew up depositions based on their witnesses' statements, they formed the last link in a chain of orally transmitted social and individual knowledge about specific people and events.[61] In the same way, the information that the *Parlement* received through its *enquêtes*, and on which it based many of its decisions, was the result of predominantly oral enquiries in the concerned locality.[62] Finally, when considering the Council of Utrecht's many brief written notices that resulted from its supervision of peace agreements established between individuals, it is crucial to realize how much non-textual interaction and negotiation they involved.[63] The textual material presented by the courts therefore forms only the small tip of an immense iceberg of communicative activities. Moreover, in putting down late medieval experiences in written form, the authors of these texts also translated such experiences, according both to their direct goals in drawing up the texts, and to their own underlying frames of reference.

Linguistic pluralism played a role in some way or another for all three courts. Not only were there several pan-European prestige languages in use, most prominently Latin, but the local variety of languages and dialects was so immense that most, if not all areas of medieval Europe could rightly be called multilingual.[64] In the case of the *Parlement* this linguistic variety comes to the fore most prominently. In the thirteenth century the expansion of the Capetian kingdom brought an increasing number of areas in the south of France under royal jurisdiction, areas where written Roman law took a more central place than in the north. This led the king to institute a new specialized commission to treat cases coming

61 Cf. Ian Forrest, "Trust and Doubt: The Late Medieval Bishop and Local Knowledge", *Studies in Church History* 52 (2016); idem, *Trustworthy Men: How Inequality and Faith Made the Medieval Church* (Princeton, NJ: Princeton University Press, 2018).

62 For more on the role of *enquêtes* in shaping the judicial power claims of the royal court, see Hilaire, *Construction*, 50–57.

63 Examples of such peace agreements can be found all over the *Raads dagelijks boek* and *Buurspraakboek*, such as HUA 701-1.16: *Buurspraakboek* 1418–1425, fol. 14v (1418) and HUA 701-1.13: *Raads dagelijks boek* 1414–1425, fol. 127v (1421). See Chapter 5 for more on the Council's role in concluding these peace agreements.

64 Ad Putter and Keith Busby, "Introduction: Medieval Francophonia", in *Medieval Multilingualism: The Francophone World and Its Neighbours*, eds. Christopher Kleinhenz and Keith Busby (Turnhout: Brepols, 2010). Cf. the contributions to Albrecht Classen, ed., *Multilingualism in the Middle Ages and Early Modern Age: Communication and Miscommunication in the Premodern World* (Berlin and Boston: De Gruyter, 2016).

from these lands in 1271, which was appropriately called the *auditoire du droit écrit*.[65] Although this body was primarily defined according to a legal difference, the distinction between the northern and southern areas of the kingdom also had a strong linguistic component. When Philip the Fair, in an ordinance usually dated to 1310, transferred the treatment of petitions coming from the south of France from the *auditoire* to his recently installed *Chambre des Requêtes*, these linguistic considerations came to the fore very explicitly. Philip divided the chamber's members into two groups, one for petitions in the *Langue françoise* and one for petitions in the *Langue d'oc*, that is, the group of languages spoken in the south of France.[66] It is unclear how long this linguistic division remained in place exactly, as it is last mentioned in a royal ordinance from 1318.[67] But it does provide a very concrete example of how linguistic concerns could influence legal practice and organization.

In the context of this linguistic diversity, the courts' relationship vis-à-vis Latin is of particular relevance. Latin played a very central role in much of the legal practice of late medieval Europe. The major sources of learned law, both from the Roman and canon law traditions, were composed in Latin, and legal theorists would for centuries to come keep writing and theorizing in Latin. However, the Latinity of this learned legal tradition contrasted sharply with the vernacular multilingualism of most societies. Latin was certainly not beyond people's reach. Besides its use by ecclesiastical elites, who were professionally trained to write and speak Latin, this language was present on many occasions in ordinary people's daily lives, from the hearing of mass to the signing of contracts over land. People from a variety of social strata had what Michael Clanchy calls 'an acquaintance with Latin'.[68] Nevertheless, such a general acquaintance is not the same as a proficiently spoken language. It says more about the ability of people to receive information in Latin than about their day-to-day use of the language. The existence of Latin court documents therefore implies the translation of words, ideas and activities originally presented in a vernacular.

Surveying the three cases we see basically three variants of the use of Latin in court texts. York's Consistory Court used Latin exclusively at least up to the end of the fifteenth century. After that time, there is a gradual shift

65 Aubert, *Histoire*, vol. 1, 6–7, 35.

66 For a modern edition of this ordinance, see Langlois, *Textes*, 178–181. The exact dating of the ordinance is uncertain, as evidenced in Aubert, "Nouvelles recherches", pt. 1, 97, n. 4.

67 See De Laurière et al., *Ordonnances*, vol. 1, 673–677, art. 7.

68 Clanchy, *Memory*, 237.

from predominantly Latin to mainly English documents.[69] In the records of the Council of Utrecht, on the other hand, (Middle) Dutch is used almost exclusively from the early fourteenth century onwards, the only exception being documents originating with other institutions that would occasionally be copied into the Council's registers in their original Latin form.[70] The *Parlement* was the most multilingual of the three courts – at least from a documentary perspective – as here both Latin and (Middle) French were intermingled in the records from an early date on. This often depended on the type of text, although particularly for the earlier fourteenth century Latin seems to predominate. Most of the formal legal acts contained in the registers – *arrêts, jugés* – were stated in Latin. At the same time, many – though certainly not the majority – of registered letters were copied in French, which may well have been their original language of composition.[71] Other texts surviving for the early-fourteenth-century *Parlement* provide a similarly diverse picture, ranging from the predominantly Latin *registres du greffe*, to the partly French *journaux* that survive in a few of the criminal registers, to the even completely French prisoners' confessions and judgements at the end of the $X^{2A}4$ register.[72] A change took place during the later fourteenth and early fifteenth centuries, as many of the new, more descriptive series of records that began to appear around that time – most prominently those of *conseil* and *plaidoiries* – were written in French.[73]

As important intermediaries between the worlds of legal theory and judicial practice, law courts were thus very much concerned with translating information from broader society. The implications of such translation for the way in which the information was received could be far-reaching. This has been shown especially in the context of inquisition records. Mark Pegg

69 Robert N. Swanson, "'...Et examinatus dicit...': Oral and Personal History in the Records of English Ecclesiastical Courts", in *Voices from the Bench: Narratives of Lesser Folk in Medieval Trials*, ed. Michael Goodich (New York: Palgrave Macmillan, 2006), 206.

70 See, for example, the *Th.2* register for 1370, where a Latin letter of hereditary lease written by the dean and chapel of St. John's Church in Utrecht is copied in full as part of an otherwise Middle Dutch entry: HUA 701-1.227, fol. 53v–54r.

71 Grün, "Notice", XXIV.

72 For the *anciens registres du greffe*, see AN $X^{1A}8844–8851^{bis}$. The *journaux* can be found in registers $X^{2A}4$, fol. 1r–135v and $X^{2A}5$, fol. 1r–40v and 144r–154r, and are inventoried in Labat-Poussin, Langlois and Lanhers, *Actes*, 126–212, 228–252, 314–327. The prisoners' confessions and judgements are edited in Langlois and Lanhers, *Confessions*.

73 For a clear example of the relation between the new (*plaidoiries, conseil*) and old (*arrêts, jugés*) types of records, see the dossier of transcribed procedural pieces in Hildesheimer and Morgat-Bonnet, *État méthodique*, XXI–XXVII, which contains examples of both regarding one case from 1427–1428.

has argued, for example, how, in the thirteenth-century inquisition records, a variety of vernacular words to characterize people would often simply be translated as 'heretics'. This showed, according to Pegg, the combination of recording practicalities – that is, conflating a range of vernacular concepts into one term for the sake of rapid recording – and the influence of preconceived notions about the nature of the people interrogated on the part of the examiners.[74] A similar standardization of translated terms can be seen in the material from York and Paris. As Claude Gauvard has noted, the documents stemming from the *Parlement* contain several fixed Latin terms for criminal acts, like *crimen* or *maleficium*, connected to their implications in the legal process rather than the exact details of the act as such.[75] In a similar way, the York depositions in marriage cases contain numerous stock phrases for sexual acts, for example, stating that a couple was seen 'alone and naked together' (*solus cum sola, nudus cum nuda*). Thus, in one (in)famous case from 1365/1366 concerning the validity of marriage between John Marrays and the twelve-year-old Alice de Rouclif, multiple witness statements contain this exact same phrase to describe the alleged consummation of the marriage, notwithstanding major differences in other details.[76] Rather than supposing that every witness used the exact same phraseology, we may interpret this standardization as a consequence of the act of translation from the vernacular to Latin. A variety of words and descriptions would be transposed by one or several fixed Latin equivalents. In this way, the court did not just capture the voices of witnesses on parchment, but also tried to control the sense in which they were used and the possible implications they had within the legal process and beyond. In translating from a vernacular – and presumably spoken – language into a language predominantly used for recording, statements, descriptions and ideas were thus fit into a specific register, ultimately determined by the interpretation and purposes of the writer.

But the impact of the transition of information from a – largely oral – social context to the written records of the court extended far beyond a translation from one language to another. Not only did the court often use a fixed court language to record its cases, but the information reaching it

74 Pegg, *Corruption*, 57–60. Cf. Arnold, *Inquisition*, 138–149, on the naming of heretics as part of a broader construction of inquisitorial discourse.

75 Gauvard, *'Grace especial'*, 111–122. See Chapter 5 for more on the implications of such terminology.

76 BIA CP.E.89. Parts of this case have been published in translation in Jeremy Goldberg, ed., *Women in England, c. 1275–1525: Documentary Sources* (Manchester: Manchester University Press, 1995), 58–80.

was also fitted within a specific court discourse. The surviving depositions from the Consistory Court of York are again a case in point. They offer some of the most detailed images of late medieval social life, yet are at the same time all the more problematic in the details they provide. Jeremy Goldberg explicitly warns against reading the York depositions as 'simple mirrors of daily life'.[77] In the context of the numerous cases regarding the validity of marriage Goldberg shows how certain social occasions are described in remarkable detail in the statements of the court's witnesses. It is, for example, striking how many witnesses in such cases allegedly observed the supposed spouses lying together in bed or even having sex.[78] Notwithstanding the possibly different norms as to the privacy of living spaces in medieval society, the ability of deponents to recall such personal details, sometimes many years later, needs to be regarded within a litigation context. For unlike the modern historian, who may be interested in the depositions in order to learn more about the lives of medieval people, those involved in the compilation of the depositions, that is, the witnesses and the court's examiners, had their own specific interests in the stories as represented in the cause papers. For the witnesses, calling upon their memory of events that may have seemed of little concern at the time, an unavoidable process of selection took place, as the specific occasion was reconstituted and reinterpreted in their mind. Furthermore, a certain bias for one of the parties was also likely, as the witnesses were in the end presented to the court by the parties in a dispute.[79] What mattered to the examiners was foremost the usefulness of the provided answers from a legal perspective. Working from a set of questions that were compiled to argue specific legal points, what the examiners focused on was to record the answers provided in a way that allowed the judges to base their legal verdicts on them. As the depositions themselves were written after the interrogation took place, based on notes taken during the interrogation, the examiners had ample time to select those aspects of the interrogations that had a bearing on the case from a purely legal perspective.[80] It was thus from the interaction – or negotiation – between questioner and questioned, both bringing their own interests and frames of reference to the table, that the depositions as they survive took shape. The legal logic that was

77 Jeremy Goldberg, "John Skatelok's Dick: Voyeurism and 'Pornography' in Late Medieval England", *Medieval Obscenities*, ed. Nicola McDonald (York: York Medieval Press, 2006), 106.

78 Ibid., 109.

79 Helmholz, *Marriage Litigation*, 127–128.

80 For an overview of the process of recording the witness statements, see ibid., 17–20.

required to prove or disprove a case led the selection and description of the details involved.

A similar interaction between social informants and the court took place in the case of the *Parlement*. The sources for this interaction are, however, often much less direct, as few texts similar to the York depositions survive. An exception is formed by the confessions and testimonies collected at the end of the fourth criminal register, and spanning the years 1319–1350.[81] These nearly 60 folia, probably attached to the register at a later date, contain small dossiers of individual cases, including transcripts of the culprits' confessions, witness testimony and, occasionally, also the judges' decisions in the case. The exceptional source gives us a view of some of the machinations of narrative construction that took place in day-to-day legal practice.[82] A first layer was formed by the story of the procedure itself. As most of these entries concerned situations in which a culprit had confessed his crime to the court, we often find a description of the circumstances of the confession. Usually such entries consist of the names of various officials, followed by a mention that the culprit has made a confession 'of his own free will' (*de sa bonne volenté*) or 'without constraint' (*sanz contrainte*). The court then contrasts this with situations where confessions – usually before other authorities – were perceived as involuntary, as in the case of Guillaume de Léans from 1333, who accused various officials of having questioned him under torture.[83]

The same theme of proper versus improper legal procedure can also be found in a second narrative layer, namely, in the subjects of the confessions themselves. For example, in the complex case of Guiart de Noireterre, treated in 1332, the alleged danger of extra-curial dispute settlement comes to the fore.[84] Guiart, himself involved in various lawsuits on the accusation of theft, pillage and murder, was mortally wounded in Paris by a group of contract killers. His murder, so we learn from various witness statements in the case, was supposedly ordered by one of his enemies, a knight called Jean de la Forêt, who had repeatedly stated to have been gravely damaged by Guiart. Instead of pursuing his grievances in court, like others appear to have done, Jean preferred to resort to private vengeance. The court's disapproval of this course of action becomes clear in several ways. In the

81 AN $X^{2A}4$, fols. 174r–232v. Published in Langlois and Lanhers, *Confessions*.

82 Cf. the multilayered narrative construction in and from trial records, as identified by Dean, *Crime and Justice*, 17–33.

83 Langlois and Lanhers, *Confessions*, 41.

84 Ibid., 51–75.

verdicts that survive in the case, some of the conspirators and killers are sentenced to death, clearly indicating the serious nature of the case. But in more subtle ways as well, the records of the case emphasize an order-disorder dichotomy. One of the main perpetrators, Jean's squire Pierre le Vicomte, had challenged Guiart to a duel prior to the murder itself, not because the latter had done him any harm, but on his master's orders.[85] Likewise, another accomplice, Bouchard d'Azai, manipulated the court of the Parisian official, requesting a summons for Guiart, in order to be able to show one of the assassins his face.[86] The documents in this case present an ingenious plot, not just to murder a rival, but above all to pursue one's justice outside of, and sometimes even by illegitimately using, the proper channels, that is, the royal court's legal process. At the same time, given that the case has now been properly incorporated into a legal procedure, the events' disordering effect is claimed to be contravened. The king's law, so the documents suggest, has caught up with the chaotic situation. As in the case of the York depositions, information coming from various social informants, each with their own motivations, is reworked into a broader narrative of legal order versus disorder.[87]

Whereas the witness testimonies and confessions suggest a particular proximity to the negotiation between social informant and court, other types of documents, like the criminal and civil registers, were no less subject to processes of narrativization. One long case from the 1340s provides a number of good examples. It concerns Jean de Dinteville, member of the *Parlement*, who together with the proctor of the king acted against a group of nobles and sergeants, including the bailiff of Vitry. The latter, according to Jean, illegally captured the fortress of Fontaine and pillaged a house belonging to him, as well as abducting several of his people. The result was a legal process covering the years 1340–1343, involving both civil claims for the personal damages of Jean and criminal legal proceedings.[88] One of the reasons for the case to be drawn out so long in the first instance was strictly procedural. The first few entries that survive are mainly concerned with allegations by Jean and the royal proctor that several of the defendants are to be declared in default for not showing up in court at the right time and

85 Ibid., 61–62.

86 Ibid., 57–58.

87 See Chapter 5 for a more extensive treatment of this socio-legal narrative as presented in the *Parlement*'s documents and practices.

88 The case is spread out over the *Parlement*'s fourth criminal register, covering many entries in the register's *journal* and two of its *arrêts*. See AN $X^{2A}4$, fols. 8v, 10v, 21r, 23r, 23v, 27v, 30v, 34r, 36v, 43v, 58v, 61r, 61v, 86v, 106r, 106v, 139v–141r.

place. These claims are initially sustained by the court.[89] Shortly thereafter, however, word reaches the court through different channels – including the defendants themselves – that the king intends to quash these initial verdicts, as the reason for the defendants' absence was that they had been serving the king in his war.[90] As in other cases, the records stress the necessity of people's presence in the courtroom, excusing their absence only in extraordinary cases.

The Dinteville case only really seems to get traction in the first half of 1341, but it remains the subject of a score of procedural decisions and orders from the *Parlement* or sometimes even from the king. *Enquêtes* are called for, people are – yet again – declared to have been in default, and the king at some point even orders the proceedings to take place on a specific day and in his presence.[91] No clear final judgement of the case has survived, the last entries being a declaration of default and mention that Dinteville's side of the case will be continued in civil proceedings.[92] But the intermediary verdicts – *arrêts* – that do survive stress more of the themes seen before, like the crime of breaching a royal safeguard and royal service as a legitimate excuse for courtroom absence. The descriptions of the case emerging from the *Parlement*'s registers present us with a limited picture of the conflict. We receive only hints of the actual politico-legal strategies and negotiations taking place between the many different parties involved, including Jean, the accused nobles, the king and the court. But in providing us with so little information, the case does show how potentially very complex social disputes were integrated into specific legal narratives – both by the litigants, in bringing particular arguments to the fore, and by the court itself – which stressed a certain social order based on royal power and justice, awarding loyalty to the king, while punishing a breaking of the king's peace. In addition to the detailed stories from the registers of confessions and witness testimony, cases such as this attest a more general textual practice whereby social information was reworked into narratives of justice. These narratives, which will be treated further in Chapter 5, provided individual cases with much broader implications by discursively linking them to extensive systems of signification, encompassing other

89 Ibid., fols. 8v, 10v, 21r, 23r.

90 Ibid., fols. 23v, 30v

91 Ibid., fols. 58r, 86v, 106v and 43v, respectively.

92 Ibid., 106v. There is one last mention of the case in the civil register dated to July 5, 1343, which delegates it to a royal sergeant in the vicinity of the alleged crime: AN $X^{1A}9$, fol. 471. Also see Henri Furgeot et al., eds., *Actes du Parlement de Paris: Deuxième série: De l'an 1328 à l'an 1350*, vol. 2 (Paris: Imprimerie Nationale, 1960), 34, nr. 5090.

texts but also, as seen in previous chapters, other features of socio-judicial practice, including spaces and ritual acts.

A similar narrative logic seems to underlie the court documents of the Council of Utrecht. Again the lack of written witness testimonies means that few direct voices – or at least texts claiming to represent such direct voices – survive. But the way in which social information is reworked in the court documents is nevertheless extensive. Two aspects clearly illustrate such processes. First there is the use of specific words. In the verdicts contained in the Council's *Buurspraakboek* the actions or general behaviour of the culprit leading to the sentence are usually specified.[93] Sometimes such descriptions are very case-specific, but often certain standardized words are used to describe the activity, like *onredelik* (unreasonable), *onstantelik* (improper) and *onsedich* (immoral). These terms sometimes appear on their own, as a description of more general intolerable behaviour that is being punished.[94] In many other cases, however, they are added as adjective to a specified other crime. So when, for example, Koenkiin van Damassche was punished for slander in 1408, the words he had spoken were recorded as being *onredelike woirde* (unreasonable words).[95] And in a case from 1418, a certain master Reyner is banished from the city for ten years, because he has committed theft and *onstantelike saeken* (improper things).[96] It is not easy to find a clear definition of these terms, or to connect them to one specific action. Berents has argued that most of them are simply indicators for more general misbehaviour, often of a violent nature.[97] Strikingly, most of these words are antonyms, as evidenced by the prefix *on-*, emphasizing that they are the opposite of generally desired forms of behaviour. A potentially large variety of acts is thus contained within several very general categories, indicated by words that already stress the transgressive character of the act.

93 As can be gathered from Berents, *Misdaad*, 130, only about 10% of the recorded verdicts up to 1455 – that is, 53% of Berents' 'other crimes' category, which constituted 18% of the total verdicts for this period – did not name the crime.

94 This is Berents' category of 'unreasonable behaviour', constituting the alleged crime for about 8% of all recorded verdicts up to 1455. See ibid., 127–129.

95 HUA 701-1.16: *Buurspraakboek* 1405–1409, 100r: *Want Koenkiin van Damassche Jan Koeken ende Gherijt van Braclede onredelike woirde opgheseit heeft die grotelic aen hoer eer dragen, die niet waer en siin, daer om is hi comen in hemde ende in broec ter cloc ende sel den Rade verghiffenisse bidden. Ende hi sel seggen wes hij hem Jan ende Gherijt voirseit geseit heeft dan van gueden luden dat hi daer aen geloghen heeft* (1408).

96 HUA 701-1.16: *Buurspraakboek* 1418–1425, 31r: *Want Reyner, die men meyster Reyner mitten kreyen heet, gestolen ende onstantelike saeken bedreven heeft, daerom verbiet men hem de stat tyen jaer lang ende een mile van der stat te wesen van dieften* (1418).

97 Berents, *Misdaad*, 127–129.

This theme of the transgression of a desired order also appears in the records' presentation of the victims of transgressive behaviour. Sometimes the victim of the crime is simply the individual directly damaged by the action, as in a case from 1386 where Wouter son of Jan stabbed Jacob son of Steffaen.[98] Not all crimes were conceptualized so clearly as victimizing private individuals. In a series of entries from 1414 five men are punished for counterfeiting. The alleged victim in this case is not so much any private individual aggrieved in a specific transaction. Instead the activities of the five men are said to have caused 'grave damage and hindrance to our communal city'.[99] Here the community as a whole is held to have been the victim of the counterfeiting. It does not need to be such a potentially extensive crime like counterfeiting for the records to extend victimhood beyond private individuals. In many subtle ways the potential harm done to the urban community is integrated into a legal narrative of disordering crime followed by just punishment. Many entries related to manslaughter describe, for example, whether the incident took place in the city or its liberty, and whether the perpetrator or the victim were citizens of Utrecht. There are procedural reasons that may have required such distinctions to be made explicit, but considering their frequent occurrence in the *Buurspraakboek* – which was not necessarily the place to develop legal argumentation – such entries shore up a broader socio-legal narrative. The alleged disorder caused by the violent death of an individual involved the urban community as a whole: both spatially through the occurrence of the crime in the city or its liberty, as well as socially through the victim's or perpetrator's status as citizen, which formalized community membership. From the many social facts involved in such potentially harmful social activities a limited selection was included in the records, emphasizing certain damaging aspects and thereby relating the occasion to a broader socio-legal discourse on order and disorder in the urban community of Utrecht.

Chapter 3 has shown how court activity – or at least the traces of this activity that are still in some way visible to us – was ritualized into chains of actions that suggested a link with previous activities in different contexts. A similar sequencing took place in the act of textually recording information from society. On the one hand, this was part of a translation between

98 HUA 701-1.16: *Buurspraakboek* 1385–1391, 34r: *Want Wouter Jans soen onredeliken ghesteken heft Jacob Steffaens soen daer omme heeft hi gheleghen inden toorn ende is hier ghecomen in hemde ende in broeke ter klocken ende zel den rade bidden verghifnisse ende gheven der stat tebeteringe V^M steens* (1386).

99 HUA 701-1.16: *Buurspraakboek* 1410–1414, 183r–v: [...] *groten schade ende hinder onser gemeenre stat* [...]' (1414).

languages, as for many courts the language in which the documents were drawn up differed from the languages spoken by a majority of the people with whom these records were concerned. More generally, however, in these documents information was selectively integrated into socio-legal narratives that echoed certain ideas about social order and disorder. Here a linguistic endeavour, related to the ritualization of actions took place. Discrete social events were taken together and logically connected within specific discursive schemata – 'sexual intercourse is the defining confirmation of marriage', 'the king represents and guarantees social order in the kingdom', 'a crime against an individual disrupts peace in the whole community' – which hinted at previous similar chains of logic constructed in the court context.[100] The court itself, as author of the documents, was the major force behind the form and contents of this textual schematization. Nevertheless, other social parties also had a role to play in the construction of the written material. In some cases – most prominently witness testimony – this influence was exerted in providing the court with specific information, modified by the interests of the party as such. More in general, however, it was often people's role as receivers of information, that is, as audiences, which strongly influenced the way in which the court conceived its documents. In order to analyse the influence of such audiences, the last part of this chapter will be concerned with the flow of information from the court back to society, placing the court documents in the context of the multimedial publishing practices of these three courts.

Text and society: Publishing practices

On September 21, 1341, the *Parlement* discussed the case of Pierre Brun. In an appealed case stemming from the town of Nonette in Auvergne, Pierre was accused of manipulating a royal letter. The court ruled that Pierre would be put in the pillory twice: once on a Saturday in Paris, and once in Nonette. On this second occasion he would have a sign above his head, stating in large lettering:

> This is Pierre Brun of Lorlange in Auvergne, who has made forgery, wrongful erasure and additions to our lord the king's letters, obtained by him for

100 Cf. the process of 'juridification of the world' as treated in Jesús R. Velasco, *Dead Voice: Law, Philosophy, and Fiction in the Iberian Middle Ages* (Philadelphia: University of Pennsylvania Press, 2020).

> an adjournment in an appeal case lodged by him and William of Lafons following a sentence given against them by the bailiff of Auvergne for Jean Aurolzer, administrator of the provost of Brioude, and for said provost, and [who] has also forged in the *executoire* of the said adjournment. And [he] has confessed this, and is therefore condemned by the court of the Parlement to be put in the pillory, once in Paris and another time in the town of Nonette in Auvergne, and he will be sent to the bailiff of Auvergne to [be] put in said pillory in Nonette for the forgery.[101]

The case of Pierre signals two fundamental aspects of the role of texts in the information dynamics of late medieval law courts. On the one hand, and echoing some of the concerns seen in the previous section, the court emphasized the importance of the reliability of the information it received and fixed in a text. Changing a validated – that is, sealed – text was considered a serious crime, judging by the extensive punishment that Pierre received. On top of that, however, this case also shows – in a rather concrete way – the way in which the court integrated written documents in its communication of information back to a specific audience. It was deemed desirable, so it seems, that people witnessing the execution of Pierre's punishment had a clear sense of what it was exactly that he was punished for. Accordingly, his crime and its consequences as narrated in the court case were broadcast physically and linguistically to all passers-by.

Pierre's case is exceptional in the registers of the *Parlement* in its explicit emphasis on the physical publication of court texts for a broader public. Few other cases place the physical text-objects used in court so crucially in the public view. But in other, more subtle ways we also see the *Parlement*'s documents implicated in the flow of information in both directions, to and from the court. The *arrêts* that the *Parlement* decided on in specific cases would, for example, be proclaimed in open court. As early as 1296 a royal ordinance stated how a named royal official, Renaut Barbou, was supposed to 'speak and bring the arrests'.[102] From 1349 onwards, the *arrêts* contained in

101 AN $X^{2A}4$, fol. 50r–v: *Cest Pierre Brun de Leulanges en Auvergne qui auoit fait farce, faussete rasure et addicion es lettres du Roy nostresire, empetre par luj sur un adiornement en cause dappel fait par luj et Guillaume de lafons dune sentence donnee contre euls par le baille dauuergne pour Jehan Aurolzer baille du preuost de Bride et pour ledit preuost et aussi lauoit fait farce en lexecutoire dudit adiornement. Et ce a confesse et pour ce est condempnez par la court du Parlement a estre mis une foiz ou pilory a Paris et une autre foiz en laville de Nonnaite en Auvergne et sera envoyez au baille dauuergne pour le farce mettre ou dit pilory a Nonnaite.*

102 Langlois, *Textes* (1888), 163: [...] *il est ordené que lidiz Renaut Barbou, se il est presens,* [...], *parleront et rendront les arrez.* Also see Aubert, "Nouvelles recherches", pt. 1, 88.

the registers bear the date of their pronouncement, leading to a clustering of *arrêts* on particular days in the registers.[103] Given the regular presence of audiences in the *Grande Chambre*, as seen in previous chapters, such readings played an important role in publishing legal narratives beyond the physical confines of the text.[104]

While these regular pronouncements were done primarily in the courtroom itself, there is evidence of a variety of court-related documents being published before potentially much larger audiences. In 1404, for example, Nicholas of Baye noted how a royal document was brought to court, forbidding two conflicting parties – one of which was the university – to publish slanderous texts in various public places. The text in its turn, so Nicholas tells us, was read aloud in the Great Hall of the *Palais de la Cité* through a window in the side of the *Grande Chambre*, which was also used for announcing the end of the *Parlement*'s pleading season.[105] In another *arrêt* from 1356, Godefroid d'Harcourt, lord of Saint-Sauveur-le-Vicomte (Normandy), and several of his accomplices, all accused of treason, were banished from the kingdom. The *arrêt* itself was said to be published in public places around the kingdom 'where it was necessary, useful or advantageous'.[106] As this last phrase reminds us, the publication of – parts of – the written text was often deemed crucial from a judicio-political viewpoint. For in order to make sure that Godefroid did not return unnoticed, it was important to inform large numbers of people of his banishment. But larger audiences could also be sought closer to the courtroom itself. Jean Guerout, for example, has argued how a marble stone that stood at the entrance to the royal castle was used for a variety of proclamations, from official summons to certain *arrêts*, like that of Godefroid d'Harcourt.[107]

None of this is to say that each and every record produced by the *Parlement* received the same degree of publicity. As argued in an earlier section, most of the surviving registers of the *Parlement* were simply collections of copies of documents used in court practice, and will likely have had a mainly internal audience of court officials. However, what the above does

103 The first *arrêts* dated like this can be found in AN $X^{1A}12$, fol. 409v. Also see Grün, "Notice", CXXXIX; Aubert, *Histoire*, vol. 2, 134–136.
104 See Chapter 2 and Chapter 3.
105 AN $X^{1A}4786$, fol. 359r. Edited in Tuetey, *Journal*, 94–95. Also see Chapter 2.
106 AN $X^{2A}6$, fol. 299v–304r: [...] *Publicabitur itaque hujusmodi bannum in locis publicis in predicto regno nostro, ubi ipsum bannum necessarium, utile aut expediens fuerit publicari.* The *arrêt* is edited in Léopold Delisle, ed., *Histoire du château et des sires de Saint-Sauveur-le-Vicomte* (Valonges: Martin, 1867), 121–141.
107 Guerout, "Le Palais: Deuxième partie", 87.

show is that many other documents – on which the surviving registers were based – were implicated both occasionally and more structurally in the flow of information from the court to various audiences, including officials, litigating parties and even a more general public in different parts of the kingdom.

What is true for the *Parlement* also holds for the other two courts considered here. The Council of Utrecht's *Buurspraakboek* offers a striking illustration of the interaction between textual and oral-performative modes of communication. The logic underlying this textual record was that it contained those matters that were to be publicly announced during the *buurspraak* occasions, thereby incorporating the public presentation of the textual record as a fundamental reason for its existence. Forming a kind of script for the *buurspraak* occasions, this record purports to bring us exceptionally close to the public oral practices of the Council, as well as to its own publication.[108] Whereas the *Buurspraakboek* formed only the basis of an otherwise oral publication, the direct physical presence of texts in the public arena was also a common phenomenon in late medieval Utrecht. The *Buurspraakboek* regularly mentions occasions on which the text of a specific decision or regulation was physically posted in a public space, usually in front of the aldermen's house on the *Plaets*. In many cases these physically published documents concerned the sale of immovable property.[109] But they could also be concerned with other matters. In 1417, for example, the Council stated how a group of former exiles had been formally reconciled with the urban authorities and that anyone who would from now on harass them extra-legally would be punished. The entry in the *Buurspraakboek* mentioned that a written document (*cedel*) on the matter had been posted at the aldermen's house to make sure 'that everyone could know it and no one would violate it'.[110] The Council seems thus to have been very concerned with the exchange of information between itself and the inhabitants of the city, and used the written word as one of several ways

108 See Chapter 3 for more on the *buurspraak* occasions. Also see Camphuijsen, "Performance of Justice".

109 For example, HUA 701-1.16: *Buurspraakboek* 1414–1418, fol. 114r: *Van den husingen, hofsteden ende eygendomme die vercoft ende voer den scoute ende scepen van onser stat in gerechte overgegeven sijn, daer sall men een cedel off uuthanghen opter Plaetsen voer der scepen huys achte dage lang zo dattet een ygelic weten mach dient aendraech ende noot is te weten* (1416). The same announcement can be found very often in the *Buurspraakboek* and seems to have formed part of a standardized series of announcements made several times each year.

110 HUA 701-1.16: *Buurspraakboek* 1414–1418, fol. 142r: [...] *dattet een ygelic weten mach ende hem daer aen niemant en versume* (1417).

to realize this. As in the previous entry, it often made this communicative goal explicit. Thus, when it turned out in 1406 that many people had not had the chance to see a public notice concerning the sale of houses because they had been on a military campaign at the time of its publication, the Council posted the notice again 'in order that everyone whom it concerns and who needs to know it may know it'.[111] The practice of bringing legal and other records to a larger public was thus very much part of broader communicative concerns on the part of the Council. Such concerns should not surprise us, considering the many instances of political instability in fourteenth- and fifteenth-century Utrecht.[112] Yet at the same time they also echoed more constant and long-term practices of informing – and being informed by – the town's inhabitants.

Unlike the *Buurspraakboek*, the documents of York's Consistory Court do not foreground further communication of textual information. Nevertheless these documents also formed part of broader communicative practices, through which the court published what had been written down in its records. Two such instances emerge from the cause paper dossier of a 1394 matrimonial case between Christina Talkan and Henry Brigg, for which only the sentence has survived.[113] The sentence, finding in favour of Christina, forms part of a letter, addressed to 'all sons of the Holy Mother Church whom the present letter might reach'.[114] Subsequently, the letter announces how, on February 9 that year, the court's commissary general had, in the consistorial place in York's cathedral church, read and brought (*legimus et tulimus*) the definite sentence in the case, which is then followed by its transcription. The document thus describes an occasion – the sentence reading – where the text is explicitly communicated beyond its physical, written form. As Chapter 3 argued, such sentence readings formed an important ritualized aspect of court procedure, involving an audience of litigants, often named witnesses of the reading and, given the setting in the cathedral church, other potential bystanders. Furthermore, since such readings could also take place in local parish churches, their role in publishing information seems even

111 HUA 701-1.16: *Buurspraakboek* 1405–1409, fol. 25v–26r: [...] *zodattet een ygelic weten mach dien 't aendraget ende noot is te weten* (1406).

112 Nor were they exceptional as compared to other reactions of premodern urban authorities on periods of social and political tension. See, for example, the communicative concerns of the Amsterdam authorities during the sixteenth-century Dutch revolt, as described in Femke Deen, *Publiek debat en propaganda in Amsterdam tijdens de Nederlandse Opstand: Amsterdam 'Moorddam' (1566–1578)* (Amsterdam: Amsterdam University Press, 2015).

113 BIA CP.E.158.

114 Ibid.: *Universis sancte matris ecclesie filiis ad quos presentes littere pervenerint* [...].

more crucial.[115] The second piece of evidence this cause paper provides of the court's communicative practices is in the form of the document itself. It was not unusual for surviving sentences to be contained within the context of a letter sent to local church officials.[116] Within the large area in which the archbishop of York held the highest jurisdiction, cases regularly moved from one court to the other as part of an appeal or in reference to a lower court. This meant that crucial information concerning a case – like the verdict reached at an earlier stage – would have to move between these courts as well. And this was where a second means of communicating information and messages outward from the court came in. Together with its sentence readings, this practice of transmitting certain aspects of the legal procedure – and most prominently the sentences – by letter to local courts, formed a crucial way in which the Consistory Court presented its textualized legal narratives to a variety of local and regional audiences.

In retrospect, it is clear that in all three cases the court used written documents not only to schematize and archive the information it received for internal use, but also involved it in its multimedial practice of bringing information to various audiences. Many of the legal narratives formed in the process of transitioning non-textual social information to a written document were thus subsequently presented back to society. Yet these publication practices were not just concerned with bringing the content of the texts to a broader audience. In many cases, as when documents were posted in public places, like town squares or churches, the physical presence of the texts was also at stake. Such published texts formed both a linguistic and physical performance of the court and its legal process. They contributed to a suggested schematization of legal proceedings, in the same way that the ritualization of these activities themselves did. Moreover, by forming a physical representative of the court-based legal process, their presence supported the court's attempt at validating a specific, text-based, format for legal practice.

With these practices of publishing documents, we touch again upon one of the fundamental, yet often overlooked participants in the socio-legal communication process of the court. Notwithstanding the way in which social information was reworked in the material according to linguistic

115 See, for example, BIA CP.E.138 (1387), where the sentence in a case is read in the consistorial place of the collegiate church of Beverley: [...] *in ecclesia collegiis beati Johannis Beverlac' Eboracencis diocesis loco consistorii eiusdem* [...].

116 Also see BIA CP.E.178.

and narrative schemes as negotiated between the court and various legal parties, one of the crucial contributors to the whole communication process surrounding these documents were its various audiences. As is often the case in reception studies of medieval texts, direct evidence of a reading or listening public is hard to come by. Much depends on reconstructions of the intended audience of a text, complemented every now and then with scarce mentions of actual audiences. Nonetheless, both types of audiences – intended and actual – can give us some insight into the logic shaping these documents, as both influenced the court in the way in which it conceived its written material.

The impression gained from the texts themselves and the available evidence on their socio-legal context actually suggests quite varied audiences for all three cases. The groups addressed in the Utrecht *Buurspraakboek*, for example, are very diverse. The Council may have presented citizenship as an advantageous status, but it certainly did not limit its texts to this one group. Many regulations written down in the book explicitly address the citizens and *ondersaten* of Utrecht, that is to say, both those who had acquired citizenship and those who had not.[117] The latter category could also include people living in the Utrecht liberty, rather than within the city walls. Likewise, both men and women appear as intended audiences of the Council's pronouncements.[118] And the audience need not be limited to inhabitants of the city. Foreigners could also be explicitly addressed by the Council, as when it opened a measure pronounced in 1425 by addressing it to 'all guests and foreigners, who have come from any other land [to] live or stay in our city or liberty'.[119] Other groups encountered as intended audience include prostitutes and beggars, groups that are often seen as standing on the margins of medieval society.[120] Measures explicitly meant

117 For example, HUA 701-1.16: *Buurspraakboek* 1405–1409, fol. 80v: *Voert gebiet die raet dat nyemant van onsen borgeren ofte ondersaten* [...] (1407). Muller, *Rechtsbronnen*, Introduction, 313, limits the term *ondersaten* to those people who did not have citizenship because they did not live within the walls, but rather in the city's liberty. This seems too limited an interpretation of this term, judging by the *Buurspraakboek* and *Raads dagelijks boek*, and I here follow Berents in extending an understanding of the term to all inhabitants of the city and the liberty without citizenship. See Berents, *Misdaad*, 18.

118 An example of the inclusion of inhabitants of the city and liberty, as well as the inclusion of both men and women, can be found in HUA 701-1.16: *Buurspraakboek* 1414–1418, fol. 120r: *Die raet van onser stat out ende nywe waernen ende laten enen ijgeliken weten mannen ende wiven die in onser stat of in onser stat vriheit woenaftich sijn* [...] (1416).

119 HUA 701-1.16: *Buurspraakboek* 1418–1425, fol. 237v: [...] *allen gasten ende vreemden luden die uut enigen anderen landen binnen onser stat ofte vrijheit woenen ofte leggen* [...] (1425).

120 Cf. Bronislaw Geremek, *Les marginaux parisiens aux XIV*e *et XV*e *siècles*, trans. Daniel Beauvois (Paris: Flammarion, 1976), for the relation between economic and social marginality in late medieval Paris.

for prostitutes actually abound in the sources, like in a regulation from 1403 where the Council forbade 'the easy women to go into any graveyard in the city by evening or by night there to commit indecent activities'.[121] Likewise, in an extensive regulation on the begging practices of the poor and leprous, agreed upon in 1413, the Council again explicitly addressed the subjects of the regulation – 'all poor people' (*allen armen luden*) and 'all leprous people' (*allen besuycten luden*) – in addition to 'ordinary' inhabitants who could be confronted with these groups' begging practices.[122] Admittedly, the addressing of specific groups by the Council does not prove that all or any of them will have been listening to its pronouncements on every occasion. But even as indirect audience, informed of certain decisions by word-of-mouth, they already had an influence on the way in which the Council shaped its socio-legal discourse and communication practices.[123] The fact that it made its pronouncements during the *buurspraak* sessions, potentially open and freely accessible events, further supports this.

There is a tendency in the historiography on the *Parlement* to consider the texts produced by this body as directed solely at an internal public of legally trained specialists, the *Parlement* being inherently secretive about its legal decisions.[124] Some evidence suggests otherwise. That is not to say that the *Parlement* was not the primary consumer of the texts it produced; most texts that survive, like its extensive registers, functioned primarily as referential material for past cases that regained relevance in later proceedings. In such cases, only those directly involved in the proceedings took note of the contents of the records.[125] But very often other groups were involved in the initial stages of the formation and reception of the textual record. As Chapter 2 has shown, the spatial practices in the *Palais de la Cité* facilitated

121 HUA 701-1.16: *Buurspraakboek* 1402–1405, fol. 29v: *Voert verbiet de raet den lichten wiven dat si savonts ende snachts nyet en gaen op enighen kerchoven binnen der stat ende onreynlicheyt daer driven* (1403). This measure is repeated in the *Buurspraakboek* on a regular basis.

122 HUA 701-1.16: *Buurspraakboek* 1410–1414, fol. 156r–157r.

123 Cf. Carol Symes, "Out in the Open in Arras: Sightlines, Soundscapes, and the Shaping of a Medieval Public Sphere", in *Cities, Texts and Social Networks 400–1500: Experiences and Perceptions of Medieval Urban Space*, eds. Caroline Goodson, Anne E. Lester and Carol Symes (Farnham and Burlington, VT: Ashgate, 2010), who interprets similar publication practices in thirteenth-century Arras in the context of the Habermasian concept of *Öffentlichkeit.*

124 Hildesheimer and Morgat-Bonnet, *État méthodique*, 22; Serge Dauchy, "Les recueils privés de 'jurisprudence' aux temps modernes", in *Case Law in the Making: The Techniques and Methods of Judicial Records and Law Reports*, vol. 1, ed. Alain Wijffels (Berlin: Duncker & Humblot, 1997), 238.

125 For an example of cross-referencing in the registers, see two mentions in the $X^{2A}3$ register, explicitly relating one entry to two cases included earlier: AN $X^{2A}3$, fol. 99r.

access to some parts of the legal process in the *Grande Chambre* itself, in particular to the audience sessions. Those sessions where certain parts of the court's records were pronounced would thus often be attended by more than just the directly involved parties. Furthermore, there were physical structures in place, like the window between the *Grande Chambre* and Great Hall, for the communication of text-based pronunciations beyond the walls of the courtroom. Thus, in and near the courtroom, various potential audiences – the court and the involved parties, but also others with business in the *Palais*, and supposedly even interested parties in general – could take note of those texts that the court deemed necessary to pronounce in open court.

The reach of many records went far beyond the direct context of the court. Since the texts produced by the *Parlement* – the highest appellate court in the kingdom, after all – often concerned cases geographically far removed, it is possible to discern various more or less conscious attempts by the *Parlement* to involve audiences beyond the *Palais*. A case from 1346 illustrates two such practices.[126] The case under scrutiny concerned the false testimony of Hugues Belin of Mussy-l'Évêque, close to Metz. Hugues had given two divergent testimonies in a case against Wiard Mignot, where the second testimony – as it turned out later – had been influenced by threats made by the son of Wiard against Hugues. The latter was punished for providing false testimony, but – as the record states – with leniency because of Hugues' 'impotence and simplicity' and because of the forceful circumstances.[127] In an act remarkably similar to the penal rituals in Utrecht, he was supposed to hold a procession in the church of Mussy-l'Évêque, barefoot, without chaperon, in shirt and pants, and with a candle in his hands.[128] As the penal occasion was to take place in Mussy-l'Évêque, the local provost had to arrange the proceedings. For this he received a letter – which was also copied into the criminal register – specifying the case, the court's considerations for leniency and the punishment to be meted out. Such letters to officials abound in the sources, and give us a first indication of the way in which the *Parlement* tried to make sure that its vision on aspects of social behaviour and morality found a broader audience beyond the Parisian courtroom. For although such letters were addressed at a local official, the fact that the sources make an explicit distinction between ordinary letters and so-called 'closed' letters, makes it

126 The case is treated in two entries in the *Parlement*'s criminal register: AN $X^{2A}5$, fol. 8r–8v.
127 AN $X^{2A}5$, fol. 8v: [...] *bene sa impotente et sa simplece et consideranz les choses dessus dites.*
128 Ibid.: [...] *miz piez senz chaperon en chemise et en braies tenent en sa main un cierge dun livre* [...].

reasonably likely that open letters found an even broader audience.[129] In the case of the letter to the provost of Mussy-l'Évêque, this potentially broader audience is involved in an exceptionally explicit way. After instructing the provost to administer Hugues' ritualized punishment, the *Parlement* also ordered him to 'be present there to tell people the things above', that is to say, the many details of the case just mentioned in the letter.[130] In addition it then asked the provost to return a sealed letter as quickly as possible, describing the things that had happened on the occasion.[131] The *Parlement*, concerned with communicating a specific penal narrative – that of the condemnation of procedural transgression and the ability of the court to show a lenient face – seems on occasion to have taken great pains to make sure that texts professing its socio-legal narrative were received by a geographically broad and diverse audience. Adding this case to the aforementioned evidence for the *Parlement*'s broader practices of publishing texts, it seems problematic to consider this court as one that was primarily concerned with the secrecy of all of its legal process. In a manner similar to other aspects of its legal practice, such as the court space dynamics seen in Chapter 2, the *Parlement*'s concern vis-à-vis the textual record was rather for the general control of access to its documents, involving the limited accessibility of some and the explicit publicity of others.

Compared to the records from Paris and Utrecht, the York court material seems to have known a much more limited audience. Being exclusively written in Latin and concerned with legal arguments before all else, the full accessibility of such texts was by definition limited to a group of legally trained specialists. Still there were occasions on which the texts would reach an audience beyond these specialists, several of which have been encountered before. Forming part of a broader ecclesiastical hierarchy, the archbishop and its Consistory Court regularly communicated with officials all over the church province and beyond. At least some of this communication was intended to be made public on a local level. In 1293, for example, the archbishop ordered his official to publish a papal bull, issued in 1286 by Honorius IV, 'in our synod and consistory as well as elsewhere throughout our diocese'.[132] The same was occasionally done with verdicts, particularly if

129 For examples of closed letters, see AN X^{2A}4, fol. 45r, and X^{2A}5, fol. 66r.

130 AN X^{2A}5, fol. 8v: [...] *y soiez presenz en disant au peuple les causes dessus dites* [...].

131 Idem: [...] *et ce que fait en sera nous rescrivez souz vostre seel le plus hastivement que vous pourrez.*

132 Brown, *John le Romeyn*, vol. 1, 38–39: *Quocirca devocioni vestre mandamus quatinus dictas litteras faciatis tam in sinodis et consistoriis nostris, quam alibi per nostram diocesim, ubi expedire videritis, puplicari, ut ipsarum series nostris subditis* [sic] *innotescat* (1293).

they concerned the integrity of the religious community. For example, one entry in the archiepiscopal registers concerning the excommunication of a certain Custance de Daneport shows the archbishop ordering his official to proclaim the excommunication publicly 'in our consistory of York as well as in every archdeaconry of our diocese and [in] their deaneries'.[133] We lack the evidence to link the cause paper verdicts specifically to such diocese-wide publication practices. What is clear, however, is the existence of a perceived need to bring certain regulations and decisions to a broader public than just the legal specialists forming part of the court community. In this we recognize a similar logic of bringing the text to society as seen for Utrecht and Paris, as well as the existence of systems to bring such a logic into practice.

But the communicative occasions most prominent in this respect were still the court's sentence readings, during which a broader audience was more or less explicitly involved in witnessing the texts and their contents. As noted before, such occasions usually took place in the cathedral church of York, although they could also be performed elsewhere.[134] At these occasions, as the *presentibus* clauses tell us, a variety of people are said to have been present, partly identifiable and partly contained within the broad and very vague mentions of 'others' (*aliis*). In a few cases the scribe even identifies a larger audience, noting how the reading took place *in multitudine copiosa* (in a great crowd), but again without giving us any further details on the individuals involved.[135] Such mentions of the presence of identified witnesses and unidentified 'others' provide us no more than a vague glimpse of the actual audience of such readings. Still, we should take care not to overlook their communicative significance. In considering medieval charters, another genre of performative texts which also often contained such mentions of a witnessing public, Michael Clanchy has argued how these mentions formed part of a system of validating the written word in a strongly oral cultural context. Together with specific written signs, seals and other extra-textual objects, these lists of known and unknown witnesses were intended to inspire trust of the text-object into its potential audience.[136] Whereas Consistory Court sentences obviously differed from the charters

133 Brown, *Thomas of Corbridge*, vol. 1, 105–106: [...] *vobis mandamus quatinus tam in nostro consistorio Ebor. quam in singulis archidiaconatibus nostre diocesis eorumque decanatibus eam sic excommunicatam denunciari pupplice faciatis* [...].

134 See Chapter 3 for more on the sentence readings.

135 BIA CP.E.107 and CP.E.124. Also see Helmholz, *Marriage Litigation*, 119, n. 16, for examples from York and several other English church courts.

136 Clanchy, *Memory*, 298.

analysed by Clanchy, they also claimed to change an external reality by performing the judgement in question. As such, they required some of the same means of validation. Thus, an indication of the presence of a broader audience witnessing the performed legal act was fundamental to the validity of the written sentence as such. Here the influence of the court's audience on its written documents worked in two ways. While the people potentially receiving information from the Consistory Court in writing influenced these documents as intended audiences, in its written sentences the court also mobilized the actual audiences present at the sentence reading to validate this written judicial performance.

This relation between publishing and validating the written word was not exclusive to the Consistory Court. The reading out of *arrêts* by officials of the *Parlement* formed an equally crucial part of the decision-taking process. Both when the *arrêt* came out of a pleading session, and when it was taken in counsel, the *Parlement* felt the need to formally confirm the decision it had taken by reading it out in open court. The practice, from 1349 onwards, to date and order arrests according to the day of their pronunciation, clearly shows the logic behind and importance of this moment of publication.[137] For Utrecht as well, the pronunciation of various verdicts, measures and other announcements, both through the reading and physical presence of texts, made up a crucial part of its public presence in the city. As Clanchy has noted for twelfth- and thirteenth-century England, trusting or even accepting writing in the context of the legal process did not come about automatically. The fundamental role of oaths and witness statements in legal procedure before the twelfth century made the process of accepting written modes of proof long and difficult.[138] Clanchy remains slightly ambiguous as to whether he considers this process of acceptance of written proof to have worked out in favour of the latter by the end of the thirteenth century. However, the impression gained from the three law courts studied here is that even if written modes of communication may have become much more commonplace in the legal process by the fourteenth century, they remained only one part of a much broader practice of validating the things said and done in a court context. Even if the written word presented a crucial means to structure and fix the information received by the court according to broader narratives of order and disorder, documents alone did not suffice to convincingly script the way of the court. Both in bringing legal information to people that did not necessarily master the literacy, let

137 Grün, "Notice", CXXXIX, CLX.

138 Clanchy, *Memory*, 295–328.

alone the specific language to read these texts, and in validating the use of documents themselves, other forms of communication remained essential. In these communicative nodes the expectations of the court's audience, as well as the courts' expectations of who constituted the latter, were crucial in shaping the documents that in their turn constitute our major source of information on these historical people and practices.

Conclusion: Courts and court records

The generation, between the late thirteenth and early fifteenth centuries, of numerous court documents forms one of the main connecting threads between the three courts selected here as case studies. Such texts play a double role for us as historians in understanding medieval – or other historical – societies. The first is concerned with the text as a historical object and its role in the development of the law court as a historically contingent forum for socio-legal communication. The logic of committing to writing aspects of legal practice that had previously been confined to the realms of orality and performance brought a new type of communication to the fore that influenced the way in which people spoke to each other about issues of social behaviour and justice with which the legal process was generally concerned. By materializing linguistic information in this way, the legal process – and through it the law court itself – became manifest in new ways. Texts could be sent over long distances to let far flung communities and individuals know about certain legal events. They could be hung in public places, to inform people of the verdicts reached by a court without its officials necessarily being present. And they could be kept in unmodified form over long spans of time, allowing later users to delve into them. What is more, texts supported the construction and preservation of legal narratives. Put in written form, a specific court-authorized interpretation of socio-legal information gained a degree of permanence similar to that seen in Chapter 2 for the construction of legal spaces. The development of a particularly institutionalized form of legal practice, as represented by late medieval law courts, thus was closely linked to the increasing use of these language-objects, that allowed for – or possibly even stimulated – a certain degree of distance between legal parties and judges, be it geographical, temporal, or otherwise, while further substantiating the latter's claim on an authoritative interpretation of justice.

None of this is to say, however, that this development entailed a simple historical process from textless to text-based practices, implemented by legal authorities on a passive society. As this chapter has shown, the documents used in and by the three law courts all functioned in the context of a much broader communicative practice, involving oral, performative and spatial elements. The text as medium was regularly combined with other types of communication, be it through reading them, through the way in which they took part in a broader judicial performance, or through the use of urban space – like a public square – in transmitting them to a specific audience. Written documents were not the dominant, let alone the only form through which most participants experienced the legal process. On the contrary, the evidence of the three courts suggests a sense of necessity on the part of the court to validate the use of documents themselves as part of its broader attempt to legitimize the legal narrative it presented in it. Furthermore, many individuals and groups beyond the court were involved in the formation of these written records. Both in the production of these texts – that is, the reshaping of social information into written form – and in their subsequent consumption, documents were shaped by the interaction between the court and various other social agents, from witnesses and culprits to different types of audiences.

And this is where the second role of court records emerges. In their quest for the voice of 'ordinary' people, historians have gratefully drawn on law courts' surviving texts, through which one appears to come deceptively close to the voices of many people that are completely absent elsewhere. This sense of vicinity, however, is problematic. We have encountered many different ways in which the text could relate to legal activity, be it by suggesting to be a description of things that had happened, a prescriptive road map of what was supposed to happen, or even a constitutive act with extra-textual consequences. Yet what a text purports to do, be it describing, prescribing or performing activity, is not necessarily how the historian working with it can interpret the document. Not only does the process of coming into being of the text present particular filters of translation and editing, such as the step from minutes to registers; but the actual role of the text in the legal process need not be limited nor correspond to what it initially claims to be doing, seeing, for example, descriptions that try to prescribe specific behaviour. Significantly, in the context of the broader communicative practices of the court as treated in earlier chapters, all of these records formed part of the physical and linguistic performance of the court and its legal process.

It is by bearing such documentary specificities in mind that historians interested in the daily lives and experiences of people in past societies may profit most from the courts' documents. These texts do not form a direct record of socio-legal practice, but are rather attempts to script activities and the discourses about them. Many layers of translation and narrativization separate us from the experiences of medieval people as reflected in these texts. However, this does not mean that these texts were produced or functioned independently from the people they purport to capture. For the same processes that brought the documents into being involved a plethora of social actors, influencing the material-linguistic objects still encountered in the archives. In this sense, we are able to gain an idea of many medieval experiences through court records, although maybe not in the direct manner often envisaged. Even though events, statements and experiences found in the records are obscured by the strategic considerations of a few contemporaries, most prominently those of the court itself, their origin in the socio-legal negotiation over practices and interpretations means that the documents provide us with at least indirect reflections of many of the voices and experiences that interest us so much. Thus, rather than considering such records in the Ladurian vein as 'testimony without intermediary', it should be the intermediary itself that receives attention. For it is through a better understanding of the court as actor in late medieval communication processes that historians can really begin to understand the full scale of historical testimony that it provides us with.

5. Court and society: The production and consumption of justice

Abstract
Late medieval law courts were neither all-powerful legal authorities nor impersonal fora for legal messaging. As complex institutions, consisting of individual functionaries with their proper interests and involvements, yet sporting an explicitly corporate identity, they sought socio-legal legitimacy by offering potential litigants and audiences a specific model of justice. To do so, they navigated a number of partially overlapping socio-legal communicative fields, each with their own participants and media. While, on the one hand, trying to define and demarcate these fields themselves, courts also engaged in them to present elaborate narratives on the nature of society and their own position therein. As such, they balanced their inherent involvement in society with the suggestion of their transcendence thereof.

Keywords: medieval law courts, medieval lawyers, legal communication, legal speech, legal narrative, field theory

Until now, the focus of this book has been on the media – be they of a spatial, enacted, oral or textual nature – constituting the process of court communication. We have seen how law courts formed the locus of an extensive communicative activity, where diverse social issues were negotiated between its participants. The latter, while present in each of the previous chapters, have not stood at the centre of attention as such. Yet it was participants' intentions and their subsequent activities that drove much of these processes of socio-legal communication. In recent years, the users of law courts have received greater attention from social and legal historians. Daniel Lord Smail, for one, has proposed to approach developments in legal practice from a consumerist perspective. While courts were traditionally considered the exclusive result of rulers' attempts at acquiring socio-political monopolies

Camphuijsen, F., *Scripting Justice in Late Medieval Europe: Legal Practice and Communication in the Law Courts of Paris, York and Utrecht.* Taylor & Francis Group, 2022
DOI 10.5117/9789463723473_CH05

of power, Smail emphasized the role of the law's consumers, that is, those pursuing their cases in court, in shaping the court-based legal system of many late medieval societies. It was at least partly because litigants actively chose to invest in a legal process that courts could become such dominant forms of legal practice. Thus, the agents of change in this period were not just authorities coercing society into using their courts, but rather the people themselves who considered it profitable to bring their disputes there, instead of looking for an alternative solution.[1]

Smail's approach brings a large and often overlooked group of historical actors into the picture. He sensitizes us to the fact that legal practice concerned the interaction between many different people, with varying motivations and interpretations of the world in which they were living. Drawing on this approach I will now explicitly extend such a consideration to what Smail calls the producers of law, that is, the courts themselves. For in addition to the fundamental role played by litigants in shaping the legal process, these courts were also more than indifferent entities catering to the needs of historical agents. As bodies consisting of multiple individuals but also having their own corporate identities, their character was more ambiguous than both the models of a uniform legal authority or an impersonal forum for legal messaging allow for. Instead, they had their own complex of interests and motivations that informed the way in which they engaged with the people potentially interested in pursuing their disputes in court. Given Smail's contention that people's investment in the court was often not coerced, the question remains as to how – to continue his metaphor of the marketplace – the producers of law then tried to convince their potential consumers to buy into their product. What – if any – was their marketing strategy? In order to gain a fuller picture of the communicative structures surrounding these courts, it is thus fundamental to consider the positions they claimed as speakers within these structures, that is, as beleaguered promoters of a product to be desired.

Building on a Bourdieuan concept of communicative activity as set out in the introduction, this chapter will trace the role of courts as strategic communicators in three steps. The first will be concerned with their habitus, that is, the pregiven socially determined factors that shaped the way in which these bodies engaged with the social world around them. This is a complex matter, as all courts had an essentially bipartite nature. They formed both an institution with particular corporate identities and motivations, and,

1 Smail, *Consumption of Justice*, 4–21; similar arguments are developed in Johnson, *Law in Common*.

at the same time, consisted of individual functionaries with their own interests and social involvement. The courts that operated in particular linguistic fields were thus the temporary results of a process of negotiation between individual and shared interests. From these composite habitus, the second part of the chapter will demarcate the various communicative fields within which the courts operated, and where they competed for the socio-linguistic capital of judicial legitimacy. Contrary to Bourdieu, I explicitly distinguish multiple fields of communicative activity, rather than identify just one. The linguistic fields on which these courts operated can be subdivided into a number of partly overlapping sub-fields, each with its own norms, media and forms of socio-linguistic capital. This is an important distinction, emphasizing that legitimating language used in one field may well have been illegitimate in another, and suggesting the fundamental importance of courts' ability to navigate multiple communicative arenas. I will consider both the forms of separation between these sub-fields and their modes of interaction, showing how strategic use of these modalities was crucial in the operation of the courts. Finally, building on such strategic considerations, the third part of the chapter looks at these courts' attempts to acquire judicial legitimacy by presenting a specific view of society and its own role within it. Echoing my interpretation of linguistic activity from the introduction, it shows how legitimate speech was at the same time the socio-linguistic capital sought and a means of acquiring it.

The court as composite unity

There is a tension in institutions of all kinds between the collective purpose of the body as such, and the individual interests of the people it comprises.[2] The first is often brought to the fore very explicitly and publicly, while the latter generally operates under the surface, being couched in terms of collectivity and general agreement or – more negatively – corruption or

2 Recent literature in institutional economics stresses the way in which actors and institutions are fundamentally co-generative: John R. Searle, "What Is an Institution?", *Journal of Institutional Economics* 1, no. 1 (2005); Gregory Jackson, "Actors and Institutions", in *The Oxford Handbook of Comparative Institutional Analysis*, eds. Glenn Morgan, John L. Campbell, Colin Crouch, Ove Kaj Pedersen and Richard Whitley (Oxford: Oxford University Press, 2010). Although I generally agree with this position, that is, that actors shape an institution while the institution in its turn influences the actors, I do believe it too easily assumes individual conformation to a broader whole. I rather argue that the tension between actors' and institutional intentions is one of the main driving forces for the latter's change over time.

rebellion.[3] For historians interested in the social history of institutions, the public institutional identity is the easiest to get hold of. It is the image presented by the court in its official communication, found in most of the surviving documents. At the same time the public presentation of these institutions also obscures much of the basic activities and processes of negotiation taking place in the court. As Chapter 4 has stressed, for the period under examination it is often difficult to obtain a clear idea of the individual interests involved in the daily practice of law courts. Many of the documents available fall under the category of official communication or are influenced by considerations of publicity. In order to get a better sense of the potential diversity of interests underlying these courts' activities, we will take a more detailed look at the socio-linguistic habitus of its members. By considering aspects such as functionaries' socio-economic backgrounds, their legal training, the possibilities for individual career paths and the role of kinship networks, this chapter will trace the communicative horizon and interests with which court members approached society as part of a broader institutional body.

For the early Consistory Court little is known about the background of the officials and other clerks serving there. Only from the late thirteenth century onwards do these men become more visible in the records. Their image is above all one of a small educated elite.[4] K.F. Burns, who has extensively traced the backgrounds of those holding the position of archi-episcopal official between the thirteenth and fifteenth centuries, names as general characteristics of these men both long careers in ecclesiastical administration and an education in Roman and/or canon law.[5] The same was true for most other judges at court, such as the commissaries general and examiners general, as well as the majority of advocates. They generally held a university degree in law and followed a longer ecclesiastical career path that spanned the different church courts of late medieval England.[6] An education, although slightly less advanced, was also required of the

3 Cf. the various contributions in Ronald Kroeze, André Vitória and Guy Geltner, eds., *Anticorruption in History: From Antiquity to the Modern Era* (Oxford: Oxford University Press, 2018).

4 As seen in Chapter 1, the statutes of Archbishop Greenfield prescribed some 25 to 30 functionaries, excluding the apparitors, but – contrary to, for example, the ordinances for the Parisian *Parlement* – including proctors and advocates.

5 Burns, "Medieval Courts", 95–97.

6 Ibid., 137–142. Helmholz, *Marriage Litigation*, 142, has shown how all functionaries judging marriage cases in the Consistory Court between the 1370s and 1420s held a university degree in canon and/or civil law, acquired in Oxford or Canterbury. For the education of church court advocates more in general, see Helmholz, *The Profession*, 40–47.

notaries and proctors of the court. They often held a master of arts degree, and were supposed to be qualified notaries public.[7] A third category of staff members of the court did not generally have any specific educational qualifications. Neither the apparitors, who were charged with summoning people to appear in court, nor the notaries' various assistant scribes were expected to have any formal legal schooling.[8]

A major ecclesiastical tribunal like York's Consistory Court could be an alluring place to work for ordained men. There were several theoretical limits for people with clerical status to practice law. Next to the more general prohibition on being involved in cases that could end in penal bloodshed, which limited their possibilities to practice in secular courts, various theorists discouraged clerics, especially above a certain rank, to work as advocate or proctor in general, as it was deemed inappropriate that they would receive riches in that way.[9] However, the York evidence suggests that these theoretical objections did not restrain clerical status holders from working in the Consistory Court. On the contrary, in the cause papers nearly all the proctors encountered are unequivocally designated as *clericus*. Furthermore, various marked examples – both from York and other English church courts – illustrate how positions in court often formed part of a broader ecclesiastical career path, sometimes even leading to deaconries or episcopates.[10] This is also supported by the available evidence for the geographical origins of court members. As Burns shows, the archiepiscopal officials about whom most information is available can be traced both to Yorkshire and beyond, suggesting the court's inclusion in a network of supra-regional career paths.[11] The ecclesiastical legal profession thus provided many an occasion for social mobility.[12]

This state of affairs had various implications for the triangular relations between the individual members of the Consistory Court, the tribunal as a whole and the social groups and individuals with which they were engaged.

7 Burns, "Medieval Courts", 143. According to Helmholz, *The Profession*, 48–49, at least a significant minority of proctors in ecclesiastical courts will have held a university degree in law. For more on notaries public, see C.R. Cheney, *Notaries Public in England in the Thirteenth and Fourteenth Centuries* (Oxford and New York: Clarendon Press, 1972); Brundage, *Medieval Origins*, 394–406.

8 Burns, "Medieval Courts", 144–145, 152–155.

9 Brundage, *Medieval Origins*, 468–471.

10 Burns, "Medieval Courts", 88–95, 137–142; James A. Brundage, "The Bar of the Ely Consistory Court in the Fourteenth Century: Advocates, Proctors and Others", *Journal of Ecclesiastical History* 43 (1992), 543–554; Brundage, *Medieval Origins*, 349–350, 391–394.

11 Burns, "Medieval Courts", 88–97.

12 Cf. Brundage, *Medieval Origins*, 349–350.

The role of education was fundamental to these men's relation to society at large. As I will argue later on, the university-trained majority of the court formed a separate communicative in-group. At the same time, however, there were also several factors potentially separating individual members of this in-group. As the careers of some individuals suggest, for these men the position in court often presented a step in their individual career paths. The inclusion of the Consistory Court in such systems of ecclesiastical career advancement thus stimulated its members' private interests over those of the body as a whole. Such dominance of individual career paths could also be seen among the staff of the chapter of York Minster, a group both physically and professionally close to the members of the Consistory Court. Here some of the most prestigious or rewarding posts were regularly negotiated between English and non-English clergymen.[13] Likewise, the prestige and opportunities for advancement that positions like that of the official or commissary general could provide, made such posts desirable. This need not imply a complete lack of embeddedness of court officials in the court and its direct York context. But it is important to keep in mind that the Consistory Court often consisted of individuals who had acquired certain privileged social positions, in many cases through an active investment or powerful benefactors of their own, and who might therefore be willing to continue working their way up within the legal or ecclesiastical hierarchy.

For ambitious French administrators, the late medieval *Parlement* of Paris could also form an important step in their professional careers. Yet, whereas members of the Consistory Court seem to have followed very individual career paths, membership of the *Parlement* became a near-hereditary post shared among a small number of influential families. The development of this curial 'milieu', as it is dubbed by Françoise Autrand, took place over some two and a half centuries. As the *Parlement* originated in the itinerant royal court, initially its members would consist of royal counsellors, both lay and clerical. They were selected by the king every time that the court gathered, and nearly always included a number of secular and ecclesiastical dignitaries, like counts, dukes, bishops and abbots.[14] This fundamentally ad hoc character of the *Parlement* began to change during the early fourteenth century. Already in the last years of the thirteenth century it is possible to identify a small, stable group of counsellors, who formed part of the *Parlement* at practically every session. This permanent core expanded

13 Dobson, "Later Middle Ages", 75–82.

14 For the – strongly fluctuating – numbers of court members in this and later periods, see Chapter 1.

during the first part of the fourteenth century, until a royal ordinance in 1345 formally made membership of the *Parlement* permanent.[15] Significantly, the appearance of a stable staff of counsellors occurred in tandem with other major changes in the constitution of the *Parlement* in the same period, such as its locational permanency in the *Palais de la Cité* and its increasing textual case load.[16]

Related to the changing character of the *Parlement* during the fourteenth century were several major developments in the background of its members, as well as in their relation to the institution of the court and to society as a whole. In the early development of the *Parlement*, in line with its role as royal council, its members formed a body of representatives from different sections of society, including the nobility, clergy and urban citizenry. As a more or less permanent core began to take shape, its members increasingly became full-time legal administrators. As Raymond Cazelles has shown, by the time of the first Valois kings, in the early fourteenth century, a great number of royal officials had received legal schooling.[17] Although local connections could and often did still play a role, the educational and social backgrounds of these officials seem to have become more uniform during the fourteenth and fifteenth centuries.[18] This development into a specific curial milieu could also be seen in the changing relations between members of the *Parlement*. Autrand distinguishes three main phases in these internal relations for the period between 1345 and 1454. At the beginning of this period, in line with the less permanent character of positions in the court, its functionaries formed part of so-called 'factions' (*équipes*), political interest groups centred around specific princes or other royal servants of great standing. These factions encompassed the royal administration as a whole, and involved the *Parlement* in broader political networks. Positions in the *Parlement* were simply one way for members of these often regionally based factions to further their particular interests in the kingdom.[19] With the development of a specific curial milieu, ties of allegiance came to be based more on the *Parlement* itself. They were mostly family-based alliances, through which sitting members tried to surround themselves with relatives or other confidants. In contrast to the extra-curial practice of the former

15 Aubert, "Nouvelles recherches", pt. 1, 88–89, 240, 268; ibid., pt. 2, 57–58.

16 See Chapter 2 and Chapter 4, respectively.

17 Raymond Cazelles, *La société politique et la crise de la royauté sous Philippe de Valois* (Paris: Libraire d'Argences, 1958), 297–300.

18 Aubert, "Nouvelles recherches", pt. 2, 199; Autrand, *Naissance*, 265–266.

19 Autrand, *Naissance*, 54, 56–57, 108.

broad factions, these networks were mostly limited to the *Parlement* itself.[20] In the third phase sketched by Autrand this trend towards the *Parlement* as a family-based network continued even further. Instead of only surrounding themselves with relatives as they had done before, members of the *Parlement* now even tried to let their sons or sons-in-law inherit their seats, creating what were effectively parliamentary dynasties.[21]

In all these phases members of the *Parlement* were involved in various social networks, either – as in the fourteenth century – cutting through or, to the contrary, forming an organizational basis for the court. Autrand connects changes in the social layout of the *Parlement* firmly to the rise of the French state. In her view there is a clear development from the fourteenth-century institution that individuals used to further their own interests, to a fifteenth-century curial milieu to which a number of important families owed their primary loyalty. It was these families, Autrand argues, working for and within their institutionalized milieu, which formed the most important basis for the establishment of the state.[22] Such a focus on the state-based development of the *Parlement*, however, is in danger of overemphasizing the apparent unity of the curial milieu vis-à-vis any signs of internal political tension. The presence of family-based alliance structures, for example, as well as the attempts by court members to pass on their seat to their relatives, does imply the existence of conflict areas within this judicial body itself. Much of what Autrand identifies as a fundamental group mentality in the fifteenth century, was, I would argue, part of a publicly professed institutional ideology rather than an all-out change in the social structures and political interests underlying this professed unity. The *Parlement* was an institution composed of multiple individuals, whose specific and kin group-based interests often overlapped, but could just as well conflict with the professed common intentionality of the body as a whole.

Finally, the character of the Council of Utrecht presents us with another particular constitution of a judicial body. As seen in Chapter 1, its annual indirect election by the local guilds meant that the Council had a very different relation to the society it judged than was the case for both York and Paris.[23] Being basically elected functionaries, the members of the Council

20 Ibid., 66, 108, 264.

21 Ibid., 103–104, 108.

22 Ibid., 108, 264–267.

23 Also see the same chapter for the varying number of court members involved in different cases.

were – formally at least – dependent on a considerable group of people for their position. That said, only a small group of Utrecht citizens – let alone of its actual inhabitants – were eligible to actually become council members. Dirk Berents has suggested, on the basis of late-fifteenth-century lists of forced loans, that the majority of council members came from the wealthiest segments of the city.[24] As in York and Paris, it is likely that a socio-economic elite provided most members of this court. An important difference, however, was the educational background of most council members. Whereas the strong reliance on learned legal traditions in the Consistory Court and the *Parlement* meant that most of their members would have had some kind of legal schooling, this was not the case in the Council of Utrecht. There was little requirement or motivation for counsellors to invest in formal legal schooling when most of the cases they dealt with concerned local customary law. Where learned legal traditions did play a role, was when external 'masters and jurists of the law' were consulted for advice in specific – mainly instance – cases.[25] But the fact that the Council made an appeal to external legal specialists in these cases confirms the rarity of formal legal schooling amongst its members. Both the process of appointment and the absence of an educational distinction of the Utrecht counsellors thus suggest a particularly strong integration of the court in its locality.

The latter impression is strengthened when considering the influence of informal social structures on the constitution and practice of the Council. Utrecht's late medieval history was rife with the intense party strife between various elite groups, leading to major conflicts and even several radical power changes within the city.[26] These parties were usually based on the heads of a few influential families, extending throughout different layers of society in the form of these leaders' relatives and dependents, not unlike the factions in the early *Parlement*.[27] The Council, with its extensive political and judicial competences, became one of the most important fora for the proliferation of these disputes. A series of political conflicts between the parties of Lichtenberg and Lokhorst spanning the years 1413–1415, illustrates the role the Council could play in these struggles. In this period both parties were locked in a fierce struggle for political influence in the city, leading to both successful and unsuccessful power takeovers. On

24 Berents, "Gegoede burgerij", 90–91.

25 Muller, *Rechtsbronnen*, Introduction, 104, 172; Berents, "Gegoede burgerij", 19.

26 Smithuis, "Politiek en geweld", 242, identifies four successful power changes and no less than ten failed ones for the period between 1400 and 1430. Also see Berents, *Misdaad*, 97–102.

27 Smithuis, "Politiek en geweld", 245–248.

each of these occasions the Council would banish or otherwise punish members of the losing party, usually for reasons of holding 'unreasonable meetings' (*onredelike vergaderinge*) or sowing discord.[28] In such cases the Council was thus very directly employed in a political conflict among the city's socio-economic elite. But even outside of such extremely politicized instances, the council members did not operate as a unified body on every occasion. The Guild Letter of 1455, which was issued after the downfall of the two most important political factions of the time had temporarily strengthened the position of the guilds vis-à-vis influential patriciates, explicitly anticipated instances of disagreement within the Council.[29] For instance, if the Council could not reach a unanimous decision in a case, it would be decided by ballot (*bonen*). The result of the ballot would then be put into practice, and individual court members who disagreed were not allowed to speak against the result, under penalty of exclusion from the Council for ten years.[30] Although this prescriptive measure cannot conclusively tell us whether and how often disagreements within the Council slowed down the decision-making process, within its direct historical context – that is, the guilds' taking back control from conflicting political factions – it was likely a concrete reaction to actual disagreements in practice. As we have seen for the Consistory Court and the *Parlement*, in the daily operation of the Council there was a constant tension between its institutional identity and the many individual interests of its members.

Whereas the Utrecht Guild Letter of 1455 provides evidence for the tension between corporate and individual interests, it likewise shows how the Council explicitly professed the ideal of speaking with one voice. While it foresaw the possibility of internal discord, the norm to be attained and confirmed was a publicly expressed communal agreement. And the same was true for the other two cases. Whereas the *Parlement* during the fourteenth and fifteenth centuries comprised members with various alternative solidarities and interests, it put forward a public face that emphasized institutional unity. Likewise, the Consistory Court's professed commonality did not preclude individual members from pursuing their own career paths by means of,

28 Berents, *Misdaad*, 102–106. Such politically motivated verdicts of banishment can be found in HUA 701-1.16: *Buurspraakboek* 1410–1414, fols. 154r, 158r.

29 The 1455 Guild Letter is edited in Johan van de Water, ed., *Groot placaatboek vervattende alle de placaten, ordonnantien en edicten der edele mogende heren staten 's lands van Utrecht: Mitsgaders van de edele groot achtbare heeren borgemeesteren en vroedschap der stad Utrecht tot het jaar 1728 ingesloten*, pt. 3 (Utrecht: Jacob van Poolsum, 1729), 80–85.

30 Ibid., 83.

rather than subject to, this one court. Despite the diverse social, economic and educational backgrounds of their members, one of the common threads in the late medieval history of these courts was their conscious attempt to present themselves as a collective, coherent body, speaking with one voice and acting uniformly. In what follows I will discuss several ways in which such idealized corporate unity was professed vis-à-vis members' potential other interests.

One means by which the three law courts sought to emphasize their uniformity was through a strong continuity in nomenclature. This is remarkable, given the fundamental changes that took place in the actual constitution and practice of these bodies over time. Such continuity of nomenclature has often misled historians in their assumptions regarding these bodies, attributing to them a continuity of character that may readily be doubted. For instance, the term 'city council' can be found in Utrecht charters as early as 1196, when a group called *consules civitatis* is said to operate as one of the representatives of the citizens of Utrecht vis-à-vis the episcopal landlord. Since that time the nomenclature has changed little. While the group alluded to changed from a body supporting the aldermen to an independent urban authority, subsequently seeing its powers wax and wane over the fourteenth and fifteenth centuries, it kept being referred to as the Council.[31]

In Paris the term *parlement* was originally a temporal designation, referring to the moment when the royal court turned itself into a judicial body. In the first *Olim* volume, for example, entries often note how a judicial act has been performed 'in this court, in a certain *parlement* (*in hac curia, in quodam parlamento*).[32] In later volumes of the *Olim*, however, the use of the term gradually expands. The fourth *Olim* volume, for instance, regularly notes how cases are brought 'to the court of the *parlement* of Paris' (*in curia parlamenti Parisiensis*), suggesting an institutional and spatial rather than purely temporal understanding of the term.[33] And this institutionalized use of the term *parlement* becomes even more explicit when entries at some point even begin to state how documents were transmitted 'to the *parlement* in Paris' (*ad parlamentum Parisius*), regarding the term *parlement* on its own as a sufficiently clear indication of the court concerned.[34] Thus, while the occasional judicial sessions of the royal court changed into a permanent

31 Muller, *Rechtsbronnen*, Introduction, 17–21.
32 AN X^{1A}1, fol. 192v (1272); Beugnot, *Les Olim*, pt. 1, 909.
33 AN X^{1A}4, fol. 288v (1315); Beugnot, *Les Olim*, pt. 3.2, 982.
34 AN X^{1A}4, fol. 301v (1315); Beugnot, *Les Olim*, pt. 3.2, 1032.

body, its most explicit form of self-identification – that is, how its members referred to their own institution – emphasized continuity.

In York a similar development took place from the court as a temporary judicial form of the more general archiepiscopal court, into a permanent legal body. Judging by the court's own sources, the term *consistorio* came over time to designate basically three separate things. One – the most common – was the old temporal denomination of the time periods during which cases would come before the court, as in 'the first consistory after the feast of the conversion of Saint Paul, beginning on the twenty-seventh day of January'.[35] Another sense in which it regularly appears, especially in the cause papers, is as a spatial indication when sessions are said to have taken place 'in the place of the consistory'.[36] But as in Paris, the documents from York too increasingly consider the indication 'consistory' as standing for the court as an institution, regularly appearing in place of the more common 'court of York' (*curia Eboracensis*).[37] Like the Utrecht Council and the *Parlement*, while the Consistory Court went through marked changes in character, constitution and competences over the centuries, in the words it used to speak about itself the suggestion of a longstanding continuity of practices came to the fore.

Such continuity of nomenclature served several purposes. First, there is the suggestion of continuity itself. Although the thirteenth-century legal gatherings of the French royal court were a completely different matter from the early-fifteenth-century judicial institution residing in the *Palais de la Cité*, the latter's labelling as *Parlement* and *Curia regis* linked it explicitly to earlier forms of judicial activity and created and kept the emphasis on a specific myth of institutional origins. Considering the increasingly independent role that the *Parlement* sought vis-à-vis the king in its daily business underscores the ideological importance of its nomenclature. Such emphasis on continuity could furthermore suggest a certain character of the court. The way in which the Council of Utrecht kept referring to itself as a 'council', that is, a body providing its lord with counsel, stressed the relative power and independence it held vis-à-vis the bishop, by emphasizing a past feudal relationship. Last, but certainly not least, the nomenclature suggested the body's corporate identity. This could have clear political overtones,

35 YML M 2(1)b, fol. 1r.: *Consistorium proximum post festum conversionis sancti Pauli incipiens xxvii die mensis Januarii.*

36 For example, BIA CP.E.259: *Ista sententia fuit lecta et lata per dominum officialum in loco consistorii pro tribunali sedenti* [...] (1368).

37 As in BIA CP.E.233: *Lata fuit ista sententia per dominum officialem infrascriptum in consistorio Eboracensis* [...] (1397).

as, for example, when the factionalism between leading Utrecht families was covered with the cloak of a unified Council representing the common interests of the city. But the suggestion of unity could also be integrated more subtly into the programme of institutional ideology. So whereas the archiepiscopal administration developed into three distinct and largely independent bodies – namely, the Consistory Court, the Court of Audience and the Exchequer – in most official documents and registers all three were usually considered together as the 'Court of York' (*Curia Eboracensis*), emphasizing a common role in the archiepiscopal household. Thus, the way in which these courts formally identified themselves emphasized aspects that could differ markedly from – or at least gave a very limited view of – the many forces that shaped their daily practice. Whereas the relation between such institutions and their individual members could take many shapes, from strong common intentionality to conflicts of interest, these naming practices emphasized institutional above private identities.

That the potential conflict of identities was a matter of concern becomes even clearer when considering the obligation – common to all three courts' officials – to take oaths. For Archbishop Greenfield, drawing up his statutes for the archiepiscopal court in 1311, the first item on his list was to decree that the presiding judge, be it the official or his commissary general, must take an oath upon assuming office. With the oath, these functionaries formally promised to avoid any external loyalty, partiality, enmity, favour or perceived profit to cloud their judgement, and to observe the court's 'laudable customs' (*laudabiles consuetudines*).[38] The advocates – most likely including the proctors – were likewise required to swear an oath, although in this case on an annual basis. In this oath, which the statutes spelled out in full, they promised to operate justly, truthfully and diligently, and not to challenge the jurisdiction or customs of the court in any way.[39] The admission oath for the York advocates developed within a broader canonical context. With the increasingly frequent use of advocates from the twelfth century onwards, ecclesiastical courts in Europe began to require oaths from these legal practitioners before they were allowed audience in the court. Although in the first instance a matter for individual courts, the Second Council of Lyons in 1274 prescribed a more general model for such oaths in its constitution *Properandum*.[40] The oath required of the

38 Wilkins, *Consilia*, vol. 2, 409.

39 Ibid., 410. See Appendix 2.2 for a full transcription of the oath.

40 Brundage, *Medieval Origins*, 283–306, including a modern English translation of the major part of the model oath at 301–302.

York advocates seems to expand on this general vow. On the one hand it echoes the *Properandum*'s exhortation that advocates should spare no effort, strength or resources to pursue what they deem right and just for their clients, while abandoning cases they find to be inherently unjust. At the same time, however, the York oath puts much more emphasis on the advocates' loyalty towards their particular institution, explicitly forbidding them to question the court's jurisdiction, customs and statutes.[41] The oath taken by the official and his commissary general reflects a similar institutional appropriation of broader principles of conduct. While the oath encompasses ethical standards that had long since been points of discussion in canon law, to unite such standards in a formal pledge, as the Greenfield statutes did, was not generally required.[42]

But the canon legal tradition was not necessarily the only source for systems of oath swearing by legal officials. As early as the second half of the thirteenth century, the French kings required officials, including sergeants, bailiffs, provosts, viscounts, mayors and judges, to publicly swear an oath before taking up their post.[43] Though not exclusively concerned with these officials' judicial activities, the topics they touched upon strongly overlap with what the York judges were supposed to swear, for example, requiring oath takers to judge indiscriminately and in keeping with royal and other laws. Thus, a second, feudal tradition formed the initial basis for practices of oath swearing in the *Parlement*. To this were added, likely under influence of the stipulations of the Council of Lyons, specific regulations for oath swearing by advocates, whether operating in the *Parlement* or other royal jurisdictions.[44] Thus, similar to the stipulations in York, the king called on advocates to operate in good faith (*bona fide*), diligently (*diligenter*) and truthfully (*fideliter*), and to drop a case if they considered it to be unjust.[45] In 1291 both oath-swearing traditions came together in an ordinance of Philip IV concerning the *Parlement*.[46] The text explicitly refers to the earlier regulations on the oath taking of royal officials (1254/1256) and advocates (1274), respectively, combining both groups under the institutional umbrella

41 Wilkins, *Consilia*, vol. 2, 410: *Nec aliquid dicam, proponam, vel faciam* [...] *contra Eborum ecclesiae jurisdictionem, aut Eborum curiae consuetudines, vel statua.* Also see Appendix 2.2.

42 Ibid., 382–384.

43 As expounded in two ordinances by Louis IX from 1254 and 1256. See De Laurière, *Ordonnances*, vol. 1, 65–75 and 77–81.

44 Stipulated in an ordinance by Philip III from 1274. See De Laurière, *Ordonnances*, vol. 1, 300–301.

45 Ibid.

46 Ibid., 320–322, esp. articles 8, 9 and 11.

of the *Parlement*.[47] That these oaths played an important role in actual legal practice is suggested by their inclusion in the *Parlement*'s registers. The 1340 criminal register, for example, contains a transcript of the extensive oaths the advocates and proctors were supposed to take before being allowed to plead in the *Parlement*.[48] These oaths covered a range of aspects of the expected behaviour of advocates and proctors, including anything from the maximum fee they were to accept for their work and their position in the courtroom, to the by now familiar exhortation not to receive nor continue unjust cases.

That practices of oath taking did not spring exclusively or even primarily from learned legal traditions is further substantiated by the major role they played in the administrative and legal practice of the Council of Utrecht. One of the fourteenth-century registers of banishments contains a transcript of the oath that council members supposedly took when assuming office.[49] During the fifteenth century, this oath was copied in a slightly adapted form into the back of the book of bylaws, called *Die Roese*, together with numerous other oaths of office, like those for the aldermen, the guild elders and a variety of special commissaries.[50] The council members' oath echoes the broad character of the Council's activities, speaking in general terms about the members' responsibility to serve the city through good and unbiased counsel, and to take an active part in the council meetings. More specific tasks are touched upon in the oaths taken by the various special commissions, either formed by a selection of council members, or by specially appointed functionaries. For example, the officials responsible for collecting the excise on beer, called *sijsmeesters* in the sources, would promise not to favour one brewer over another.[51] In the same vein, members of the *vive*, responsible for judicial investigations, took an oath not to withhold any information in a case, notwithstanding their own or their relatives' interests.[52] A common theme in these oaths was thus the obligation to put the interests of the city, its guilds and the Council before those of ones relatives, friends, or oneself. In daily practice such oaths were regularly called upon to morally impede self-serving or otherwise inadequate behaviour from officials. Thus, when

47 See Telliez, *Officiers*, 85–90, for a comparison with oath-taking practices in several other French officialities.

48 AN $X^{2A}4$, fol. 18v–19v (1340). See Appendix 3.1 and 3.2 for a full transcription.

49 The oath is transcribed on the unfoliated front fly leaf of the Council's *Th.2* register: HUA 701-1.227. See Appendix 1.4 for a full transcription.

50 Muller, *Rechtsbronnen*, vol. 1, 386–394.

51 Ibid., 386.

52 Ibid., 393–394.

the Council decreed in 1417 that all its members and city servants (*alle rade, alle der statknapen ende knechten*) were supposed to fine anyone driving his cart in the city, all were to accept this responsibility 'on their oath and trade' (*bij horen eede en bij horen ambacht*).[53]

Oaths served various functions. First, the court made its officials formally – that is to say, legally – and publicly accountable for their actions through them. If a member of the court behaved in a way that was considered to be contrary to the interests of the entity that gave him his power – be it in the form of a kingdom, an (urban) community or the court itself – he could be penalized on the basis of breaking his oath.[54] Oaths thus ideally intended to prevent practices perceived as unaccountable amongst court officials, in particular those that put private interests before those of the court.[55] At the same time, in singling out wrong activities, oaths formed a guideline for the behaviour officials were supposed to display. By distinguishing categories of good and bad behaviour, oaths in a sense created and defined both the practices they attempted to further and those they intended to extirpate.[56] The sources suggest, furthermore, that the message of these oaths was meant to be received by a broader public. The 1254 and 1256 regulations of the French king, for example, required officials to take their oath during a public session of the court (*en pleine assise* or *en pleine place*), to make sure that it would be observed more strictly.[57] Likewise, Archbishop Greenfield, in drawing up the court statutes that set out the oaths for various functionaries, specified how these same statutes were to be read out publicly on a yearly basis.[58] Such oaths could thus be a public display of court ideology, binding officials to the ideals of the institution they served. What is more, through this same process of ideological binding they also functioned to define the court itself. For in requiring an oath of office from its officials, the court – here understood as the complex of expectations of the people working in and otherwise using the court – explicitly singled out these individuals from general society, and related them to each other according to their specific role in the legal process. It thus emphasized the *esprit de corps* of the group of individuals constituting the court, lauding their collective morals and contrasting these explicitly with the private interests that might threaten this unity.

53 HUA 701-1.16: *BSB* 1414–1418, fol. 128v.

54 See Brundage, *Medieval Origins*, 302–303, for examples of the penalization of oath breakers.

55 Helmholz, *Marriage Litigation*, 152.

56 Telliez, *Officiers*, 85–90.

57 De Laurière, *Ordonnances*, 70, 79.

58 Wilkins, *Consilia*, vol. 2, 413.

Late medieval law courts tried to curb the individual interests of their many members within an overarching whole of common intentionality and identity. That is not to say that they always succeeded. There were alternative forms of organization and practice – such as kinship networks or opportunities for individual career paths – that could cause tensions between what the institution was said to stand for, and the interests and loyalties of the individuals working within it. In order to counter potential disunity and mitigate conflicts of interest, courts – or, more precisely, those profiting most from their univocal appearance – performed curial unity in several ways. Through their stable nomenclature – *Parlement*, Council, *Curia* – they identified themselves with certain past structures of organization, echoing a particular foundational myth. In a way reminiscent of the ritualization of legal practices as seen in Chapter 3, the repeated application of certain terms to designate a specific judicial gathering of men suggested a continuity that provided the court with an ideological permanency vis-à-vis the ever-changing socio-political relations of its members. The oaths that court officials were required to take worked in a similar way. By formally promising to fulfil their role in a particular manner, these functionaries performed the submission of their individual interests to those of the institution as a whole. They did so linguistically, that is, by speaking certain words, but in many cases also enacted these words bodily, by taking the oath in a publicly staged setting. The producers of justice were thus complex constellations. Integrated into society through the social habitus of their members, ideologically they tried to stress their transcendence of such private interests and alternative loyalties. This tension, between forming an essential part of society and claiming to be impartially surveying it from a distance, was also one of the central issues in these courts' interaction with the law's many potential consumers.

Fields of legal speech

Bourdieu, in discussing communicative activity, considers linguistic markets as separate arenas of speech activity with their own particular characteristics. When a social actor performs a speech act, its form and implications are determined by the interaction between the actor's habitus and the specific linguistic field where the utterance is done.[59] Late medieval law courts were often not limited to only one linguistic field in this sense.

59 Bourdieu, *Language*, 37–65.

Rather, they interacted in several different social and institutional contexts, from the internal forum of the court itself to interregional networks of legal specialists, communal dynamics of *fama* and other public knowledge, or even outright political arenas. Each of these formed its own field of communication, with specific participants, norms and media. Building on Bourdieu's concept of speech activity, in what follows I will trace the different communicative fields on which these courts operated, sketching the positions of their participants and the linguistic norms and media governing participation in them. Strictly delimiting these fields of communicative action is often impossible. On the contrary, much of the courts' legal activity was specifically concerned with defining and redefining the limits of fields of communicative activity. For it was through such practices that the court and other social actors attempted to manipulate their positions on these fields, as well as the fields themselves. Thus, next to tracing the arenas of speech activity, I will also consider the attempts by the court to influence the scope and character of these fields. Through this twofold analysis of the courts' communicative landscape, we gain a better understanding of the way in which they related to and positioned themselves within their broader social contexts.

Both the *Parlement* of Paris and York's Consistory Court comprised for a large part university-trained lawyers. This background strongly influenced the types of language and rhetoric used, which thereby came to function as linguistic boundaries of a specific curial speech community. The Consistory Court is a case in point. The cause papers produced by this court strongly emphasize the closed character of its professional speech community. The fact that they were written in Latin was not necessarily the main factor limiting their accessibility for outsiders. But the Latin of these records is highly abbreviated, requiring a specialized vocabulary (Figure 14). Furthermore, studying this court's records is like entering a completely different world, with its own language and system of logic. For the average litigant, seeking or being forced to bring his conflict to court, much of this legal discourse was difficult to follow, let alone participate in. The procedural requirements as constantly encountered in the sources, such as the parties' presentation of *positiones* or *responsiones* to state or refute the exact points on which the legal argumentation would proceed, stood far from the terms in which the conflict was conceptualized outside of the courtroom.[60] And the same can be said of a legal measure like the abjuration *sub pena nubendi*. According to

60 See Helmholz, *Marriage Litigation*, 14–16, for more on the presentation of *positiones* and *responsiones* in English church courts.

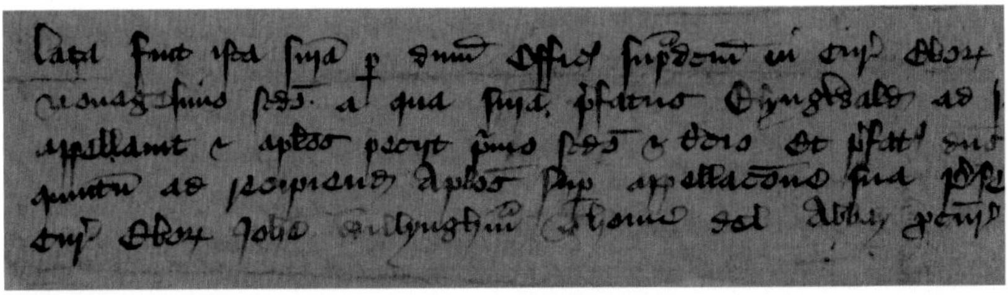

Figure 14: Abbreviated latin in a (*Lecta et*) *lata*-entry in the Consistory Court's cause papers (BIA CP.E.193).

this procedure, two litigants, appearing in court on charges of fornication, could be forced to contract a conditional marriage. This meant that if they had sexual relations, they would, after that point, automatically be married.[61] Although, from the point of view of canon law, such measures followed a clear series of causal relationships, in the specific social setting where the stated events took place, very different concerns underlay people's thoughts and actions.

This was, after all, the discourse of legal professionals who were attempting to apply their theoretical knowledge to the complexities of social life. It was a university-bred discourse, whose mastery formed the main capital required – though never explicitly stated – for participating in the legal business of the court. Both linguistic forms and the media used to communicate them limited participation to those actually trained in this kind of language. Within this linguistic field the court interacted with other groups of trained legal specialists. In appeal procedures the Consistory Court communicated with both superior and inferior courts in the ecclesiastical court hierarchy, evidenced, for example, by the survival of sentences contained in letters to court officials.[62] This same field could also encompass interactions with a broader range of legal actors. In the case of the English church courts, this concerned principally the system of royal courts, with which they regularly competed for jurisdiction.[63] These royal courts were also increasingly staffed by university-trained legal professionals, thus creating a common linguistic ground for interaction in a specific communicative field.

However, the field of university-trained legal discourse was not the only speech arena within which the Consistory Court was involved. For, far

61 R.H. Helmholz, "Abjuration *sub pena nubendi* in the Church Courts of Medieval England", *The Jurist* 32 (1972).

62 See the treatment of such letter-sentences in Chapter 4.

63 R.H. Helmholz, "Writs of Prohibition and Ecclesiastical Sanctions in the English Courts Christian", *Minnesota Law Review* 60 (1976).

from being completely detached from ordinary society by walls of professionalized discourse and language, it interacted with it in several ways. This interaction was often of a non-textual character, building on oral and enacted media. The sentence readings, for example, orally performing the court's written legal process in the Minster or another church, were more than a formalization of the textual sentence. They also engaged another, lay audience, such as the litigants, their friends and relatives, and even broader groups witnessing these events, in a discussion about the solutions for social conflict and the role of the court in providing them.[64] And the same was true for other publicly performed aspects of the legal process, such as public penitence for contumacy or formal oaths of compurgation.[65] On the face of it, this field of communication may appear to be one-directional, emanating from the court outwards. However, a strong argument for the essentially multidirectionality of communication in this field is provided by the extensive role of both witness testimony and its more general variant of public repute – or *fama publica* – in the procedure of the court.[66]

An often-cited suit from 1328 provides a case in point. In it Elizabeth, daughter of Simon Lovell, claimed to have contracted a valid marriage with Thomas, son of Robert of Marton. The latter, however, denied having done so, claiming to have consented to no more than a conditional marriage.[67] In attempting to make her case, Elizabeth drew on two forms of evidence, the first provided by individual witnesses, and the second by the alleged common knowledge in the deanery of Ryedale. Nine people testified on her behalf, presenting their accounts of a number of occasions that were considered crucial for the case, in particular because of the words of consent supposedly spoken by Thomas and Elizabeth in these situations. In addition, the libel and positions presented in the case also mentioned explicitly how this alleged consent was not just known by these nine individuals, but was 'public, notorious and manifest' (*publica, notoria et manifesta*) in the whole deanery, and that there was 'public speech and rumour' (*publica vox*

64 See Chapter 3 and Chapter 4 for more on the sentence readings.

65 For the practice of public penitence, see Chapter 3. For compurgation oaths, see R.H. Helmholz, *The Oxford History of the Laws of England: The Canon Law and Ecclesiastical Jurisdiction from 597 to the 1640s* (Oxford: Oxford University Press, 2004), 599–642.

66 For the practice of taking testimony, see Chapter 4. For the role of *fama publica* in the English church courts, see Helmholz, *Marriage Litigation*, 46. Also see Thelma Fenster and Daniel Lord Smail, eds., *Fama: The Politics of Talk and Reputation in Medieval Europe* (Ithaca, NY: Cornell University Press, 2003).

67 BIA CP.E.18. Several documents from the case have been edited in Helmholz, *Marriage Litigation*, 191–195. The case is discussed at length in Pedersen, *Marriage Disputes*, 110–114; Donahue, *Law, Marriage and Society*, 96–97.

et fama) about it. Here, different social groups and individuals thus spoke to the court directly or indirectly, providing their interpretation of events and norms of behaviour.[68] There existed a bi-directional flow of messaging between the court and other segments of society, which was concerned not only with the evaluation of certain ways of behaving, but also with promoting the social legitimacy of the court in judging this behaviour. In short, there are at least three different fields of socio-legal communication to account for when treating the Consistory Court: the field that it itself constituted as overarching institution to which individual court members had to relate themselves, a field of university-bred legal discourse on which it negotiated with other legal authorities over categories of jurisdiction and judicial power, and a field of broader social legitimacy where it interacted with those whose behaviour it claimed to judge.

It would be pointless to fix strict boundaries to the foregone communicative fields, as becomes even clearer when comparing the analysis of the Consistory Court with that of the other two courts under scrutiny. Although it is in some cases possible to distinguish fields similar to those identified in York, the overall picture differs markedly. The *Parlement*, like the Consistory Court, contained a large – and growing – group of university-trained lawyers. It thus participated in a linguistic field similar to that of the York case, where legal specialists talked to other specialists about social conflicts, placing them in a particular legal framework to look for a legitimate means to resolve them. Again, the media used shaped the limits of this particular communicative field, as much communication was conducted in judicially moulded Latin texts. The criminal register from 1345 contains an *arrêt*, briefly touched upon in Chapter 4, in a case initiated by Isabelle de Blanot, lady of Uxelles, following the attack by several armed men on the village of Ougy-sous-Uxelles, which fell within her jurisdiction.[69] The entry is built around the procedural decision that the *Parlement* made, to join Isabelle as plaintiff to the royal proctor and thereby extend the scope of the case beyond that of a purely civil suit. The *arrêt* sets out the legal issue, namely, that the attackers have possibly breached a royal safeguard by their action against the village, specifies the procedural steps undertaken so far, that is, that the court has received and assessed multiple pieces of information (*plures informationes*) concerning the case, and notes its final decision. The information provided is limited to what is relevant for the current legal argument, leaving out such things as the exact outcome of the enquiries or

68 Cf. Forrest, "Trust and Doubt"; idem, *Trustworthy Men*.

69 AN $X^{2A}5$, fol. 74r. For a full transcription, see Appendix 3.2.

the precise events that have taken place in Ougy. Thus, both in its language – that is, juridical Latin – and its rhetorical structure, this entry was targeted at a field of specialized legal discourse. However, the *arrêt* likewise hints at how the *Parlement* engaged in a communicative field beyond that of legal specialists. In the stress it lays on the role of the information received by the court in formulating a decision in the case, this entry shows how the *Parlement* depended on the interaction with many groups and individuals outside a court context. And, as seen for the Consistory Court, the interaction in this field was bi-directional. The *Parlement* performed its claim to a legitimate definition of justice, be it through the publication of some of its legal documents, as discussed in Chapter 4, or through the public enactment of parts of its legal process.[70]

Yet the above *arrêt* also nods at a third field of communicative activity with which the *Parlement* was particularly concerned. In the case of Isabelle de Blanot, the main issue at stake was the alleged breach of royal safeguard. Such legal subjects, being concerned with an ideal social order in the realm that was supposed to be guaranteed by the king, engaged the *Parlement* in a communicative field that had a more politico-ideological character. Late medieval French kings claimed power over an increasingly large geographical area, including Normandy, Champagne and the Languedoc.[71] As a major instance of the kings' claim on supreme judicial power, the *Parlement* was thus also strongly involved in its field of politico-ideological language. An example of this can be found in its practice of regularly holding *Grands Jours*, that is, parliamentary sessions in other places than the Parisian *Palais de la Cité*.[72] In performing royal justice the *Parlement* not only vied for the social legitimacy of its own position as assessor of social behaviour, but also engaged in the political language of royal power, that is to say, it claimed these areas fell within the political constellation of the French kingdom with the king at its head. It thus essentially shared in the many forms by which this royal ideology came to be propagated and challenged, be it architecturally, as in the campaign to visualize the royal presence in Paris by expanding the *Palais de la Cité*, enacted, in the form of Joyous Entries, or otherwise.[73]

70 For the *Parlement*'s publication practices, see Chapter 4. For examples of judicial enactment in Paris, see Cohen, "To Die a Criminal"; Gauvard, "Pendre et dépendre".

71 For a general history of the late Capetians, see Menant, Martin, Merdrignac and Chauvin, *Les Capétiens*, 315–446.

72 See Chapter 3 for the practice of holding *Grands Jours*.

73 On the rebuilding of the *Palais de la Cité*, see Chapter 2. As argued in Chapter 3, the *Grands Jours* are closely related to various forms of political performance, like the Joyous Entries held

The Council of Utrecht likewise offers a complex picture of courts' fields of communicative activity. The most striking difference with the other two courts, and in particular with the Consistory Court, is the foreignness of university-schooled lawyers. Professional lawyers from outside were occasionally called upon, but they did not form an intricate part of the judicial body itself. Having received legal training at a university was no formal or informal prerequisite to participating in the curial speech community, as it did in York and Paris. The particularities of these officials' nomination – that is, an indirect election by the political community, influenced by oligarchic interests – put up very different criteria for admission to the judiciary. The surviving documents support this view of a modest importance attributed to learned legal discourse. From their oldest surviving exemplars at the beginning of the fourteenth century, the Council's many registers are almost exclusively written in Dutch. Furthermore, the learned legal categories according to which social reality is often conceptualized in the York and Paris sources are hardly present in the Utrecht material. For example, the vocabulary applied to distinguish various types of crimes, like *onstantelike saken* (improper things) or *vredebrake* (breach of peace), echoes very specific moral and political ideas rather than a learned taxonomy.[74]

It is, however, still possible to distinguish different fields of communicative activity in which the Council was engaged. Although less defined by a formal training in legal theory, there was an important difference between the court's internal and external speech contexts. This difference becomes particularly clear when comparing the two major written sources surviving for the Council, the *Raads dagelijks boek* and the *Buurspraakboek*.[75] The former, constituting a register of the court's daily business, is mainly concerned with matters internal to the Council or otherwise limited to a small group of people involved in a specific case concerning, for example, private debt, marriage or inheritance. Thus, in 1417 the Council, aldermen and guild elders recorded a decision taken in a conflict between Jan van Damassche and the relatives of Alfer van Woudegem over the claim of a debt owed by Alfer to Jan since 1399.[76] Likewise, in 1418 the Council intervened in what seems to have been a problematic marriage between Gerijt van Vroenenstein and his wife, Lady Haze van Vroenenstein, when it learned that Gerijt had taken excessive control of his

by many late medieval rulers.

74 For the category of *onstantelike saken*, see Chapter 4.

75 See Chapter 1 and Chapter 4 for more on the *Raads dagelijks boek* and *Buurspraakboek*.

76 HUA 701-1.13: *Raads dagelijks boek* 1414–1425, fol. 54v (1417).

wife's property.[77] Finally, when in 1416 Nellen, the mother of late Jan de Witte's bastard children, claimed to be missing 300 guilders from Jan's inheritance, it was the Council who investigated and decided in the matter.[78] In such instances, the Council took part in a field of internal or private speech, seeing a small group of insiders negotiate about socio-legal truth in a specific case.

The *Buurspraakboek*, meanwhile, was involved in a completely different kind of communicative field. As part of the regular *buurspraak* occasions, this register functioned within an explicitly public setting, involving large numbers of local inhabitants. It was part of a field of external speech, where social actors posed their claims and counter-claims on the constitution of Utrecht society. This did not simply encompass the official *buurspraak* occasions, but also the many forms of non-official public speech that formed part of socio-political life in the city. The Council, for example, regularly punished people for causing unrest with public utterances, such as 'unreasonable' (*onredelike*) shouting by night,[79] words damaging people's honour,[80] or speech directed against the Council.[81] Although in these cases, the Council painted such public speech acts as illegitimate behaviour, they nevertheless formed part of the same field of public socio-political speech, where claims for truth were publicly uttered and negotiated. What is more, in discrediting others' use of such public forms of speech, the Council was essentially claiming the field's capital of legitimate public speech as its own.[82] Thus, in using specific media in particular settings, various social actors, including the Council, participated in a particular field of communicative action, while at the same time negotiating their own position in as well as the boundaries of the field itself.

Interaction and mediation between fields

The communicative fields sketched above are strongly simplified conceptions of social practice. Where the previous analysis has shown the

77 Ibid., fol. 74r (1418).
78 Ibid., fol. 32r (1416).
79 HUA 701-1.16: *Buurspraakboek* 1396–1402, fol. 326v (1401).
80 HUA 701-1.16: *Buurspraakboek* 1405–1409, fol. 100r (1408).
81 HUA 701-1.16: *Buurspraakboek* 1414–1418, fol. 118r (1416).
82 Cf. Daniel Lord Smail, "Hatred as a Social Institution in Late Medieval Society", *Speculum: A Journal of Medieval Studies* 76 (2001); idem, *Consumption of Justice*; Jan Dumolyn, "'Criers and Shouters': The Discourse on Radical Urban Rebels in Late Medieval Flanders", *Journal of Social History* 42 (2008); Deen, *Publiek debat.*

variety of communicative structures between the three cases – and thus the limited applicability of one single model to all three – in what follows I will complicate the picture in another way. For despite the clear differences between the communicative fields on which these courts operated, in all three cases there was a strong correspondence between the ways in which separate fields overlapped and interacted with each other.

Such interaction could take the form of linguistic mediators, that is, individuals positioned at certain crucial points between speech fields and able to convert the linguistic capital of the one into that of the other. Proctors and advocates are the prime example here. Both in the Consistory Court and the *Parlement* these men played an important role in the interaction between the court and its litigants. Advocates generally took the role of legal advisors, while proctors were essentially legal representatives of one of the parties.[83] They thus formed, each in their own way, a link between legal and extra-legal linguistic fields. Advocates would develop legal arguments and plead these before the courts, thereby navigating the troubled waters of legal speech and argument for their clients. Proctors, in their turn, could increase the accessibility of the court geographically and financially, by allowing litigants who lived far away from the court to be represented without the costs and trouble of a personal appearance at every session. At the same time, proctors and advocates could also function as gatekeepers to the legal field by assessing whether a case brought before them would be legally tenable. Numerous surviving oaths of admission echo this gatekeeping ideal by their stipulation that proctors and advocates ought to refuse or abandon cases they think to be flawed, hopeless or otherwise untenable from a legal point of view.[84] They were thus the first to determine the possibility or impossibility of translation between the legal and extra-legal communicative fields. The role of proctors as legal intermediaries had its limits in various courts. The *Parlement* often required plaintiffs to acquire a special letter of approval before they could appoint a proctor to plead in their stead.[85] And various church courts incentivized litigants to appear in person during the first and last session of a case.[86] But such limits show

83 See Chapter 1 and Chapter 3. Aubert, *Histoire*, vol. 1, 205–228; Aubert, "Nouvelles recherches", pt. 1, 282–286; Helmholz, *Marriage Litigation*, 147–154; Brundage, *Medieval Origins*, 344–370. However, Helmholz also shows how the roles of advocates and proctors could overlap in some courts: Helmholz, *Marriage Litigation*, 150.

84 De Laurière, *Ordonnances*, vol. 1, 300; Wilkins, *Consilia*, vol. 2, 410; Aubert, *Histoire*, vol. 1, 220; Brundage, *Medieval Origins*, 295–305.

85 Aubert, "Nouvelles recherches", pt. 1, 282–284.

86 Helmholz, *Marriage Litigation*, 124.

that courts were conscious of the crucial role these speech intermediaries played in managing the boundaries between linguistic fields. This could be facilitated through individuals, but an overreliance on their mediating role could also have the adverse effect of completely estranging both linguistic fields from each other, by separating litigants too strongly from what was actually going on in court. Hence the emphasis on litigants' presence or absence in some of our courts, as seen in Chapter 3.

Advocates and proctors are not as visible in the sources from Utrecht, although there is occasional evidence for their presence both in the Council's books of bylaws and in the aldermen's register.[87] Another type of intermediary, however, took centre stage in the communication processes in Utrecht. The functionaries called *stadsknapen* formed the most important officials employed to facilitate the day-to-day functioning of the Council. Their roles included such diverse tasks as guarding the entrance to the council room and arresting contumacious individuals. But their main job consisted of summoning the parties in a case and bringing messages to and from the Council.[88] They thus functioned as crucial mediators between the internal speech arena of the council room and the world outside, be it in a much more practical sense than the proctors and advocates. This role of communicative intermediaries was far from unique for Utrecht. Both the *Parlement* and the Consistory Court employed similar functionaries, who put flesh on the flow of information between the internal speech world of the court, and the external parties interacting with it. The intermediary role that the *Parlement*'s *huissiers* played has already come to the fore in considering the spatial practices in the *Palais de la Cité* in Chapter 2. Yet their activities extended far beyond the courtroom itself. In the documents from the *Parlement* they are seen to be tasked with many operational matters: summoning litigants, confiscating property, overseeing the payment of debts and bringing letters and arrests to and from the *Parlement*.[89] Evidence for the precise activities of the apparitors or summoners of the Consistory Court is less prominent in the records. But the focus of their tasks on the summoning of litigants and the reporting of its results back to the court was again concerned with the communication between two speech fields.[90]

87 Muller, *Rechtsbronnen*, vol. 1, 190; ibid., vol. 2, 50. Both refer to lawyers' role in the aldermen's legal process.

88 Muller, *Rechtsbronnen*, Introduction, 210, n. 2; ibid., vol. 1, 203–204.

89 For an extensive overview of these tasks, see Félix Aubert, "Les huissiers du parlement de Paris, 1300–1420", *Bibliothèque de l'école des chartes*, 47 (1886), esp. 377–381.

90 Burns, "Medieval Courts", 152–153. On the role of apparitors in church courts more in general, see Brundage, *Medieval Origins*, 148–149, 417.

Both within and beyond the courtroom, functionaries like the *stadsknapen*, the *huissiers* and the apparitors facilitated the interaction between a restricted world of legal technicalities and a world outside where such technicalities were to be translated into communicative practice. At the same time, it was through their functioning, and its limits, that the courts in fact emphasized the boundaries between the various speech fields concerned. Both the *stadsknapen* in Utrecht and the Parisian *huissiers*, for example, had only limited accessibility to the court room. The late-fourteenth-century *Liber hirsutus minor* forbade those *stadsknapen* charged with guarding the entrance to the council room, to enter the same room unless explicitly called for. Instead, it ordered them to remain 'between the two doors', suggesting the existence of a kind of lobby outside the courtroom.[91] Likewise, at least since the royal ordinance of January 27, 1360, the *huissiers* were not allowed to enter the *Grande Chambre* during counsel sessions.[92] At the same time, as seen in Chapter 2, their role in audience sessions was deemed very important. They could even be formally reprimanded if they failed to deliver on this front, as shown by an entry in the 1386 counsel register which threatened to punish the then *huissiers* 'gravely' (*griefment*) if they continued to neglect their duties. For, so the court stated, their failure to guard the entrance to the *Grand Chambre* and to the *parquet* within it had resulted in 'great noise' (*grant noise*) in the place where court sessions took place, upsetting the communicative order as envisioned by the *Parlement*.[93] A line was thus drawn in the operation of these communicative intermediaries between where mediation was desirable – or even fundamental – and where it was not. By suggesting the necessity of intermediaries in certain cases, the courts not only tried to facilitate interaction between linguistic fields, but also carried out these fields' separation.

Next to specific mediators, particular speech situations could also form a link between the various linguistic fields in which courts were engaged. Such occasions were often connected to the gathering or spreading of information. The taking of witness testimony, for example, saw a strong reliance – one might even say dependence – of the court on the interaction between speech fields.[94] All three courts knew these kinds of communicative occasions, although their visibility in the surviving records differs

91 Muller, *Rechtsbronnen*, vol. 1, 73–74.

92 Aubert, "Huissiers", 377.

93 AN X^{1A}1473, fol. 202v (1386). Also published in Aubert, "Huissiers", 385.

94 Also see Forrest, "Trust and Doubt" and idem, *Trustworthy Men* for the crucial role of social informants for late medieval episcopal administrations.

significantly. Chapter 4 has shown that depositions form a major part of the surviving cause papers from York's Consistory Court. In the elaborate process of drafting the depositions, the experience and information of social informants was reworked within a learned legal framework, thus facilitating the interaction between both types of speech.[95] Although less visible in the court records, in Utrecht the procedure of taking witness statements entailed a similar linking of diverse linguistic fields. Time and again, the *Liber albus* noted how transgressions of many of the city's bylaws could only be proven through the testimony of two 'honest persons' (*reckeliken luden*). Only if this turned out to be impossible, the alleged transgressor was sometimes given the option of proving his innocence by taking an oath, thus emphasizing the importance attributed to linking diverse speech fields in legal practice.[96] The role of testimony in connecting speech fields becomes even more explicit in one specific type of procedure, noted both in the *Liber albus* and the *Roede boeck*. Through this procedure, the defendant in a case brought before an ecclesiastical court could force the plaintiff to have the case adjudicated by the Council instead. The *Roede boeck* in particular details the way in which the Council proceeded in such cases. Mirroring the procedure in York, the Council would examine witnesses on a number of specific topics, partly determined by the defendant in the case. What is more, the officer in charge of the examinations would then subject these testimonies to the scrutiny of 'masters and jurists' to determine their legal implications, and present their assessment to the Council.[97] In this procedure, the court actively and explicitly tried to connect three separate linguistic fields: that of its social informants, that of the legally schooled specialists, and its own internal linguistic context.

For the *Parlement* of Paris the extensive procedure of *enquêtes* constitutes one of the most concrete forms of overlap between several speech contexts. The exact nature of the inquiries undertaken by the *Parlement*'s officials could vary widely, but the hearing of witnesses played a major part in many of them. As was the case in York, in accusatory cases, witnesses – usually summoned by the parties involved – would come in court to respond to a set of statements drawn up on the basis of the points of disagreement between both parties.[98] Several forms of social information also played an

95 See Chapter 4.

96 Muller, *Rechtsbronnen*, vol. 1, 6–11, 15.

97 Ibid., 65–66, 168. On the practice of bringing an ecclesiastical 'libel' before the Council, see Muller, *Rechtsbronnen*, Introduction, 98–100.

98 On the procedure of *enquêtes*, see Aubert, *Histoire*, vol. 2, 79–123, and, in particular, 100–110 on the role of testimony therein.

important part in *ex officio* cases. The interrogations of *Châtelet* prisoners at the end of the $X^{2A}4$ register suggest, for example, how proving culprits' crimes depended not only on their own confessions, but also on information brought directly by witnesses or through inquiries by local authorities.[99] In other parts of the criminal registers the role of social information in the judicial process is also evident. An ordinance from 1349 in a case of alleged abuse of power and corruption by the former bailiff of Auvergne, Pierre du Port, gives some insight into the practice of hearing witness testimony. In it the *Parlement* specified not only that the parties could produce witnesses, who would be sworn in and whose testimony would subsequently be received by the court on a specific date, but also that earlier testimony, over which doubts had arisen during the case, would be verified.[100] In this case, confessions, testimony and their reliability took a prominent place, forming a central issue in at least seven of the eight entries devoted to the case in the *Parlement*'s register.[101] Next to such individual testimony, more general types of social information were also taken into account. Thus, in another ordinance, this time from 1339, the *Parlement* ordered the bailiff of Vermandois to make an enquiry into the *fama publica* surrounding Reims citizen Thomas Maigret and his alleged accomplices. The *fama* on Thomas, so the court related, accused him of kidnapping and imprisoning fellow Reims inhabitant Gesson Roti and of blaming several others for Gesson's subsequent death.[102] What emerges from such cases, is that both the gathering of individual testimony and the more general 'word on the street' formed an intricate part of the *enquête* process, linking different fields of communicative activity together.

The media that were used by and in relation to the courts – be they oral, textual, enacted or otherwise – operated in constellations of multiple and partly overlapping linguistic fields in which these courts were engaged. There they were often used to emphasize the separation of fields, by raising linguistic, conceptual or even physical boundaries between them. Thus, by producing documents in a relatively inaccessible style or language (Chapter 4), or by limiting people's access to particular places or sessions (Chapter 2), courts stressed the difference between curial and extra-curial speech contexts. Yet in their communicative practice they also actively tried

99 Langlois and Lanhers, *Confessions*, 17–19.

100 AN $X^{2A}5$, fol. 171v.

101 The case is spread over the AN $X^{2A}5$ register, receiving mentions between 1346 and 1350 at fols. 10r, 13r, 136v, 153v, 167r, 171r, 193v and 194v.

102 AN $X^{2A}2$, fol. 7r.

to bridge gaps between fields, either through particular intermediators or on specific speech occasions in the legal process. While advocates, proctors and various court functionaries facilitated communication between the court and its potential litigants and audiences, the interaction between fields was likewise stimulated on occasions like sentence readings and during the taking of testimony. In line with what the first part of this chapter has suggested, courts, in their interaction with the law's consumers, thus showed a tension between the professed detachment from and the practical involvement in society. Consequently, they used the media at their disposal not only to navigate between linguistic fields, but also to try and define the fields, that is, to script the way in which participants acted, spoke and interpreted the things said and done in particular speech contexts. By suggesting which forms of communication belonged to a particular field and which fell outside of it – for example, because they needed translation into a different form – the courts claimed specific types of speech to be legitimate in certain communicative contexts, while others were not. In attempting to define the boundaries of the linguistic fields in which they took part, the courts were thus involved in a negotiation over the capital of these fields, that is, over the nature of legitimate speech in each of them, as well as their own and others' possession of this capital.

The legal process as socio-legal narrative

In their attempts to define the nature and relative possession of socio-linguistic capital in different communicative fields, the courts under study not only tried to influence concrete communicative practice, but also propagated specific socio-legal narratives. These narratives were essentially conglomerates of truth claims, which were linked together by strands of common logic. They encompassed claims on the essential ordering of society, the potential threats to this order, as well as the role of the court in safeguarding the latter. While reflecting institutional ideals about the world, such narratives were at the same time constructed to influence it. They formed, like the communicative practices treated above, part of the attempt to gather socio-linguistic capital in the form of legitimate judicial speech. Through propagating specific socio-legal narratives, courts tried to become a logical and inevitable part of the late medieval legal landscape. Chapter 4 has already shown the discursive strategies used in the production of legal documents to incorporate separate social events into these narratives. In what follows, the conglomerates of truth claims themselves will take centre stage. By reviewing some of the central elements of the narratives found in York, Utrecht and Paris, I will show how all three courts, despite constructing their narratives differently, expressed similar concerns, thus suggesting a broader court-related development in the propagation of late medieval socio-legal narratives.

At the basis of many forms of judicial practice and logic lies the conception of ordering a potentially disordered society.[103] However, what 'disorder' – and for that matter 'order' – exactly entails differs from case to case and is subject to linguistic claims. In her *'De grace especial'*, Claude Gauvard studies the discourse on criminality in the sources of the *Parlement* of Paris. Her analysis of its late-fourteenth- and fifteenth-century registers and other procedural documents suggests that these sources often resist classifying the acts treated in a case according to modern categories of crimes. Instead, they describe and moralize the criminal event and characterize the offender. Acts are said to be *scelus* (sinful) or *mala* (bad), while the offender is portrayed as a socially and morally transgressive individual. The definition of crimes in these judicial sources is thus primarily concerned with the perturbation of an assumed social and moral order.[104] Such ideas on the nature of crime were not isolated. They formed part of a broader conception of society as encompassing both social and moral aspects, that is to say, forming both a worldly and religious community. The ideal community, furthermore, was given geographical shape in the French kingdom, with a king at its head as guarantor of the political, social and religious order.[105] A clear example of this relation between social and political order are the many legal cases concerned with the breach of royal safeguard.[106] In such cases, like that of Isabelle de Blanot treated in the previous section, otherwise private conflicts were provided with a particular public significance. The men attacking a village within Isabelle's jurisdiction were not just causing unrest in one community, they were transgressing a socio-political order guaranteed by the king. In line with the expanding territorial and centralizing ambitions of the French kings, the *Parlement* defined social order and disorder in relation to a political ideology that presented the French kingdom as a natural, logical and sacred unity. Referring to this broader narrative could be of interest to litigants as well. Thus, in the above-mentioned 1349 case

103 Cf. Smith, *Punishment and Culture*, 13.

104 Gauvard, *'Grace especial'*, 111–143.

105 Ibid., 789–847.

106 A survey of the criminal registers $X^{2A}2$–5, as analysed in Labat-Poussin, Langlois and Lanhers, *Actes*, results in 184 entries concerned with breaches of the royal safeguard for the period 1330–1350, making it one of the most frequently appearing types of crime in these registers.

of alleged abuse of power by the former bailiff of Auvergne, said bailiff, Pierre du Port, defended his actions by stating that he performed them 'for and in name of the king' and in line with the justice and needs of his former bailiwick.[107]

A similar link between narratives of social and political order in Utrecht emerges from the description of forgiveness rituals as commonly recorded in the *Buurspraakboek*. In 1385, the Council punished Hughe de Kraen and his son, Aernt, for killing a man within the city. The entry relating this event reveals many of the broader ideological claims posed in such cases:

> Because Hughe de Kraen and Aernt son of Hughe have killed a man within the city, without bringing charges [against him] to the Council, they have lain in the tower and have come here to the clock in shirt and pants and ask the Council forgiveness and give the city 60,000 stones in compensation.[108]

Reconstructing the legal and penal logic of this account, we notice an apparent dichotomy between the subject of the crime and the entity or entities receiving redress for the murder. While the unnamed victim may well have had relatives or friends who could be eligible for redress, this entry speaks only of a compensation to the city and reconciliation with the Council. It thus presents the city and its governing council as the main victims of the crime. Contrary to such entries in the *Buurspraakboek*, the various bylaws relating to manslaughter often do stress the obligation of the convict to reconcile with the relatives of the deceased.[109] Describing the event in such a way thus constitutes a conscious choice to emphasize those aspects of the crime that are deemed important in the situation. And that situation was the public gathering of citizens at a *buurspraak*. Like the *Parlement*, the Council propagated a specific idea about who or what was damaged by a criminal act. The heinous acts of individuals brought the urban community and its representative, the Council, into disarray. It was thus these entities, according to the *Buurspraakboek*, that were to be compensated by the offenders. This reasoning was also in line with the call on all citizens to keep the 'peace of

107 AN $X^{2A}5$, fol. 136r: [...] *pro et nomine regio per viam et modum ac bonum racionis et justicie et necessitate sui tunc temporis officii baillie predicte* [...].

108 HUA 701-1.16: *Buurspraakboek* 1385–1391, fol. 16v: *Want hughe de kraen ende aernt hughen zoen enen man binnen der stat doot ghesleghen hebben onvervolcht vanden Rade daer omme hebben zi gheleghen inden toorn ende zijn hier ghecomen in hemde ende in broeke ter klocken ende bidden den rade verghifnisse ende gheven der Stat tebeteringhe* LX^{M} *steens.*

109 HUA 701-1.227: *Th.2* register, fol. 69v; Muller, *Rechtsbronnen*, vol. 1, 100, 161.

our citizens' (*vrede van onsen borgeren*) that was proclaimed several times a year.[110] The idea of a semi-permanent peaceful state of affairs between all citizens of Utrecht formed the ideological basis for the judicial system of which the Council formed the main proponent.[111] Where the *Parlement* took the political ideal of the French kingdom as its point of departure, the socio-legal narrative professed by the Council was based on the idea of the city of Utrecht as peaceful communal body endangered by transgressive behaviour.

The Consistory Court, being primarily concerned with accusatory cases, was less explicit in presenting its ideal of an orderly society. Nevertheless, traces of such ideas do survive in the available sources. Considering again, for example, the court statutes drawn up in 1311 by Archbishop Greenfield, we notice how the broader aim of the document was predicated upon the needs of society. The statutes, which were supposed to be read publicly in court twice a year, formed the ideological basis for the existence of the archiepiscopal courts.[112] In the prologue, the archbishop notes the importance of regulating the court of York, 'to which our subjects flow together from everywhere, from the city, the diocese and the province, in order to obtain fair justice in their causes and disputes'.[113] The statutes portray the archiepiscopal subjects as being in dire need of someone or something to provide a fair solution to their mutual disagreements. The society thus presented is again one threatened by disorder. In this case, however, the threat comes not from transgressive individuals, but from disputes between ordinary individuals. Such disputes, judging by the statutes, appear to be rife, requiring an impartial – maybe even superhuman – arbiter. The images of society presented by the various courts differ in the specific characterization of what constitutes social order as well as the potential threats to this order. But the general sense one gets from these – often implicit – social characterizations is that of a society full of challenges, to which the court in question may just be the best solution. In short, while the nature and scope of the concerned community varied between the narratives of the three courts, from the inhabitants of a kingdom to those of one town, the concept of a potentially threatened social order in need of safeguarding returns in all of them.

110 See, for example, HUA 701-1.16: *Buurspraakboek* 1414–1418, fol. 81r (1415).

111 Muller, *Rechtsbronnen*, Introduction, 46–49.

112 Burns, "Medieval Courts", 113–114.

113 Wilkins, *Consilia*, 409: […] *ut in curia nostra Eborum, ad quam undique confluunt subditi nostrarum civitatis, diocesis, et provinciae, pro justitia in suis causis et negotiis fiducialiter obtinenda,* […].

Late medieval law courts coexisted with other socio-legal stakeholders in their communities. These could include formal legal authorities and their representatives, but also many alternative forms of dispute settlement. Law courts in general began to form an important constitutive factor of the late medieval legal landscape, and several of them played a part in each of the cases studied here. At the same time feuding and other socio-legal practices that took kinship or patronage structures as their main point of reference were also omnipresent. There were, in short, alternative, sometimes competing, solutions available to quell the threat of social disorder that the law courts signalled, and to which they had to relate themselves. In the narratives presented by the three courts, such alternatives therefore received ample attention.

Evidence for a concern with feuding practices and other forms of private justice can be found in all three cases. In Utrecht we have seen how the idea of a threatened urban peace formed a central legitimization for the political and jurisdictional state of affairs. In day-to-day practice, however, this general urban peace knew a more specific manifestation. In cases where two or more citizens got involved in a dispute, the urban authorities could demand a temporary peace from the fighting parties, their relatives and friends. Refusal or transgression of this case-specific peace could result in anything from a monetary fine to corporal punishment.[114] Such measures were concerned with limiting feuds between groups of citizens, which, taking the frequency of these peace demands as a measure, seem to have been common practice. Yet their character, as Muller rightly notes, was hardly an all-out imposition of one system over the other. Rather, it tried to integrate the Council within an existing system of socio-legal practice, by claiming supervision over practices of appeasement between parties.[115] In the above account of the punishment of Hughe and Aernt de Kraen for manslaughter, the Council specified how the two men were convicted for killing a man 'without bringing charges [against him] to the Council' (*onvervolcht van den Rade*).[116] The same wording returns in one of the regulations in the *Liber albus*:

114 Muller, *Rechtsbronnen*, vol. 1, 43–46.

115 Muller, *Rechtsbronnen*, Introduction, 49–52.

116 The translation of the term *onvervolcht* is slightly ambiguous, as the *Middelnederlandsch Woordenboek* (searchable through http://gtb.inl.nl) attests, appearing both in a legal context as actions taken outside of a judicial procedure and in the more general sense of 'without foreknowledge'. Given the legal issues at stake in these cases, I have chosen to follow the first meaning.

> Any citizen living in our city, who hits any man in relation to a feud that he pursues against him without bringing charges [against him] to the city council, will forfeit three pounds.[117]

What is presented as problematic – and therefore eligible for punishment – in these cases is not so much the feuding practice itself, but the non-involvement of the Council in these conflicts. These rules and accounts show an authority trying to assert its own position within existing means of conflict resolution. This is also how one can interpret the wording of the regulations in the books of bylaws through which the Council tried to appease the parties in a conflict. Instead of simply ordering an end to the conflict, it 'demanded' (*eyschen*) peace from both parties. In addition, a system of fines was put in place that would penalize a party that refused to give this peace once, twice or even three times.[118] Refusal by one – or both – of the parties was thus considered a real possibility. Again, what may seem at first like a forceful measure to control private vengeance, can rather be read as an attempt by the urban authorities to tap into and assert its own role within existing discourses of socio-legal practice.[119]

That courts did not simply replace existing forms of socio-legal practice is also clear in the case of the *Parlement*. In Paris, various forms of conflict resolution and socio-legal reasoning existed next to and often even in tandem with the court's legal procedure, including such practices as trial by ordeal and judicial duelling.[120] On a more fundamental level, however, the *Parlement* was also involved in a broader economy of honour, a socio-legal rationale in terms of which people conceptualized many of the conflicts between individuals and groups.[121] This rationale of honour – understood both on a personal and kinship level – formed the basis for an extensive system of private vengeance, within which social standing was publicly negotiated according to unwritten rules. Such rules provided a framework to limit uncontrolled violent excesses between conflicting parties and achieve a truce or peace, often mediated by these parties' kin-groups.[122] The 1332 case

117 Muller, *Rechtsbronnen*, vol. 1, 28: *Waer enich onser borgher of de in onser stat woenachtich is, de enighen man sloeghe om enighe vete, de hi te voeren op hem hadde onvervolghet den raet vander stat, verboerde drie pont.*

118 Ibid., 44.

119 Cf. Glaudemans, *Om die wrake wille*, esp. 66–115, who traces similar concerns with practices of feuding and private vengeance for the late medieval law courts of Holland and Zeeland.

120 Gauvard, *'Grace especial'*, 172–189.

121 Ibid., 734–752.

122 Ibid., 753–779.

of the attack on Guiart de Noireterre, considered in Chapter 4, provides a glimpse of the court's concerns with these extra-curial practices and ways of reasoning.[123] In the statement that Guiart himself made on his deathbed, he told the court that he believed his long-time enemy Jean de la Fôret and Jean's esquire, Pierre le Viconte, to have organized the attack against him:

> Both on account of [his] cousin, called Jehan de Noireterre, who pleaded against said knight [Jean de la Fôret] in an appeal case, which [Guiart] supported, and because said Pierre le Viconte had challenged [Guiart] to a judicial duel for reasons of his master.[124]

Although providing little detailed information on the exact motivations for the conflict between Guiart and his attackers, this statement – supposedly essentialized from Guiart's own words, given its formalized structure – does clearly show the intertwinement of curial and extra-curial forms of dispute resolution. According to this entry, the conflict was fought out in multiple arenas, from a curial appeal procedure to a judicial duel and even in an outright attack on the streets of Paris, during which Guiart was mortally wounded. By presenting Guiart's suggestion of causality in this way, the *Parlement* thus acknowledged the existence of such extra-curial solutions to a conflict.

That is not to say, however, that the court unquestioningly accepted all alternatives to its own dispute resolution. As the Noireterre case shows, the *Parlement* explicitly condemned this extra-curial attack, sentencing both conspirators and assassins to death. Yet in many cases, the court's approach of such alternatives was subtler. Judicial duels, for example, while formally abolished by Louis IX in 1260, still appeared on a regular basis in the fourteenth-century registers of the *Parlement*, where they were treated as a legitimate option to solve a conflict.[125] For example, in a case from 1338, Jean Le Charlier appealed to the *Parlement* after the provost of Laon had decided not to grant him the right to a duel with Guillaume Rouvel.[126]

123 Langlois and Lanhers, *Confessions*, 51–75.

124 Ibid., 52–53: [...] *tant parce que le cousin germain de lui qui parle, qui est appelé Jehan de Noireterre, qui plaidoit contre ledit chevalier en cause dáppel, et lequel il qui parle soustenoit, comme pour ce que ledit Pierre le Viconte avoit appellé de lui qui parle de gage de bataille pour raison de son maistre.*

125 Cf. Gauvard, *'Grace especial'*, 173–179. For the legislation of Louis IX on judicial duels, see P. Guilhiermoz, "Saint Louis, les gages de bataille et la procédure civile", *Bibliothèque de l'école des chartes* 48, no. 1 (1887), 111–120.

126 See AN $X^{2A}2$, fol. 1.

While the court did not explicitly approve of Jean's wish for a judicial duel, by treating his appeal as a legitimate legal action, it implicitly accepted the duel as practice for solving disputes. Rather than forcefully replacing alternative socio-legal rationales with a logic of court-centred litigation or criminalization, the *Parlement* attempted to claim its own role within them. To this end, it used means similar to those of the Council of Utrecht. Parties involved in a conflict had the option of acquiring a formal guarantee (*asseurement*) of peace between them from the *Parlement*. Guarantees were sometimes requested by only one of the parties, in which case the other side would be urged to comply as well.[127] This was also often the case in litigation concerning requests for judicial duels. Although the request to hold such a duel is accepted as legitimate action, in most of these cases the court tried to push for a court-guided solution to the conflict, through appointing mediators.[128] As in the case of Utrecht, the *Parlement* thus sought to enter into existing systems of dispute resolution by taking over a specific discourse and logic, while claiming its own role within the process as such.

Next to these informal or semi-formal systems of dispute resolution, other law courts – most of them also of fairly recent date – formed important entities to which the courts under scrutiny had to relate themselves. These relations and the courts' discursive strategies in them become particularly clear in the case of York's Consistory Court. Despite its position at the summit of the English ecclesiastical court hierarchy, within the context of the kingdom itself the Consistory Court had to situate itself vis-à-vis several other legal entities. Prominent among those were the royal courts. Much has been written about the relation between English ecclesiastical and royal courts. W.R. Jones, for instance, set out the many areas of jurisdiction where the crown and ecclesiastical courts confronted each other, including topics as diverse as ecclesiastical benefices, debts and excommunication.[129] Although both spheres generally accepted each other's spheres of competence, Jones argued that in cases of conflict the royal courts held the upper hand. Their main instrument in this was the so-called writ of prohibition, a writ that litigants in the church courts could request from the king to halt a case, as it was said to belong to the royal jurisdiction.[130] Thus, by offering litigants

127 Gauvard, *'Grace especial'*, 779–788.

128 For example, $X^{2A}5$, fol. 1v (1345), where Savrai de Vivonne, lord of Thors, is appointed as mediator in a conflict in which a judicial duel has been requested.

129 Jones, "Two Jurisdictions", 100–101.

130 Ibid., 80–87.

the possibility to strategically adapt a case's legal definition, the royal court indirectly tried to extend its legal authority.

Richard Helmholz finds the same kinds of discursive strategies, although he questions the alleged royal dominance in using them. Instead, he stresses how the church courts had procedural 'weapons of their own' to discourage litigants – and through them the royal courts – from trying to take cases away from persecution in an ecclesiastical court.[131] Jones and Helmholz, while disagreeing on the relative position of royal and ecclesiastical courts in jurisdictional disputes, both present a very similar picture of the way in which they negotiated this power. First, the struggle for jurisdictional supremacy was fought indirectly by trying to influence the actions of litigants in pursuing their cases, rather than through outright coercion of the latter. Second, it was primarily a semantic struggle, that is to say, a negotiation over the definition of actions according to specific legal categories. A case of debt, for example, could very well be claimed to concern a case of breach of faith, and thus be eligible to pursue in an ecclesiastical court.[132] The Consistory Court and other curial stakeholders used a subtle strategy of legal semantics to negotiate their own place vis-à-vis each other. Both in their relations towards other tribunals and towards the many non-curial forms of socio-legal logic and practice, courts did not – and probably could not – simply impose themselves on an existing field of potential solutions for social disorder. Instead, they tried to tap into existing systems of legal practice and rationale, manipulating both actions and semantic categories in order to legitimize their own position vis-à-vis these other potential solutions.

As courts acknowledged the existence and even legitimacy of alternative solutions to potential social disorder, they were faced with the need to define themselves and the legitimacy of their role in quelling disarray. In order to do so, the socio-legal narratives propagated by them engaged implicitly or explicitly with the question as to the source of their legitimacy as guardians of social order. As seen for the other discursive building blocks of this narrative, that is, these courts' definitions of social order and disorder, as well as the mechanisms to guarantee the latter, the conceptualization of their own role in this story and the font of justice on which they allegedly based it, differed from case to case. Yet a basic concern with such topics of institutional legitimacy occupied all three courts, as their documentary sources attest.

131 Helmholz, "Writs of Prohibition", 87–90.

132 Jones, "Two Jurisdictions", 165–169.

Between the thirteenth and fifteenth centuries, the *Parlement* of Paris developed from a small advisory committee to the French kings to an immense bureaucratic institution, consisting of numerous subdivisions and involved in legal proceedings all over the French kingdom. At the same time, the kings had spatially detached themselves from their supreme court of law, hardly ever staying at the *Palais de la Cité* anymore from the early fifteenth century onwards.[133] Consequently, they had also become less directly involved in the daily affairs of the *Parlement*. Yet narratively the king still played a very central role as font of legal power. The many royal letters included in the *Parlement*'s registers from early on are a marked example.[134] By copying documents that were explicitly drawn up in name of the king, the court textually confirmed the latter's symbolic role in the legal process. And the symbolic legitimacy provided by the person of the king took other shapes as well, as in the inclusion of a royal throne, the *lit de justice*, in the *Grande Chambre*, physically emphasizing the role of the king in the legal process even in his absence.[135] However, one of the most prominent forms in which the king appeared in the *Parlement*'s legal procedure is as a focal point in the definition of various crimes. Gauvard notes how in the late-fourteenth- and early-fifteenth-century remission letters, several crimes are distinguished as being particularly serious. Among them were those acts that involved threatening the socio-political order of the realm and could thus be styled public crimes. These crimes, Gauvard argues, were semantically related to the body and honour of the king. So whereas rape, violence and defamation would compromise the bodily integrity and reputation of an individual, acts like *lèse-majesté*, rebellion and warfare could be considered as infringements of the royal body and honour, and therefore as fundamentally threatening the integrity of the realm.[136] The many cases involving breach of royal safeguard, like that of Isabelle de Blanot above, clearly show this discursive link between the royal persona and the ideal political unity of the French realm. By violently entering land under royal safeguard, the attackers are argued to have transgressed against the king himself, thus turning the event into an act of public criminality liable to be judged by the *Parlement*. In short, despite the minimal involvement of

133 Guerout, "Le Palais: Troisième et dernier article", 29–30.

134 See Chapter 4 for more on the *lettres* sections in the *Parlement*'s registers.

135 See Chapter 2; cf. Brown and Famiglietti, *The* lit de justice.

136 Gauvard, *'Grace especial'*, 832–847. The same was true for attacks on royal officials, whose honour was explicitly linked to that of the king. See Telliez, *Officiers*, 419–424. Cf. Ernst H. Kantorowicz, *The King's Two Bodies: A Study in Medieval Political Theology* (Princeton, NJ: Princeton University Press, 1957), for the theological basis of such ideas.

the French kings in the day-to-day business of the *Parlement*, their role as legitimizers of the court was nonetheless emphasized in the latter's socio-legal narrative as propagated on many occasions.

From a medieval theological viewpoint true judgement could only come from God, while human judges were at best its earthly delegates. For the ecclesiastical courts in particular this matter played an important part in their legitimization as legal authorities. As the York statutes of Archbishop Greenfield stressed, fallible men were a problematic entity to trust with fair judgement all by themselves. At the same time, the court itself consisted of just such fallible men. In this context, there was thus a need both to emphasize the non-fallible, almost superhuman character of the court, and to legitimately include the activities of fallible men into its daily operation. Attempts at achieving the first can be found both explicitly and implicitly throughout the Consistory Court's written documentation. As noted in Chapter 3, the surviving sentences in the York cause papers are very formulaic, and provide little information on the actual cases. Most of their contents are instead devoted to a detailed description of the procedural steps leading to the final sentence. I have argued how this focus on procedure functioned in ritualizing court procedure, by linking it to a broader idealized structure of practices.[137] Integrated in the broader court narrative of order versus disorder, however, these oft-repeated formulae also emphasized the superhuman character of the legal process itself. Rather than expounding on the individual motivations for judges and lawyers in taking certain actions, the legal process was presented as impersonal. These sentences thus emphasized above all the absence of human agency, thereby focusing on an allegedly non-fallible procedural structure as intermediary between God and men. At the same time, as Ian Forrest has shown, following the growth of ecclesiastical administrations after 1100, fundamental aspects of the legal process, like testimony or judgement, came to rely on the integrity of an increasingly large network of potentially fallible individuals. In order to counter the problem of relying on less than certain – that is to say, non-divine – information, clerics and laymen alike began to use a language of belief in their dealings within this system, putting 'faith' in the words heard from others. Fallible men were deified, in the sense that – for practical considerations at least – their words were considered as reliable as God's own.[138] Thus, both by dehumanizing the legal process and deifying the

137 See Chapter 3.
138 Forrest, "Trust and Doubt"; idem, *Trustworthy Men*.

activities of otherwise fallible men, ecclesiastical courts tried to legitimize their position as guardians of social order.

In the 1385 manslaughter case of Hughe and Aernt de Kraen the Council situated itself as the main representative of the urban community, explicitly receiving the moral compensation for a transgression of the social order in general. This idea, however, need not be self-evident. As seen concretely in the development of forgiveness rituals in Chapter 3, the spiritual and political authority of the Utrecht bishop often loomed in the background. When the Council felt confident at some point to present itself as communal representative, this was based upon a long-developed narrative of the Council's legitimacy. As an elected body, much of the Council's legitimization was initially focused on the city's political structure, based as it was around the guilds and their representatives. Looking, for example, at the way in which newly instituted regulations are described we notice how these are often presented as being decided upon in tandem with the general assembly (*morghensprake*) of all the guilds or with their representatives, the guild elders. So it is that a decision on the sale of the wine tax in 1342 is described as being agreed upon 'with the old Council and the new and in the general assembly of all guilds'.[139] Such oft-repeated explicit legitimization of new regulations shows us a concern for the suggestion of (semi-)democratic decision-making, directly involving the relevant elective bodies in the city. Over time, however, the Council appears to have regarded this explicit legitimization through the city's elective institutions as less of a necessity. In the later books of bylaws, mention of the *morghensprake* and the guild representatives becomes infrequent. For example, in a measure taken in 1410 to limit freeloaders abusing the city's right of citizenship, the measure is said to have been taken by the old and new Council, 'for the benefit of our city'.[140] It is as if the position of the Council as the community's problem-solver has become self-evident. And this is the same message as propagated in the many different entries in the *Buurspraakboek*. The link between Council and urban community, though at first explicated through the guild-based elective system, has come to form the Council's legitimization by itself.

The *Parlement* of Paris, York's Consistory Court and the Council of Utrecht characterized their society, as well as their own position within it, in unique ways. Between the legal head of a kingdom-wide socio-political order, the

139 Muller, *Rechtsbronnen*, vol. 1, 36–37: [...] *mitten ouden rade ende mitten nywe ende bi ghemeenre morghensprake van allen ghilden* [...].

140 Ibid., 260: *Die raet vander stat out ende nye hebben eendrachtelic overdragen voer nutscap onser stat* [...].

superhuman arbiter of a Christian community or an urban society's representative in judicial matters, contemporaries encountering these courts will have been presented with very different idealized images. Still, there were also crucial common elements in the socio-legal narratives these courts promoted. In each case some concept of an ordered society is present, as well as the potential threats it faced. Thus, while the *Parlement* presented the ideal political unity of the French kingdom as a social and moral community in danger of being thrown in disarray, the Council of Utrecht attached a similar socio-moral connotation to its city, and the York archbishops presented their subjects' alleged lack of 'fair justice' in disputes as the primary challenge to overcome. Subsequently, each court claimed to be a solution to these threats, which was not necessarily a replacement of other forms of socio-legal practices and rationales, but a particularly legitimate and attractive part of the broader socio-legal landscape. In Utrecht, the Council presented itself as an arbiter in disputes, representing the communal interest to limit these struggles' disordering consequences, without denying people's right to pursue satisfaction. The *Parlement* propagated a similar narrative, in which it acknowledged people's need for redress, while putting itself forward as the royally sanctioned intermediate to acquire it. Finally, the Consistory Court stressed the deified, almost extra-human character of its judicial services in an attempt to entice potential litigants to bring their disputes to it, instead of searching for other resolutions. Each court thus tried to market itself to its potential litigants and audiences through the propagation of a normalizing court narrative. In addition to their attempts to influence people's performance and perception of proper communicative practice, the courts negotiated their position in society by presenting a constellation of claims on their and others' role within it.

Conclusion: Producing and consuming justice

Late medieval law courts were in the business of selling a court-centred model of socio-legal practice and logic. They promoted a way of doing and thinking about justice that was not self-evident to many of the individuals confronted with it. The courts' strategy to engage potential litigants and audiences was twofold. On the one hand, they tried to influence the forms and arenas of socio-legal communication. By suggesting specific definitions for the communicative fields in which they operated, as concerned participants, linguistic norms and media used, the courts attempted to manipulate people's experience and use of these fields and claim a position as legitimate communicators in them. On the other hand, they presented narratives on the constitution and character of society and their role within it. Such constellations of interlinked truth claims detailed the alleged nature of social order, the forces threatening it and the role of the court in facing the latter. Through the propagation of these socio-legal narratives the courts tried to script a discourse on justice, which shaped what people considered just and unjust solutions to particular social issues, from violent disputes to conflicts over marriage.

In both of the above areas, courts showed a particular tension between being fundamentally involved in and, at the same time, trying to transcend ordinary human practices and experiences. In communicative practice, courts on the one hand emphasized the boundaries between communicative fields by complicating mutual accessibility through the use of a specific language or jargon, or by limiting access to certain speech situations physically. Yet at the same time, they also facilitated attempts to bridge these boundaries, providing occasions on which people could engage with other communicative fields, or deploying intermediaries, such as advocates, to mediate between forms of speech. Discursively, a similar tension was present. In their socio-legal narratives, courts acknowledged many of the alternative solutions for the prevention and overcoming of social disorder, from other courts to feuding practices and forms of private vengeance. While thus stressing their embeddedness in socially ingrained systems of dispute resolution, their own role in these narratives was always that of supreme guardian and arbiter, catering to people's individual desire for justice, while surveying its broader social implications. Be it on the basis of royal supremacy, a God-given jurisdictional hierarchy, or the representation of an urban community, these courts in the end staked a fundamental claim to social transcendence. The tension between social embeddedness and transcendence could furthermore be seen in the courts' internal forum. Within these institutions, members' private interests were often at loggerheads with the professed corporate identity and intentionality of the body as a whole. Court communities knew a range of enacted and discursive measures to counter such internal tensions, including the use of nomenclature that emphasized institutional continuity and practices of oath swearing. Thus, both internally and externally, courts tried to script the relation and interaction between themselves and the social structures in which they operated, attempting to control the measure of involvement in or transcendence of society.

The courts' embeddedness in social structures thus had strong implications for the matters that concerned them in daily practice and the related activities that they employed. As Smail and others have argued, courts' success as socio-legal format was dependent on the law's consumers. The latter stimulated the growth of courts by investing in individual legal processes to pursue their private socio-economic interests. Yet that does not mean that the courts themselves can be left out of the picture. In trying to sell potential consumers, either litigants or audiences, their solutions to alleged social issues, these bodies directed their attention and means at influencing communicative flows and their contents. To become an attractive solution for settling disputes and guaranteeing social order, these courts needed to press a successful claim on socio-legal legitimacy. In order to do so, they both made active use of and tried to define the linguistic capital of a number of interconnected communicative fields. As such, the law's consumers were not only enticed to accept the socio-legal authority of courts, but also to reconsider their definitions of justice.

General conclusion

Abstract
During the later Middle Ages law courts were established in numerous urban localities, following broader demographic and intellectual trends, as well as local or regional socio-political modalities. The comparative study of three courts of varying size and character in Utrecht, York and Paris shows how these courts' search for institutional legitimacy led them to employ specific scripts of justice to influence people's legal literacy. The five scripts distinguished here, those of accessibility, physicality, rituality, semantic linking and narrativity, combined multiple media, including texts, spaces, oral statements and physical acts, while actively engaging different agents beyond the court in performing them. Given this multi-authored character of judicial performance, courts' textual records should be understood in terms of negotiations over the concepts and practices of justice.

Keywords: medieval law courts, legal communication, legal theatre, comparative history, medieval court records

'There is no doubt', said K., 'there is no doubt, that behind all the statements of this court, and in my case also behind the arrest and the current investigation, there stands a large organization. One that comprises not only bribable guards, oafish supervisors and at best unpretentious magistrates, but that also maintains a judiciary of a high or even the highest level, along with its myriad, inescapable entourage of servants, scribes, policemen and other assistants, perhaps even executioners – I'm not afraid of using that word. And the purpose of this organization, gentlemen? Its purpose is to arrest innocent people and to begin a pointless procedure against them which, as in my case, usually leads to no result.'[1]

1 Translated from Franz Kafka, *Sämtliche Werke* (Frankfurt am Main: Suhrkamp, 2008), 271–272.

Camphuijsen, F., *Scripting Justice in Late Medieval Europe: Legal Practice and Communication in the Law Courts of Paris, York and Utrecht.* Taylor & Francis Group, 2022
DOI 10.5117/9789463723473_CONC

Thus Franz Kafka, often considered the father of modern bureaucratic horror, imagined justice. In his novel *Der Prozess* he sketched the vicissitudes of a man caught in a legal process whose exact cause and procedure remain obscure. Notwithstanding people's best intentions to help the protagonist with his case, no character in the story ever seems able to fully understand or work the system behind these proceedings. Kafka gave words to a fear of being caught up in the infernal machinations of a faceless legal bureaucracy, whose sole reason for existence was the realization of a purposeless show called the legal process.

Despite a chronological distance of some four and a half centuries, Kafka's image of legal practice in the early twentieth century echoes much of the criticism uttered at law courts by François Villon and his contemporaries in the later Middle Ages. Central to these images is a fundamental criticism of the court itself. Be it as a Kafkaesque organization capturing people in a web of legal proceedings, or as Villon's godlike entity that has the power to pardon and punish at will, courts are conceptualized as particularly inaccessible forms of justice. In such depictions, people are at the mercy of an institution that defines both the nature of justice and the means of achieving it, without allowing individuals any real influence on the process as such.

Institutional legitimacy is not a given, either in a modern or in a medieval context. Countering such criticisms as uttered by Kafka and Villon, legal bureaucracies are and have been in need of legitimizing their role as authorities – that is to say, entities with a norm-setting voice and practice – in the pursuit of justice. The later Middle Ages formed a particularly formative period for the creation of such a discourse and practice of institutional legitimization that continues to play a role to this very day. Late medieval societies saw a change in the ways of working with and the ways of speaking about justice, in which a specific format for organizing legal practice, the law court, was propagated as the socio-legal norm. Yet it was no self-evident norm, regularly clashing with people's sense of what justice entailed and how one should go about achieving it. To trace and explain this process of negotiation between a specific court-centred discourse and practice of justice and its many alternatives has been the goal of the current book.

Medieval law courts: General and local developments

Law courts, as spatially fixed and text-producing fora for social disputes, were established in numerous urban localities, following both broader and more case-specific developments. Some of these were related to demographic and socio-economic trends. The growing number of case loads, for example, which led many rulers, both secular and ecclesiastical, to instigate textual procedures, coincided with a more general demographic growth in many parts of Europe that had its peak in the late thirteenth and early fourteenth centuries. More people meant more potential conflicts, which subsequently translated into more possible litigants. Another factor of importance was urban growth, which had kicked off at the turn of the second millennium. With the increase in cities' size and number, urban residents became a particularly relevant public for the socio-legal claims of rulers. Thus, the establishment of permanent courts in an urban context could be a very effective communication strategy, bringing legal presence to places with a relatively high population density. Other influences on the establishment of law courts can be traced to the procedural realm. From the eleventh century onwards, interest in the canon and Roman procedural traditions increased. As the early universities began to incorporate the study of both legal traditions, lawyers came to play a dominant role in urban and princely administrations and at the courts of both secular and ecclesiastical rulers. Efforts to standardize legal procedure made these traditions and their representatives attractive bases for claims to centralized authority. Furthermore, the substantial attention for textual procedure also stimulated the use of documents in daily legal practice.

These general developments impacted all three courts studied here. Yet, zooming in on them individually also shows how particular case-specific conditions merged with these broader trends to shape the way in which each court came into being. In France, the Capetian monarchy's increasing politico-judicial claims brought with it an expansion of the territories from which it would hear legal cases. As the feasibility of personally visiting each region where the king claimed power diminished, the itinerant royal court established a more permanent residence in Paris where it could receive those seeking judgement from all over the realm. At the same time, a system of judicial representatives was set up, along which socio-legal information could flow to and from the court, often in the form of texts. These factors formed the basis for the development of the *Parlement* of Paris, a permanent law court with a fixed staff.

Growing case loads were also at the heart of the institutional changes in the ecclesiastical province of York. Eleventh- and twelfth-century attempts at the standardization of religious practice stimulated the expansion and textualization of episcopal administrations in many regions of western Christendom. In York the formerly itinerant archiepiscopal court became part of a broader administrative block in and around the expanded cathedral church, combining the archiepiscopal residence with scriptoria and a law court. By operating in and around a place like the York Minster, the Consistory Court combined administrative permanence with a presence at the ideological heart of the church province. This symbolic centrality formed a crucial part of its claim to legitimacy in conflicts of jurisdiction with other socio-legal claimants, like the royal courts or local urban authorities.

The Council of Utrecht, also a former episcopal advisory board, took a different path. In the process of gaining independence from its ecclesiastical landlord, the socio-economic elite of Utrecht preferred the Council as representative body over a bench of aldermen appointed by the bishop. As a judicial and governmental body indirectly elected by the Utrecht citizenry, the Council came to constitute the main forum for communicating political and legal messages both within the community and vis-à-vis its rural hinterland, where it had to consider the interests of noble elites and other urban communities. Questions about the role of Utrecht's outlying jurisdictions (*buitengerechten*), the implications of citizenship and the relative position of non-citizens, underlay many of the Council's activities. But at the same time, the Council also formed the main venue for the city's internal power struggles. It was over and through this institution that political factions in Utrecht denied each other's claims for legitimate authority.

The establishment of law courts across late medieval Europe thus followed both broader and case-specific developments. While demographic and intellectual trends shaped the general framework within which these bodies were realized, differences of scale, legal tradition and socio-political context all influenced the particular motivations that brought each court into existence. Law courts could develop as part of kingdom- or province-wide administrations, like the *Parlement* or York's Consistory Court, treating conflicts in localities tens to hundreds of kilometres removed from the court proper. However, they might also be very locally oriented institutions, like the Council of Utrecht, concerned mainly with conflicts and social order in one specific community. Nor were courts limited to one legal tradition only. In the judicial practice of the cases treated in this book we have seen traces of learned legal traditions, like canon law (York and Paris) and Roman law (Paris), as well as a variety of regional, local or even court-specific rules and customs. Notably, these courts were also staffed by very different groups of functionaries, representing a diversity of social elites with their proper motivations. Whereas York's Consistory Court was based around a group of university-trained clergymen, presenting themselves as the moral compass of a religious community, the Parisian *Parlement*'s personnel consisted of a score of noble, clerical and other functionaries, involved in the major judicio-political project of the French kingdom, while the prominent citizens staffing the Council of Utrecht sought a position as representatives of the urban community vis-à-vis external and internal threats. The establishment and operation of these spatially fixed, text-producing judicial bodies, thus proves to be a remarkably similar response to diverse socio-communicative challenges faced by different claimants to legal legitimacy.

Scripting justice

Despite courts' popularity as forms of legal practice, their role in late medieval societies was contested. Alternative practices and discourses of justice existed, including feuding and other forms of private vengeance. Courts therefore had to market themselves, enticing both potential litigants and audiences to consider them as legitimate forms of socio-legal practice over and above the available alternatives. To do so, they engaged in what I have dubbed the scripting of justice. In a manner akin to a theatrical piece, specific constellations of acts, actors and/or matter, as well as related discourses, were put forward as normative ways to perform justice. These scripts constituted consistent communication strategies, incorporating spaces, texts, speech and activity, through which courts presented a specific idealized image of socio-legal practice. With them, courts tried to influence people's legal literacy, that is, their conceptualization of the nature of justice and how to achieve it. I have identified five of these legal scripts, each engaging with particular challenges that the courts faced to their legitimacy. They are provisionally styled the scripts of accessibility, physicality, rituality, semantic linking and narrativity.

As the discussion of Villon and Kafka has suggested, one of the main issues facing institutionalized courts was the negotiation of the accessibility versus the opacity of the legal process. Thus, the first script which courts employed concerned the degree of access which various participants had to their process. The court space had a fundamental part to play in this. As physical stage on which the courts' proceedings took place it was part and parcel of people's experience with the daily practice of law. The question of which parts of the legal process were to be experienced by whom, was to a large extent negotiated in space. This involved not only the layout of the physical spaces in which the court operated – be it a royal castle, a cathedral or a market square – but also the way in which such spaces were employed. The physical separation of two rooms by means of walls and doors could as easily be used to make a point about the publicity of the legal process, as could limiting access to one of these rooms for a certain group. Other media were also used in scripting the accessibility of legal practice. Certain parts of the legal process, like the *buurspraak* events in Utrecht or the sentence readings in York, formed an explicitly public performance of this process. Here space, activity and speech were combined in order to create a highly visible and audible experience of the court and its activities. Accessibility could likewise be limited by the strategic use of several modes of expression. Texts written in abbreviated Latin or the use of jargon could seriously impede large groups from participating fully in the processes of signification – that is, the attribution of meaning – that took place in court, establishing a dominant role for legal professionals, like advocates and proctors, in managing such participation.

Whereas the accessibility script was primarily concerned with people's access to the legal process, in a related way courts scripted the presence of this process in society. Through a multitude of media courts reified their presence in the world. The most prominent form of this script was again played out in space. By creating or appropriating physical spaces in the urban landscape, thereby establishing permanent fora of justice, courts made their presence concrete for potential audiences and litigants alike. The courtroom became a physical imprint on society, communicating the court's claim for prominence in the socio-legal field. And the same was true for its texts. As language-objects, these documents of practice not only communicated the contents of a legal case, but also physicalized its proceedings. The many registers, writs, letters and other records produced, used and archived by a court provided it with a presence and permanency unlike many non-physical aspects of the legal process. Finally, a third form in which courts took physical shape was in the enactment of their legal process. Occasions like the Utrecht forgiveness procedures, the York sentence readings and the *Grands Jours* of the *Parlement* of Paris, despite having less permanency than spaces or texts, made the court and its way of doing things physically present in the socio-legal arena.

Considering legal enactments leads to a third form of scripting, namely, the ritualization of legal acts. Within this script, otherwise separate acts were suggested to belong to an overarching and pre-existing structure – that is, a ritual – in an attempt to convincingly imbue them with specific meanings. Thus, public reconciliations between offenders and their community in the city of Utrecht would be framed according to a model of spiritual penance, echoing the moral power claim of the Council. Likewise, the individual *Grands Jours* held by the *Parlement* of Paris referred in the constellation of their activities to the ordinary sessions of this court, despite taking place in a completely different setting. And in York, the Consistory Court's sentence readings focused on the way that individual acts fitted within the overarching whole of canon law procedure. Although primarily concerned with physical activities, these scripts of rituality also drew on their textual record. A text could pose a particularly strong claim on the existence of a ritual whole, by suggesting a uniformity of practice and by fixing this suggestion on a written surface, allowing later audiences – including historians – to take note of the court's ritual myth. Thus, the involvement of written documents in the legal process was also part of an attempt to ritually script the events taking place.

Closely involved in all previous forms of scripting was the semantic linkage of entities and concepts involved in the legal process. Thus, when the Council of Utrecht demanded the compensation for a crime to be paid in 'stones', or the Consistory Court earmarked a certain fine to be used for the fabric of the church, they directly related monetary reconciliation to the (re)construction of specific meaningful structures, like town walls or the cathedral church. Likewise, the use of labels like *scelus* (sinful), *mala* (bad), *onredelik* (unreasonable) and *onstantelik* (improper) to describe certain acts as objectionable and thus fit for persecution, linked these acts to certain categories of thought, suggesting a specific meaning and valuation for them. In this fourth script, court records had a fundamental role to play. Even more than was the case in other forms of scripting, semantic links were particularly pronounced in writing. The endless repetition of the 'stone fine', or 'sinful acts' in the records, formed part of a campaign for the felicity of a particular semantic script.

Whereas semantic scripting focused on individual utterances and their suggested meanings, in a related way a much broader discursive framework was set up to encapsulate the meanings attributed to the court and its legal process as a whole. Often involving many of the previously identified forms of scripting, the courts presented what can best be called a court narrative, that is, a more or less cohesive story on the nature of social order and the role of the court itself in facilitating that order. Thus, the *Parlement*'s negotiation of its public and secluded spaces, ritualization of its legal procedure and moralization of the deeds of its litigants all contributed to positioning itself in relation to a society where it claimed the highest form of judiciary power. It wrote and performed a script that asserted its role as an experienced and at the same time detached – because royal – justice. And it underscored the logic of the legal manners of the *Parlement* and of the socio-moral character of the political constellation that was the French kingdom. Similarly, the Consistory Court in York combined its use of the cathedral with an oral and textual performance of the procedure of canon law in order to narrate its role in society. Taking place in the province's religious centre par excellence, and forming the realization of an ideal system of behaviour, the court's sessions were presented as the community's fundamental moral compass representing a judicial hierarchy whose highest arbiter was God himself. The Council of Utrecht, finally, mobilized everything from urban space to penitential references and categories of improper behaviour to claim a role as representative and guardian of its community. Narrative scripts, although mostly explicated in court documents, incorporated a large array of other media in bringing a broad and more or less coherent story about the court and the crucial role it allegedly played in guaranteeing social order.

Communication processes and the negotiation of justice

Courts' attempts at scripting socio-legal activity and discourse involved a range of modes of expression, including the use of texts, spaces, physical activities and the spoken word. In distinguishing between various scripts, we have seen how each of them was expressed through several if not all of these forms of communication. Each medium had its own character, influencing the way in which it was engaged in the communication process. Spaces, while forming the stage on which other means of expression operated, were themselves also used as a medium to conceptualize and communicate messages. Their obdurate materiality – that is, the relative complexity of changing them after their initial formation – gave them a particular role in scripting the court's accessibility and physicality, while also lending itself to semantic linking, as evidenced most clearly in the case of the Utrecht stone fines. Physical acts, while possessing a less permanent character than spaces, were also important means to make the court physically present and negotiate its accessibility, through the visualization or – on the contrary – concealment of its process. Just as important, however, was the performative role of these activities, that is, the courts' attempts to speak by acting, which was most pronounced in their ritualization of court practice. Performance also played its part in texts and oral statements, although in the reverse meaning of acting through speech. Common to both oral and textual modes of expression were the attempts to make concrete changes to the world by means of linguistic utterances. This could take the form of the attribution of meaning to specific acts, objects or people, or by explicating their interconnectedness in broader structures of practice and thought. In the case of texts, the medium's materiality further influenced its application in the process of communication. Having both a physical permanency similar to spaces, and the linguistic explicitness of speech, court documents added a specific dimension to the communicative activity of the court and were involved in all forms of scripting as identified above.

Court records' particular place in these socio-judicial communication processes makes it all the more relevant to see their numbers and application in legal practice increase markedly with the development of law courts. While taking care not to overstress the uniqueness or novelty of the use of texts in socio-legal practice, the scale of producing, using and archiving these linguistic artefacts rose drastically over the years in each of our three cases. This development of the textual record was in its turn related to other changes in the socio-legal communication processes related to the establishment of law courts. The link with physical permanence, a feature common to all courts treated here, is particularly pronounced. Not only did a set space for the court facilitate the production, handling and archiving of extensive records, it can also be argued to have sprung from a similar tendency to fix and thereby control the course of legal practice. Just as court space was actively used in scripting legal practice – negotiating accessibility, suggesting ritual structures – so the court record reduced the complexity of practice to a fixed scheme of operations.

These newly developing forms of communicative action built on and interacted with many existing practices. Contrary to the idea of an absolute shift from orality to textuality in legal practice by the late medieval period, the courts under scrutiny here continued to rely on existing forms of oral presentation and validation. Witness testimony, *fama* and other kinds of social information may have been increasingly translated into a textual format, yet their role as validators of the legal process worked because of, rather than despite, their oral character. Likewise, in reporting the legal process back to society, these courts made extensive use of oral modes of communication, publicly reading sentences, oaths and other parts of legal procedure. And the same is true for physical enactment, which is often found in close relation to such acts of public orality. The public staging of decisive moments in legal truth finding and dispute resolution processes had a long extra-textual history before being incorporated in court practice, encompassing, for example, various forms of ordeals and systems of public feuding. Such continuation of practices was even regularly explicated as part of courts' strategies of legitimization. Scripting rituality, for example, relied on the suggestion of a relation between one specific instance and a pre-existing structure of communication. Thus, while new modalities were gradually introduced in the legal format of the court, many practices and ideas about practices that had formed a central part of earlier socio-legal communication processes remained relevant in attempts to script justice.

The development of new modes of socio-legal communication, even when incorporating familiar practices and ideas, required people to adopt and accept new forms of expression, that is, the acquisition of a new kind of legal literacy. The logic of relying on a textualized procedure to achieve a just resolution in one's dispute, for example, was not self-evident, nor easily practicable, for those used to the private solution of conflicts through oral and enacted feuding practices. Over time people's legal literacy changed to incorporate the specific format of socio-legal communication that the court represented, even though – as the fears expressed by Kafka suggest – its acceptance was never a given. This process, at any rate, was hardly a top-down movement, forcing people to submit to externally implemented socio-legal modalities. Rather, it was the interaction of different agents, including the courts, their litigants and audiences, which shaped the forms and content of communication. All had their motivations to participate in particular socio-legal practices, be it in an attempt to claim legitimacy, in pursuit of specific socio-economic goals, or to seek confirmation of the proper functioning of justice. At the same time, each participant influenced the actions of the others. This could be done directly, by demanding specific activity from others, or, likewise, refusing to follow others' demands. Yet agents' actions were also often shaped in an indirect manner, as seen in audiences' influence on the courts' publication strategies. Thus, in the process that gradually changed people's legal literacy, individual socio-legal strategies were combined with a public negotiation of the nature and means of achieving justice.

It is in the context of this negotiated development of new legal literacies, that the courts played out their strategies of scripting justice. These scripts were highly participatory by nature. Many people could, so to speak, become co-authors, by bringing suits, acting as witnesses, forming audiences and so on. Society at large was actively engaged in legitimizing the courts' claims to socio-legal authority. Consequently, to speak in Bourdieuan terms, such claims were not just concerned with achieving a certain amount of socio-linguistic capital on an existing and stable field of communication. Instead, by involving the participation of so many potential speakers in their scripts of justice, the courts put the constitution of the field itself at stake. Rather than forcing themselves on a potentially unwilling society, courts tried to convince their potential consumers that their show of justice was the most legitimate by enticing them to contribute to and thus participate in it. While courts could and did draw on forceful means to summon, arrest, punish or otherwise incorporate individuals in the scripts of justice as they envisaged them, for the legitimacy of these scripts they depended on the voluntary cooperation, contribution and interest of the many people witnessing and participating in them.

Scripted justice and historians

The questions underlying this book have sprung from a desire to trace and understand people's experiences in engaging with behavioural norms, moralities and socio-legal practices in their daily lives, while acknowledging the problematic character of the sources used to do so. Such questions interest a growing group of social, legal and cultural historians. In the context of this field of the socio-cultural history of legal mentality and practice, a consideration of courts' scripting strategies can sharpen historians' understanding of past societies, the socio-legal processes taking place there and the written remains used to trace these. Firstly, a focus on scripting takes the explanation for actions back to where they actually take place. Rather than consider the socio-legal actions and considerations of historical individuals as merely derivative of external processes in the social, economic, political or other spheres, it takes these actions and considerations as main *explanans* for the changes taking place. In the historical narrative presented here, the communicative interaction between historical agents, including the staking and refuting of claims, the performance of acts and words and the suggestion of meaning for them, is the main process driving the development of people's socio-legal environment. Whether we consider Utrecht culprits publicly begging forgiveness for their deeds in a penitential garb, Parisian *huissiers* preventing people from making a racket in the royal courtroom or court examiners in York trying to distil a legal essence from the stories of multiple witnesses, we find ourselves in the thick of the action. Here people's concepts of justice and injustice were actively negotiated and renegotiated, subsequently influencing the activities employed in other fields of practice.

Secondly, an awareness of processes of judicial scripting is crucial for understanding key records on which historians base their claims about past societies. Among the sources – both textual and non-textual – available for the study of late medieval legal practice, court records form an impressively rich sediment of past human action and interaction, generally increasing in volume as we move further in time. Yet, their sedimentary nature also means that anyone wishing to use these sources to reconstruct broader patterns of thought and action must be aware of the texts' conditions of coming into being. Forming part of processes of judicial scripting, these documents were engaged in the interaction between a multiplicity of actors and modes of communication, complicating the relation of these sources to the social activities and ideas one tries to gather from them. Court records, despite their claim to describe events as they have taken place, are no untroubled mirrors of social activity. Rather, in describing certain practices, they also prescribe how such acts are supposed to proceed and even perform part of these idealized proceedings. They thus constitute an active attempt at reshaping an external reality by textually organizing the things that have supposedly taken place.

In this sense, court records are elaborate speech acts, that is, the textual performance of an idealized course of events. Whereas Austinian theories of performance focus on the one-directional, simple character of performative speech, court records can be conceived of as constitutive speech acts, that is, multi-authored and multidirectional speech acts. When witness testimony was drawn up, for example, a chain of agents, from the witness through to the examiner and the lawyer, each with their own strategies and motivations for speaking, made what they considered a felicitous contribution to the speech act as it has survived in writing. A particular form of influence was furthermore provided by the records' audiences. As many of these texts were written with a certain public in mind, these groups, without necessarily actively engaging in the construction of the historical record, had a major influence on what its authors eventually put into writing and how. The felicity conditions of a speech act were to a large extent dependent on the intended audience of the act as such, which thereby contributed to shaping the record in a similar fashion as its authors. Admittedly, the various voices represented in the material – direct and indirect authors as well as audiences – do not carry the same weight, and it is the court that speaks to us most directly. Nevertheless, even this dominant voice was not impervious to external influences. As such, the court records basically form a textualized, and thus more or less fixed, stage in a process of negotiation between multiple social agents, each contributing in some way or another to the document under scrutiny. They reflect attempts to script justice, that is, to assert and communicate a definition and practice of justice in a manner considered sufficiently legitimate by its potential participants and audiences.

Court records and the courts producing them thus form a crucial intermediary between historians and the historical actors, actions and mentalities that they try to understand. By taking such sources at face value, one takes the risk of reproducing the court's narrative of justice and idealized socio-legal practice. Yet, assuming that the records were produced in a complete curial vacuum, reflecting only the learned concepts of a small legal elite denies the influence of many direct and especially indirect actors on the constitution of ideas and practices of justice. Rather, by acknowledging the underlying communication processes – as well as their respective power relations – historians may recognize both the complexities and opportunities that these sources offer for those interested in historical understandings and experiences of justice. Reading mere fragments of lives long past, it is unreasonable to expect a complete, let alone unmediated view of people's lives and concerns. Yet the textual mediation that hides so many aspects of the past from our view is itself also a product of that past. In negotiating concepts and practices of justice, courts and other socio-judicial stakeholders found it opportune to invest in linguistic artefacts, including them in a broader complex of strategic activity. The records that form the result of this socio-legal scripting confront us with the sometimes strikingly familiar attempts of past generations to cope with the ambiguity of justice.

Appendix 1: Utrecht

1.1 Stone fines (1385–1425)

The number of entries in the Utrecht *Buurspraakboek* (BSB) presenting stone fines varies greatly per year. Table 1.1 distinguishes between the number of entries and the number of actual fines per year, as many entries concern multiple people being fined at once. It furthermore specifies the total number of stones allegedly collected each year, although it is important to keep in mind that an imposed fine does not need to equal the amount eventually collected. For each year, the table also gives an average number of stones per entry and per fine. The years 1392–1395 are left out, because the register covering those years is missing.

Table 1.1: Number and amount of stone fines (BSB)

Year	Entries	Fines	Stones (total) x1000	Stones (average per entry) x1000	Stones (avg. per fine) x1000
1385	13	13	255	19.6	19.6
1386	7	9	167	23.9	18.6
1387	7	8	258	36.9	32.3
1388	4	14	153	38.3	10.9
1389	9	18	333	37.0	18.5
1390	7	13	150	21.4	11.5
1391	3	5	54	18.0	10.8
-	-	-	-	-	-
1396	0	0	0	0.0	0.0
1397	8	8	104	13.0	13.0
1398	4	6	34	8.5	5.7
1399	4	5	105	26.3	21.0
1400	3	4	87	29.0	21.8
1401	5	7	80	16.0	11.4
1402	4	10	105	26.3	10.5
1403	1	1	10	10.0	10.0
1404	4	4	170	42.5	42.5
1405	1	1	20	20.0	20.0
1406	1	1	73	73.0	73.0
1407	4	6	185	46.3	30.8
1408	1	1	5	5.0	5.0
1409	2	2	45	22.5	22.5
1410	0	0	0	0.0	0.0

Year	Entries	Fines	Stones (total) x1000	Stones (average per entry) x1000	Stones (avg. per fine) x1000
1411	3	25	305	101.7	12.2
1412	4	13	105	26.3	8.1
1413	0	0	0	0.0	0.0
1414	6	7	595	99.2	85.0
1415	4	5	137	34.3	27.4
1416	2	2	65	32.5	32.5
1417	2	2	15	7.5	7.5
1418	0	0	0	0.0	0.0
1419	2	2	20	10.0	10.0
1420	1	1	5	5.0	5.0
1421	0	0	0	0.0	0.0
1422	2	2	30	15.0	15.0
1423	4	4	45	11.3	11.3
1424	6	10	270	45.0	27.0
1425	0	0	0	0.0	0.0
Total	**128**	**209**	**3985**	**31.1**	**19.1**

1.2 Utrecht banishments (1385–1425)

Table 1.2 and Diagram 1 show the number of banishments recorded in the *Buurspraakboek* between 1385 and 1425, as well as the indicated range beyond the city walls, if any. This could be the city mile, the range of its excise (*sijs*) or liberty (*vrijheit*), which appear to be synonymous, or the land of Utrecht. The register covering the years 1392–1395 is missing.

Table 1.2: Number and range of banishments (BSB)

Year	Total	Distance			
		City	City and city mile	City and range of excise and/or liberty	City and land of Utrecht
1385	23	22	0	0	1
1386	16	15	1	0	0
1387	10	8	1	0	1
1388	17	16	0	0	1
1389	26	25	0	0	1
1390	25	25	0	0	0
1391	4	4	0	0	0

Year	Total	Distance			
		City	City and city mile	City and range of excise and/or liberty	City and land of Utrecht
-	-	-	-	-	-
1396	5	5	0	0	0
1397	21	14	4	2	1
1398	21	15	2	3	1
1399	25	22	2	1	0
1400	16	13	0	2	1
1401	12	6	3	3	0
1402	14	12	1	1	0
1403	8	2	2	3	1
1404	6	2	1	1	2
1405	9	1	7	1	0
1406	2	0	0	0	2
1407	33	32	0	0	1
1408	10	9	1	0	0
1409	1	1	0	0	0
1410	13	8	4	1	0
1411	10	3	5	1	1
1412	13	10	2	0	1
1413	39	22	11	4	2
1414	17	10	6	0	1
1415	28	10	13	4	1
1416	13	5	7	0	1
1417	10	5	4	0	1
1418	16	5	11	0	0
1419	14	4	8	2	0
1420	7	0	5	0	2
1421	7	2	4	0	1
1422	1	0	0	1	0
1423	14	3	9	1	1
1424	8	0	7	1	0
1425	4	0	4	0	0
	518	336	125	32	25

Diagram 1: Number and range of banishments (BSB)

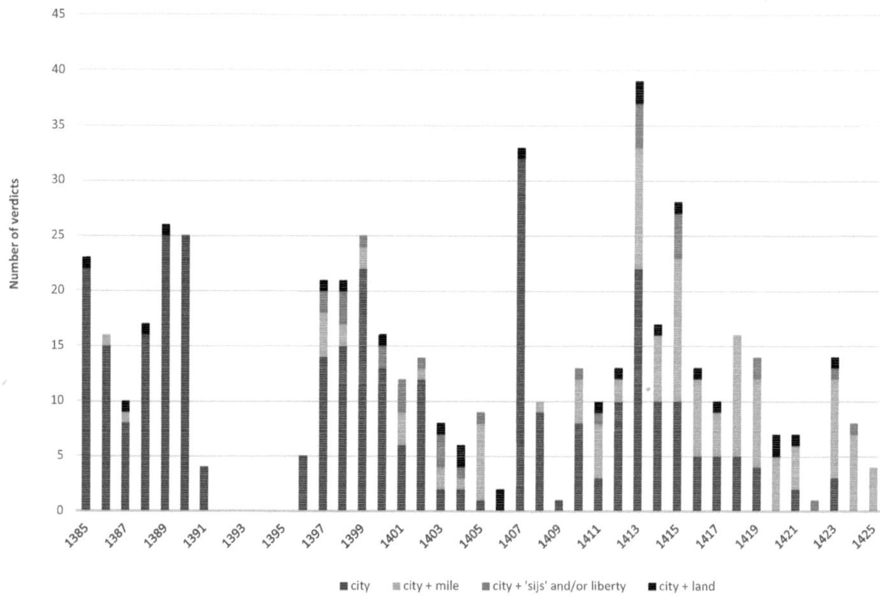

1.3 Procedure of forgiveness (1385–1425)

Table 1.3 traces the elements constituting the procedure of forgiveness. The descriptions of the procedure are built up of varieties of a number of main elements: custody in one of the city prisons, movement towards the *Buurkerk* in special attire, asking the Council and/or the victim for forgiveness and paying a compensation for the crime committed. Not every description contains all main aspects of the procedure. In other cases, several sub-elements are combined in one entry (for example, paying compensation to the city and to the victim). Some elements, like the loss of citizenship, appear in very few descriptions, and are therefore considered extraordinary additions to the core procedure.

Table 1.3: Elements of the procedure of forgiveness (1385–1425)

	BSB (1385–1425)	RDB (1402–1425)	Total
Total instances of a procedure of forgiveness	**220**	**174**	**394**
Imprisonment			
Imprisoned	190	87	**277**
Dress			
In 'shirt and pants' before the Council	156	54	**210**
Bareheaded before the Council	63	68	**131**
Bareheaded before the victim	1	3	**4**
Asking for forgiveness			
Asking the Council for forgiveness	215	162	**377**
Asking the victim for forgiveness	4	45	**49**
Declaring one's life forfeit with a bare sword in hand, asking the Council for forgiveness	4	2	**6**
Compensation			
Compensation to the city	122	65	**187**
Compensation to the Council	8	47	**55**
Compensation to the victim	16	42	**58**
Other elements			
Loss of citizenship	22	19	**41**
Making an *oorvede*[1]	0	9	**9**
Willekeur to atone with a deceased person's relatives before the Council	10	11	**21**
Other *willekeur*	42	43	**85**
Other elements	27	38	**65**

1.4 Oath of the Utrecht council members

The unfoliated front fly leaf of the *Th.2* register (HUA 701-1.227) contains a transcript of the oath allegedly sworn by new Council members. The oath, originally written in the third-person singular (*gi*), shows evidence of having been adapted to be read in the first-person singular (*ic*). A later copy at the back of the book of bylaws *Die Roese*, is entirely written in the first-person singular.

1 A formal promise to abstain from vengeance.

[Dat z]weer[t] gi	So you will swear
[d]at gi van deser tiid voert	that from now on
tot onser vrouwen lichtmisse toe over een iaer	until our lady's lightmass in a year
der stat enten menen ghilden van utrecht	you will counsel the city and all guilds of Utrecht
hoer beste raden zelt	what is good for them
hoer qwaetste waernen zelt	warn them for what is bad
ter stat rade comen zelt	come to the city council
alst gi daer gheeyschet wert	when your presence is wanted
der stat raet helen zelt	bring unity to the city council
den armen ghelike den riken voerraden zelt	supply the poor like the rich
der stat scout van hoers selfs b[etal]en zelt	do your duty to the city
ende ten naesten iaer also gi out raet sijt	and next year when you are part of the old council
ende gi ten rade gheroepen wert	and you are called to the [new] council
der stat beste raden zelt	[you shall] counsel the city what is good
der stat raet oec dan helen zelt	again bringing unity to the city council
alse gi in deser iare sculdich z[elt we]sen	as you are obliged to in this year
des en zel gi laten	you will not refrain from doing so
om lieve	neither because of your life
noch om lede	nor because of your body
noch om maesscap	nor because of kinship
noch om zwagherscap	nor because of affinity
noch om anxt van uwen live	nor for fear of your life
noch om anxt van uwen ghoede	nor for fear of your goods
noch om gheenrehande zaken	nor for any reason
dat u god also helpe	that God may help you
[ende sij]n hilighen	as well as his saints

Appendix 2: York

2.1 Cause papers (fourteenth century)

The 254 fourteenth century cause papers can be divided into seven main categories according to their subject matter: matrimonial, tithes, defamation, benefices, testamentary, church rights and breach of faith. Each category contains both cases heard in first instance and on appeal. Table 2.1 distinguishes between first instance and appealed cases, while Table 2.2 takes both together. Table 2.3 shows the number and percentage of cases originating in each of the ten decades between 1300 and 1400. Each of the three tables furthermore shows the number and percentage of surviving depositions and sentences among these cause papers. The 'Depositions' row gives the depositions of each category or decade both as percentage of all cause papers from that category or decade (DP) and as percentage of the total number of surviving depositions (PD). The 'Sentences' row does the same for the sentences, indicating both their weight among all cause papers from that category or decade (SP) and among the total number of surviving sentences (PS).

Table 2.1: First instance/appeal

			Depositions				Sentences			
			Yes	No	DP	PD	Yes	No	SP	PS
Matrimonial	**48**	19%	37	11	77%	24%	22	26	46%	25%
Matrimonial app.	**40**	16%	31	9	78%	20%	30	10	75%	34%
Tithes	**22**	9%	15	7	68%	10%	4	18	18%	5%
Tithes appeal	**12**	5%	8	4	67%	5%	7	5	58%	8%
Defamation	**15**	6%	8	7	53%	5%	3	12	20%	3%
Defamation app.	**5**	2%	4	1	80%	3%	2	3	40%	2%
Benefice	**12**	5%	6	6	50%	4%	1	11	8%	1%
Benefice appeal	**23**	9%	10	13	43%	7%	1	22	4%	1%
Testamentary	**16**	6%	6	10	38%	4%	1	15	6%	1%
Testament. app.	**7**	3%	6	1	86%	4%	6	1	86%	7%
Church rights	**12**	5%	5	7	42%	3%	2	10	17%	2%
Church r. app.	**18**	7%	8	10	44%	5%	2	16	11%	2%
Breach of faith	**10**	4%	3	7	30%	2%	2	8	20%	2%
Breach of f. app.	**4**	2%	2	2	50%	1%	4	0	100%	5%
Appeal other	**6**	2%	3	3	50%	2%	0	6	0%	0%
Undefined	**4**	2%	0	4	0%	0%	0	4	0%	0%
Total	**254**	**100%**	**152**	**102**	60%	**100%**	**87**	**167**	34%	**100%**

Table 2.2: First instance + appeal

			Depositions				Sentences			
			Yes	No	DP	PD	Yes	No	SP	PS
Matrimonial	**88**	35%	68	20	77%	45%	52	36	59%	60%
Tithes	**34**	13%	23	11	68%	15%	11	23	32%	13%
Defamation	**20**	8%	12	8	60%	8%	5	15	25%	6%
Benefice	**35**	14%	16	19	46%	11%	2	33	6%	2%
Testamentary	**23**	9%	12	11	52%	8%	7	16	30%	8%
Church rights	**30**	12%	13	17	43%	9%	4	26	13%	5%
Breach of faith	**14**	6%	5	9	36%	3%	6	8	43%	7%
Other/undefined	**10**	4%	3	7	30%	2%	0	10	0%	0%
Total	**254**	**100%**	**152**	**102**	60%	**100%**	**87**	**167**	34%	**100%**

Table 2.3: Cause papers per decade

			Depositions				Sentences			
			Yes	No	DP	PD	Yes	No	SP	PS
1300–1309	4	2%	3	1	75%	2%	3	1	75%	3%
1310–1319	9	4%	3	6	33%	2%	1	8	11%	1%
1320–1329	9	4%	4	5	44%	3%	4	5	44%	5%
1330–1339	18	7%	16	2	89%	11%	4	14	22%	5%
1340–1349	23	9%	16	7	70%	11%	2	21	9%	2%
1350–1359	24	9%	18	6	75%	12%	9	15	38%	10%
1360–1369	32	13%	25	7	78%	16%	13	19	41%	15%
1370–1379	20	8%	13	7	65%	9%	12	8	60%	14%
1380–1389	36	14%	18	18	50%	12%	7	29	19%	8%
1390–1399	79	31%	36	43	46%	24%	32	47	41%	37%
Total	**254**	**100%**	**152**	**102**	60%	**100%**	**87**	**167**	34%	**100%**

2.2 Oath of the Consistory Court advocates

The following oath, allegedly taken by the advocates of the Consistory Court of York, was included in the court statutes drawn up under archbishop William Greenfield in 1311. They were published by David Wilkins in the second volume of his *Consilia magnae britanniae et hiberniae ab anno MDXLVI ad annum MDCCXVII* (1737), 409–415. Wilkins based his edition on two surviving manuscripts: Cotton MS. Vitellius D V[1] and MS. penes Tho. episc. Assaven.[2]

> *Ego N. juro ad haec sancta Dei evangelia quod in omnibus causis, quarum patronus sum et ero in hoc consistorio, vel coram domino archiepiscopo, vel ipsius spiritualibus commissariis, fidele patrocinium praestabo. Quodque omni opere ac diligentia id, quod justum et verum aestimavero, meis clientibus in suis causis et negotiis procurabo, et circa hoc, quatenus est mihi possibile, fideliter laborabo. Nec aliquid dicam, proponam, vel faciam, seu per alium dici, proponi, vel fieri, quantum in me est, scienter et malitiose permittam, ad partis alterius justitiam auferendam, vel etiam indebite differendam. Nec etiam contra Eborum ecclesiae jurisdictionem, aut Eborum curiae consuetudines, vel statua. Ita quod si in quacunque parte judicii mihi innotuerit clientulos meos malam, seu injustam causam fovere, seu defendere, quae mihi visa fuerit desperata, amplius non patrocinabor eidem, nec in eadem praestabo consilium, vel auxilium clam vel palam. Sic me Deus adjuvet, et haec sancta Dei evangelia.*

1 This manuscript was reported lost after the fire that hit the Cotton Library on October 23, 1731. Still, some remnants seem to have survived. They were later split between British Library (BL) Cotton MS. Vitellius D V, BL Cotton MS. Vespasian D XIII and Corpus Christi College, Oxford, MS. 155.

2 This is assumedly manuscript number 365 of the Lansdowne manuscript collection of the British Museum.

Appendix 3: Paris

3.1 Oath of the advocates of the *Parlement* of Paris

Below follows the oath taken by the *Parlement*'s advocates as recorded in 1340 on fols. 18v–19r of the fourth criminal register of the *Parlement* (AN $X^{2A}4$). The oath follows a list with the names of all the advocates working in the *Parlement*, and is followed by a comparable name list and oath for the proctors (see Appendix 3.2).

Aduocati istius curie iurabunt articulos qui sequntur videlicet:

- *Quod diligenter et fideliter istud officium exercebunt.*
- *Quod causarum iniustarum patrocinium scientur non recipient.*
- *Quod et si non ab inicio ex post facto tamen viderint causam esse iniustam statim eam dimittent.*
- *Quod in causis quas fovebunt si viderint tangi regem ipsi de hanc curiam avisabunt.*
- *Quod causa placitata et factis negatis ipsi de recenti infra biduum uel trium facient et curie tradent articulos suos iusi ex causa de licencia curie defferent.*
- *Quod impertinentes articulos scienter non facient.*
- *Quod consuetudines quas veras non coediderint non proponent nec sustinebunt.*
- *Quod causas quas suscipient cito expedient pro posse suo.*
- *Quod in eis dilaciones et subterfugia maliciose non quarent.*
- *Quod pro salario suo quantumcumque sit magna causa ultra triginta libras Turonensis non recipient nec etiam aliquod ultra in salarii maioris fraudem minus tamen recipere possunt.*
- *Quod pro mediocri minus et pro minori causa multo minus recipient secundum quantitatem cause et condiciones personarum.*
- *Hoc idem iuramentum prestabunt illi qui aduocatis proponentibus ut consiliarii assistent.*
- *Iniungatur eis preter iuramentum.*
- *Quod bene mane venient et bene mane venire faciant partes suas.*
- *Quod illum cui data fuerit audientia non impediant.*
- *Quod stando et retro primum scamium patrocinentur.*
- *Quod primum scamium non occupant.*
- *Quod licet plures sint aduocati in vna causa vnus tantummodo loquatur.*

- *Quod facta impertinencia non proponant.*
- *Quod ipsi de curia non recedant quamdiu magistri in camera erunt.*
- *Et est sciendum quod nullus aduocatus ad patrocinandum recipietur nisi fit iuratus et in rotulo nominum aduocatorum scriptus. Et prohibet curia ne ipsi ingerant se ad patrocinandum nisi sint iurati.*

3.2 Oath of the proctors of the *Parlement* of Paris

Like for the advocates, the fourth criminal register (AN $X^{2a}4$) contains a transcript of the oath allegedly sworn by the proctors operating in the *Parlement*. It is written on fols. 19r–19v and follows a list of names of all the general proctors working in the *Parlement* in 1340.

Procuratores predicti iurauerunt hec qui sequntur:

- *Quod diligenter et fideliter officium procuracionis exercebunt.*
- *Quod causarum iniustarum onus seu officium procuracionis scienter non recipient.*
- *Quod et si non ab inicio ex post facto viderint causam esse iniustam statim eam dimittent.*
- *Quod in causis quas fouebunt si viderint tangi ius regis ipsi de hanc curiam auisabunt.*
- *Quod causa placitata et factis negatis ipsi de recenti infra biduum vel triduum fieri et tradi procurabunt articulos suos nisi ex causa de licencia curie ulterius different.*
- *Quod impertinentes articulos scienter non facient nec fieri facient seu permittent.*
- *Quod facta nec consuetudines quas veras non crediderint non proponent nec proponi facient.*
- *Quod causas quas suscipient cito expediri procurabunt pro posse suo.*
- *Quod in eis dilaciones et subterfugia maliciose non querent.*
- *Quod pro salario suo quantumcumque fit magna causa ultra decem libris Parisiensis pro uno parlamento non recipient nec etiam aliquid in salarii maioris fraudem minus tamen recipient secundum qualitatem causarum et condiciones personarum.*
- *Quod non pascicentur de quota parte liti.*
- *Quod non facient forum de causa ducenda seu consilio querendo in fraudem salarij aduocatoris nec alii.*
- *Quod non impetrabunt seu impetrari facient litteras iniustas et iniquas contra racionem et stilum curie.*

- *Quod non inducent magistros suos ad corrupcionem aliquam faciendum nec eciam informandum aliquos dominorum de causis suis ad partem extra iudicium.*
- *Quod per favorem preces pecuniam aut alie indebite non querent aduocatos ad modum prosenete uel mediatoris.*
- *Iniungatur eis preter iuramentum:*
- *Quod bene mane veniant.*
- *Quod illum cui data fuerit audientia non impediant.*
- *Quod retro aduocatos stent vel sedeant.*
- *Quod primum scamium non occupent.*
- *Quod ipsi de curia non recedant quamdiu magistri erunt in camera.*
- *Et est sciendum quod nullus procurator generalis parlamenti admittetur ad officium procuracionis exercendi nisi sit iuratus et in rotulo procuratorum generalium scriptus.*
- *Et prohibet curia ne ipsi ingerant se ad procurator generaliter in parlamento nisi fuit iurati.*

3.3 *Arrêt* in the case of Isabelle de Blanot (1345)

The following *arrêt* is part of a case from 1345 involving Isabelle de Blanot, lady of Uxelles, and a group of men who have attacked the village Ougy-sous-Uxelles, which fell under her jurisdiction. The *arrêt* concerns the question of whether the royal proctor will join Isabelle as plaintiff against the attackers, because the latter have breached a royal safeguard. Based on the information received about the case, the *Parlement* eventually decides to do so. The *arrêt* is recorded in the fifth criminal register (AN $X^{2A}5$) on fol. 74r. Also see Labat-Poussin, Langlois and Lanhers, *Actes*, 273.

> *Cum dudum Ysabellis de Blanesco domina de huissellis nobis conquerendo monstrasset quod licet ipsa cum familia hominibus justiciabilibus et subditis suis esse in nostra gardia principali sufficienter significata et publicata in ballivo Matisconensis, Nicholus Benedictus quadrigarius, Jaquestus Jasset et plures alii malefactores venerant cum armis prohibitis in villa de Ongiers subtus Huissellas in alta et bassa jurisdictione dicte Ysabellis, ibique vulneraverant, mutilaverant ac occiderant nostram salvam gardiam infringendo in dicte gardie et superioritatis nostre vituperium et contemptum dicteque Ysabellis grande providicium et iaccuram super quibus delictis plures informationes facte fuerant, ipsis demum ad curiam nostram asportatis et ad finem si procurator noster cum dicta Ysabelli adiungeretur vel ut*

adiunctus remaneret, receptis. Quadam informatione super predictis facta per arrestum curie nostre reiecta. Aliis informationibus super predictis factis visis et diligenter examinatis per judicium dicte curie nostre dictum fuit quod dictus procurator noster cum dicta Ysabelli adiungetur vel ut alii adiunctus remanebit.

Ludovicus Wauterche reportator *pronunciatum xxiii[a] die decembris anno xlv[to]*

Bibliography

Primary Sources

Het Utrechts Archief, Utrecht (HUA)

HUA 701-1.13	*Raads dagelijks boek* (RDB)	1402–1577 (non-continuous)
HUA 701-1.16	*Buurspraakboek* (BSB)	1385–1579 (non-continuous)
HUA 701-1.226	*Register van den raad Th.1*	[1315] 1342–1374
HUA 701-1.227	*Register van den raad Th.2*	[1315] 1342–1403

Borthwick Institute for Archives, York (BIA)

BIA CP.E	*Cause papers, 14th c.*	1301–1399

York Minster Library, York (YML)

YML M 2(1)b	*Consistory Court act book*	Jan–July 1371
YML M 2(1)c	*Consistory Court act book*	Oct 1371–Oct 1375

Archives Nationales, Paris (AN)

AN X^{1A} 1–4	*Olim registers*	1254–1318
AN X^{1A} 5–156	*Civil registers (lettres, arrêts, jugés)*	1319–1515
AN X^{1A} 8844–8851bis	*'Anciens registres du greffe'*	1319–1713
AN X^{2A} 1–900, 906	*Criminal registers*	1312–1784

Edited Sources

Beugnot, Arthur Auguste, ed. *Les Olim ou registres des arrêts rendus par la cour du roi sous les règnes de Saint Louis, de Philippe le Hardi, de Philippe le Bel, de Louis le Hutin et de Philippe le Long.* 3 parts/4 vols. Paris: Imprimerie Royale, 1839–1848.

Boutaric, Edgar, ed. *Actes du Parlement de Paris: Première série: De l'an 1254 à l'an 1328.* 2 vols. Paris: Henri Plon, 1863–1867.

Brown, William, ed. *The Register of John le Romeyn, Lord Archbishop of York, 1286–1296.* 2 vols. Durham: Surtees Society, 1913–1917.

Brown, William, ed. *The Register of Thomas of Corbridge, Lord Archbishop of York, 1300–1304.* 2 vols. Durham: Surtees Society, 1925–1928.

Brown, William, ed. *The Register of William Wickwane, Lord Archbishop of York, 1279–1285.* Durham: Surtees Society, 1907.

Brown, William, and A. Hamilton Thompson, eds. *The Register of William Greenfield, Lord Archbishop of York, 1306–1315.* 5 vols. Durham: Surtees Society, 1931–1940.

Cohn, Samuel K., Jr., ed. *Popular Protest in Late Medieval Europe: Italy, France and Flanders*. Manchester and New York: Manchester University Press, 2004.

De Laurière, Eusèbe Jacques et al., eds. *Ordonnances des roys de France de la troisième race, recueillies par ordre chronologique, avec des renvoys des unes aux autres, des sommaires, & des observations sur le Texte*. 21 vols. Paris: Imprimerie royale, 1723–1849.

Delisle, Léopold, ed. *Histoire du château et des sires de Saint-Sauveur-le-Vicomte*. Valonges: Martin, 1867.

Du Breuil, Guillaume. *Stilus curie parlamenti*. Edited by Félix Aubert. Paris: Alphonse Picard, 1909.

Emerton, Ephraim, ed. *The Correspondence of Pope Gregory VII: Selected Letters from the Registrum*. New York: Columbia University Press, 1932.

Furgeot, Henri, et al., eds. *Actes du Parlement de Paris: Deuxième série: De l'an 1328 à l'an 1350*. 2 vols. Paris: Plon-Nourrit and Imprimerie Nationale, 1920–1960.

Goldberg, Jeremy, ed. *Women in England, c. 1275–1525: Documentary Sources*. Manchester: Manchester University Press, 1995.

Hill, Rosalind, et al., eds. *The Register of William Melton, Archbishop of York, 1317–1340*. 6 vols. Torquay and Woodbridge: Boydell Press, 1977–2011.

Kafka, Franz, *Sämtliche Werke*. Frankfurt am Main: Suhrkamp, 2008.

Langlois, C. V., ed. *Textes relatifs à l'histoire du Parlement depuis les origines jusqu'en 1314*. Paris: Alphonse Picard, 1888.

Langlois, Monique, and Yvonne Lanhers, eds. *Confessions et jugements de criminels au Parlement de Paris (1319–1350)*. Paris: S.E.V.P.E.N., 1971.

Muller, Samuel, ed. *De middeleeuwsche rechtsbronnen der stad Utrecht*. 2 vols., introduction and register. The Hague: Nijhoff, 1883–1885.

Overvoorde, J.C., and J.G.C. Joosting, eds. *De gilden van Utrecht tot 1528*. 2 vols. The Hague: Nijhoff, 1896–1897.

Raine, James, ed. *The Fabric Rolls of York Minster*. London and Edinburgh: Surtees Society, 1859.

Raine, James, ed. *Historical Papers and Letters from the Northern Registers*. London: Longman, 1873.

Tuetey, Alexandre, ed. *Journal de Nicolas de Baye, greffier du Parlement de Paris 1400–1417*. 2 vols. Paris: Renouard, 1885–1889.

Van de Water, Johan, ed. *Groot placaatboek vervattende alle de placaten, ordonnantien en edicten der edele mogende heren staten 's lands van Utrecht: Mitsgaders van de edele groot achtbare heeren borgemeesteren en vroedschap der stad Utrecht tot het jaar 1728 ingesloten*. 3 vols. Utrecht: Jacob van Poolsum, 1729.

Villon, François. *Lais, testament, poésies diverses/Ballades en jargon*. Edited by Jean-Claude Mühlethaler and Eric Hicks. Paris: Champion, 2004.

Villon, François. *Poems*. Translated by Peter Dale. London: Carcanet Press, 2001.
Wilkins, David, ed. *Consilia magnae britanniae et hiberniae ab anno MDXLVI ad annum MDCCXVII*. 4 vols. London, 1737.

Literature

Althoff, Gerd. *Spielregeln der Politik im Mittelalter: Kommunikation in Friede un Fehde*. Darmstadt: Darmstadt Wissenschaftliche Buchgesellschaft, 1997.
Arnold, John. *Inquisition and Power: Catharism and the Confessing Subject in Medieval Languedoc*. Philadelphia: University of Pennsylvania Press, 2001.
Aubert, Félix. *Histoire du Parlement de Paris de l'origine à François Ier: 1250–1515*. 2 vols. Paris: Picard, 1894.
Aubert, Félix. "Les huissiers du parlement de Paris, 1300–1420". *Bibliothèque de l'école des chartes* 47 (1886): 370–393.
Aubert, Félix. "Nouvelles recherches sur le Parlement de Paris: Période d'organisation". Pt. 1. *Nouvelle revue historique de droit Français et étranger* 40 (1916): 62–109, 229–290.
Aubert, Félix. "Nouvelles recherches sur le Parlement de Paris: Période d'organisation". Pt. 2. *Nouvelle revue historique de droit Français et étranger* 41 (1917): 48–72, 181–208.
Austin, John. *How to Do Things with Words*. Edited by J.O. Urmson. Cambridge, MA: Harvard University Press, 1962.
Autrand, Françoise. *Naissance d'un grand corps de l'Etat: Les gens du Parlement de Paris, 1345–1454*. Paris: Publications de la Sorbonne, 1981.
Baildon, William Paley. *Notes on the Religious and Secular Houses of Yorkshire*. 2 vols. London: Yorkshire Archaeological Society, 1895–1931.
Bartlett, Robert. *The Hanged Man: A Story of Miracle, Memory, and Colonialism*. Princeton, NJ: Princeton University Press, 2004.
Beattie, John. "Ritual and Social Change". *Man, new series* 1 (1966): 60–74.
Bednarski, Steven. *Curia: A Social History of a Provençal Criminal Court in the Fourteenth Century*. Montpellier: Presses universitaires de la Méditerranée, 2013.
Bednarski, Steven. *A Poisoned Past: The Life and Times of Margarida de Portu, a Fourteenth-Century Accused Poisoner*. Toronto: University of Toronto Press, 2014.
Bell, Catherine. *Ritual Theory, Ritual Practice*. Oxford: Oxford University Press, 1992.
Benders, J.F. *Bestuursstructuur en schriftcultuur: Een analyse van de bestuurlijke verschriftelijking in Deventer tot het eind van de 15e eeuw*. Kampen: IJsselacademie, 2004.
Benders, J.F. "Urban Administrative Literacy in the Northeastern Low Countries: A Comparison of Groningen, Kampen, Deventer, and Zutphen, Twelfth–Fifteenth

Centuries". In *Writing and the Administration of Medieval Towns*, edited by Marco Mostert and Anna Adamska, 97–121. Turnhout: Brepols, 2014.

Benton, John F. "Philip the Fair and the Jours of Troyes". *Studies in Medieval and Renaissance History* 6 (1969): 279–344.

Berents, D.A. "Gegoede burgerij in Utrecht in de 15e eeuw". *Jaarboek Oud-Utrecht* (1972): 78–92.

Berents, D.A. *Misdaad in de Middeleeuwen: Een onderzoek naar de criminaliteit in het laat-middeleeuwse Utrecht*. Utrecht: Stichting Stichtse Historische Reeks, 1976.

Berman, Harold J. *Law and Revolution: The Formation of the Western Legal Tradition*. Cambridge, MA: Harvard University Press, 1983.

Bisson, Thomas N. *Tormented Voices: Power, Crisis and Humanity in Rural Catalonia 1140–1200*. Cambridge, MA, and London: Harvard University Press, 1998.

Bloch, Claudine, and Jean-Marie Carbasse. "Aux origines de la série criminelle du Parlement: Le registre $X^{2A}1$". *Histoire et archives* 12 (2002): 7–26.

Bloch, Marc. "Pour une histoire comparée des sociétiés Européennes". In Marc Bloch, *Mélanges historiques*. Vol. 1, 16–40. Paris: Fleuris, 1963. Translated by J.E. Anderson as "A Contribution Towards a Comparative History of European Societies". In *Land and Work in Mediaeval Europe: Selected Papers by Marc Bloch*, 44–81. London: Routledge and Kegan Paul, 1967.

Blockmans, Wim. "Les pouvoirs publics dans des régions de haute urbanisation: 'Flandre' et 'Italie' aux XIVe–XVIe siècles". In *Villes de Flandre et d'Italie (XIIIe–XVIe siècle): Les enseignements d'une comparaison*, edited by Élisabeth Crouzet-Pavan and Élodie Lecuppre-Desjardin, 65–74. Turnhout: Brepols, 2008.

Blockmans, Wim. "Voracious States and Obstructing Cities: An Aspect of State Formation in Preindustrial Europe". *Theory and Society* 18, no. 5 (1989): 733–755.

Blockmans, Wim, André Holenstein and Jon Mathieu, eds. *Empowering Interactions: Political Cultures and the Emergence of the State in Europe 1300–1900*. Farnham and Burlington, VT: Ashgate, 2009.

Bossy, John, ed. *Disputes and Settlements: Law and Human Relations in the West*. Cambridge: Cambridge University Press, 1983.

Bourdieu, Pierre. *Language and Symbolic Power*. Edited by John Thompson. Translated by Gino Raymond and Matthew Adamson. Cambridge, MA: Harvard University Press, 1991.

Boyle, Leonard E. "Montaillou Revisited: *Mentalité* and Methodology". In *Pathways to Medieval Peasants*, edited by J.A. Raftis, 119–140. Toronto: Pontifical Institute of Medieval Studies, 1981.

Brand, Paul. *The Origins of the English Legal Profession*. Oxford and Cambridge, MA: Blackwell, 1992.

Braun, Georg, and Frans Hogenberg. *Civitates orbis terrarum*. 6 vols. Cologne: 1572–1617.

Brett, Martin. "Canon Law and Litigation: The Century before Gratian". In *Medieval Ecclesiastical Studies in Honour of Dorothy M. Owen*, edited by Michael Franklin and Christopher Harper-Brill, 21–40. Woodbridge and Rochester, NY: Boydell & Brewer, 1995.

Brown, Alison. "Insiders and Outsiders: The Changing Boundaries of Exile". In *Society and Individual in Renaissance Florence*, edited by William Connell, 337–383. Berkeley: University of California Press, 2002.

Brown, Elizabeth A.R., and Richard C. Famiglietti. *The* lit de justice*: Semantics, Ceremonial and the Parlement of Paris 1300–1600*. Sigmaringen: J. Thorbecke, 1994.

Brown, Sandra. *The Medieval Courts of the York Minster Peculiar*. York: University of York, 1984.

Brown, Sarah. *'Our Magnificent Fabrick': York Minster: An Architectural History c. 1220–1500*. Swindon: English Heritage, 2003.

Brown, Warren C., and Piotr Górecki, eds. *Conflict in Medieval Europe: Changing Perspectives on Society and Culture*. Aldershot and Burlington, VT: Ashgate, 2003.

Brundage, James A. "The Bar of the Ely Consistory Court in the Fourteenth Century: Advocates, Proctors and Others". *Journal of Ecclesiastical History* 43 (1992): 541–560.

Brundage, James A. *Medieval Canon Law*. London and New York: Longman, 1995.

Brundage, James A. *The Medieval Origins of the Legal Profession: Canonists, Civilians and Courts*. Chicago and London: Chicago University Press, 2008.

Bubenicek, Michelle, and Richard Partington. "Justice, Law and Lawyers". In *Government and Political Life in England and France, c. 1300–c. 1500*, edited by Christopher Fletcher, Jean-Philippe Genet and John Watts, 150–182. Cambridge: Cambridge University Press, 2015.

Buc, Philip. *The Dangers of Ritual: Between Early Medieval Texts and Social Scientific Theory*. Princeton, NJ, and Oxford: Princeton University Press, 2001.

Bulst, Neithard and Jean-Philippe Genet, eds. *La ville, la bourgeoisie et la genèse de l'état moderne (XIIe–XVIIIe siècles): Actes du colloque de Bielefeld (29 novembre–1er décembre 1985)*. Paris: Centre National de la Recherche Scientifique, 1988.

Burns, K.F. "The Administrative System of the Ecclesiastical Courts in the Diocese and Province of York: Part I: The Medieval Courts". Unpublished manuscript, 1962.

Butler, Judith. *Notes Toward a Performative Theory of Assembly*. Cambridge, MA, and London: Harvard University Press, 2015.

Butler, R.M. "Notes on the Minster Close at York". *York Historian* 14 (1997): 10–25.

Caby, Cécile. "Hermits for Communes: The Camaldolese in the Service of the Communes of Central and Northern Italy in the Thirteenth to Fifteenth Centuries". In *Churchmen and Urban Government in Late Medieval Italy c. 1200–c. 1450: Cases and Contexts*, edited by Frances Andrews and Maria Agata Pincelli, 268–284. Cambridge: Cambridge University Press, 2013.

Camphuijsen, Frans. "'*In hemde ende in broeck*': The Performance of Justice in Late Medieval Utrecht". In *La permission et la sanction: Théories légales et pratiques du théatre (XIVe–XVIIe siècle)*, edited by Marie Bouhaïk-Gironès, Jelle Koopmans and Katell Lavéant, 219–247. Paris: Classiques Garnier, 2017.

Camphuijsen, Frans, and Jamie Page, "Introduction: New Approaches to Late Medieval Court Records". *Open Library of Humanities*, 5(1), no. 69 (2019): 1–26. DOI: http://doi.org/10.16995/olh.505.

Camphuijsen, Frans, and Janna Coomans, "De middeleeuwse stad en zijn varkens". *Madoc* 28, no. 3 (2014): 140–148.

Carbonnières, Louis de. *La procédure devant la chambre criminelle du Parlement de Paris au XIVe siècle*. Paris: Champion, 2004.

Cazelles, Raymond. *La société politique et la crise de la royauté sous Philippe de Valois*. Paris: Libraire d'Argences, 1958.

Cazelles, Raymond. *Nouvelle histoire de Paris: De la fin du règne de Philippe Auguste à la mort de Charles V, 1223–1380*. Paris: Hachette, 1972.

Cheney, C.R. *Notaries Public in England in the Thirteenth and Fourteenth Centuries*. Oxford and New York: Clarendon Press, 1972.

Clanchy, Michael. *From Memory to Written Record: England 1066–1307*, 3rd ed. Chichester and Malden, MA: Wiley-Blackwell, 2013. Originally published in 1979 by Edward Arnold (London).

Clanchy, Michael. "Law and Love in the Middle Ages". In *Disputes and Settlements: Law and Human Relations in the West*, edited by John Bossy, 47–67. Cambridge: Cambridge University Press, 1983.

Classen, Albrecht, ed. *Multilingualism in the Middle Ages and Early Modern Age: Communication and Miscommunication in the Premodern World*. Berlin and Boston: De Gruyter, 2016.

Cohen, Esther. "To Die a Criminal for the Public Good: The Execution Ritual in Late Medieval Paris". In *Law, Custom and the Social Fabric in Medieval Europe: Essays in Honour of Bryce Lyon*, edited by Bernard S. Bachrach and David Nicholas, 285–304. Kalamazoo: Medieval Institute Publications, Western Michigan University, 1990.

Colilli, P. "Texts: Semiotic Theory". In *Encyclopedia of Language & Linguistics*. 2nd ed. Vol. 12, edited by Keith Brown, 630–642. Oxford: Elsevier, 2006.

Coomans, Janna. "In Pursuit of a Healthy City: Sanitation and the Common Good in the Late Medieval Low Countries". PhD diss., University of Amsterdam, 2018.

Dauchy, Serge. "Les recueils privés de 'jurisprudence' aux temps modernes". In *Case Law in the Making: The Techniques and Methods of Judicial Records and Law Reports*. Vol. 1, edited by Alain Wijffels, 237–247. Berlin: Duncker & Humblot, 1997.

Dauphant, Léonard. "'Si grant charté a Paris … par defaulté du roy': Governmental Practice and the Customary Geography of the Absence and Presence of the King in France (1364–1525)". In *Absentee Authority across Medieval Europe*, edited by Frédérique Lachaud and Michael Penman, 153–170. Woodbridge: The Boydell Press, 2017.

Davies, Wendy. "Judges and Judging: Truth and Justice in Northern Iberia on the Eve of the Millennium". *Journal of Medieval History* 36, no. 3 (2010): 193–203.

Dean, Trevor. *Crime and Justice in Late Medieval Italy*. Cambridge: Cambridge University Press, 2007.

De Bruijn, Martin. *Husinghe ende hofstede: Een institutioneel-geografische studie van de rechtspraak over onroerend goed in de stad Utrecht in de Middeleeuwen*. Utrecht: Het Spectrum, 1994.

De Bruin, R.E., P.D. 't Hart, A.J. van den Hoven van Genderen, A. Pietersma and J.E.A.L. Struick, eds. *'Een paradijs vol weelde': Geschiedenis van de stad Utrecht*. Utrecht: Matrijs, 2000.

De Certeau, Michel. *The Practice of Everyday Life*. Translated by Steven Rendall. Berkeley: University of California Press, 1984.

Deen, Femke. *Publiek debat en propaganda in Amsterdam tijdens de Nederlandse Opstand: Amsterdam 'Moorddam' (1566–1578)*. Amsterdam: Amsterdam University Press, 2015.

De Groot, H.L. "Van strijdhamer tot bisschopsstaf: De vroegste geschiedenis tot circa 925". In *'Een paradijs vol weelde': Geschiedenis van de stad Utrecht*, edited by Renger de Bruin et al., 10–43. Utrecht: Matrijs, 2000.

De Jong, Mayke. *The Penitential State: Authority and Atonement in the Age of Louis the Pious, 814–840*. Cambridge: Cambridge University Press, 2009.

De Kam, René. *De ommuurde stad: Geschiedenis van een stadsverdediging*. Amsterdam: Spectrum, 2020.

De Kam, René. *Dwars door Utrecht: Opgravingen langs de HOV-busbaan*. Utrecht: Matrijs, 2003.

De Waal, Frans. *Peacemaking among Primates*. Cambridge, MA: Harvard University Press, 1990.

De Win, Paul. *De schandstraffen in het wereldlijk strafrecht in de Zuidelijke Nederlanden van de Middeleeuwen tot de Franse Tijd bestudeerd in Europees perspectief*. Brussel: Paleis der Academiën, 1991.

Dobson, Barrie. "The Later Middle Ages 1215–1500". In *A History of York Minster*, edited by G.E. Aylmer and Reginald Cant, 44–109. Oxford: Clarendon Press, 1977.

Donahue, Charles. *Law, Marriage and Society in the Later Middle Ages: Arguments about Marriage in Five Courts*. Cambridge: Cambridge University Press, 2007.

Donahue, Charles. "Roman Canon Law in the Medieval English Church: Stubbs vs. Maitland Re-examined after 75 Years in the Light of Some Records from the Church Courts". *Michigan Law Review* 72, no. 4 (1974): 647–716.

Ducoudray, Gustave. *Les origines du Parlement de Paris et la justice aux XIIIe et XIVe siècles*. Paris: Hachette, 1902.

Dumolyn, Jan. "'Criers and Shouters': The Discourse on Radical Urban Rebels in Late Medieval Flanders". *Journal of Social History* 42 (2008): 111–137.

Durkheim, Émile. *De la division du travail social*. 5th ed. Paris: Félix Alcan, 1926. Originally published in 1893 by Félix Alcan (Paris). Translated by George Simpson as *The Division of Labor in Society*. Glencoe, IL: Free Press, 1960.

Durkheim, Émile. *Les formes élémentaires de la vie religieuse: Le système totémique en Australie*. Paris: Alcan, 1912.

Elias, Norbert. *Über den Prozess der Zivilisation*. Basel: Haus zum Falken, 1939. Translated by Edmund Jephcott as *The Civilizing Process: The History of Manners and State Formation and Civilization*. Oxford and Cambridge, MA: Blackwell, 1994.

Fenster, Thelma, and Daniel Lord Smail, eds. *Fama: The Politics of Talk and Reputation in Medieval Europe*. Ithaca, NY: Cornell University Press, 2003.

Fischer Taylor, Katherine, "Le code et l'équité: La transformation du palais de justice de Paris au XIXe siècle". In *La justice en ses temples: Regards sur l'architecture judiciaire en France*, edited by Association Française pour l'histoire de la justice, 81–128. Paris: Éditions Errance and Poitiers: Éditions Brissaud, 1992.

Fletcher, Christopher, Jean-Philippe Genet and John Watts, eds. *Government and Political Life in England and France, c. 1300–c. 1500*. Cambridge: Cambridge University Press, 2015.

Forrest, Ian. "Trust and Doubt: The Late Medieval Bishop and Local Knowledge". *Studies in Church History* 52 (2016): 152–174.

Forrest, Ian. *Trustworthy Men: How Inequality and Faith Made the Medieval Church*. Princeton, NJ: Princeton University Press, 2018.

Foucault, Michel. *Surveiller et punir: Naissance de la prison*. Paris: Gallimard, 1975. Translated by Alan Sheridan as *Discipline and Punish: The Birth of the Prison*. London: Penguin Books, 1991.

Fournier, Paul. *Les Officialités au Moyen-Age: Étude sur l'organisation, la compétence et la procédure des tribunaux ecclésiastiques ordinaires en France de 1180 à 1328*. Paris: E. Plon, 1880.

Frankot, Edda. *Banishment in the Late Medieval Eastern Netherlands: Exile and Redemption in Kampen*. Cham: Palgrave Macmillan, 2022.

Gauvard, Claude. *'De grace especial': Crime, état et société en France à la fin du Moyen Âge*. Paris: Publications de la Sorbonne, 1991.

Gauvard, Claude. "Pendre et dépendre à la fin du Moyen Âge: Les exigences d'un ritual judiciaire". In *Riti e rituali nelle società medievali*, edited by Jacques Chiffoleau, Lauro Martines and Agostino Paravicini Bagliani, 191–211. Spoleto: Centro Italiano di Studi sull'alto Medioevo, 1994.

Gauvard, Claude, and Robert Jacob. "Introduction: Le rite, la justice et l'historien". In *Les rites de la justice: Gestes et rituels judiciaires au Moyen Âge occidental*, edited by Claude Gauvard and Robert Jacob, 5–18. Paris: Léopard d'or, 2000.

Geertz, Clifford. *Local Knowledge: Further Essays in Interpretive Anthropology.* New York: Basic Books, 1983.

Geltner, Guy. "*Detrusio*: Penal Cloistering in the Middle Ages". *Revue Bénédictine* 118 (2008): 89–108.

Geltner, Guy. *The Medieval Prison: A Social History.* Princeton, NJ, and Oxford: Princeton University Press, 2008.

Genet, Jean-Philippe, ed. *L'état moderne: Genese: Bilans et perspectives: Actes du colloque tenu au CNRS à Paris les 19–20 septembre 1989*. Paris: CNRS Éditions, 1990.

Geremek, Bronislaw. *Les marginaux parisiens aux XIV*e *et XV*e *siècles*. Translated by Daniel Beauvois. Paris: Flammarion, 1976.

Giles, Katherine. *An Archaeology of Social Identity: Guildhalls in York, c. 1350–1630.* Oxford: Archaeopress, 2000.

Ginzburg, Carlo. *Il formaggio e i vermi. Il cosmo di un mugnaio del '500*. Turin: Einaudi, 1976. Translated by John and Anne Tedeschi as *The Cheese and the Worms: The Cosmos of a Sixteenth-Century Miller.* Baltimore: Johns Hopkins University Press, 1980.

Given, James. "The Inquisitors of Languedoc and the Medieval Technology of Power". *American Historical Review* 94, no. 2 (1989): 336–359.

Glaudemans, Corien. *Om die wrake wille: Eigenrichting, veten en verzoening in laat-middeleeuws Holland en Zeeland.* Hilversum: Verloren, 2004.

Goldberg, Jeremy. *Communal Discord, Child Abduction and Rape in the Later Middle Ages.* New York and Basingstoke: Palgrave Macmillan, 2008.

Goldberg, Jeremy. "John Skatelok's Dick: Voyeurism and 'Pornography' in Late Medieval England". In *Medieval Obscenities*, edited by Nicola McDonald, 105–123. York: York Medieval Press, 2006.

Goodich, Michael, ed. *Voices from the Bench: Narratives of Lesser Folk in Medieval Trials.* New York: Palgrave Macmillan, 2006.

Grün, Alphonse. "Notice sur les archives du Parlement de Paris". In *Actes du Parlement de Paris: Première série: De l'an 1254 à l'an 1328*. Vol. 1, edited by Edgar Boutaric, I–CCXC. Paris: Henri Plon, 1863.

Guerout, Jean. "Le palais de la cité à Paris des origines à 1417: Essai topographique et archéologique: Première partie: Des origines à 1285". *Mémoires de la fédération des sociétés historiques et archéologiques de Paris et de l'Ile-de-France* 1 (1949): 57–212.

Guerout, Jean. "Le palais de la cité à Paris des origines à 1417: Essai topographique et archéologique: Deuxième partie: de 1285 à 1350". *Mémoires de la fédération des sociétés historiques et archéologiques de Paris et de l'Ile-de-France* 2 (1950): 21–204.

Guerout, Jean. "Le palais de la cité à Paris des origines à 1417: Essai topographique et archéologique: Troisième et dernier article". *Mémoires de la fédération des sociétés historiques et archéologiques de Paris et de l'Ile-de-France* 3 (1951): 7–101.

Guilhiermoz, P. *Enquètes et procès: Étude sur la procedure et le fonctionnement du Parlement au XIVe siècle*. Paris: Alphonse Picard, 1892.

Guilhiermoz, P. "Saint Louis, les gages de bataille et la procédure civile". *Bibliothèque de l'école des chartes* 48, no. 1 (1887): 111–120.

Gulliver, Philip. *Disputes and Negotiations: A Cross-cultural Perspective*. New York and London: Academic Press, 1979.

Haines, Roy Martin. *Ecclesia anglicana: Studies in the English Church of the Later Middle Ages*. Toronto: University of Toronto Press, 1989.

Harding, Alan. "The Revolt against the Justices". In *The English Rising of 1381*, edited by R.H. Hilton and T.H. Aston, 165–193. Cambridge: Cambridge University Press, 1981.

Harris, Roy. "The Semiology of Textualization". *Language Sciences* 6, no. 2 (1984): 271–286.

Helmholz, R.H. "Abjuration *sub pena nubendi* in the Church Courts of Medieval England". *The Jurist* 32 (1972): 80–90.

Helmholz, R.H. *Marriage Litigation in Medieval England*. Cambridge: Cambridge University Press, 1974.

Helmholz, R.H. *The Oxford History of the Laws of England: The Canon Law and Ecclesiastical Jurisdiction from 597 to the 1640s*. Oxford: Oxford University Press, 2004.

Helmholz, R.H. *The Profession of Ecclesiastical Lawyers: An Historical Introduction*. Cambridge and New York: Cambridge University Press, 2019.

Helmholz, R.H. "Writs of Prohibition and Ecclesiastical Sanctions in the English Courts Christian". *Minnesota Law Review* 60 (1976): 1011–1033.

Hilaire, Jean. *La construction de l'état de droit dans les archives judiciaires de la cour de France au XIIIe siècle*. Paris: Dalloz, 2011.

Hildesheimer, Françoise. "Les deux premiers registres des 'ordonnances' ou la logique floue de l'enregistrement". *Histoire et archives* 12 (2002): 79–114.

Hildesheimer, Françoise, and Monique Morgat-Bonnet, eds. *État méthodique des archives du Parlement de Paris*. Paris: Archives Nationales, 2011.

Hildesheimer, Françoise, and Monique Morgat-Bonnet, eds. *Le Parlement de Paris: Histoire d'un grand corps de l'État monarchique XIIIe–XVIIIe siècle*. Paris: Honoré Champion, 2018.

Hoekstra, Tarquinus J., and A.F.E. Kipp "Archeologische en bouwhistorische kroniek van de gemeente Utrecht over 1984". *Maandblad Oud-Utrecht* 58, no. 4 (1985): 41–191.

Humphrey, Caroline, and James Laidlaw. *The Archetypal Actions of Ritual: A Theory of Ritual Illustrated by the Jain Rite Worship*. Oxford: Clarendon Press, 1994.

Hyams, Paul R. *Rancor and Reconciliation in Medieval England*. Ithaca, NY: Cornell University Press, 2003.

Jackson, Gregory. "Actors and Institutions". In *The Oxford Handbook of Comparative Institutional Analysis*, edited by Glenn Morgan et al., 63–81. Oxford: Oxford University Press, 2010.

Jacob, Robert, and Nadine Marchal-Jacob. "Jalons pour une histoire de l'architecture judiciaire". In *La justice en ses temples: Regards sur l'architecture judiciaire en France*, edited by Association Française pour l'histoire de la justice, 23–68. Paris: Éditions Errance and Poitiers: Éditions Brissaud, 1992.

Jerram, Leif. "Space: A Useless Category of Analysis?" *History and Theory* 52 (2013): 400–419.

Johnson, Tom. *Law in Common: Legal Cultures in Late-Medieval England*. Oxford: Oxford University Press, 2020.

Johnson, Tom. "Legal Ephemera in the Ecclesiastical Courts of Late-Medieval England". *Open Library of Humanities* 5(1), no. 17 (2019): 1–27. DOI: https://doi.org/10.16995/olh.334.

Jones, Sarah Rees. "York's Civic Administration, 1354–1464". In *The Government of Medieval York: Essays in Commemoration of the 1396 Royal Charter*, edited by Sarah Rees Jones, 108–140. York: Borthwick Institute of Historical Research, University of York, 1997.

Jones, Sarah Rees. *York: The Making of a City 1068–1350*. New York and Oxford: Oxford University Press, 2013.

Jones, Sarah Rees, ed. *The Government of Medieval York: Essays in Commemoration of the 1396 Royal Charter*. York: Borthwick Institute of Historical Research, University of York, 1997.

Jones, Sarah Rees, and David M. Palliser. "York 1066–1272". In *York: British Historic Towns Atlas*, edited by Peter Addyman, 27–36. Oxford: Historic Towns Trust, 2015.

Jones, Sarah Rees, and David M. Palliser. "York 1272–1536". In *York: British Historic Towns Atlas*, edited by Peter Addyman, 37–48. Oxford: Historic Towns Trust, 2015.

Jones, W.R. "Relations of the Two Jurisdictions: Conflict and Cooperation in England during the Thirteenth and Fourteenth Centuries". *Studies in Medieval and Renaissance History* 7 (1970): 77–210.

Jordan, William Chester. "A Fresh Look at Medieval Sanctuary". In *Law and the Illicit in Medieval Europe*, edited by Ruth Mazo Karras, Joel Kaye and E. Ann Matter, 17–32. Philadelphia: University of Pennsylvania Press, 2008.

Jordan, William Chester. *From England to France: Felony and Exile in the High Middle Ages*. Princeton, NJ: Princeton University Press, 2015.

Kaeuper, Richard W. *War, Justice and Public Order: England and France in the Later Middle Ages*. Oxford: Clarendon Press, 1988.

Kantorowicz, Ernst H. *The King's Two Bodies: A Study in Medieval Political Theology*. Princeton, NJ: Princeton University Press, 1957.

Korpiola, Mia, ed. *Regional Variations in Matrimonial Law and Custom in Europe, 1150–1600*. Leiden and Boston: Brill, 2011.

Kroeze, Ronald, André Vitória and Guy Geltner, eds. *Anticorruption in History: From Antiquity to the Modern Era*. Oxford: Oxford University Press, 2018.

Labat-Poussin, Brigitte, Monique Langlois and Yvonne Lanhers, eds. *Actes du Parlement de Paris: Parlement criminel, règne de Philippe VI de Valois: Inventaire analytique des registres X^{2A} 2 à 5*. Paris: Archives Nationales, 1987.

Langlois, Monique, "Parlement de Paris". In *Guide des recherches dans les fonds judiciaires de l'ancien régime*, edited by Michel Antoine et al., 65–160. Paris: Imprimerie nationale, 1958.

Latour, Bruno. *La fabrique du droit*. Paris: La Découverte, 2002. Translated by Marina Brilman and Alain Pottage as *The Making of Law: An Ethnography of the* Conseil d'état. Cambridge and Malden: Polity Press, 2010.

Latour, Bruno. *Reassembling the Social: An Introduction to Actor-Network-Theory*. Oxford: Oxford University Press, 2005.

Leach, Edmund. *Political Systems of Highland Burma: A Study of Kachin Social Structure*. London: G. Bell, 1954.

Lecuppre-Desjardin, Élodie. *La ville des cérémonies: Essai sur la communication politique dans les anciens Pays-Bas bourguignons*. Turnhout: Brepols, 2004.

Lecuppre-Desjardin, Élodie. "The Space of Punishments: Reflections on the Expression and Perception of Judgment and Punishment in the Cities of the Low Countries in the Late Middle Ages". In *The Power of Space in Late Medieval and Early Modern Europe: The Cities of Italy, Northern France and the Low Countries*, edited by Marc Boone and Martha Howell, 139–151. Turnhout: Brepols, 2013.

Lefebvre, Henri. *La production de l'espace*. Paris: Éditions Anthropos, 1974. Translated by Donald Nicholson-Smith as *The Production of Space*. Malden, MA: Blackwell, 1991.

Le Roy Ladurie, Emmanuel. *Montaillou: Village occitan de 1294 à 1324*. Paris: Gallimard, 1982. Originally published in 1975 by Gallimard.

Loxley, James. *Performativity*. London and New York: Routledge, 2007.

Maes, Louis T. *Vijf eeuwen stedelijk strafrecht: Bijdrage tot de rechts- en cultuurgeschiedenis der Nederlanden*. Antwerp: De Sikkel and The Hague: Martinus Nijhoff, 1947.

Mansfield, Mary C. *The Humiliation of Sinners: Public Penance in Thirteenth-Century France*. Ithaca, NY, and London: Cornell University Press, 1995.

Masschaele, James. "The Public Space of the Marketplace in Medieval England". *Speculum* 77, no. 2 (2002): 383–421.

Meens, Rob. "Penitential Varieties". In *The Oxford Handbook of Medieval Christianity*, edited by John Arnold, 254–268. Oxford: Oxford University Press, 2014.

Menant, François, Hervé Martin, Bernard Merdrignac and Monique Chauvin. *Les Capétiens: Histoire et dictionnaire, 987–1328*. Paris: Robert Laffont, 1999.

Merry, Sally Engle. "What Is Legal Culture? An Anthropological Perspective". *Journal of Comparative Law* 5 (2010): 40–58.

Mostert, Marco. *A Bibliography of Works on Medieval Communication*. Turnhout: Brepols, 2012.

Mostert, Marco, and P.S. Barnwell, eds. *Medieval Legal Process: Physical, Spoken and Written Performance in the Middle Ages*. Turnhout: Brepols, 2011.

Musin, Aude. *Sociabilité urbaine et criminalisation étatique: La justice namuroise face à la violence de 1360 à 1555*. Turnhout: Brepols, 2017.

Musson, Anthony. *Medieval Law in Context: The Growth of Legal Consciousness from Magna Carta to the Peasant's Revolt*. Manchester and New York: Manchester University Press, 2001.

Musson, Anthony, and W.M. Ormrod. *The Evolution of English Justice: Law, Politics and Society in the Fourteenth Century*. Basingstoke: Macmillan Press and St. Martin's Press, 1999.

Netterstrøm, Jeppe Büchert, and Bjørn Poulsen, eds. *Feud in Medieval and Early Modern Europe*. Aarhus: Aarhus University Press, 2007.

Nirenberg, David. *Communities of Violence: Persecution of Minorities in the Middle Ages*. Princeton, NJ: Princeton University Press, 1996.

Ormrod, W.M. "The Peasants' Revolt and the Government of England". *Journal of British Studies* 29, no. 1 (1990): 1–30.

Overlaet, Kim. "The 'Joyous Entry' of Archduke Maximilian into Antwerp (13 January 1478): An Analysis of a 'Most Elegant and Dignified' Dialogue". *Journal of Medieval History* 44, no. 2 (2018): 231–249.

Palliser, David M. "The Birth of York's Civic Liberties, c. 1200–1354". In *The Government of Medieval York: Essays in Commemoration of the 1396 Royal Charter*, edited by Sarah Rees Jones, 88–107. York: Borthwick Institute of Historical Research, University of York, 1997.

Pantin, W. "The Fourteenth Century". In *The English Church and the Papacy in the Middle Ages*, edited by C.H. Lawrence, 157–194. London: Burns & Oates, 1965.

Parkin, D. "Ritual". In *International Encyclopedia of the Social & Behavioral Sciences*, edited by Neil J. Smelser and Paul B. Baltes, 13368–13371. Amsterdam: Elsevier, 2001.

Pazzaglini, Peter Raymond. *The Criminal Ban of the Sienese Commune, 1225–1310*. Milan: A. Giuffrè, 1979.

Pedersen, Frederik. *Marriage Disputes in Medieval England*. London and New York: Hambledon and London, 2000.

Pegg, Mark G. *The Corruption of Angels: The Great Inquisition of 1245–1246*. Princeton, NJ, and Oxford: Princeton University Press, 2001.

Perrot, Ernest. *Les cas royaux: Origine et développement de la théorie aux XIIIe et XIVe siècles*. Paris: A. Rousseau, 1910.

Postles, Dave. "Penance and the Market Place: A Reformation Dialogue with the Medieval Church (c. 1250–c. 1600)". *The Journal of Ecclesiastical History* 54, no. 3 (2003): 441–468.

Putter, Ad, and Keith Busby. "Introduction: Medieval Francophonia". In *Medieval Multilingualism: The Francophone World and Its Neighbours*, edited by Christopher Kleinhenz and Keith Busby, 1–13. Turnhout: Brepols, 2010.

Reynolds, Susan. "The Emergence of Professional Law in the Long Twelfth Century". *Law and History Review* 21, no. 2 (2003): 347–366.

Reynolds, Susan. *Kingdoms and Communities in Western Europe, 900–1300*. Oxford: Clarendon Press, 1984.

Roberts, Simon. "The Study of Dispute: Anthropological Perspectives". In *Disputes and Settlements: Law and Human Relations in the West*, edited by John Bossy, 1–24. Cambridge: Cambridge University Press, 1983.

Rosen, Lawrence. *The Anthropology of Justice: Law as Culture in Islamic Society*. Cambridge: Cambridge University Press, 1989.

Rosen, Lawrence. *Law as Culture: An Invitation*. Princeton, NJ: Princeton University Press, 2006.

Schmit, Elisabeth. "'En bon trayn de justice': Les grands jours du parlement de Paris au lendemain de la guerre de Cent Ans (1454–1459)". PhD diss., Paris I Panthéon-Sorbonne University, 2019.

Schwob, Marcel. "Date de la condamnation à mort de Villon". In Marcel Schwob, *Œuvres complètes*. Vol. 6, *Mélanges d'histoire littéraires et de linguistique: L'Argot, Villon, Rabelais*, 201–210. Paris: François Bernouard, 1928.

Searle, John R. "What Is an Institution?" *Journal of Institutional Economics* 1, no. 1 (2005): 1–22.

Shaw, Christine. *The Politics of Exile in Renaissance Italy*. Cambridge: Cambridge University Press, 2000.

Shoemaker, Karl. *Sanctuary and Crime in the Middle Ages, 400–1500*. Ashland, OH: Fordham University Press, 2011.

Silbey, Susan S. "Legal Culture and Legal Consciousness". In *International Encyclopedia of the Social & Behavioral Sciences*, edited by Neil J. Smelser and Paul B. Baltes, 8623–8629. Amsterdam: Elsevier, 2001.

Smail, Daniel Lord. "Aspects of Procedural Documentation in Marseille (14th–15th Centuries)". In *Als die Welt in die Akten kam: Prozeßschriftgut im europäischen*

Mittelalter, edited by Susanne Lepsius and Thomas Wetzstein, 139–169. Frankfurt am Main: Vittorio Klostermann, 2008.

Smail, Daniel Lord. *The Consumption of Justice: Emotions, Publicity, and Legal Culture in Marseille, 1264–1423*. Ithaca, NY, and London: Cornell University Press, 2003.

Smail, Daniel Lord. "Hatred as a Social Institution in Late Medieval Society". *Speculum: A Journal of Medieval Studies* 76 (2001): 90–126.

Smith, D.M. *Ecclesiastical Cause Papers at York: The Court of York 1301–1399*. York: Borthwick Institute of Historical Research, University of York, 1988.

Smith, Jonathan Z. "The Bare Facts of Ritual". *History of Religions* 20 (1980): 112–127.

Smith, Philip. *Punishment and Culture*. Chicago and London: University of Chicago Press, 2008.

Smithuis, Justine. "Gildevertegenwoordiging of oligarchie? De samenstelling van het Utrechtse stadsbestuur in de late Middeleeuwen (1304–ca. 1450)". *Jaarboek Oud-Utrecht* (2014): 209–236.

Smithuis, Justine. "Politiek en geweld in een laatmiddeleeuwse stad, Utrecht, 1400–1430". *Tijdschrift voor geschiedenis* 123, no. 2 (2010): 240–253.

Smithuis, Justine. "Urban Politics and the Role of Guilds in the City of Utrecht (1250–1450)". PhD diss., University of Leiden, 2019.

Société des historiens médiévistes de l'enseignement supérieur public. *Le règlement des conflits au Moyen Âge: Actes du XXXI*[e] *congrès de la SHMES, Angers, juin 2000*. Paris: Publications de la Sorbonne, 2001.

Soly, H. "Plechtige intochten in de steden van de Zuidelijke Nederlanden tijdens de overgang van Middeleeuwen naar Nieuwe Tijd: Communicatie, propaganda, spektakel". *Tijdschrift voor Geschiedenis* 97 (1984): 341–361.

Spilsbury, Sarah. "Villon's *Louenge a la court* Reconsidered". *Neophilologus* 59, no. 4 (1975): 482–493.

Stanford, Charlotte A. "Archbishop Melton's Donations to York Minster: Strengthening the See". *Yorkshire Archaeological Journal* 75 (2003): 77–89.

Swanson, Robert N. *Church and Society in Late Medieval England*. Oxford and New York: Blackwell, 1989.

Swanson, Robert N. "'...Et examinatus dicit...' Oral and Personal History in the Records of English Ecclesiastical Courts". In *Voices from the Bench: Narratives of Lesser Folk in Medieval Trials*, edited by Michael Goodich, 203–225. New York: Palgrave Macmillan, 2006.

Swanson, Robert N. *Indulgences in Late Medieval England: Passports to Paradise?* Cambridge: Cambridge University Press, 2007.

Symes, Carol. "Out in the Open, in Arras: Sightlines, Soundscapes, and the Shaping of a Medieval Public Sphere". In *Cities, Texts and Social Networks 400–1500: Experiences and Perceptions of Medieval Urban Space*, edited by Caroline Goodson, Anne E. Lester and Carol Symes, 279–302. Farnham and Burlington, VT: Ashgate, 2010.

Telliez, Romain. *'Per potentiam officii': Les officiers devant la justice dans le Royaume de France au XIVe siècle*. Paris: Champion, 2005.
Tilly, Charles, and Wim Blockmans, eds. *Cities and the Rise of States in Europe, A.D. 1000 to 1800*. Boulder, CO: Westview Press, 1994.
Trachtenberg, Marvin. *Building-in-Time: From Giotto to Alberti and Modern Oblivion*. New Haven, CT, and London, 2010.
Trexler, Richard C. *Public Life in Renaissance Florence*. New York: Academic Press, 1980.
Turner, Victor. *The Forest of Symbols: Aspects of Ndembu Ritual*. Ithaca, NY: Cornell University Press, 1967.
Turning, Patricia. *Municipal Officials, Their Public and the Negotiation of Justice in Medieval Languedoc: 'Fear Not the Madness of the Raging Mob'*. Leiden and Boston: Brill, 2013.
Vale, Malcolm. "Courts". In *Government and Political Life in England and France, c. 1300–c. 1500*, edited by Christopher Fletcher, Jean-Philippe Genet and John Watts, 24–40. Cambridge: Cambridge University Press, 2015.
Vallerani, Massimo. *Medieval Public Justice*. Translated by Sarah Rubin Blanshei. Washington, DC: The Catholic University of America Press, 2012.
Van den Hoven van Genderen, A.J., "Op het toppunt van de macht: 1304–1528". In *'Een paradijs vol weelde': Geschiedenis van de stad Utrecht*, edited by Renger de Bruin et al., 112–189. Utrecht: Matrijs, 2000.
Van der Monde, N. *Geschied- en oudheidkundige beschrijving van de pleinen, straten, stegen, waterleidingen, wedden, putten en pompen der stad Utrecht*. 3 vols. Utrecht: N. van der Monde, 1844–1846.
Van Gennep, Arnold. *Les rites de passage: étude systématique des rites de la porte et du seuil, de l'hospitalité, de l'adoption, etc*. Paris: Émile Noury, 1909.
Van Herwaarden, Jan, *Opgelegde bedevaarten: Een studie over de praktijk van opleggen van bedevaarten (met name in de stedelijke rechtspraak) in de Nederlanden gedurende de late Middeleeuwen (ca. 1300–ca. 1550)*. Assen and Amsterdam: Van Gorcum, 1978.
Van Kleij, Nathan. "Beyond the Façade: Town Halls, Publicity and Urban Society in the Fifteenth-Century Low Countries". PhD diss., University of Amsterdam, 2021.
Van Schaik, A.H.M. "Een nieuwe heer en een andere leer (1528–1618)". In *'Een paradijs vol weelde': Geschiedenis van de stad Utrecht*, edited by Renger de Bruin et al., 191–249. Utrecht: Matrijs, 2000.
Van Vliet, K. "De stad van de bisschop: Circa 925–1122". In *'Een paradijs vol weelde': Geschiedenis van de stad Utrecht*, edited by Renger de Bruin et al., 44–71. Utrecht: Matrijs, 2000.

Van Vliet, K. "De stad van de burgers: 1122–1304". In *'Een paradijs vol weelde': Geschiedenis van de stad Utrecht*, edited by Renger de Bruin et al., 72–111. Utrecht: Matrijs, 2000.

Velasco, Jesús R. *Dead Voice: Law, Philosophy, and Fiction in the Iberian Middle Ages.* Philadelphia: University of Pennsylvania Press, 2020.

Vollrath, Hanna. "Rebels and Rituals: From Demonstrations of Enmity to Criminal Justice". In *Medieval Concepts of the Past: Ritual, Memory, Historiography*, edited by Gerd Althoff, Johannes Fried and Patrick Geary, 89–110. Cambridge: Cambridge University Press and Washington, DC: German Historical Institute, 2002.

Weber, Max. *Economy and Society: An Outline of Interpretive Sociology.* Translated and Edited by Guenther Roth and Claus Wittich. New York: Bedminster Press, 1968.

Wettlaufer, Jörg, and Yasuhiro Nishimura. "The History of Shaming Punishments and Public Exposure in Penal Law (1200–1800): A Comparative Perspective (Western Europe and East Asia)". In *Shame between Punishment and Penance: The Social Usages of Shame in the Middle Ages and Early Modern Times*, edited by Bénédicte Sère and Jörg Wettlaufer, 197–228. Florence: SISMEL edizioni del Galluzzo, 2013.

Wickham, Chris. *Courts and Conflict in Twelfth-Century Tuscany.* Oxford: Oxford University Press, 2003.

Zaremska, Hanna. *Les bannis au Moyen Âge.* Translated by Thérèse Douchy. Paris: Aubier, 1996.

Zemon Davis, Natalie. *Fiction in the Archives: Pardon Tales and Their Tellers in Sixteenth-Century France.* Stanford: Stanford University Press, 1987.

Zemon Davis, Natalie. *The Return of Martin Guerre.* Cambridge, MA, and London: Harvard University Press, 1983.

Index

Entries that are of particular interest for one of the three case studies, are noted as such, where (U) = Utrecht, (Y) = York and (P) = Paris.

For Product Safety Concerns and Information please contact our EU representative GPSR@taylorandfrancis.com Taylor & Francis Verlag GmbH, Kaufingerstraße 24, 80331 München, Germany

Batch number: 10722100

Printed by Printforce, the Netherlands